Peter Pan

The Forgotten Story of Phar Lap's Successor

Jessica Owers

16

EasyRead Large

RHYW

Copyright Page from the Original Book

An Ebury Press book
Published by Random House Australia Pty Ltd
Level 3, 100 Pacific Highway, North Sydney NSW 2060
www.randomhouse.com.au

First published by Ebury Press in 2011

Addresses for companies within the Random House Group can be found at www.randomhouse.com.au/offices

National Library of Australia
Cataloguing-in-Publication Entry

Owers, Jessica.
Peter Pan/Jessica Owers.

ISBN: 978 1 74275 021 7 (pbk).

Melbourne Cup (Horse race) – History.
Peter Pan (Race horse).
Race horses – Australia – History.
Horse racing – Australia – History.

Dewey Number: 798.400994

Cover design by Adam Yazxhi/MAXCO
Front cover image: Peter Pan and Darby Munro after winning the 1934 Melbourne Cup
Back cover image: Peter Pan and Jim Pike winning the 1933 AJC St Leger at Randwick
Internal design and typesetting by Xou, www.xou.com.au
Printed in Australia by Griffin Press, an Accredited ISO AS/NZS 14001:2004 Environmental Management System printer.

10 9 8 7 6 5 4 3 2 1

FSC
www.fsc.org
MIX
Paper from responsible sources
FSC® C009448

The paper this book is printed on is certified against the Forest Stewardship Council® Standards. Griffin Press holds FSC chain of custody certification SGS-COC-005088. FSC promotes environmentally responsible, socially beneficial and economically viable management of the world's forests.

Set in 16 pt. Verdana

TABLE OF CONTENTS

JESSICA OWERS was born the year Kingston Town won his first Cox Plate. In 1988 she was introduced to Phar Lap on the school curriculum, and she has been writing about racehorses ever since. After completing a degree in environmental science and journalism from the University of Stirling, Scotland, Jessica worked as a riding instructor, then staff-writer for the Sydney-based magazines *R.M. Williams' Outback* and *Breeding& Racing.* Her work has since been published in *Inside Breeding, The Thoroughbred, Turf Monthly* and *Racing Life,* along with various other books and publications across the Australian racing industry. Jessica lives in Sydney's Eastern Suburbs. *Peter Pan: The Forgotten Story of Phar Lap's Successor* is her first book, and the result of five years of work. She is currently writing her second racing book.

For Maurice, the wind in my sails

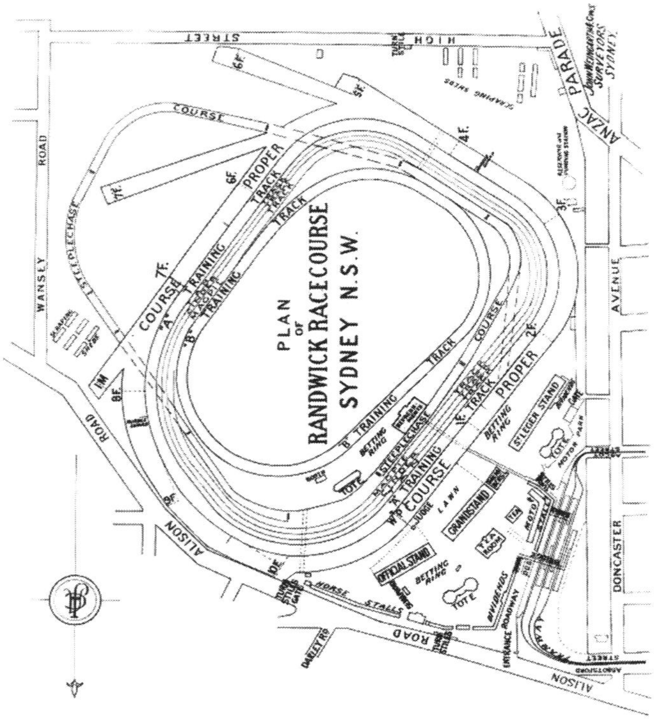

Reproduced with the permission of the Australian Turf Club

Conversions

Weight

Stones and pounds	Kilograms (approximate)
6st 10lb	42.6kg
6st 11lb	43kg
6st 12lb	43.5kg
6st 13lb	44kg
7st	44.5kg
7st 1lb	45kg
7st 2lb	45.3kg
7st 3lb	45.8kg
7st 4lb	46.2kg
7st 5lb	46.7kg
7st 6lb	47kg
7st 7lb	47.6kg
7st 8lb	48kg
7st 9lb	48.5kg
7st 10lb	48.9kg
7st 11lb	49.4kg
7st 12lb	49.9kg
7st 13lb	50.3kg
8st	50.8kg
8st 1lb	51.2kg
8st 2lb	51.7kg
8st 3lb	52.1kg
8st 4lb	52.6kg
8st 5lb	53kg
8st 6lb	53.5kg
8st 7lb	53.9kg
8st 8lb	54.4kg

Stones and pounds	Kilograms (approximate)
8st 9lb	54.8kg
8st 10lb	55.3kg
8st 11lb	55.7kg
8st 12lb	56.2kg
8st 13lb	56.7kg
9st	57.1kg
9st 1lb	57.6kg
9st 2lb	58kg
9st 3lb	58.1kg
9st 4lb	59kg
9st 5lb	59.5kg
9st 6lb	59.8kg
9st 7lb	60.3kg
9st 8lb	60.7kg
9st 9lb	61.2kg
9st 10lb	61.6kg
9st 11lb	62.1kg
9st 12lb	62.6kg
9st 13lb	63kg
10st	63.5kg
10st 1lb	63.9kg
10st 2lb	64.4kg
10st 3lb	64.8kg
10st 4lb	65.3kg
10st 5lb	65.7kg
10st 6lb	66.2kg
10st 7lb	66.6kg
10st 8lb	67.1kg
10st 9lb	67.5kg
10st 10lb	68kg
10st 11lb	68.5kg

Stones and pounds	Kilograms (approximate)
10st 12lb	68.9kg
10st 13lb	69.4kg
11st	69.8kg

Racetrack Distances

Furlongs	Metres (approximate)
5	1000
6	1200
7	1400
8 (1 mile)	1600
9	1800
10 (1 1/4 miles)	2000
11	2200
12 (1 1/2 miles)	2400
13	2600
14 (1 3/4 miles)	2800
16 (2 miles)	3200
20 (2 1/2 miles)	4000

Pedigree of Peter Pan (AUS) 1929

Pantheon (GB) 1921	Tracery (USA) 1909	Rock Sand (GB) 1900	Sainfoin (GB) 1887	Springfield (GB) 1873	St Albans (GB) 1857
					Viridis (GB) 1864
				Sanda (GB) 1878	Wenlock (GB) 1869
					Sandal (GB) 1861
			Roquebrune (GB) 1893	St Simon (GB) 1881	Galopin (GB) 1872
					St Angela (GB) 1865
				St Marguerite (GB) 1879	Hermit (GB) 1864
					Devotion (GB) 1869
		Topiary (GB) 1901	Orme (GB) 1889	Ormonde (GB) 1883	Bend Or (GB) 1877
					Lily Agnes (GB) 1871
				Angelica (GB) 1879	Galopin (GB) 1872
					St Angela (GB) 1865
			Plaisanterie (FR) 1882	Wellingtonia (GB) 1869	Chattanooga (GB) 1862
					Araucaria (GB) 1862
				Poetess (FR) 1875	Trocadero (FR) 1864
					La Dorette (FR) 1867
	Scotch Rose (IRE) 1912	Your Majesty (GB) 1905	Persimmon (GB) 1893	St Simon (GB) 1881	Galopin (GB) 1872
					St Angela (GB) 1865
				Perdita II (GB) 1881	Hampton (GB) 1872
					Hermione (GB) 1875
			Yours (ITY) 1894	Melton (GB) 1882	Master Kildare (GB) 1875
					Violet Melrose (GB) 1875
				Your Grace (GB) 1886	Galliard (GB) 1880
					Grand Duchess (GB) 1871
		Rose Of Ayrshire (GB) 1905	Ayrshire (GB) 1885	Hampton (GB) 1872	Lord Clifden (GB) 1860
					Lady Langden (GB) 1868
				Atalanta (GB) 1878	Galopin (GB) 1872
					Feronia (GB) 1868
			Pink Flower (GB) 1891	Melton (GB) 1882	Master Kildare (GB) 1875
					Violet Melrose (GB) 1875
				Saponaria (GB) 1883	The Duke (GB) 1862
					Festival (GB) 1877
Alwina (AUS) 1923	St Alwyne (GB) 1899	St Frusquin (GB) 1893	St Simon (GB) 1881	Galopin (GB) 1872	Vedette (GB) 1854
					Flying Duchess (GB) 1853
				St Angela (GB) 1865	King Tom (GB) 1851
					Adeline (GB) 1851
			Isabel (GB) 1879	Plebeian (GB) 1872	Joskin (GB) 1856
					Queen Elizabeth (GB) 1859
				Parma (GB) 1864	Parmesan (GB) 1857
					Archeress (GB) 1858
		Lady Alwyne (GB) 1887	Camballo (GB) 1872	Cambuscan (GB) 1861	Newminster (GB) 1848
					The Arrow (GB) 1850
				Little Lady (GB) 1858	Orlando (GB) 1841
					Volley (GB) 1845
			Florence Aislabie (GB) 1865	Young Melbourne (GB) 1855	Melbourne (GB) 1834
					Clarissa (GB) 1846
				Mary Aislabie (GB) 1850	Malcolm (GB) 1843
					Actaeon Mare (GB) 1834
	Formaliter (NZ) 1911	Boniform (NZ) 1904	Multiform (NZ) 1894	Hotchkiss (NZ) 1885	Musket (GB) 1867
					Petroleuse (GB) 1869
				Formo (NZ) 1884	Sterlingworth (GB) 1875
					Pulchra (GB) 1874
			Otterden (GB) 1896	Sheen (GB) 1885	Hampton (GB) 1872
					Radiancy (GB) 1876
				Spring Morn (GB) 1881	Springfield (GB) 1873
					Sunray (GB) 1874
		Waitemata (AUS) 1891	Eiridspord (GB) 1884	Isonomy (GB) 1875	Sterling (GB) 1868
					Isola Bella (GB) 1868
				Sonsie Queen (GB) 1875	Musket (GB) 1867
					Highland Lassie (GB) 1869
			Aorere (AUS) 1887	Chester (AUS) 1874	Yattendon (AUS) 1861
					Lady Chester (GB) 1870
				Kaipara (AUS) 1880	Goldsbrough (AUS) 1870
					Maritana (AUS) 1870

'Help me to win if I may, but if I may not win make me a good loser.'

RODNEY ROUSE DANGAR

Prologue

A little after midnight on Wednesday 6 April 1932, a furious change rolled over Sydney. It was purple and dangerous, a wild electrical storm, and it burst over the city's Eastern Suburbs, belting the gardener's cottage at Randwick Racecourse and derailing a tram on the Marrickville line. Its ferocity, the likes of which had not been seen for years, was a glimpse of things to come that day. By ten o'clock in the morning, as Sydney swept away an unruly mess, word trickled through that Phar Lap was dead.

'Phar Lap has died at Menlo Park, California,' reported popular journalist Bert 'Cardigan' Wolfe from San Diego. On street corners, in hotel doorways and along the docks of Sydney's Circular Quay, the ringing truth numbed everyone. 'Phar Lap's mystery death,' reported the afternoon dailies, 'so sudden was it that the question was asked all over America whether he had been poisoned.' Though initial autopsies on the great thoroughbred suggested otherwise, and though the best clinical authorities in America refuted it, there was a sneaking suspicion among Australians that their hero had been murdered.

The news struck an already troubled nation. It was 1932, and amid the Great Depression the giant, near-invincible galloping machine that was Phar Lap had fought his way to 39 wins on the racetrack. He had won a Melbourne Cup, two Derbies and an international handicap. Here was the only horse in

Australian history that had changed the weight-for-age rules. Here was the only horse that had closed the books on betting. He had been a battler, an ugly duckling colt that had spawned rare brilliance, a horse neither bred into richness nor lavished with it. He had slaved for every penny he had won, and while he did, he had furrowed into the affections of working-class Australia. Now suddenly he was gone.

Rodney Rouse Dangar was at home that morning when he heard the news. It spilled from the wireless at his home on Edgecliff Road in Sydney's plush east. He was shocked, but he was reasonable. He wasn't about to think the world would never be the same. In fact, Phar Lap had left Australia for America nearly six months before. Hadn't racing moved on? Nevertheless, he decided he would drive over to Doncaster Avenue to visit his racehorse trainer and catch up on this Phar Lap business.

The weather was a balmy 22 degrees, about average for an autumn afternoon. Dangar drove along the opulent, tree-lined avenues of Woollahra towards the racing suburb of Kensington, before parking outside 156 Doncaster Avenue, a two-storey Federation house with a neat front yard. It was the home of racehorse trainer Frank McGrath. 'A national loss,' McGrath said as the two men sat on McGrath's verandah. 'Phar Lap was one of the greatest advertisements Australia could have had. But I wonder if it was colic at all. A strapping beast like that. I wonder whether he got blood poisoning.'

The two gentlemen talked the subject over a while, then rose and walked down to McGrath's stables. Stepping through the main gates they found the yard quiet, as it always was at that time of day, the horses respiting through the afternoon heat. The boxes were aligned on the left and right, and there was a hayloft at the end of the row, a wash bay halfway down and a feed room in the far right corner. The yard, as was typical of Frank McGrath, was bright, neat and orderly. The two men walked over to box number three, third on the left of the shed row. The horse inside turned his head to look at them. He was only a two-year-old, narrow and undeveloped, and still raw to racing. He would make his first start in a few weeks' time. But clapping eyes on him was like suddenly spotting a magnificent woman. One tended to forget one's self. He had a light chestnut coat and an almost-perfect white diamond on his forehead, hidden behind a tumble of blond hair that fell down his face. Both the mane and tail were an extraordinary flaxen colour. McGrath had never seen anything like him.

Dangar stretched his hand out to his young horse and the colt nosed his fingers in greeting. 'Hello my boy Peter Pan,' Dangar said. 'Did you hear the news about Phar Lap?'

1

Alwina

A slow drizzle fell on the roof of the sale ring like a thousand dripping taps. It made raincoats limp and umbrellas heavy, and it had settled in for the afternoon. Men ducked from it in all directions, into the already crowded auditorium. They shook themselves under the shelter, cursed the blasted Easter weather, and settled down for the business of horse trading.

It was Wednesday 16 April 1925, the second-last day of the yearling sales in Sydney. Auctions had begun a week earlier, divided between the bloodstock firms of William Inglis & Sons and Harry Chisholm & Co. The Inglis yards were at rest today, but here at King Street, behind the tram depot north of Randwick Racecourse, a good crowd had gathered for the Chisholm sales. Rodney Dangar huddled in the middle of the packed auditorium, his umbrella propped between his knees. He clutched the H. Chisholm & Co. catalogue, his fingers wedged in one of its pages. He was here to buy a horse, and one filly in particular. She was Lot 276: a chestnut by the ageing, imported stallion St Alwyne out of Formaliter, daughter of the unbeaten New Zealand racehorse Boniform.

Dangar was 53 years old, tall, with broad shoulders and a smock of silver hair. He was a pastoralist, the son and heir of an old English family in New South Wales, and he was one of the wealthiest men in the state. He peered out at the world through privileged eyes, and being of good breeding, moved in all the right social circles. But he possessed few airs and graces. He would shake the hand of any man, and lived his life by rules of humility. He feared growing stodgy and unimaginative, and so, despite his wealth and status, that morning in the Chisholm pavilion he fitted right in.

Dangar lived in the opulent mansion Arlington in Woollahra, east Sydney, and ran his businesses from 4 O'Connell Street downtown. But he also had a vast estate in the Hunter Valley, some 2000 acres outside of Singleton. He had been born there, at the grand homestead Baroona in the tiny hamlet of Whittingham, and nowadays it was the home of his small thoroughbred empire. He hoped to add to it this afternoon.

Dangar glanced around the ring as bidding began for the afternoon. Auctioneer Harry Chisholm was reciting pedigrees with wild, babbling enthusiasm. Dangar flipped to Lot 276 in his catalogue and stared at the page, though he knew it almost by heart. The filly was on account of Mr John Hudson Keys, whose property Bengalla was in Muswellbrook, in the heart of the Hunter Valley. Keys had purchased the filly, at foot to Formaliter, at the dispersal of Arrowfield Stud the previous year. The sale had been the most prolific event in breeding for decades, for the stock sold had been the highest quality horses there was. The stallion

Valais had set a record price for a thoroughbred in Australasia, some 3000 guineas more than the record sale of Carbine 35 years before. Keys had purchased the filly and her dam for 150 guineas, and if Dangar could get her for that price today, he would consider it a bargain.

Dangar believed he had here a thoroughbred with all the right building blocks. If a man had Melbourne Cup pretensions, this was the filly for him. Lot 276 was from a proven racing family, which had as many wins as runners, but she was also impeccably bred. She had some of the finest colonial lines in her, horses that had run all day and come back for more the next morning. The youngster was a full sister to the racehorse Sir Alwyne, an early fancy for the West Australian Derby. She was a lovely type, a solid filly with clean conformation, but it wasn't her looks that appealed to Dangar. It was her pedigree.

She was by St Alwyne, now an old stallion in Victoria, who had sired Melbourne Cup winners Night Watch and Poitrel, and Sydney Cup winner Moorilla. On the dam side, Lot 276 was an exciting cocktail of old blood. Formaliter, a New Zealand-bred mare, had Carbine's sire twice in her fifth remove. She traced through to Chester, Yattendon and Goldsbrough – the corner stallions of Australian breeding – but the real gilt in her pedigree came from her fifth dam, the New Zealand mare Mermaid. Mermaid had been the great grand-dam of Wallace, champion son of Carbine and a brilliant sire himself. On her sire side, Formaliter was by Boniform, who was a half-brother to Martian, the sire of the legendary winners Rapine, The Hawk, Star Stranger, and 1916 Melbourne Cup winner Sasanof. These were extraordinary staying lines, lines that Dangar hadn't seen for a long time.

The sky outside hung very low, and the rain had not stopped drumming on the roof. Harry Chisholm was singing above the drone of droplets, and he was more than halfway through his schedule when he arrived at Lot 276. He would sell 139 horses that day, but this filly was the only one by St Alwyne. When she stepped into the ring beside her handler, few men bid her any attention. They hadn't looked deep into her pedigree as Dangar had, and there was nothing immediate in her. She came in without as much as a hush from the crowd.

The filly was up for sale for the second time in her short life. It was on the very same date the year before that she had been sold at Arrowfield. She was familiar with the hordes of people, with their animated chatter and the clang of the gavel, and she was more relaxed than most of the other yearlings. Dangar watched closely as horse and handler walked around under Harry Chisholm's calls.

'Who'll give me 50 guineas?' the auctioneer boomed. 'Fifty guineas for this well-bred daughter of an unbeaten stallion.' Bidding was slow on the filly, and Dangar glanced nervously around the sale ring to see where the money would come from. A spotter's call punctured the silence, and Chisholm tickled the bidding to 100 guineas. Into triple figures, a few more buyers joined the fray. The filly went to 160, 170, then 180 guineas. Dangar raised his catalogue to signal 190. Immediately, a call came from the other side of the sale ring. 'At 200 guineas,' Chisholm called, and he hung there, his gavel suspended above his podium. Dangar thought quickly. He could afford the price, but whoever was bidding against him was as keen as he was, and he couldn't guarantee the man would not go higher. He wondered how much the filly was worth, and wondered if two bidders had just pushed her price over her value. He shook his head at Chisholm, and the gavel clattered down on Lot 276.

The filly had been sold to Elwyn Darworth Bloomfield, the secretary of the Bong Bong Picnic Race Club. He was a distinguished man, with as much in his pocket as Dangar, the type who dined with prime ministers and governors and played golf every other day. But he was a racing man, not a breeder, so when he purchased Lot 276 he had paid little attention to her potential powers of reproduction. He had wanted a racehorse, not a broodmare, and he had become the official recorded buyer for 200 guineas.

Dangar left the crowded auditorium and walked out into the rain. He was agitated, struggling to see the good in what had just happened. He pitched his umbrella and strode towards the shed rows, looking for the chestnut filly. He had made a decision during bidding, but he couldn't tell himself it was the right one. It galled him that he had surrendered the youngster for the silly sum of 10 guineas. When he looked at her in her stable, she looked better than he remembered. She was so solidly built, so square and straight, a perfect complement to her pedigree. Dangar regretted his decision immediately and went in search of Elwyn Bloomfield.

He was familiar with Bloomfield through the Southern Highlands district. Dangar had a country residence at Sutton Forest called Rotherwood, which wasn't far from Bloomfield's home at Moss Vale. It was an intimate locale, populated by wealthy graziers, governors and the Sydney noblesse, and because Dangar spent Christmases at Rotherwood, he usually attended the annual Bong Bong meeting in January. Bloomfield greeted Dangar like an old friend, and Dangar explained his situation. He said he would pay a good price for the St Alwyne filly, and Bloomfield nodded. A man is always curious about the value of his stock when another man comes knocking for it. But the Bong Bong secretary didn't press the matter. He had traded racehorses for much of his life, and this filly was just another that someone else wanted more than he did. He happily accepted 210 guineas from Rodney Dangar, a profit of a little more than £10 in as many minutes, and exchanged the sale papers with his neighbour. Lot 276 was bound for Baroona.

***

The train carrying Lot 276 from Sydney eased into Whittingham railway siding shortly after seven in the evening, when the light had all but faded across the upper Hunter Valley. There was a subtle April breeze, and Rodney Dangar's new filly stepped from her boxcar into the crisp country air. William Shade was waiting for her, ready to walk her home to Baroona.

Shade was a thin man in his early fifties, an upright fellow with a wiry moustache. He was kind with horses and a stellar farmhand. He had worked at Baroona since 1896, and tonight, tucked into the pocket of his trousers was a telegram from the boss: NEW FILLY ARRIVING. GOODS TRAIN TO MUSWELLBROOK. DANGAR. The filly had been put on the freight train from Sydney, so the only people that joined Shade at the station that evening were those expecting merchandise. The unloading dock was a little further along from the passenger platforms, and from here the goods and livestock were dispersed to waiting parties. Shade collected his jittery cargo as crates and cattle scurried in all directions, and he hurried her gently off the platform.

Shade led the filly away by lantern. The pair headed along the road west for a short time, then crossed the open paddocks towards Baroona. They climbed the long driveway towards the house, an extravagant avenue lined with elm and pine trees, jacarandas and thick oleander plants, and they skirted around the back towards the stables. Shade turned the filly into a spacious loose box, settling her with a manger of sweet lucerne and hot mash. Then he shut the stable door, and left her alone in the pallid silence of the night.

***

Nearly a month after the Easter sales, on 11 May 1925, Dangar stepped off Bligh Street, Sydney, into the offices of the Australian Jockey Club (AJC). He was here to collect his new filly's registration papers. He had named the chestnut 'Alwina', and whether Dangar intended to race her or not, her registration was a compulsory element of her ownership. The registrar was the custodian of all identifying information pertaining to racehorses in New South Wales, and that included broodmares and stallions. Dangar had fronted to the registrar many times before, and he would do so many times again.

Dangar left the AJC offices and swung north. He looped around Bent Street and into the financial district of O'Connell Street. It was a lively part of town, and today was a Monday, so there were motorcars tooting and people rushing about. He could hear the rattle of trams on nearby Castlereagh Street, could feel the rush of Sydney skywards. It was the roaring twenties and progress was everywhere. Dangar was excited about it, even embraced it, despite his age. Electrical poles had replaced gas lanterns, and telephones were on the way. The tender for the Harbour Bridge had been granted last year, and the construction was a never-ending subject in the newspapers. Nothing quite so grand had ever been planned in the colony, and pictorials tracked its progress at least every week.

Dangar walked into the Pitt Son & Badgery building at 4 O'Connell, and slipped up the stairs to his office on the top floor. It was at this time of year that his senses came alive, when his English roots began to crave the country air again. He missed the pace of rural life when he was in Sydney, the smells during harvest and the willowy whiffs of cattle. About this time every year, as the trees began to toss their leaves around glorious Hyde Park, Dangar craved a passage to Baroona.

***

Whittingham was 145 miles north of Sydney, on the railway line that ran between Newcastle and Muswellbrook. When Dangar was born here in 1873, Baroona had belonged to his father, Albert Augustus Dangar, only three years. Then, it was a humble homestead, a compact little residence of untold potential, sitting on a hillside overlooking the east and the rich flats of the Hunter River. By the time Dangar was 13, Baroona had become the grandest home in the district. It had rich, Italianate features, a piazza out the front and an imposing watch tower. There were servant wings, a tennis court and greenhouse, and 1400 acres surrounding the house. Albert had even created an artificial lake in the front paddock. There were 16 boxes in the stable yard, gas lighting throughout, and four windmills pumping water. It was a palace, a pastoralist's playground, worthy of the family that lived inside.

Albert Dangar was the fourth son of Henry Dangar, the first pioneer of the Hunter region. He was a famous man, decorated by queen and country, and his children grew up similarly distinguished. Henry Cary Dangar, Albert's older brother, became the longest-serving AJC committeeman in memory, one of a long list of Dangars tied to horse racing. Albert was a wildly successful pastoralist. By the age of 22 he was managing some 300,000 acres of Henry Dangar land, runs that extended from the Hunter to the New England districts and northern Queensland. When he married, in 1866, Mary Phoebe Rouse of the Rouse Hill family, he forever interconnected two of the finest families in New South Wales.

Albert and Mary's home at Baroona was a family one. They had three sons, the first of whom was Rodney Rouse Dangar, who grew up under the moral wisdom of his father. Albert was a fair and honest employer, a man of thick and proper code. 'No man in Australia has more sympathy with the real, honest, straightforward worker,' wrote the *Pastoral Review* of Albert in 1910. 'Few have worked harder than he himself.' Despite thousands of men in his employ up and down the country, Albert had never found himself in a court of law with a single one, and that was a rare attribute of the times. He was also a generous philanthropist. Because of him, Singleton could boast the Dangar Cottage Hospital and the All Saints Anglican Church, and when he died in 1913, he was buried under the altar he had paid for, only after the funeral cortege choked the streets of Singleton for many hours.

Rodney Dangar was 40 years old when he finally inherited Baroona. He had waited a long time for the homestead, and had lingered for years in his father's long shadow. But Albert, though an imposing and often daunting role model for young Rodney, was an excellent and generous father. Rodney was well-educated and well-travelled, and had spent most of 1905 in England. He had learned, during his time in the motherland, all about the 'empire and her dominions', and royalism became a strong part of his character. He began to swear by it, and it would later influence his racing career. He adored Australia, but Australia was a servant of England, and he rarely saw it otherwise.

Though Dangar resembled his father in looks, with the same tall stature and deep eyes, it was in character that he was most like Albert. Dangar was upstanding and honourable, a man of excellent manners, and a rather dashing sort. When he met Elsie Winifred Macdonald in Sydney, the daughter of a respectable Double Bay surveyor, he was smitten.

She was a patron of the arts, a conservationist and an independent, forward-thinking young woman. He married her during the war in 1914.

When Baroona came into Dangar's hands, he was a wealthy man already, but he possessed the intelligence to protect his fortune. He rarely gambled (even though his interest in horse racing was extensive), and he invested a large chunk of income in mining and tobacco shares, and large Australian businesses such as the Colonial Sugar Refining Co. He sat on the board of directors for the Australian Mutual Provident Society (later AMP), and was a founding member of the Royal Geographical Society. Like his father, he never forgot the charitable cause. Though he was rich beyond the wildest dreams of the common man, he never flaunted it. Character rarely deserted Dangar. He was always the English gentleman.

Dangar and Elsie bought Arlington in 1920 as a city home when they weren't at Baroona. They lost an infant son at this time, a child that didn't live long enough to be named, but in 1922 Elsie gave birth to a little girl. They named her Roslyn, and Dangar was devoted to her. He named horses after her, as well as the little lane that ran alongside Arlington, and he took her everywhere. As his father had been, Dangar was a wonderful role model. But he differed heavily from Albert on one single issue. Thoroughbreds.

For decades, the districts of Singleton had produced Melbourne Cup winners. Glencoe, Lord Cardigan, Poseidon, Lord Nolan and Piastre had all come from local breeders. But at the bottom of the hillside from Baroona, on the flanks of the Hunter River, the original homestead Neotsfield, the home of Dangar's grandfather Henry, was where it had all begun for the racehorses in the Dangar family. Henry's sons, including Albert, had stood Positano here, one of the greatest stallions ever in Australia, and racing in Dangar colours, Positano won the AJC Spring Stakes and VRC Veterans' Stakes before retiring. At Neotsfield, he sired four Melbourne Cup winners, a record that would stand for a long time. In 1869, Albert and his brothers imported an English colt called Grandmaster, an extravagant son of the English Triple Crown winner Gladiateur. They stood Grandmaster at Baroona for three seasons, but Albert was an impatient man. He sold the horse before the winners arrived – and arrive they did, in the form of 39 stakes races.

In addition to Positano and Grandmaster, the Dangars were also responsible for Welcome Jack, a New Zealand champion and the winner of 11 stakes events. They stood the horse at Neotsfield for many years, producing the winners of the AJC Derby and Epsom Handicap near the turn of the century. Such was the success of the Dangars that their colours became as famous as any on Sydney racecourses. But Albert was not a man to wait on horse racing. Convinced that his luck lay elsewhere, exeunt the thoroughbreds from Baroona, replaced by Arab and Suffolk Punch breeds.

Rodney Dangar was frustrated at his father's shortsightedness, but Albert's word was law. It would not be questioned. Nevertheless, young Rodney couldn't understand why the successes of Neotsfield could not be duplicated at Baroona. The land was rich with limestone, good for breeding bone into horses, and there was plenty of space to rotate stock. But it was only in 1913 that he was finally able to test his suspicions. After Albert died, Dangar began to sell off the Arabs and draughts and collect a small band of thoroughbreds. By the mid-1920s he had a select string of broodmares, and a racehorse here and there.

He was also the last Dangar standing at Whittingham, for Neotsfield had been dispersed in 1924, subdivided into various estates. Local breeder Percy Brown had set up his Randwick Lodge stud on part of it, and Dangar and his neighbour became good friends. By 1926, in the autumn after Alwina arrived at Baroona, Dangar was looking for something for his pretty new filly. He wanted a stallion, a match that would produce another Poseidon or Positano, but he couldn't choose which one. In the end, fate refused to leave him scratching around in the dark. It presented him, in 1928, with a horse called Pantheon.

2

Pantheon

It was a stubborn prejudice but there was no shifting it. The bias against locally bred stallions was thick and netted to Australia's bloodstock industry, and it was the reason that Joseph E. Brien, the 58-year-old master of Kingsfield Stud, found himself on a steamship to England in late 1924. Brien was a self-creation, a hardworking, astute businessman who had delved into horse racing headfirst. He craved the respectability that came with success in the Sport of Kings. With his son Cecil, he had raced the brilliant horses Malt King and Beragoon and, by 1925, he was standing the imported English stallion Rossendale. By nature of being an English import, and not an unfashionable Australian, Rossendale was doing very well and making money. With this in mind, J.E. Brien thought the expense and labour of a round trip to England worth every penny. When he spotted a handsome, masculine-looking bay colt called Spalpeen, a horse who was already campaigning the English racetracks, he liked what he saw very much.

Spalpeen was born in 1921, by Tracery out of Scotch Rose, a nicely bred mare by St Leger and Eclipse winner Your Majesty. He was owned by English newspaper baron Sir Edward Hulton and trained by Matthew Dawson Waugh. The colt started racing on

14 June 1923, in the Berkshire Foal Plate at Newbury. The two-year-old began at odds of 11/4, probably because of his attractive breeding and Hulton ownership, and he ran third in the five-furlong sprint. It was a promising start, and Spalpeen was stepped up for the July Stakes three weeks later. He ran third. When he resumed racing the following season as a three year-old, he won first up in the Spring Stakes over a mile and a quarter. His next two starts came in the 2000 Guineas at Newmarket, where he managed only seventh of 20, and then the Epsom Derby, finishing eighteenth of 27 runners.

Hulton must have been at a loss with his horse, for Spalpeen was suggesting great potential. He could win, just not in the races that really counted. J.E. Brien had his chequebook at the ready.

On paper, Spalpeen was an attractive candidate for Brien. Progeny of Tracery were yet to make their way to Australia, so the market was raw. Tracery himself was an outstanding piece of pedigree. Actually an American-bred horse, he was born in 1909 by the great Rock Sand, and owned by arguably the most influential racing identity in America, August Belmont II. Racing in England, Tracery ran third in the Derby before winning the St Leger, the Eclipse and the Champion Stakes. For Brien, the fact that Tracery had won the mile-and-three-quarter St Leger meant that staying lines were strong in Spalpeen, and that was a good thing for Australia's distance races. Sir Edward Hulton relinquished Spalpeen to the Australian for 2400 guineas, and Brien readied the shipping papers.

***

On the long crossing back to Australia in February 1925, J.E. Brien had plenty of time to consider Spalpeen's future. Already the Australian press had labelled his new horse 'an important purchase' so, electing to campaign his four year-old colt, Brien sent Spalpeen to Randwick trainer Fred Williams. But there was one small detail demanding attention. The horse had a ridiculous name.

A 'spalpeen' was a workman or labourer, even a rascal to some, and not so long ago Brien had changed his own name from O'Brien to refresh his reputation in racing. He didn't want anything to do with working-class connotations, so he arrived upon the name 'Pantheon' for his new horse – a different innuendo altogether. Here was a word associated with the gods, and that seemed to suit the owner and his aspirations much better.

Pantheon spent the early part of his arrival acclimatising. By September he was ready for his first start, and it came in the Chelmsford Stakes at Randwick where he finished eighth. Next was the AJC Warwick Stakes, and he ran a creditable third. Williams then started the horse in the AJC Craven Plate, and he ran third again. Shipping south, Pantheon started in the weight-for-age W.S. Cox Plate against the brilliant, irascible Manfred and the consistent The Night Patrol. Manfred stuck his nose out on the line to win by a short head from The Night Patrol, with Pantheon three lengths away third.

Trainer and owner were pleased after the Cox Plate. There was no disgrace in losing to Manfred, but in as many starts, Pantheon had finished third three times. He was about ripe for a win. On the first day of the VRC carnival at Flemington, the horse lined up for the mile-and-a-quarter Melbourne Stakes (renamed the Mackinnon Stakes in 1936). But when victory looked certain, Pilliewinkie edged past Pantheon in the shadow of the line and snatched the win by a neck.

Pantheon ran fourth in the Linlithgow Stakes that week, and on the final day of the meeting he contested the C.B. Fisher Plate. Yet again, he finished third, and he was returned to Sydney to rest. Brien was frustrated with his horse, though not discouraged. Pantheon had started six times since arriving in Australia for places no worse than fourth. When he started racing again in February 1926, he was a fitter and more experienced horse, and Williams started him at Caulfield, in the St George Stakes over nine furlongs. Again he ran second. He followed this with another second, this time at Flemington, and then another second in the Governor's Plate. At Rosehill on 20 March he ran third in the Rawson Stakes and, unbelievably, another third in the Chipping Norton Stakes at Warwick Farm. When the AJC autumn carnival began at Randwick, Pantheon was again beaten. Brien was finding it hard to shrug off his doubts by now. But on the final day, his horse stepped out in the Dangar Handicap over a mile and a half. The race was an honorary event for none other than the late AJC committeeman Henry Cary Dangar, and Pantheon finally broke his drought in the colony, winning by a short head. Both J.E. Brien and Fred Williams heaved an almighty sigh of relief that their expensive import had finally won a race.

Pantheon returned in September 1926 to win the Spring Handicap at Warwick Farm first up. On the opening day of the AJC spring meeting, when he met Spearfelt for the first time, he ran third. The following Monday, Pantheon ran second in the Metropolitan, but on the Saturday he won the two-mile Randwick Plate by three lengths. Williams had no doubt now that the imported horse would stay the Melbourne Cup distance. With ordinary luck, he might even win it.

Pantheon ran second again in the Melbourne Stakes on the first day of the Cup meeting. Brien and Williams had cause to be confident for the big race on Tuesday. Their horse had already won over two miles, and he was carrying one of Australia's best jockeys in Jim Pike. But to Brien's grief, Spearfelt prevailed by half a length, with Pantheon a breath away in third. The time, 3:22 3/4, equalled the course record.

Brien didn't know whether to be thrilled or annoyed with his import. Pantheon had returned a tidy profit already, but the horse lingered ceaselessly on the fringes of greatness. He had been racing solidly for nearly two years, not including his two seasons in England. He had contested each of the major spring and autumn carnivals in New South Wales and Victoria, and had run true and honest over every distance, from seven furlongs to more than two miles. He was, by March 1927, six years old, and it was on Brien's mind that his horse should soon go to stud. Just when was the veritable question.

Still, Pantheon was prepared for another racing season, and in the spring of 1927 he won the Rosehill Cup and the Spring Stakes. Brien allowed himself to hope again. Vying for another Melbourne Cup, Williams shipped the horse to Melbourne, but on the morning of 20 October, Pantheon was lame after a track gallop. Brien announced the horse's withdrawal from the Melbourne Cup, and though Pantheon was returned to training the following autumn, a new swathe of talent had appeared on the racecourse. The son of Tracery was now too old to compete with them. Valuing his horse too good a stud prospect, J.E. Brien retired Pantheon in the autumn of 1928.

The imported stallion had won nine races in Australia, for 10 seconds and eight thirds. He had won a fortune in place money for Brien, and it was hard to be disappointed with him, as inconsistent as his winning pattern was. He had won £15,990 in winnings, and had started 34 times in Australia, finishing in the money 27 times. Combined with his English record,

Pantheon finished third or better in 35 of his 46 starts. He had proved an excellent racehorse, against no less champions than Windbag, Spearfelt, Heroic and Manfred, and when he arrived at Kingsfield Stud in 1928, at Aberdeen in the Hunter Valley, promise was laid out like a magic carpet before him.

***

Across the paddocks from Baroona, on land subdivided from Neotsfield, Percy Brown had a predicament at his Randwick Lodge farm. It was well into the breeding season and he had booked five mares to go to Kingsfield, to this exciting new stallion Pantheon. It was November 1928, only a few months into the stallion's first season. Brown's problem lay with his having only four mares that morning, and he needed another to fill the quota he had paid for. He hurried up the hill to his affluent neighbour Rodney Dangar, and the two men discussed the predicament. Brown offered to take one of Dangar's mares with him to Kingsfield that afternoon.

Dangar chewed over his neighbour's suggestion. He wasn't the greatest fan of Joseph Brien, a man of suspect beginnings and deceptive pedigree, but more than that it didn't please Dangar to make bloodstock decisions on a whim. He preferred to think long and hard about his thoroughbreds, scouring their pedigrees for the perfect match. He also knew little about Pantheon as a stud prospect, and hadn't planned on complementing the stallion to any of his mares that season because he didn't send stock to Kingsfield Stud. Nonetheless, his good friend was in a bind, and Dangar's mind ran over the mares that were still dry.

Alwina, now a five-year-old, had not been covered. Dangar had sent the filly to Randwick trainer J. Whitton in 1926, but she hadn't stayed long. She showed no interest in running, nor possessed the will to even try, so she had come back to Baroona shortly after. Dangar had sent her to Percy Brown's imported stallion Rosewing, and the resultant foal, a little thing called Rosabel, was in training now. But Dangar didn't want Alwina breeding every year. He had rested the young mare in 1927, and in fact she was one of the only empty mares on the farm. He motioned to Brown to take her. 'I don't want to appear in the matter,' he said to his neighbour. 'Take her to fill up the number, and let me know the sum owing.'

And so became one of the greatest accidents of the Australian turf. Alwina was sent to Pantheon in the stallion's first season, an unplanned, providential match, and she was returned to Dangar a few days later in foal.

3

Good fortune is as necessary as a good racehorse

The trees around Baroona hung hot and still on 17 October 1929 when Peter Pan was born. It was sticky, oppressive spring heat, the kind that makes the crickets sing like an orchestra. Pantheon and Alwina, an accidental union, produced that day a colt of light chestnut colouring with a blond mane and tail, so blond he could have been palomino; it was at odds with almost every genetic combination in the thoroughbred breed. This colt was, quite simply, extraordinary to look at. Rodney Dangar noticed him immediately. From the beginning he was smitten with his new horse, and in later years he would admit that it was the colt's glamourous good looks that made him keep him.

The colt remained with Alwina until a weanling, gambolling and fooling about the paddocks of fair Baroona. He had an idyllic youth, and when it was time to be separated from the broodmares, at eight months old, he was sent to a small paddock of his own on the other side of the property. He sprouted into a massive weanling: all legs, and each straight as a rake. It was almost impossible for the Baroona residents to ignore him as his classy looks and pleasant nature endeared him to everyone. Even Dangar's mother, at 84, ambled out to visit him every morning. Still, the boss was insistent. The youngster was to receive no special treatment. He was never rugged or handfed, and he grew into an independent and curious yearling. When he had developed the necessary skeleton to carry a man, he was slowly, patiently broken in by William Shade and readied to become a racehorse. The boss had hopes for this one.

Dangar *did* have hopes. One evening, just after the colt had turned two, he found himself leaning on a fence post watching his horse trot across the paddock. It was one of those frozen moments for Dangar, a photograph that would come to him again later on. 'I've got him there,' he said quite aloud. 'That's my Cup horse.' His cousin, Richard Halifax Dangar, had left Baroona a few weeks before with high praise for the Pantheon youngster. 'Tell my cousin,' R.H. Dangar had said, 'that he has the best foal I've seen since Poseidon.' It was praise indeed. On 2 April 1920, on a hot, oily day in downtown Sydney, Dangar walked into the offices of the AJC and registered his new colt 'Peter Pan', certificate number B1906.

Dangar's choice of the name was obvious, as it was a connection to his sire Pantheon. However, it was Dangar's wife, Elsie, who chose it, as in her eyes it was perfect. Here was the young boy of a colt with brilliant blond hair who, she hoped, would later fly like J.M. Barrie's magical character. Fearing the name would be taken by other Pantheon progeny, Dangar wasted no time in registering it. But he had to think twice, because America already had its own celebrated racehorse called Peter Pan. He had won the Belmont Stakes in 1907 and had since become a notable sire. Fortunately, there were no rules in Australia preventing Dangar from using it too.

At Baroona, Peter Pan developed into a fine thoroughbred. He was lean, straight in the forelegs and unblemished. At the end of 1931, when Dangar shipped him to Sydney to the stables of trainer Frank McGrath, he looked every bit the stayer he was bred to be. He was ridiculously tall, and long and narrow in the shoulders. He had a beautiful eye, kind and inquisitive with a high arch, and his silver hair fell over his face like some flirtatious Hollywood starlet. He was Jean Harlow on four legs. Each and every time he walked out of the yard, people stopped to stare at this flashy new horse.

***

Frank McGrath leaned against the redbrick stable wall and listened to Rodney Dangar chatter. It was the morning of Phar Lap's death, four months after Peter Pan had arrived at McGrath's yard. Over the stable door beside him, in box number four, the old fellow Amounis beckoned for attention. McGrath had had Amounis since 1926, when his bookmaker friend William 'Bill' Pearson had obtained the tried horse from the sale ring. The gelding had gone on to win a trove of top races, including the 1930 Caulfield Cup and Futurity Stakes. Until Phar Lap, he was the highest earning racehorse in Australian history. McGrath was certain that he was, excepting Phar Lap, the best racehorse of these times.

Frank McGrath believed that good fortune in training was as necessary as a good racehorse, and the 65-year-old trainer had had good racehorses. Fortune had simply followed suit. McGrath was the centre of the Randwick racing scene, the epicentre of the racetrack's commotions. He was one of the most successful trainers there had ever been, but he was polite and pleasant. Success had not bloated his ego. These days he kept a team of nearly 20 horses, a huge number for these times. McGrath's age had not wearied him, for he was still bright and energetic. He had soft, amenable facial features, thick round spectacles, and there wasn't a more likeable, or more liked, man on Doncaster Avenue.

McGrath had been born in 1866 in the New South Wales rural district of Binalong, not far from Yass, the oldest of three sons. His father, an Irishman with a roving eye, kept a handful of horses on the country circuit, and this early exposure to racing was the start of Frank McGrath's life among horses. He moved into Randwick trainer John Allsop's stables as a riding apprentice and earned his grub like the rest of the lads, mucking stables and riding out, climbing the ranks. He moved soon after to the yard of Edward Keys, a Waverley trainer who had up to 50 horses at any one time, but McGrath's riding merits didn't arrive until he moved up the coast to Newcastle, to the yards of the respectably famous John Mayo, when he was 18 years old.

Mayo was impressed by the young horseman in his yard, and he gave Frank the ride on a horse called Prince Imperial, and together the pair landed the Grand Handicap at Hawkesbury, and when they lined up for the 1885 Caulfield Cup later in the year, a 10/1 joint favourite, McGrath's life changed forever. Approaching the straight, Prince Imperial was one of 41 horses going hell for leather, and when the two frontrunners fell they brought down 14 others, Prince Imperial and Frank McGrath among them. McGrath lay unconscious on the turf, but it was a lucky escape. Fellow jockey Donald Nicholson was killed, along with a horse called Uarah, and the race, forever labelled 'Grace Darling's Caulfield Cup' (after the winner), would remain the worst pile-up in Australian racing history. McGrath, crippled with injury, didn't ride again for six months.

He returned to the Newcastle and country circuits after that, and met with moderate success. His confidence had wavered, though he never admitted it. Each spring he hiked to Melbourne to ride trackwork for Flemington trainer Walter Hickenbotham. Track riding was easy, less dangerous, and during these mornings he was tossed aboard Carbine for a spurt around the course proper, and he swore he never saw a greater horse again. 'Old Jack' was the best there had ever been, he would say for the rest of his life.

By now settled in Randwick, the young rider could have scratched a living for many years this way, but he was bitten by constant headaches. The Caulfield crash had left a nasty legacy, so McGrath retired his irons and moved into training. At first he based himself in Goulburn, out in the sticks of New South Wales, but he moved back to the bright lights of Sydney in 1895, training on the pony circuits at Canterbury for several years with great success. A horse called Stormy was his first major success. The dashing little racehorse won enough races for McGrath to send him on his merry way to the top.

Success on the pony circuit allowed the young trainer to purchase a house and stables on Doncaster Avenue in Kensington, a suburb that hung off the western end of Randwick Racecourse. Doncaster Avenue ran parallel to the course, behind the grandstands and the tramlines, and it was the hub of the racing community. It was home to illustrious jockeys and colourful trainers, their wives, sons and daughters. Every morning, the street came alive with the sound of delivery carts, feed merchants and farriers, and the clippity-clop of racehorses in and out of the racetrack. Towards the southern end sat Frank McGrath's stately home, Stormy, named after his little pony, and two doors along was his stable yard.

It was nearly the end of the century when McGrath moved in to Doncaster Avenue, about the same time the AJC passed a life-altering law unto its trainers. Overnight, it became forbidden to train, ride or compete ponies at Randwick Racecourse and its sister track Warwick Farm, and McGrath was faced with a decision. He could stick to the ponies he knew so well, or he could concentrate on the registered racing of thoroughbreds. Attracted by the better prizemoney and lured by the glamour of horse racing, McGrath relinquished his smaller horses, and therein began the life a trainer only dreams about. McGrath had, in succession, AJC Derby and Victoria Derby winner Abundance, then Little Toy and Kingloch. Little Toy belonged to McGrath outright, and when the horse won the 1906 Doncaster, the trainer built a row of four cottages on the northern end of his house. McGrath also coupled the Doncaster result that year into the Sydney Cup result, and collected. It made him a fortune overnight, and triggered a life of huge betting plunges that often broke the ring on a Saturday afternoon.

In 1909, when rich, opinionated coal magnate John 'Baron' Brown sent Prince Foote to McGrath's yard, success took on new meaning for the trainer. Prince Foote broke his maiden in the 1909 AJC Sires' Produce Stakes, and in his three-year-old season won nine of 11 starts, including the AJC Derby. In the autumn, McGrath took the horse to Melbourne where he won the Victoria Derby by six lengths and fell into favouritism for the Melbourne Cup. McGrath placed his bets on Prince Foote early and secured excellent odds, but owner Brown was not so quick. When he couldn't get anything better than 4/1 about his horse, he demanded Prince Foote be scratched. Brown was a spoilt man who liked to win. What is more, he liked to be the *only* winner. McGrath refused, and at the intervention of racing stewards, Prince Foote took his place in the field of 1909. He ran away with the race by three lengths. The colt trained on to win the Cumberland Stakes, AJC Plate, VRC Champion Stakes, and the VRC and AJC St Legers in 1910. The relationship between owner and trainer, however, remained strained.

The same year, McGrath won the AJC Derby for the second successive year with his own horse, Tanami. But it came at a cost for the trainer. Of the two runners McGrath had entered in the Derby, the other was a Baron Brown colt. The quarrelsome owner did not accept defeat lightly, and was furious that McGrath had pitted another horse against his own. The morning following Tanami's win, McGrath lost all of Brown's horses from his stable. The whole episode was a comedy to McGrath. Brown was terse, blunt and bullish. He was not an easy man to train for, even stipulating to McGrath which horses he wanted his own to gallop with each morning. When the two men parted ways after the Derby, they remained good friends, though McGrath was quite relieved to be rid of him.

After 1910, McGrath trained a flurry of decent horses, notably the jumpers Grafnax and Honeydew.

It was a compliment to him that he could work both disciplines of racing and it was due, almost wholly, to his individual assessment of horses. 'Hard and fast rules are impossible,' he would later tell the *Argus* about training racehorses. 'One must first study a horse and regard it as an individual.' Through the war years and into the booming twenties, McGrath trained horses that won the December Stakes, Maribyrnong Plate and successive Gimcrack Stakes. He moonlighted with betting coups that raked him a fortune, but in 1926, when Amounis arrived in his yard, he was reacquainted with wild success. Amounis amounted 25 principal race wins under McGrath, including successive VRC Cantala and Linlithgow Stakes, the AJC Craven Plate and Epsom Handicap, the Caulfield Stakes and Caulfield Cup of 1930. When he won the Futurity of that year with an impost of 10st 4lb, it left no doubt in McGrath's mind that Amounis was out of the ordinary.

In any other year Amounis would have been a supreme champion. But fortune had pitted him against Phar Lap, and there had been no room at the top. Phar Lap, completely and convincingly, had won nearly everything, and had allowed Amounis very little space. Nonetheless, this grand gelding had made the hard times of the Depression the good times for McGrath, when all around him had hung dispossession and dejection. At 65 years of age, the old trainer was a proven success. He was enthusiastic, a glass half-full sort of man, kind and approachable. Most of the time, he ‘forgot’ to collect the rent for his little cottages down the street, especially when he saw his tenants doing it tough.

Looking down the shed row that sunny afternoon, McGrath had a glimpse of the season to come. There was an Irish horse called Denis Boy in stable number one, and Rosehill Guineas winner Lightning March across the way, as well as a promising bay horse called Satmoth. And there was this new horse, Peter Pan. McGrath had to concede the hard times hadn’t come through his gates. The same could be said for Mr Dangar, he thought. In tailored trousers and polished shoes, the pastoralist looked every bit as well-bred as his colt. The old trainer gave Amounis one last scratch, and he wrapped up his afternoon with Dangar. The boys were arriving for their duties, and with the latest bustle around the yard, the curious Peter Pan had stuck his nose out of his stall for a look.

4

The first start

Early on the morning of 13 May 1932, Frank McGrath leaned over the running rail of Randwick Racecourse and watched as Peter Pan drummed four furlongs around the middle grass, a training track inside the course proper, in 51 seconds. It wasn't an extraordinary time. The flags were out 30 feet from the rail and the going was fast, and two other horses galloped the same time for the distance. Nevertheless, it was the fastest half-mile clocked that morning. McGrath watched as jockey E. 'Jock' Reynolds eased the colt down, then signalled to Reynolds to bring Peter Pan in. All's well, McGrath mused as he headed back to the yard. It was, after all, Friday the 13th.

McGrath exited the racecourse via McGrath's Lane, a strip of land he had given the AJC that allowed horses access to the racetrack from Doncaster Avenue. Heading south, McGrath reached his yard in minutes, where boys and horses moved in all directions between the boxes, the wash bay and the tack room. The last handful of horses arrived back to the yard, among them Jock Reynolds aboard Peter Pan. The blond colt had hardly turned a hair. He was fit and full of beans and it was just as well. Tomorrow was Tattersall's Club raceday at Randwick, and Peter Pan's first race start.

McGrath and Dangar had deliberated the colt's first-race options for months. There were attractive prizes for two-year-old racing in Sydney, notably the Sires' Produce Stakes. But McGrath had elected to bypass it with Peter Pan because the colt hadn't yet grown into himself. He was leggy and undeveloped, and had only started on fast work at the end of March. Now he was better built to withstand racing. He had a grasp of galloping with other horses and of going ahead alone, and was ready to start racing. McGrath, not hopeful of a first-up win, had selected the fourth event on the next day's card for Peter Pan's debut: the Tattersall's Two-Year-Old Handicap over six furlongs at Randwick.

The yard was winding down by mid-morning when McGrath headed home for a cup of tea, and that was when he heard the latest news. Up and down Doncaster Avenue, like electricity zipping through water, people cheered that the mulish New South Wales premier Jack Lang had been forced from office by the state governor.

McGrath took a raincheck on that cup of tea and hurried back to the racecourse. He knew that the dismissal of the Lang government would have terrific consequences for horse racing. Slowly, doggedly, Lang had been choking racing in New South Wales. In 1930 he had introduced the Winning Bets Tax, a 10 per cent levy on all winning tickets at the racecourse, and it had done a marvellous job of driving down oncourse betting. In contrast, business was booming in the illegal offcourse establishments. The tax had had a rippling effect across racing. When the sport most needed it, attendance had plummeted. The previous week, the totalisator at Randwick had been banned altogether, but it was a happy scene that greeted Frank McGrath when he joined the other trainers on Randwick Racecourse.

Lang hadn't had an easy time in office. The crash of the stock markets in 1929 had left Australia in a sorry heap. The federal government, in the years preceding the crisis, had spent lavishly on telegraph and telephone lines, railways and road works. Some £350 million had been borrowed from England to pay for it all, but when the Depression set in, the mother country came calling on its debt. The states of Australia were forced to honour their interest payments, and in most respects, human life suffered. By 1932, the fallout was catastrophic. There were lines for food, for rations and for work. Families were hiked onto the streets when they couldn't pay their rents. Lonely, demoralised men stood on street corners selling shoes, or battled with their neighbours for a day's work. The jobless accounted for a staggering 32 per cent of all Australians. The price of butter had gone up by a halfpenny a pound, following recent hikes in the cost of jam and eggs. Onions would be next. So that morning, even as a change of government promised to lift the spirit of New South Wales, people were tired and trodden from hardship.

Word spread among the trainers that the tote ban had been lifted right away. The totalisator had been a successful element of Randwick racing since 1917, turning over half-a-million pounds in its first season. At its peak in 1924, it had made over £1.5 million, though the Depression had nipped that figure in half. Still, if the powers at Randwick could reinstate the machine for the next day's racing, Tattersall's Club could have a profitable day in store.

McGrath shook his head in disbelief as he strolled back to Doncaster Avenue. If 24 hours was a short time in racing, it was obviously a short time in politics too. What else would they see in this turbulent year of 1932? The state government had collapsed overnight; Phar Lap had died. McGrath was grateful that he had ducked the worst of the Depression. His big owners like Bill Pearson and Rodney Dangar had ensured that by giving him brilliant horses and paying him swiftly and generously. But his smaller owners were doing it tough, barely managing the £3 and 10 pence (£3/10d) training fee per horse. Few trainers were as lucky as McGrath. The feed merchant was banging on doors up and down Doncaster Avenue, but he had yet to call at 156.

***

A little after 9am the following morning, the *Referee* journalist Jack F. Dexter, or 'Pilot', strolled into the administrative offices at Randwick Racecourse to check on the progress of the tote machine. Bookmakers were already setting up in their respective enclosures around the racetrack, and most were readying for a day's betting minus the tote. To them, and to 'Pilot' too, it looked unlikely the machine would be operating. It seemed too great a task to organise its reinstatement. But within the hour, the Automatic Totalisator Company had rounded up its staff and by noon its manager, Mr J. Wilkinson, was ready to open the booths. He had organised an 11th-hour delivery of cash from the bank, which included £4000 in silver coin, and as patrons began to stream through the racecourse gates, there was renewed vigour in the air. The tote was up and operating.

The race meeting was occurring on behalf of the Sydney Tattersall's Club, a distinguished league for gentlemen that had strong ties to betting, horse racing and general sporting. The club's headquarters overlooked Hyde Park, and in any given day on any given week, gentlemen of the city could be found inside, sucking on expensive cigars, playing billiards or swimming. Among its members were top trainers William Kelso and Mick Polson, and Phar Lap's American owner, David Davis. But though it was a playground for the wealthy and well to do, Sydney Tattersall's was in the oppressive grip of the Depression. Profits had dropped to just £680 by early 1932, when two years earlier the club's surplus had been a record £7930. Membership had also been affected, so race meetings, like the one it had scheduled at Randwick for Saturday 14 May, were an opportunity to generate revenue. With the tote spinning, Tattersall's could expect a better turnout than previous meetings.

Randwick Racecourse had swelled to 17,000 racegoers by mid-afternoon, and the weather was autumnal and glorious, so the track was good, firm under foot. The Two-Year-Old Handicap, Peter Pan's race, was due off at 3.10pm, and 20 minutes before start time Peter Pan was in the parade ring with 17 other horses. He peered around at the thousands of faces clamouring the yard and they, in turn, peered back, fascinated by the uncommonly handsome racehorse with the silver hair. The bookies, however, were disenchanted with the son of Pantheon. He looked immature and foalish. Betting on the two-year-old event offered plenty of value, with four horses sharing favouritism at 6/1, but Peter Pan wasn't among them.

The colt was one of two horses in the field starting for the first time. The other was Maltdale, a black Rossendale colt, and the two youngsters were carrying equal weights of 7st 7lb. McGrath had asked Jock Reynolds to pilot Peter Pan, and the jockey donned Dangar's silks for the first time: orange with green hoops and orange cap. The pair cantered to the six-furlong start with plenty to do. In the betting they had drifted beyond 20/1, and it would be the only race in which Peter Pan, beyond his looks, attracted little attention.

Reynolds lined up the colt at the six-furlong start and stood before the starting barrier. The tape, a five-stranded elastic system, was stretched across the track in front of them. The AJC starter, Jack Gaxieu, placed his hand on the lever, and Reynolds looked down the track ahead of him. He was drawn midfield, and beside him, Diamond de Rouge was giving trouble. At two minutes after start time, Gaxieu sent the tapes into the air, and the 17 horses surged forward. Peter Pan, jumping for the first time in a race, followed their lead and took off too.

The field thundered straight for nearly three furlongs, sorting itself into running order. Diamond de Rouge worked his way across to the rails, and by the half-mile post he was a length in front of Vista, with Delmond and Chiefava on his heels. Jock Reynolds was having a hard time with the inexperienced Peter Pan. The colt was all running in the early stages, and Reynolds tucked him between horses right back in the field. But into the home turn, with three furlongs to go, Peter Pan lost all concentration. Staring into the grandstands on his left, the colt galloped awkwardly down the straight with his neck skewed and a tired Reynolds coaxing him back to the rails. Ahead of them, Diamond de Rouge was fighting out the finish with Vista. The two leaders were level within the shadow of the judge, but Diamond de Rouge dug deep to prevail by a half-neck in the time of 1:11 3/4. Peter Pan, overwhelmed by the task asked of him, finished eighth.

McGrath was not concerned. In fact, he was rather pleased. He had had no illusions that Peter Pan would win the race, and the colt had finished the race with the field. McGrath had noticed during trackwork that Peter Pan had developed a curious habit of staring into the grandstands down the straight, and that was when they were empty. Today, the stands buzzed with thousands of bobbing faces. On any given day, Peter Pan was aggressively curious – but experience and maturity would knock that out of him. The colt trotted back to scale tired but sound, and McGrath exchanged a few words with his jockey, learning nothing he hadn't seen from the stands. He then headed back to the yard, for he didn't have another runner that day.

The race had been run true and quick, the winning time very smart for two-year-olds. Peter Pan hadn't shown anything remarkable, though he had beaten home half the field. McGrath knew the horse needed time, and racing, to figure out his new career. Dangar agreed. He had expected no miracles from his new colt, and he hadn't got any. He knew that Peter would only improve.

***

Peter Pan was rested on Sunday morning. A first race was a big change to a young horse's routine, both physically and psychologically, and McGrath had learned right away that this colt – this dexterous, sharp-minded son of Pantheon – suited light work and often. Amounis, on the other hand, devoured hard work without salt. But McGrath's great maxim was that every horse was different, and their individual attention was what made them win or lose. In Peter Pan's case, his light frame required only light exercise to remain fit, so on this Sunday, when most of the Randwick horses were rested, Peter Pan enjoyed a stroll in the afternoon and a roll in the sandbox, then it was business as usual on Monday.

For the first few mornings after raceday, the course officials directed trackwork away from the course proper as it was the only way to repair the grass after 127 or so horses had ripped through it. McGrath's team cantered over the middle grasses on Monday and Tuesday morning, and on Wednesday they used the tan track. The tan was a sand course that ran inside the A grass, shorter in circumference but heavier in going. It was a fact that galloping horses on sandy surfaces worked them harder, but on this Wednesday morning McGrath couldn't have planned his bad luck better. Peter Pan, clipping along at a leisurely gallop, ran onto something that drove itself into the delicate tissues of a hind foot. When Jock Reynolds felt the colt baulk underneath him, he pulled up straight away.

Peter Pan was instantly lame, and it took McGrath moments to arrive on the scene. He signalled for a horse float to be called in, and they sent Peter Pan back to the yard to gauge a diagnosis. It was impossible to tell how serious the injury was. Neither Reynolds nor McGrath knew if the colt had snapped a tendon, broke a bone or stepped on a shoe, but back in the yard it was plain as day what had happened. The frog in Peter Pan's near-hind foot, the fleshy triangular part on the underside of the hoof, was swollen and sensitive and there, quite clearly, was an old rusted nail from a horseshoe. McGrath called the track veterinarian Roy Stewart right away.

The adage 'no foot, no horse' was firmly on the minds of those that surrounded Peter Pan's box, watching Roy Stewart pry the nail out. There was McGrath and his brother Maurice, who was the foreman of the yard, and Amounis's attendant George Phillips. Peter Pan was in a nervous sweat over the situation he had found himself in, and McGrath was anxious to calm the colt. After an injection of antitoxin, and another for tetanus, and concerns of infection firmly on McGrath's mind, the trainer prepared a poultice for the injury. Using meal mixed with cold water, and adding a menthol agent like eucalyptus, he blended the poultice in a bucket on the stable floor and packed Peter Pan's injured foot. The colt stood trembling beside him. With luck, the concoction would draw out any abscess or infection, soothing the injured area until it was able to heal on its own. But luck was nowhere to be seen in the days that followed Wednesday 18 May. Quite clearly the foot was infected, and Peter Pan grew dangerously ill.

McGrath was no physician, but he suspected the colt had blood poisoning. Within a few days Peter Pan was running a fever – one minute his temperature was off the charts and the next deceptively normal, coupled with a lack of appetite and restlessness. The colt's light chestnut colour had turned a distressed, sweaty red. There had either been inflammation of the pedal bone, which the nail had hit when the colt drove it into his foot, or the wound itself was unhealthy. Either way, blood poisoning had killed many a racehorse, and McGrath was taking no chances. He stationed a round-the-clock watch on Peter Pan, and painstakingly, carefully, he set about trying to purify the colt's blood.

If McGrath had moved 10 years through time he would have had the miracle of penicillin at hand, but that antibiotic wouldn't present itself until the mid-1940s, and he therefore had to rely on traditional wisdom. He treated the hoof with diluted household disinfectant, then dusted it with iodoform, an iodine compound that was widely used as an antiseptic on wounds. Then he wrapped the foot in stable bandages and repeated the process twice a day. It was difficult to make the sick colt eat. He was listless and feverish and partially exhausted, so McGrath made his food as digestible as possible – ground oats and chopped hay, and cornmeal moistened with warm water. Despite the relentless attention, though, Peter Pan lay on death's door. McGrath kept Dangar on alert about the colt's condition and wore a path between his house, the telephone, and the stable, then waited.

Peter Pan fought for his life bullishly. There was stubbornness in him that rejected his illness. Though he was supposed to stay confined, he tried to barge out of his stable when the door opened. He didn't want to lie down, or slip into a comfortable state of comatose. He was difficult, and because of that he began to win the battle. Slowly, and with McGrath's vigilant nursing, the infection drained from the colt and Peter Pan began to recover. McGrath and Dangar were overcome with relief. The colt started to eat, and walk, until his trainer was no longer concerned. But for many weeks, Peter Pan didn't glimpse the rail at Randwick. His two-year-old season disappeared from whence it had come. Sending the horse out to grass for four weeks, McGrath decided to start all over again in the spring. He had now glimpsed Peter Pan's resilience, had witnessed his tenacious, uncompromising spirit, and he was excited. The colt headed to a spelling property at Doonside, west of Sydney, not to return until the end of June.

5

The first win

It was after four o'clock on the wintry afternoon of 17 August 1932 when Colin Stephen, respected chairman of the Australian Jockey Club, drew a hush over the committee gathered before him. The club, for the racing season 1931–32, had tallied a loss of £6347, and the committee was appalled. Members had gathered at 6 Bligh Street, Sydney, to discuss it. Admission was down, so revenue was down, and the club had paid over £2 million in state taxes. That afternoon, fingers wagged at the ailing Warwick Farm Racecourse.

Warwick Farm was the AJC's secondary track after Randwick, and it sat on a rural plot some 22 miles southwest of Sydney. The AJC, under Colin Stephen, had negotiated its purchase in 1922, and racing in its officialdom began there in 1925. The track was an attractive one. It wasn't flanked by creeping industry or urban sprawl, as was Randwick. Rather, Warwick Farm felt like a picnic racecourse with AJC trimmings. It had wattle trees and scrubby, open spaces, but the straight could be shallow and burnt; that was the price of its west country climate. Stephen bellowed in its defence that afternoon. Though its accumulated loss since 1922 was estimated at £76,000, the racetrack offered, on a regular basis, contests for good horses to compete in high-class company and, as such, the AJC chairman had little difficulty in reminding his committee of its value. In better economic times, he reasoned, the banknotes would roll through the turnstiles again.

Peter Pan, meanwhile, had returned from Doonside. On 1 August, with a speckle of rain dripping over the Eastern Suburbs, he had aged a year with every thoroughbred in Australia. The birthday rule had been introduced by the AJC in 1859 to validate the weight-for-age scale, so though not actually three years old until 17 October, Peter Pan was a three-year-old on paper.

During his spell, he matured as McGrath knew he would. His girth had deepened and his shoulders grown, and he was now a streamlined, loose-limbed racehorse of 16 hands. There was nothing squatty or sprinter about him. He had wide, deep nostrils, an angular nose and his tell-tale silver mane, which fell in tousled order and gave him such easy beauty as to be almost human. To boot, he had figured out this whole racing thing. The colt had been back in training since the middle of July, but he had slung such energy at his trackwork that word had spread among the clockers about 'Macker' McGrath's new horse. Each morning, McGrath would send Peter Pan out with his sparring partner, Queen's Pilot, and each morning the colt produced racy brilliance.

The old trainer was convinced he had the best prospect since Prince Foote 25 years before. Early in

August, he sent Peter Pan to Rosebery, a pony track a few miles southwest of Randwick, and with Dangar in the audience, Peter surged from behind in a seven-furlong pipe opener. He beat Denis Boy and Satmoth, his stablemates, without breaking a sweat. What was better was that McGrath had arranged the workout at midday, so the only eyes to this early brilliance were those of owner, trainer and riders. On 16 August, Peter galloped four furlongs over the middle grass at Randwick in 1:10, with the flags out 18 feet. Two days later, he covered the same distance in 1:07. On 23 August, with McGrath's stable jockey Andy Knox in the saddle, Peter Pan galloped four furlongs in 51 seconds. It was a smart effort.

The benchmark for track times lay with the rule of running a furlong in 12 seconds. A standard racehorse, carrying a standard weight over six furlongs, would ideally race at the rate of 12 seconds per furlong. That meant that a six-furlong sprint would be run in 1:12. But it was loose ideology. Firstly, Australian races were rarely run flatchat from post to post. An Australian horse-race over six furlongs typically began with a jostle for position in the first quarter-mile (two furlongs), then an easing of pace for the second quarter, and inside the two-furlong post the race began with earnest, so that the final two furlongs were usually the fastest. At Randwick, the six-furlong course record was 1:10 1/4, while the world record, dubiously run in 1929 at Brighton, England, was a fraction over 1:06. None of these times factored in the incline of the straight, or the racecourse itself, or the headwind conditions that some horses ran into. They didn't explain what a standard weight was either. But even if Andy Knox had been sparing Peter Pan over the four furlongs of 23 August, his 51 seconds was smart going.

Knox was a local jockey of working-class background, and he wasn't beneath the early starts for trackwork. He had been a successful pony hoop before defecting to thoroughbreds, and had since won his way into serious contention for top-jockey honours. The 28-year-old was a hard worker and an earnest competitor, and such character made him McGrath's first choice. He was at trackwork most mornings, piloting horses from all strings at Randwick, and his commitment made him prominent in selections. But among the jockeys of the day, with his steely expression and iron nerve and nickname of 'The Basher', it was generally conceded there was none that could give a horse a greater hiding than Andrew Reginald Knox.

McGrath had swung Knox into Peter Pan's saddle because the colt needed an experienced, unnegotiable hand on the reins. As the pair grew acquainted during their early morning workouts, McGrath nominated Peter Pan for the Farm Novice Handicap at Warwick Farm on Saturday 27 August. It would be the colt's second start, and his first run in 105 days.

***

Raceday, and Frank McGrath's yard was a different place. It buzzed with restrained excitement, and on the morning of the Warwick Farm meeting there was extra special nuance. Amounis was racing. McGrath had commissioned a large horse float to ferry his team to Warwick Farm, and by mid-morning it was parked on Doncaster Avenue. The driver opened the flap doors and dropped the two ramps on the pavement. Rugged and ready, Peter Pan, Satmoth, Lightning March and Amounis stepped up the wooden gangway into their compartments. The journey to Warwick Farm was a long one. The float rattled out of the residential labyrinth of the Eastern Suburbs and into the industrial fields of the west, trundling down the Hume Highway with Frank McGrath in tow in his Hupmobile motorcar. By the time they arrived at the racecourse, which flanked the west shore of the Georges River, the morning had grown obstinately hot.

Racegoers were spilling into Warwick Farm from the nearby train station, peeling off their layers at the unexpected heatwave. By midday, Warwick Farm's grandstands were buzzing, its lawns dotted with picnic blankets and the soundtrack of cheerful banter everywhere. It was the first big race meeting of the new season, and Peter Pan's Farm Novice Handicap was the second race. Then there were the Hobartville Stakes being contested by the state's top three-year-old, Kuvera; the Warwick Stakes, in which McGrath's Amounis and Satmoth were racing against the 1929 Melbourne Cup winner, Nightmarch; the Campbelltown

Handicap, which Lightning March was contesting; and the Spring and Glenlee handicaps. The meeting had attracted Sydney's best racehorses, as it was a good trial for the AJC's spring races in October.

Peter Pan entered the mounting yard about 20 minutes before start time. The afternoon had become terribly hot, and it would tell on the track. There were already bald patches on the home straight where the grass had given up, and a shallow cloud of dust had tracked the hurdle race all the way around. The going would be fast. Peter Pan had drawn an inside position in the field of 20, and the handicapper had given him 7st 10lb. It was relative weight. Top weight in the field was 8st 7lb, while the lightest was 7st 2lb, and Peter Pan was to start the most inexperienced in the field.

The ring had not been fooled. Green he may have been, but Peter Pan had skinnied into favouritism. By the time Andy Knox was boosted into the saddle, the colt was paying 5/2 against. McGrath's plunge had been felt somewhere. The trainer was certain his colt would account in this race, and had laid large on him doing so. He had worked hard since July to keep Peter Pan away from beady eyes, but whispers had leaked from the McGrath stable all week. Money had also come for Archmel, who was getting 9/2, and a brown colt called Babili was circling the ring. Babili, trained by top Randwick man William Kelso, was offering 5/1, and the Kelso stable had laid on him.

Knox eased Peter Pan down to the start on a tight rein. The one-mile point was from a chute in the extreme left corner of the racecourse. There was no doubt Warwick Farm was a tighter track than Randwick. The straight was 19 feet narrower and 275 feet shorter. The course itself was a triangle. The far turn was sharper than any turn at Randwick, and it needed to be ridden differently. Post positions came to account, fast starters factored, and there was less room to make one's own luck. Knox had a job ahead of him on this track with the fractious, over-thinking Peter Pan.

The starter threw the tape up at two minutes after two o'clock and 20 horses, Peter Pan drawn inside, leaned on their hindquarters and dashed up and away. Knox, ready for the jump, got Peter away fairly, but the early speed of Western Sky, Gold Joy and Samian King cut him off. The sprinters in the field simply ran around Peter Pan and moved across him to the rails, and Knox found himself behind a wall of horses early on.

The field settled into the first turn, tightly bunched with Western Sky showing the way. Babili, a small horse, was lodged halfway back, and Knox was having a hard time keeping Peter Pan off heels. The colt, bounding over the turf, had absolutely nowhere to go, and was finding it impossible to get into stride. His head was in the air, and he was annoyed. When the horse on his outside shoved him against the running rail at the six furlongs, Peter Pan had had enough. Knox felt the horse go flat beneath him, and knew exactly what had happened. Peter Pan, seeing he was sandwiched, had reasoned there was no point to this battle and had simply stopped racing. Knox did the only thing he could. He pulled the colt out and galloped him wide. When the field swung into the home turn, Peter Pan was in front of only seven horses.

Knox had a dilemma. He could coax the colt along near the back of the field and wait for a run between horses, or he could send Peter Pan after the leaders right away. Because Knox could bleed the last ounce out of his mounts, he decided to go after the lead right away. He drew his whip and hit the colt once behind the saddle, and Peter was jolted out of his sulk. He set off for the front of the field in a panic. The response was so quick, so devastating, that Knox rode hands and heels off the turn for home.

Peter Pan swept towards the leaders in a few kicks, making full use of the 75-foot lane. He ran down the middle of the straight, and at this rate he would swallow the field. Western Sky and Gold Joy had dropped away beaten, and Samian King was also tiring. But Babili had challenged for the lead, and with two furlongs to go William Kelso's horse was in front. Knox shook Peter Pan to go after Babili, but to his horror, the colt had begun to stare into the grandstands. He was drifting to the outside rail, his inattention wasting his chances in the dying stages of the race, and Knox cracked the colt a second time. He planted his whip on Peter's flank, and jolted once again by the sting of Knox's hand, Peter Pan dashed like a scalded cat down the straight. His speed was so tremendous that jockey Edgar Britt, riding Babili, didn't see him coming. Peter Pan rushed past the judge in the middle of the straight, with Babili near the rails, and not a stride later, Peter Pan left Babili for dust. But it was too late. Neither the jockeys, nor Frank McGrath in the stands, nor the thousands that had cheered themselves senseless, knew which horse had won. They threw their eyes to the semaphore board and awaited the judge's response.

On this day, with thousands of nervous ticket holders on the verge of bursting the ring, the photo-finish camera would have been a useful contraption. But such progress was not to be made until 1946 – 14 years later – and when Peter Pan's number appeared beside that of Babili, the judges unable to split the colts, the dead-heat result sent a cheer across Warwick Farm. But Edgar Britt was spitting chips. Jumping off Babili in the mounting yard, he swore at the result. 'I thought I beat him easily by a head,' he spat, within earshot of a dozen journalists.

Dead-heat results were a common occurrence, and it meant that both horses shared the first prize equally, but it also meant that even though Peter Pan took half the prize, he would carry forth the full measure of the handicapper when the time came to race again. As the colt returned to scale, Frank McGrath was bewildered. His disbelief was peppered with relief, but nonetheless, he had been certain his horse was a sure winner on the day. He hadn't expected Peter to gallop so green. The colt stood in a curious trance in the mounting yard, staring across the infield to the spot where he had been put on the rails. He had a white stain on his offside, the evidence of his collision in running, and McGrath thought he might be surveying the site of the mishap, as if for future reference. He would not put it past the son of Pantheon.

The Novice Handicap had been run in 1:40 flat, and earned Peter Pan £99 of the winner's purse. The fact that he'd won at all was remarkable. He'd had every excuse to get left behind. He'd been sandwiched, bumped, checked and distracted, and still made it to the line on time. 'Peter Pan was the cove who never *grew* up,' *Truth* newspaper would say the following day. 'Yesterday punters thought Peter Pan would never *get* up, but he did.' Peter was led off the racecourse and back to the stalls.

Amounis was starting in the Warwick Stakes in an hour or so, for possibly his last start. McGrath wasn't confident in the old horse's constitution, and he was right. Amounis ran well in his race, for a moment suggesting the old dash that had once downed Phar Lap. As the crowd bellowed its approval, the 10-year-old flew into the picture on the home turn, but could manage only sixth. He had been ridden wide and couldn't sustain Johnnie Jason, Veilmond and New Zealand champion Nightmarch. McGrath declared the horse 'splendid' after the race, and Amounis cooled off well, but the doubts didn't evaporate from the trainer's mind. He would talk to Bill Pearson about them later. After the Campbelltown Handicap, in which crack miler Chatham left Lightning March in a spin, McGrath packed up his team and sent them home.

On Monday, McGrath nominated Peter Pan for the Hill Stakes at Rosehill on 17 September, and on Tuesday, a little before the deadline of four o'clock, he strode into the offices of the AJC and declared the colt for the AJC Derby. It was an ambitious itinerary. The Hill Stakes had attracted no less than Nightmarch and Warwick Stakes–winner Johnnie Jason, and the AJC Derby of 1 October was the blue riband event for three-year-olds. Peter Pan had only won a novice contest, but McGrath had unwavering faith. He was certain that Peter Pan was his next Melbourne Cup winner.

Over at the offices of the upmarket weekly magazine, the *Sydney Mail,* 'Musket', chief turf reporter, had the Derby nominations before him. He twirled the list of three-year-olds through his fingers, and arrived on a hollow prophecy. 'The gulf separating a Novice Handicap from a Derby is fairly wide, and success in the former would not entitle the winner to be regarded as a Derby candidate,' he said. 'However, the sensational run that Peter Pan unwound when he dead-heated with Babili drew pointed attention to his prospects as a blue riband rival to Kuvera and co. The style in which he flew over the final furlong was conclusive proof that Peter Pan has pretensions to staying, for he certainly would have won had the race been another ten yards further.'

McGrath's little secret was out. Peter Pan was ready for the spring.

6

Rising to Fame

Saturday morning at Central Station, and a loose crowd was milling on platform 10 for the 11.06am train to Rosehill Racecourse. It was Guineas Day, 17 September 1932, and though it was two-and-a-bit weeks into spring, a September chill stuck close and cold. The 11.06 wound west along the Carlingford line, stopping briefly at Lidcombe, then eased into Rosehill racetrack 32 minutes after departure, 14 miles west of Sydneytown. The racecourse was just starting to come alive. By the time the 11.06 passengers had disappeared through the turnstiles, thousands of racegoers had descended on Rosehill for its high-profile spring race meeting.

Rosehill was a unique club in Sydney. Unlike the AJC racecourses, it was privately owned, but it was a registered proprietary racecourse for thoroughbreds, and as such a step above the many proprietary pony clubs that dotted Sydney's suburbs. Operating as the Rosehill Racing Club (RRC), contests had begun there on 18 April 1885, with £100,000 shovelled into the promotion of its first meeting. It now hosted the prestigious Rawson Stakes, a classy nine-furlong test won by Poseidon, Artilleryman, Poitrel and Nightmarch, as well as the Canterbury Stakes, won by Amounis. Today was the biggest day of them all. The eight-race card featured the Camellia Stakes first and second divisions, the Rosehill Guineas, Rosehill Cup and the Hill Stakes, the latter being Frank McGrath's target for the inexpert Peter Pan.

The wily old trainer was suspected that afternoon, by more than a few, of over-ambition. The Hill Stakes, an open weight-forage event over a mile, had attracted top class racehorses, but that was not unusual in the race's history. First run in 1921, the Hill Stakes had been won by Beauford, Gloaming, Limerick (twice) and Phar Lap (also twice). This year, Peter Pan was facing Nightmarch, Veilmond and Johnnie Jason, and for good measure, Waterline, onetime vanquisher of Phar Lap, and up-and-coming Queensland hero Lough Neagh. McGrath, unwavering as ever, was indifferent about all that. In the race stalls, his team rested quietly. Denis Boy and Lightning March were contesting the Camellia Stakes, and Satmoth was engaged in the Rosehill Cup. Only Amounis was missing, but though no official retirement had yet been announced, and the old horse was still appearing in light work each morning, McGrath suspected his champion had raced for the last time.

Peter Pan's race at Warwick Farm three weeks before had not gone unnoticed. Babili had since come out and won a handicap at Canterbury Park, indicating there was form on Peter Pan's side. But the Hill Stakes was a huge step-up in class for the Pantheon colt, and it was a weight-for-age event. That meant that all horses engaged in it carried only what their age demanded, rather than what the handicapper deemed they should carry. As the youngest horse in the race, Peter Pan was lightly weighted with 7st 7lb. Nightmarch, on the other hand, now a seven-year-old, was allotted 9st 3lb. In fact, of the eight horses in the race, only three carried less than 9st, Peter Pan among them, and that meant that most, if not all, of the colt's competition was well-raced older horses. 'Entries for the Hill Stakes give promise of a splendid race,' wrote the *Sun* newspaper. 'The list includes the best of the Sydney horses and representatives from Queensland, New Zealand and Victoria.'

McGrath had got vigorous with Peter Pan since his Warwick Farm win. He had upped the ante during the colt's morning workouts, and had witnessed some fine gallops as a result. The horse showed a tenacity to be in front, and dug deep during his short bursts around Randwick. He was running six furlongs in 1.18 or better, and he was faster, fitter, and bigger. McGrath suspected that the Hill Stakes, older horses or not, would be a walk in the park. The press, however, didn't completely concur with the old trainer. 'Eastern Chief and Peter Pan will be having their Derby trial in this event,' wrote the *Sun,* 'and that is no mean trying tackle.' The *Arrow* was also realistic. In its form guide for Rosehill, the paper stated that Peter Pan was 'highly promising, but hardly up to weight-for-age standard yet'.

Andy Knox had the job of riding the colt into such standards. The Warwick Farm handicap had showed him that Peter Pan was young, inexperienced and awkward to handle, but very, very fast. He was also a rare horse to overcome trouble in racing, and only the best horses could do that. Knox also had to remind himself that the Hill Stakes was only Peter Pan's third start. Not even Phar Lap, the yardstick these days for greatness, had tackled decent opposition until well into his eighth or ninth.

Unluckily, Peter Pan had drawn an outside position for the race, and McGrath had instructed Knox to take the colt out fast and furiously. The trainer did not question that the horse could go the mile. Rather, he questioned interference if Peter Pan got stuck out the back. He recalled, quite clearly, seeing Peter Pan go flat at Warwick Farm when he found himself in a pocket on the rails. So when Andy Knox was legged into Peter Pan's saddle for the Hill Stakes, McGrath said it one last time. 'Take him to the front, Andy. Ask him early, and he'll go.'

Knox had won the Rosehill Cup on Satmoth half an hour earlier, and McGrath had laid a huge sum of money on Satmoth's victory into Peter Pan winning the Hill Stakes. The weight of the coup had been felt in the betting ring, and Peter Pan had come down to 5/1. Veilmond was favourite at 9/4, Johnnie Jason was at 9/2, while Nightmarch was getting 12s. Not a single newspaper, however, had tipped Peter to win, and only the *Sydney Morning Herald* paid him any attention: 'If he has any chance in the classics it is only reasonable to expect him to make a bold showing here.'

Knox was waiting on the opportunity to make it so. As the starter climbed his podium to send the field away, the jockey stood Peter Pan before the tapes. He was nearly widest on the track, but he snatched a handful of the colt's mane, ready to send him flying. Peter Pan twitched with excitement. At 3.30pm, the barrier flew up and the Hill Stakes began in slow motion.

The eight horses leaned on their hindquarters as one. Down they went together, then up in the air in front, and as they dashed out of their standstill and into their first strides, a head bobbed out. Nightmarch had outjumped the rest of the field. Knox bustled Peter Pan after him. There was going to be no dawdling this time, and the colt could feel the pressure from his rider. With Nightmarch leading into the first furlong, Peter Pan crossed over the course to join the leading group, and into the first turn on the backstretch he raced with Johnnie Jason, Autopay, Lough Neagh and Veilmond.

Nightmarch settled and came back to the field, and Johnnie Jason swept away by two lengths. Belting out of the first two furlongs in 26 1/2 seconds, the horses swung into the far turn, Johnnie Jason out by two, followed by Nightmarch, Lough Neagh, Autopay and Peter Pan. Knox was shuffling his horse so that with each stride Peter Pan was gaining on the leader. He had loose, fluid strokes that carried his light frame beautifully. There had been no interruptions, no interference or checks, and along the backstretch, one off the rails, Knox was in good contention. But the boss's orders were to get a clear run, and the only way to get that was in front. So as the horses galloped off the backstretch, Johnnie Jason burning oil up front, Knox asked Peter Pan to race to the lead.

Approaching the half-mile post, Peter Pan had inched in to second spot, a length off Johnnie Jason. Knox kept punching him out, though he hadn't yet drawn the whip. Peter Pan was full of running. The colt could see the home turn approaching, and the grandstands on the right of the track, but today he wasn't distracted. In a few kicks he had swallowed Johnnie Jason's lead, and the two horses burst onto the straight together. Peter Pan swept past his rival, and with a clear alley ahead, he pricked his ears and ran for home.

The colt covered the last three furlongs in 38 seconds, and only Nightmarch managed to get close to him. At the winning post, the Melbourne Cup winner was a length behind the Pantheon colt, and only because Peter Pan, still green, drifted across the track at the line. But Knox was still riding for his worth, and the pair dashed past the post in 1.42 flat, with Johnnie Jason three-quarters of a length behind Nightmarch. Peter had hardly raised an effort.

Andy Knox stood in his irons and punched the air. This brilliant colt had won so easily, and had earned him a tidy double with the Satmoth win. It was also the jockey's first victory in a weight-for-age event, and as he returned to scale he relished the reception proffered by the crowd at Rosehill. In the paddock, McGrath was ecstatic, and Dangar was almost overwhelmed by the rise of his new star. The bookies, plain and simple, were tickled. The 6/4 favourite, Veilmond, had run dead last, beaten by a novice at only his third start.

The Hill Stakes was worth £405 to the winner, and Peter Pan's winnings now totalled £504. The time of 1:42 was a fair effort, because the track had received a soaking only minutes before start time, and the sectionals were adequate: 26 1/2 seconds for the first two furlongs, three covered in 39 seconds, five in 1:04, and the final three in 38 seconds. Peter Pan had wrestled the lead from the four-furlongs post, and in mowing down Johnnie Jason, he had outstayed his peers for half a mile.

In the paddock, McGrath idled in the aftermath of the race. His ecstasy had fermented into relief that Peter Pan had proved himself the colt McGrath suspected all along. As he enjoyed the validation, he was joined by racing identity Jim Kingsley. Kingsley was a colourful man in turf circles, for he was on the wrong side of racing more than he was on the right side of it. In 1903 he had been disqualified for life for his involvement in the rigging of the Newcastle weight scales, though the AJC had reinstated him in 1918. The club had simply tired of Kingsley's persistence, for on any given raceday at Randwick during his debarring he was escorted from the course by AJC officials up to 16 times. Nevertheless, Kingsley's dubious, usually not-so-legal activities had continued, often in the betting ring. It was, in fact, his scallywagging that had earned him the nickname of 'Grafter'.

'You've got a good colt there,' Kingsley motioned to McGrath as Peter Pan disappeared from the paddock. 'You ought to secure Jim Pike to ride him for you.' Kingsley, a gross man of nearly 20st, was hardly a character one could ignore, even if McGrath wanted to. The trainer simply nodded. The same thought had crossed his mind too.

'In fact, I've a good mind to engage him for you,' said Kingsley, and before McGrath could respond, Grafter was striding away, ambling towards the jockeys' room. Kingsley found Pike, and told him about McGrath's colt. 'I've engaged you for Peter Pan in the Derby,' he boomed at the jockey. Kingsley didn't believe in negotiation.

'Has he got any chance, Jim?' Pike asked.

'Well,' breathed Kingsley, 'I'll bet you an even £50 right now that Peter Pan beats the horse they've got favourite.' That was enough for Pike. When Grafter named a horse and money in the same breath, he was rarely off the mark.

'In that case,' Pike replied, 'I'll take the ride.' Kingsley relayed the news to the horse's trainer. In fact, McGrath had already conferred with Dangar on their Derby rider, and agreed that Jim Pike was the preferred man for the task. Kingsley was simply faster than McGrath at proposing the ride to Pike.

On his way home, McGrath stopped to buy the *Sun* newspaper, whose afternoon edition carried the racing results. 'Peter Pan in the Hill Stakes, fine win. Satmoth scores in the Rosehill Cup,' it said. He tossed the paper onto the passenger seat of the Hupmobile and went on his way. These were good times indeed.

***

Sunlight tumbled across the lawns of beautiful Arlington the following Wednesday as Rodney Dangar read the newspapers. Arlington was Dangar's magnificent three-storey Woollahra mansion at 351 Edgecliff Road. It was his Sydney home, a gentleman's residence with three reception rooms, five bedrooms, three maids' rooms and offices. When he bought it at auction in December 1920, it had electric lighting, power points and, boasted the catalogue, was 'within a few minutes of the tram on Ocean Road, commanding extensive harbour views'. Dangar had relaxed into his favourite white cane chair in the garden, and gentlemanly, stately, with his legs crossed and a cigar perched between his fingers, he read all about the newspaper opinions of his young colt.

Peter Pan was engaged for the AJC Derby on 1 October, against top three-year-olds Oro and Gaine Carrington, and as such each review of the Hill Stakes was written in lieu of his chances in the Derby. 'For a green colt like Peter Pan to dispute the lead for over five furlongs, and then gain the upper hand of such a horse [as Johnnie Jason] places him on a very high pedestal among the Derby hopes,' wrote 'Musket' in the *Sydney Mail.*

A.B. 'Banjo' Paterson was 'Musket's' colleague at the *Mail.* He was a famous turf man, as passionate about racing and breeding as he was poetry, and he was a famous Australian poet. About the 1932 Derby, however, he had no definite favourite. 'Supporters of Peter Pan argued that their horse was drawn nearly as wide as Oro [who ran third in the Rosehill Guineas], but he did not waste any time in getting into his stride,' Paterson wrote. 'He was travelling in high-class company, and yet he not only got to the lead, but he stayed there.' Paterson added, though, that the track was so wet for the Hill Stakes it was no form guide at all, so his loyalty lay with Oro for the Derby. Dangar was surprised at that. With Jim Pike engaged, Peter Pan's prospects in the blue riband event were bright. The *Sun* agreed: 'As J.E. Pike is to ride Peter Pan, he will have the benefit of a most experienced rider who has selected Peter Pan in preference to other Derby mounts.'

Dangar considered the Derby for a moment. He knew that his horse could stay the mile and a half and had the best jockey, so the only question unanswered at this point was the weight. The AJC Derby was a set-weights affair, which meant that each colt would carry equal burden of 8st 10lb and each filly 8st 7lb, regardless of ability. To date, Peter Pan had carried a maximum 7st 10lb, so the Derby weight was a full stone heavier than anything he had burdened before. The *Argus* iterated such thoughts: 'Peter Pan's appearance suggests that his 8st 10lb in the Derby will trouble him more than the distance. He is tall, but rather lightly framed and leggy.'

Weight was a curious thing in the racing game. It slowed a galloping horse, but there were many things that could slow a galloping horse, including interference or heavy going. The effect of weight also changed with distance. If a horse was carrying a 7lb penalty in a race, as was Johnnie Jason when Peter Pan cruised past him on Saturday, that 7lb was of little consequence over four or five furlongs. Carrying it over 10 furlongs, however, altered a horse's fortunes remarkably. It was common, therefore, for punters to ignore weight altogether over short tracks. Given also that horses tire at a cumulative rate, each furlong galloped would be slower than the one before it, if ridden out, and in the circumstances of a race it was therefore impossible to say if weight had decided a horse. It took many a handicap to bring Phar Lap back to the field, as added weight made little difference to him. But he was a giant beast from every angle, and large-framed horses carried weight more easily than slightly set ones. Again, thresholds varied, but it remained a punting philosophy that if the weight range was small and the horse good, a few pounds would not contribute to the winning or losing of a race.

The AJC Derby, however, was different. Because the handicapper played no part in the field, nor did previous ability, all horses lined up equally despite the spread in weight-carrying aptitude. Nevertheless, well-backed runners usually won the Derby, and history did not argue with that. Gloaming, Rivoli, Heroic, Manfred, Rampion and Phar Lap had all won the race as favourites. So, while weight was a variable to consider, the chief philosophy behind the winner of the Derby was whether the horse could run out the mile and a half. Of that, Dangar was not concerned.

7

'A regular bobby dazzler'

It was a Thursday morning in Sydney, two days before the Derby at Randwick, and the rain had been tumbling all week. It was also unseasonably cool, but this morning Jim Pike stole a glance through the windscreen of his motorcar and he liked what he saw – bursts of blue sky. He ambled down Old South Head Road towards the Royal Sydney Golf Club, where he was to meet an old friend for a round of the links.

Jim Pike was Sydney's leading jockey, a rider so good and experienced that he was almost unbackable. He rode the best horses in Sydney for the best prizes. In the Sydney spring of 1931, James Edward Pike partnered Phar Lap through three straight wins at the AJC meeting – the Spring Stakes, Craven Plate and Randwick Plate, nearly five miles of glorious victory in seven days. His partnership with the Red Terror had been so successful, so lethal, that the maxim of sure things and horse racing had been swiftly deserted, and the bookies had simply refused to take bets on the pair. Pike couldn't imagine it ever occurring again. Phar Lap was too good, too fast, too consistent. He'd been unbeatable on fair terms, unbackable on most terms, and in less than a year he was gone. Yes, Pike thought, horse racing had changed in just 12 months.

The jockey was 39 years old. He had been race riding at Randwick since 1906, and had scores of huge wins to his credit. He had won every major race in Australia, many several times over, and Pike could go for weeks without a win, yet still hold the best winning average for the season. Success, though, had not boiled his ego. He remained one of the most humble, most approachable hoops on the circuit. But he was getting on now, and making the weights for his races had become a daily battle. He was taller than most jockeys, a long stick of a man who had earned, through years of hard wasting, a wan and skeletal expression. He spent hours in the steam rooms sweating away his health, and couldn't recall the last time he had dined on meat and three veg. Amazingly, none of this affected his riding. Mild-mannered and pleasant on the ground, on horseback Pike's mind was a steel trap.

Pike swung his motorcar into the parking lot at Royal Sydney, hauled his clubs from the trunk space and waited for Mick Polson. Polson was one of Pike's closest friends, a Randwick trainer who had the promising galloper Winooka, and their friendship had lasted for years. Pike had ridden his first winner for Polson, and the young jockey had matured under the fostered care of the Randwick-based trainer. They were also judicious golfers, though Pike also played to stay fit. Out on the greens five or six times a week, there was scarcely a morning when he didn't cover 10 miles across the links.

'It's a different spring for you this year, Jim,' said Polson, 'No Phar Lap to shut the place down.' Pike was sure the whole of Randwick was thinking the same thing.

***

Most of Randwick *was* thinking that, as Phar Lap had been whitewashing the last two spring meetings. No one had wished for the big horse's demise, but it was with renewed excitement that horse racing looked forward to Derby Day on 1 October. 'There will be no Phar Lap barring the way in the weight-for-age races at the AJC carnival this time,' wrote the *Arrow.*

With the Winning Bets Tax retired, and punters now free to gamble without a taxation on their winnings, the AJC was hopeful of a vigorous turnout this year. But in place of the old levy, the new state government had installed a bookies tax just in time for Saturday. For every £100 earned by the books, £1 was to go straight into parliament coffers. The usual chorus of protest had sprung up from the ring at the announcement of the new situation, but within hours, money poured into the ring for Saturday's Epsom Handicap as punters realised that the burden of taxation was no longer on their shoulders – it was henceforth on those of the bag swingers.

Every top galloper in New South Wales was running at Randwick over the next couple of weeks, and many more from Queensland and New Zealand. There was the nation's expert miler Chatham, and the promising stayer Rogilla, and there was Winooka, Autopay and Johnnie Jason, Veilmond, Nightmarch, Whittingham, Lough Neagh from Queensland, and McGrath's twins Satmoth and Denis Boy.

But the Melbourne horses were conspicuous by their absence. Victorian owners like Eric Connolly and Cecil Godby, and owner-trainer Jack Holt, had no entries at the AJC carnival, and it was all put down to prizemoney. 'Events that formerly carried £1000 in added money are now down to £200,' reasoned the *Sportsman,* demonstrating the choking effect of the Depression. 'Why then would they [Victorians] go away from home?' In addition, there was a ludicrous clash of meetings that saw the last day of the Randwick spring meeting occur on the first day of the Caulfield spring meeting in Victoria. Because the Caulfield meeting was second only to the Melbourne Cup in importance, local horses dashed south after the running of the AJC's Craven Plate on the Wednesday.

The biggest races occurred early on the AJC card. The Derby, Epsom and Spring Stakes went off on the first day, a Saturday, followed by the Shorts, Metropolitan and Breeder's Plate the following Monday. On Wednesday, the Craven Plate and the Gimcrack took place, and on the following Saturday was the Randwick Plate, the only two-miler on the card.

While the Epsom–Metropolitan double was the betting highlight of the week, the Derby carried the highest purse of them all (£4420 to the winner, with an additional £250 to the breeder). The Derby was a sacred event, a race restricted to the elite three-year-olds of the country, and it attracted its own sort of buzz. It had been first run as the Randwick Derby Stakes on 12 September 1861. The race was, in effect, as old as the Melbourne Cup, and it was a contest created to imitate the great Epsom Derby Stakes in England, a mile-and-a-half marathon for three-year-olds. From its outset, the Derby at Randwick found brilliant winners, and due to it being a set-weights affair, the best horses usually won it.

There was, however, a situation this year that had made the race controversial. For the first time in AJC history, geldings had been barred from the Derby. The powers in racing were trying to discourage the gelding of good racehorses which, though making individuals easier to train, eliminated them as stud prospects. But the ban was controversial for one specific reason: in the last decade, the three most brilliant horses – Gloaming, Amounis and Phar Lap – had all been geldings, and it was unthinkable that Phar Lap could have been barred from the classics. There would have been a national outcry. The day that Peter Pan had won the Hill Stakes, a good gelding called Bronze Hawk had won the Rosehill Guineas, and as a three-year-old he was eligible for the Derby. But not in 1932. 'The strange thing about Bronze Hawk being debarred from the Derby this year is that it will probably make a gift of it to Gaine Carrington,' observed *Smith's Weekly*.

Gaine Carrington was favourite for the AJC Derby, and so sure of him were backers that they looked around for something to beat him. He was indeed a fine horse, a New Zealand colt. He had won the Chelmsford Stakes in scintillating form at the Tattersall's meeting some weeks before. Oro and Kuvera were also in the Derby, and they had run third and second to Bronze Hawk in the Rosehill Guineas. There was also Ruach, an Adelaide Guineas winner, and Regal Son, a third-place finisher in the Chelmsford Stakes. Eastern Chief, a two-year-old winner at Flemington in July, was also in, as was the other Pantheon galloper Milantheon. The 1932 AJC Derby was a smart one, even without Bronze Hawk.

Frank McGrath kept an eye on the line-up, for the Derby was a great test for the young colt. Peter was still only two years old, was carrying 1st more than he had ever carried and running a half-mile further than he had ever run. But quietly, privately, McGrath knew Peter Pan had the Derby's measure, and each morning at dawn the young horse proved it. At Rosebery on 23 September, Peter Pan gave Denis Boy and Satmoth a searching trial, and the *Sun* was on hand this time to comment. 'Peter Pan never let 'em in,' it wrote, 'and there's not the slightest doubt that next Saturday he will be the fittest horse in the Derby.'

Sydney, in the meantime, geared up for spring racing. Despite the sullen weather, there was energy in the air. Thanks to the relentless downpours of recent weeks, flowers had sprouted everywhere, but even they could mask only a little of the hardship that still stuck close to the city's flanks. Due to the Depression, for the first time in 17 years, tram fares had been cut for racegoers, along with the price of bread. Train workers' rates had dropped by 15 per cent the previous Monday, so in the face of such adversities, of such overwhelming struggles for the everyday man, horse racing was a terrific distraction.

***

By mid-morning of Derby Day, McGrath's yard was bustling. With the retirement of Amounis only weeks ago, Peter Pan had been assigned to the care of strapper George Phillips. Phillips had worked for McGrath for many years, and was one of the trainer's tried and trusted handlers. He was in his late forties, an astute and dedicated fellow, and he had been shattered at the loss of Amounis. He needed a new project, something to propel him from his despondency, and the young son of Pantheon was it. The strapper had taken to the colt right away. Peter Pan was no Amounis – he was neither affectionate nor humble – but that mattered little to George Phillips. The two became fast friends.

Phillips led the colt to the race stalls a little after one o'clock. He ran a cloth over Peter Pan, working out the tension in his body. It was still only the colt's fourth race start, and he had never seen so many thousands of people milling around Randwick before. Phillips worked quietly, and under his firm hand and soft voice Peter Pan stood still. He stroked the knots out of the colt's blond mane, allowing it to fold neatly over his off side, and he rubbed a shine into the pale chestnut coat. Then Phillips set about tacking up. He fixed the bit-lifter on Peter Pan's bridle, a tidy strap that ran from each bit ring up the middle of the colt's face and attached behind his ears. It was a device that kept the bit high in the horse's mouth, and would prevent Peter Pan from putting his tongue over it. Next, Phillips placed a light towel across the horse's back, then the AJC's white saddlecloth, and finally Jim Pike's little racing saddle. There were no lead weights required. The 8st 10lb was Pike's minimum riding weight, and after Phillips fixed the girth, the colt was ready to go. Phillips donned his white strapper's coat over his smart suit and shoes, and the two headed out to the saddling paddock.

The paddock was actually a huge lawn in front of the Members' stand, and McGrath stood at the edge of it, a picture of smart coolness in his Sunday suit. He wasn't nervous. He'd won the Derby three times already and he was a high-stakes trainer. The pressures of big races were familiar territory. Beside him, though, stood Rodney Dangar, a towering figure in a single-breasted brown suit with waistcoat and tie, trilby, and a pair of binoculars. The pressure was fairly new to him. Dangar could move in the most powerful social circles any day of the week, but he had never had a horse that could win the AJC Derby. He smiled confidently at everyone who wished him luck, though he was churning with nerves inside. No one noticed. Amid the expensive furs and fancy tailoring of the Members' stand, Dangar looked smooth and secure.

Randwick was filled to capacity. There were thousands crammed into the grandstand and the St Leger stand, the more affordable accommodation. There was also the Flat, the infield enclosure on the other side of the racetrack where the colourful, working-class Sydneyites flocked. Approaching 2.40pm in the afternoon, the bugle sounded and jockeys moved towards their horses. Jim Pike, who had huddled with McGrath and Dangar, strode over to Peter Pan, and with a quick leg-up from McGrath, he was astride the Pantheon colt for the first time.

As was his way, Pike revealed nothing in his expression. Though Peter Pan was narrow, still a streamlined bullet of a thoroughbred, he was definitely tall, way over 16 hands, and his height helped Pike sit down. Still, the jockey looked gangly on him. Peter was growing yet. The veteran jockey and the inexperienced racehorse set off down the straight for their preliminary gallop, and arrived at the mile-and-a-half start. It was almost opposite the Leger stand, about halfway down the home straight.

As the horses milled around behind the starter, the barrier strand was dropped across the track and the horses were called to order. This time, Peter Pan had drawn fairly. He was positioned five off the rail in the field of 11 horses. 'Alright jockeys, bring them up,' called the AJC starter Jack Gaxieu, and Pike turned Peter Pan into line. Gaxieu shuffled the horses forward, and when all 11 entrants were standing still and straight, he pushed the lever of the starting tape and the strands flew up before them.

Pike leaned into Peter Pan's neck as the colt rose from his standstill, buoyed by the cheers of the thousands that surrounded them. But the track was heavy on the inside, even heavier from days and days of rain, and it took Peter Pan several strides to get his feet out of the squelch. As a result, a wall of horses crossed over him onto the rails, and almost instantly Pike found himself on the heels of a dozen runners. Quickly, he peeled away from the rails and found running widest of all. He hoped the firmer surface would relax Peter Pan into stride.

The long shots Prince Pombal and Bombastic had found their way to the lead, and coming out of the straight for the first time they were setting a lively tempo. Peter Pan remained the widest out. Galloping past the 10-furlong pole, Pike saw something grey and shiny go flying. Peter Pan had thrown a shoe from one of his front feet. The jockey panicked for a moment. Often, this spelled the end of a horse's race. Pike had no idea if the shoe had come off clean, or if it had taken away some of Peter's hoof with it, as sometimes happened. He waited for signs of unbalance in the young horse, but Peter Pan didn't miss a skip. Pike relaxed, and the pair flew out of the turn.

Down the back, Gaine Carrington suddenly dropped out, and as he slipped back through the field he checked half-a-dozen runners. Regal Son, Maltdale and Kuvera had to dive out of the way, and Oro was almost brought down. From his outside spot, Peter Pan bypassed all the trouble and Pike urged the colt forward. Within strides, Peter had moved into third position on the rails, with Prince Pombal and Bombastic in his sights.

Down the backstretch they thundered, three horses clear of the pack, and as they swept into the far turn Peter Pan picked off Bombastic. Prince Pombal had opened a decent lead, and he was on his own at the half-mile pole, but Pike hadn't even moved. The veteran rider could feel his horse had plenty in reserve. Behind him, some 20 lengths spread the field. Approaching the home turn, Pike could see the leader was tiring, and still he sat quietly on Peter Pan. Into the turn and they were side by side, Peter travelling the better. At the top of the straight, Pike niggled at the colt to hurry up, and the silver-tailed son of Pantheon burst into the lead. He rushed away from Prince Pombal, and thousands of voices swamped the air around him.

Pike saw the straight opening up, the lonely, glorious path to victory, but suddenly, he felt Peter Pan falter. It wasn't the colt's stamina, or even anything physical. As he had done in his first race, and his second, Peter Pan had stopped racing to have a good old look around him. Pike was not ready for it, and was shocked to feel his mount go cold in his hands. But then he realised what Peter Pan was at, and that steel-trap brain of Pike's kicked in. He drew the whip and slapped the distracted colt hard on his left shoulder. Behind him, Oro was coming. Coolly, calmly, without shifting his weight, Pike hit Peter Pan again and then shook his whip in the horse's face. That was all it took. Peter Pan bolted away from the closing Oro and dashed towards the winning post. He clattered over the line a length and a half in front, with Kuvera plugging into third another three lengths behind. In two minutes and 34 seconds, Peter Pan had raced into stardom.

Up in the Members', Rodney Dangar felt the swell of nearly 30,000 people as they hollered his racehorse home. Beside him, his wife Elsie was nearly over the railing with excitement. Dangar didn't know what to do with himself. Here was a lifelong ambition, a racing ambition that had dawdled in the family for two generations, and now he had bred a classic winner. He had succeeded where his father had failed. Brushing past the congratulations that came from every angle, he and Elsie skipped down the stairs from the Members' and into the saddling paddock, in time for Pike and Peter Pan as they trotted back to scale. The colt was on his toes, hardly blowing at the effort, and as George Phillips snapped a lead shank to Peter Pan, Pike slid to the ground. The crowds were packed around the fences, cheering and applauding and yelling at Pike as if this afternoon it had dawned on them that something new and special had arrived on the scene.

Phillips was beaming as he congratulated Pike, and the jockey was cool as ever, no smile on his face or crack in his armour. He bundled the saddle off Peter Pan and over his arm, and moved across the paddock to the weigh room. Both McGrath and Dangar stepped in to pump his hand. 'He's a good colt, Mr Dangar,' Pike said as the warm admiration of the owner swept over him. Dangar and McGrath smiled widely and nodded, and the jockey moved inside to weigh in.

A *Truth* journalist pressed the jockey for more. 'I got the shock of my life when Peter Pan ran to the front,' Pike said. 'He simply dropped dead in my hands and I thought he was beaten. I hit him with the stick and from the furlong post he finished with the gameness of a tiger cat. He's some colt alright, but a little roguish.'

The *Truth* reporter bustled his way back to Frank McGrath, and asked for a few comments. 'Well, well, well,' McGrath replied, 'I knew he would win, and he has certainly done the trick. I can't say anything more except that I am a happy man, and that the little colt is a regular bobby dazzler.' Peter Pan was actually a big colt, but such was McGrath's style.

The buzz in the saddling paddock continued for many minutes, at least until the presentation had been made, and Rodney Dangar, proud as pink punch, accepted the Derby sash from the cheerful governor, Sir Philip Game. With the sash came the £4420 first prize, along with the £250 bonus for the breeder, bringing Peter Pan's tally in four races to £5174. It was small change for Dangar, but the prestige that came with it ... that was priceless. Peter had started four times now for three wins, and suddenly he had pocketed the richest prize for three-year-olds. This time yesterday so many had suspected he was great, but today they knew for sure.

George Phillips led Peter Pan out of the paddock and back to the stalls, and he was met with a sea of excited fans all along the way. Everyone wanted a glimpse of this terrific blond racehorse that had suddenly emerged, and only as the horses for the Epsom began to file away to the paddock was Phillips able to lead his charge back to Doncaster Avenue. He prepared the colt's box, set his feed, and watched him lick every drop from the manger. When the stable lads goaded him for his luck with another Amounis, Phillips calmly replied, 'Amounis was a wonder galloper, but Peter's going to be even greater.'

***

The afternoon got better for Jim Pike. In the Epsom, he guided Chatham to a scintillating victory, and in the Spring Stakes, the third big race of the day, he brought Veilmond home by two lengths to second-placed Satmoth. McGrath was equally pleased. Denis Boy ran a respectable fifth in the Epsom, and with Satmoth's second and Peter Pan's first, McGrath's top trio had produced the goods indeed. And they weren't the only ones. The AJC had managed to attract a colossal crowd for Derby Day, the largest Randwick crowd since the start of the Depression, and much of it had to do with the death of the Winning Bets Tax.

By and large, the first day of the spring meeting was a success. Investments on the totalisator amounted to £49,563, and the Spring Stakes alone was extraordinary by comparison. In 1931, with Phar Lap collapsing the betting, £958 was invested on that race in the paddock tote. This year, punters had shovelled £3521 into it, and by the time the Randwick meeting concluded the following Saturday, the AJC had made a round profit of £8000. Racing in New South Wales had finally crawled out of its hole.

In the days that followed the Derby, the newspapers piled lavish praise on Peter Pan, and none more so than the *Guardian.* 'Another star shines brightly,' splashed Bert 'Cardigan' Wolfe in its racing pages. 'Phar Laps may die and champions and near champions retire from the racecourse, but there is always another one to carry on. Peter Pan, the AJC Derby winner, is the latest star.'

'The style in which Peter Pan won the AJC Derby indicates that he is going to be a horse of the highest class,' wrote 'Musket', and *Smith's Weekly* agreed: 'In less than a month Peter Pan has stepped from complete obscurity to the forefront of thoroughbred class. Physically he is capable of much development, and with this development must come improved form. So perhaps there is no idle boast in the forecast of his shrewd trainer, Frank McGrath, that here he has a champion of the future who will dominate the great events.'

McGrath was certain that he had such a champion, and had been for months, but now that the secret was out it was open to all sorts of comment. 'While it is customary to hail the new champion as the greatest of all, Peter Pan has yet to prove himself,' wrote 'Cardigan' on 9 October. 'The opportunity is waiting for him to do so.' The opportunity referred to was the big spring races in Melbourne, notably the Caulfield and Melbourne cups, and McGrath had to make some quick decisions about Peter Pan's career. But on the Monday after the Derby, it was a wonder he had time to think at all. Denis Boy won the Metropolitan Handicap that day, and Lightning March won the Shorts at 20/1. And because McGrath had a tidy coup on Chatham for the Epsom into Denis Boy for the Metropolitan, and he had gotten his odds when the irons were cool, the trainer was an even richer man on Monday night.

Jim Pike, on the other hand, felt fortune turn against him. After a halcyon run on the first day of the meeting, Sydney's leading jockey was charged with careless riding on Monday in the Centennial Park Handicap. The penalty was severe. Pike was handed a two-month suspension and ruled out of Melbourne's spring racing. All of a sudden, the ride on Peter Pan was wide open.

8

'Not even the celestial horses could have won from there'

The clatter of hooves rattled across Central Station as Peter Pan made his way along the livestock platform towards the 6.20pm express train to Melbourne. It was Tuesday night, the day after Denis Boy's Metropolitan, and McGrath was wasting no time in Sydney. He was shipping Peter Pan south before the end of the AJC meeting, and George Phillips hurried the colt to his boxcar. The platform hands were loading horses everywhere; the Melbourne Express was a busy service just before spring racing. George Phillips led the rugged and bandaged Peter Pan coolly up the gangway, calming the big colt with his quiet words and firm hand. He tethered the horse inside the boxcar and stuffed his manger with hay, then settled in for the 17 hours to Melbourne.

The boxcar swayed gently as it rattled out of Sydney, winding down the tracks towards Victoria and pulling into Albury in the wee hours of the morning. Albury was the border town between New South Wales and Victoria, and because the rail gauges were different between the two states, Peter Pan had to change trains. It was an hour before the Melbourne Express continued on its way, but at eleven o'clock the following morning it eased into St Albans station, nine miles northwest of Melbourne. This was the point where horses disembarked and from here, they were floated to the various racecourses dotting the southern city. On 5 October 1932, Peter Pan was going to Flemington. Phillips loaded the colt into the float that awaited them before jumping in the front with the driver, and the engine roared to life, taking the pair towards Flemington.

Phillips eyed the familiar surrounds of Melbourne as they drove through the northwest suburbs. He had been coming to Melbourne with McGrath's charges for a long time, but had come to know the place particularly well during Amounis's years. This was a different city from Sydney, with a different feel. The population had passed the one million mark, but there was still a sense of physical space about. Somehow, it didn't feel as tight and fast as its northern rival. Eventually, the float pulled into Flemington Racecourse and the driver offloaded them at the Mackinnon & Cox yards. Before he left them, he said he would have a bob on Peter Pan for the Cup. 'Good for you,' Phillips replied. 'You won't be sorry for it, I tell you.'

Mackinnon & Cox was a bloodstock auction company, and their boxes were sited at the end of the straight six at Flemington. Peter Pan arrived to a vacant row of stalls, but that would change by the middle of the following week. Satmoth, Denis Boy and

Lightning March would arrive over the weekend, and on Monday a flotilla of Sydney horses were due – Winooka, Oro, Gaine Carrington, Peter Jackson and Rogilla. Bronze Hawk was already here, and Lough Neagh's owner, who was keeping his horse in Sydney for the two-mile Randwick Plate, was as yet undecided about bringing his charge down south. McGrath had left strict orders for George Phillips. The trainer wanted Peter Pan into a routine by the time he arrived on Friday, and the strapper set about straight away.

The morning after they arrived, Phillips rode Peter Pan onto the Flemington course for the first time, trotting him round a few times to give the colt a look. On Friday 7 October, Peter Pan took his first gallop in Melbourne. Under the guidance of lightweight rider Ron Bones, the son of Pantheon went twice around the Flemington tan, taking it easy for the first nine furlongs, and stretching out in the remaining six to put 1.26 on the clock. It was an easy trial. Peter Pan was full of gusto, stretching his legs for the first time since Monday morning, and the Flemington clockers were on hand all the way. The gallop was nothing to set the headlines alight, but there was plenty of chitchat over the horse's appearance.

'At first glance the AJC Derby winner does not impress,' wrote the *Sporting Globe,* Melbourne's chief sporting paper. 'But on closer examination he has most of the make and shape required in a thoroughbred.' The *Globe* went on to describe Peter Pan's straight legs, and added in his splendid length and deep girth for measure, but it also repeated a comment made in Sydney. 'Some critics are of the opinion that Peter Pan is short in the hindquarters.' A similar observation had been made by 'Banjo' Paterson in the *Sydney Mail.*

Nevertheless, Peter Pan had certainly developed. He was a fit, rippling racehorse, although the legginess about him hadn't gone away. He still had a narrow body on iron pins, and he was found to be 'foalish' compared to his older Melbourne rivals. In Sydney, he had raced against older horses only once, in the weight-for-age Hill Stakes at Rosehill, and had more than accounted for them. Down here, though, his age was really sticking out. McGrath and Dangar had elected Peter Pan for three tough races – the Caulfield Cup, the Melbourne Stakes and the gruelling Melbourne Cup, four-and-three-quarter miles in all – and none of these contests would be favourable to his age. They were all open to older horses, and suddenly the three-year-old who was actually only two seemed very juvenile indeed.

The usual path for AJC Derby winners was the three-year-olds' Victoria Derby, run on the first day of the Melbourne Cup carnival, always a Saturday. Through some terrible oversight, though, Peter Pan had not been nominated for the race. Dangar had thought that McGrath had done it, and McGrath had thought that Dangar had done it, as he had done with the AJC Derby. It was a rare mistake for the two men, as they usually had all angles covered when it came to Peter Pan's career. It was also an expensive one, as the Derby was a rich purse. However, neither man was upset by it, even when they were left with little option but to run their horse in the Caulfield Cup first, and the Mackinnon Stakes on Derby Day. If Peter Pan had been aimed for the three-year-old classic he would have skated home, for he would have met Gaine Carrington and Ruach again, and a promising Victorian youngster called Liberal. He was more than a match for these. But as it stood, the young colt was meeting much older, stronger horses in the Caulfield competition, and the task set him was the stiffest yet.

McGrath had few concerns. He took the overnight train from Sydney and arrived in Melbourne on Friday, and before he'd even checked into his lodgings in the city he was at Flemington, diligent and thorough, taking a look at Peter Pan. The trainer was no stranger in these parts. He'd been coming here since his calamitous fall in Grace Darling's 1885 Caulfield Cup, and though that had been disastrous for him, his subsequent visits had been far better. The previous year he'd taken the Caulfield Cup with Denis Boy, and the year before with Amounis. 'Peter Pan has come along in great style since he came over from Sydney,' McGrath told *Truth* that first day in Melbourne. 'I expect the colt to follow up his Derby success in next Saturday's Caulfield Cup.'

Actually, it was a half-truth. McGrath had been sure of the AJC Derby result, but of the Caulfield Cup on 15 October he wasn't so sure. He knew what it took to win the mile-and-a-half handicap, and the Caulfield racetrack would be no gift to Peter Pan. It was tight and egg-shaped and suited the shorter horses, and his long-striding colt would have to be lucky to get a run. But Peter Pan had lifted himself from trouble in three of his four races, and McGrath had no reason to doubt it would be any different at Caulfield. With only moderate luck he felt Peter Pan would prevail, but nevertheless he toned down his confidence when talking to the newspapers. Rodney Dangar, on the other hand, did not. There was no dampening his enthusiasm, or his faith in his horse. 'Peter is a great colt and in my opinion he is as good as Poseidon,' Dangar told *Truth* on the Saturday night. Speaking to the *Sporting Globe,* he said, 'I don't think he will be beaten this spring.'

Not everyone was as confident as Rodney Dangar. 'Peter Pan needs to be the equal of Poseidon to overcome his handicap in the Caulfield Cup, and Poseidon is acclaimed the greatest three-year-old Australia has known,' wrote the *Referee* on 9 October. It was a fair statement. Poseidon was the brilliant son of the Neotsfield stallion Positano. In 1906 he had pillaged the AJC Derby, Caulfield Cup, Victoria Derby and Melbourne Cup, all within six weeks of each other, and the feat had never been equalled. If Peter Pan could take both Cups and the Melbourne Stakes during his sojourn in the south, he could equal the merits of Poseidon. But the *Referee* was guarded. 'Peter Pan is to face the Caulfield Cup barrier without any experience of the course and the reverse style of going,' it debated. The fact that horses in Victoria ran anticlockwise was a big deal for New South Wales runners (who galloped clockwise), and on a tight-turning track like Caulfield, matters were made worse.

The handicapper had given Peter Pan 7st 7lb for the Caulfield Cup. The conditions of both the Caulfield and Flemington cups stated that a Derby winner would carry weight-for-age for the distance, which meant 7st 7lb at Caulfield and 7st 6lb at Flemington. But the Melbourne Cup conditions also stated that the winner of any handicap worth £1000 or more to the winner would carry additional weight up to 10lb. That meant that if Peter Pan won the Caulfield, he could be re-handicapped to the extent of 10lb. Thankfully, that adjustment was based on his original declaration, which was 7st before his win in the AJC Derby. That meant that the most Peter Pan could be given for the Melbourne Cup, if he won the Caulfield, was 7st 10lb.

The Caulfield Cup was as old as its racecourse, a handicap of a mile and a half first staged in 1879. It didn't have auspicious beginnings, and in its list of winners there was no outstanding thoroughbred until Poseidon in 1906. But it had since become a highlight of Victoria's racing calendar. The 1932 field was a big one, 21 runners so far, and the scramble for good positions would occur quickly. 'Luck in running counts for more in a Caulfield Cup than in any other big turf event,' wrote 'Banjo' Paterson in the *Sydney Mail* on 12 October. This was especially true for Peter Pan.

He was drawn second from the outside, and luck, confidence and clever riding were just the beginning.

After McGrath's arrival on Friday, things became routine for Peter – trackwork in the morning, food and rest, a walk in the afternoon – and he remained as relaxed and happy as when he had arrived. McGrath noticed the horse's affinity for Flemington. His long stride suited the course, and it wasn't long before he was burning up the workouts, fully relaxed in the reverse way of going. Knox breezed the colt through easy sectionals, sometimes against Satmoth, sometimes on his own. McGrath was careful, however, not to overtax his colt. There would be no over-racing or over-training of this horse, and Dangar would insist on that. He was very protective of Peter Pan. If the horse showed any sign of unease he would be rested, but at the moment, the colt was electric. 'The battle is half-won with a horse of this disposition,' McGrath told the *Sportsman* in the lead-up to the Caulfield Cup. 'He's as clean-winded as a yearling and a more fit horse would be hard to find. I once said dear old Amounis was the made-to-order thoroughbred, but Peter has him licked to a frazzle. He is one of the kindest horses I've ever had anything to do with. He doesn't know how to do anything that's wrong.'

Peter Pan's biggest worry was getting enough to eat, and before McGrath arrived on Friday the colt had put on condition with the trip to Melbourne. But a few pipe openers in the days that followed got rid of that, and in no time the horse was racing fit. 'In my opinion he will stay for a week,' McGrath said. 'Whether it be a mile or two miles, I don't think Peter worries very much. Of course, I'm too old in the head to say that any horse is a certainty, but if Peter Pan is beaten on Saturday then my optimism will be destroyed for all time.'

On Wednesday morning there were other reasons for the destruction of McGrath's optimism. The weather that had moved over Melbourne was so wet it broke the October rainfall records. Buckets of water fell over the city and suburbs, and by nightfall it was hammering the roof over Peter Pan's head. In the morning it was no better. The Flemington course was properly saturated, and the tan track, though firmer, was little safe. It was a ridiculous situation given that the Caulfield Cup was two days away. McGrath boxed up his four horses and floated them to Williamstown, a suburban course he knew could withstand the drenching. Sending Peter Pan out with Andy Knox, he galloped the colt over seven furlongs with Satmoth, and the stablemate had no chance. The son of Pantheon had a monstrous advantage by the finish, running the seven in 1:28 1/2, only half-a-second off the course record set in 1917. The trainers and clockers that watched the trial that morning were amazed, declaring it the best-ever performed on the Williamstown grounds. Knox knew it had been scintillating. The Sydney lightweight was back on Peter Pan for the Caulfield Cup, grateful for the absence of Jim Pike.

McGrath had been impressed with Pike's Derby ride, and would have liked to retain the jockey for the Melbourne campaign were it not for his reckless riding ban. Even so, Pike never would have made the weights to ride Peter Pan, for anything below 8st 10lb was beyond him. As Knox was McGrath's stable jockey, the trainer saw no need to search about for a new rider. Still, McGrath watched with keen eyes all that was happening when it came to jockeys. The shuffle for rides was a constant aspect of spring racing, and it could change as suddenly as Melbourne's weather. Darby Munro was supposedly on his way from Sydney, while Billy Duncan, Melbourne's leading hoop, was still not declared for a runner. Many of the top hoops were waiting for the results of the Caulfield Cup before they declared themselves. The day was not long arriving.

***

Arthur Hiskens was the popular secretary of the Victoria Amateur Turf Club (VATC), the organising body over Caulfield Racecourse, and on Saturday morning he went to inspect his racetrack. The club had spent a pretty penny on drainage and regrading and, after two days of tumultuous rain, the track was found to be good. Though it was probably sodden, Hiskens declared, it was not unduly heavy or in the least degree unsafe. He even showed his boots to prove his point.

By noon, the racecourse was alive with people. The trams that arrived out front had barely stopped before thousands of racegoers fell out of them, spilling through the turnstiles in a steady throng until 40,600 people jammed the racecourse. There was not a patch of ground unclaimed. Even the infield inside the steeplechase course was humming. The paddock bookies were parked on the edge of the parade ring, and under their white umbrellas men shuffled forward and back placing bets, laying commissions and watching the odds for the Caulfield Cup. The South Australian horse Induna was favourite, with Peter Pan second choice and Rogilla after him, and the nearest to that group were Dermid, K. Cid, Top Hole and Satmoth. The interest in Peter Pan was relentless. His track times had been published in every paper, his Sydney feats stated and restated for the Victorian audience, his physicality admired and criticised.

Peter Pan and Satmoth had been floated to Caulfield late in the morning, and as race time approached the frenzied air of excitement could be felt in the wind. The Cup was due off at 3.50 in the afternoon, and by three o'clock Peter Pan was tacked up, a pair of neat brushing boots on his forelegs. McGrath, very concerned about the tight-turning Caulfield and Peter Pan's outside draw, felt the long-striding colt could fall over himself in the scrimmage for positions, and he wanted to keep his legs protected. When they reached the parade ring, the crowd wondered if McGrath was sending the horse for a track gallop.

Induna had remained favourite for the Caulfield Cup. He had run second in the Caulfield Stakes the previous Saturday, and had won the South Australian Derby earlier in the season. He had also run a trial at Mentone during the week that had set a course record, so as far as his trainer was concerned, he was the winner. Rogilla, however, had earned many friends. He had placed second in both the Epsom and Metropolitan handicaps at Randwick in the last few weeks, and on paper he was due for a win. He was a big, rangy horse from Newcastle, one of the least attractive animals in racing. Injury and accidents had hampered the gelding's success at all points of his five-year-old life, and come raceday it was a miracle he had declared. His owner-trainer, Les Haigh, who was actually leasing the big gelding, had almost scratched him. Rogilla had suffered a foot injury before coming to Melbourne from Sydney.

The 1932 Caulfield Cup was the 55th running of the handicap. The field was a good one. Outside of Induna, Peter Pan and Rogilla, there was the Sydney Cup winner Johnnie Jason, and High Brae, winner of the Memsie Stakes the previous month. There was Dermid, a consistent racehorse with questionable stamina, and Top Hole, the mount of leading Victorian rider William Duncan. There was also K. Cid, winner of the Toorak Handicap last Saturday. Including Peter Pan, five three-year-olds were in the race, among them a lovely Manfred filly called Segati, and Ruach, the horse that had chased home Peter Pan in the Derby. Shortly after noon, the four-year-old Stephen was scratched, and the field fell to 20.

McGrath and Dangar stood with Andy Knox in the mounting yard. Dangar had arrived from Sydney on Thursday evening, and was relaxed and confident in the Caulfield enclosure. The three men talked loosely as they watched the 20 horses walking around. There was no order to the procession, just finely tuned thoroughbreds weaving everywhere, and McGrath reiterated his instructions to his jockey. He wanted Peter Pan in the leading bunch immediately, which would be no small effort given he had drawn almost the widest alley. Knox nodded, and crossed the paddock towards George Phillips and Peter Pan.

Knox was a good jockey, and a good boy. He had a solid friendship with Frank McGrath, but it was built on professionalism, not necessarily affection. Knox had ridden McGrath's top-notch horses for two years. He had brought home Denis Boy in the 1931 Caulfield Cup, which had been the jockey's first major win. The race hadn't been without incident. Ten minutes before post time, Knox was hauled in from the mounting yard to face the stewards. An anonymous messenger had declared that Knox intended on riding with a battery whip, an electric device at the end of his crop that would shock the horse each time it was used. The stewards completed a thorough search of Knox's equipment, but they found nothing. They dismissed the tip-off as nothing more than an insidious attempt to throw the jockey off his game that day. It hadn't worked. The young rider composed his nerves enough to steer Denis Boy to victory. He had relentless instincts for riding, but today he sensed something was wrong. As soon as Peter Pan stepped on to the track at Caulfield, Knox knew the colt wasn't himself. He was antsy, almost upset in his surroundings.

The mile-and-a-half start of the Caulfield Cup was at the top of the straight, right in front of the Leger reserve. Tens of thousands of shrill cheers deafened the young colt. Derby Day at Randwick had been just as loud, but that, at least, was a track Peter Pan had seen before, and he was facing the wrong way this time. The VATC starter, Rupert Greene, called the 20 horses to order, and the jockeys assembled into a line. In Victoria, races were begun from a walk-up start, rather than the standstill start employed in Sydney. While the walk-up start had its benefits, a horse that reached the starting tape before the others was forced to stop momentarily, and was often caught flat-footed as the tape went up. There was a very fine line between getting the jump right, and getting it terribly wrong. 'Steady jockeys,' called Greene as the horses walked up. Lancegay was drawn on the rail, with Rogilla in postposition 11. Dermid was drawn 19, Peter Pan beside him in 20, and Lady Pam was on the outside. In the middle, a flurry of itching horses waited to jump.

Peter Pan wasn't ready to race. He dived in and out of the line, swinging out of place just as Greene called him in. It wasn't that the colt was having a tantrum, for he wasn't that kind of racehorse. It was just that things felt wrong to him, and as he grumbled, bubbles of sweat building on his neck, so started Rogilla until Greene had had enough of the two Sydney horses. He ordered the clerk of the course to catch hold of Peter Pan's bridle, and with an impatient tug the colt was led into line. They stepped forward, but when the tape went up and the field lurched away, Peter Pan's mind was somewhere else. He was tilted towards the outside rail, and in the split of a second McGrath's orders went up in smoke.

The field deserted Peter Pan in an instant. As he lurched into stride he was panicked, and so was Andy Knox. It was the worst possible start. Hauling on the inside rein, Knox yanked Peter Pan across the course towards the rail, and when they met it they were galloping dead last, an army of horses running away in front of them. Johnnie Jason had jumped straight to the lead, as he had in the Hill Stakes, and thundering away from the grandstands he was leading Top Hole, with Induna just behind. Right down the back, with Prince Dayton running beside him, Knox was punching Peter Pan. He urged the colt to make up ground, but Peter just couldn't find his stride. The odd turns of the Caulfield course, and the reverse way of going, had left him in a spin, and Peter Pan ran with his head skewed, hanging to the outside rail like he was trying to get to it. It didn't help that the track was sticky from days of rain. At the seven-pole, Knox had pushed the colt around two horses, but at the five he was last again. As the field hurtled away from Peter Pan like hounds on a fox, Knox gave up the relentless driving and tried to settle his racehorse.

Induna had moved up to Johnnie Jason, and Dermid, Movie Star and Top Hole were prominent. When the field moved onto the railway side, the longest stretch of running on the racecourse, the order of racing changed dramatically. From nowhere, Rogilla motored around the field and barrelled down on the leaders, so that by the half-mile he was breathing all over Johnnie Jason, with Induna and Top Hole still fresh, and Segati behind them. Then the cry went up from the grandstands: 'Here comes Peter Pan!' Knox had used the railway stretch to bring Peter Pan around the field, and for a furlong or two the colt was in stride. He had levelled his body, dropping like a horse in top gear, and he was picking off runners like they were hobbled. His ears were flat, his eyes set on the leaders, aggressive. He had run around the field in two furlongs.

They clattered into the home turn, and Rogilla ranged along the outside, hitting the front and cutting over to the rails. As he did, he stopped short Induna and Johnnie Jason. On the extreme outside of horses, Peter Pan, who had been travelling brilliantly, suddenly hung to the outside. He left room for Induna, Top Hole, Satmoth and Segati to sneak through, and Knox pleaded with the colt to stay in touch. He hauled on his inside rein, but it was no use. Peter Pan couldn't handle the tight turn, and as he ran wide a wall of horses came through on the inside.

Rogilla surged ahead as they straightened for home, with Segati and Top Hole chasing. Down the middle of the course, Knox wrung the last drop from Peter Pan. The colt scrambled down the track, finally galloping straight. Knox walloped him once, then again and again, and they levelled with Top Hole. Every stride was an effort now, but Peter began to inch forward into third. He had summoned terrific speed, though he was tired, when suddenly he baulked in the final furlong. Billy Duncan, riding hell for leather on Top Hole, had lashed Peter Pan in the face. It was an accident, for the colt had gone too close to his rival, but the sting stopped the colt for a moment, a moment long enough to cost him third place. As Rogilla dived past the judge three-and-a-half lengths to Segati ahead of him, Peter Pan fell short by a head. Top Hole flashed past the post in third place, and Peter Pan was fourth. The effort, all of 2:34 1/4, had just about burst his heart.

McGrath was seething up in the grandstand. He had known the horse had been set a task after the start, but he hadn't counted on Andy Knox destroying the chances that remained. He had watched the jockey pound Peter Pan furiously down the backstretch, making him run wide when he should have slotted in at the back and waited for a gap to open, and it was a wonder the colt had any wind to finish the race at all. As it was, McGrath felt he had witnessed a minor miracle in Peter Pan's finishing fourth. Up in the owner's box, Rodney Dangar was also appalled. Disgusted, he headed for the stairs.

Knox's ride had cost Peter Pan £300 in stakes money, more than the average yearly wage of a working man in New South Wales. It had robbed him of a placing for the first time in his three-year-old career. It wasn't the jockey's finest hour. When Peter Pan returned to scale, he was dripping with sweat. George Phillips hurried him away from the enclosure and back to his stall, and Satmoth wasn't far behind. Though he'd had a clean run in the Caulfield Cup, Satmoth had managed only twelfth, and it demonstrated the vast difference between McGrath's two horses.

The trainer arrived at the stalls to check the colt over, and found him clean and injury-free. But there were deep lines in McGrath's face, dark furrows in his brow. The Caulfield Cup had been a terrible struggle for Peter Pan, and he was still only two years old (he would turn three on Monday). McGrath knew that it took only one hard race to ruin a horse sometimes. Back in 1931, many had said that the Futurity Stakes had altered Phar Lap forever, and McGrath tried to shake off the association in his mind. He ordered the two horses back to Flemington, and told George Phillips to do nothing extra with Peter Pan. He suspected the colt was fine and, if he wasn't, Peter Pan would tell him straight away. But when the colt licked up every morsel of his food that night and fell asleep at his usual time, not stirring until the birds so did, McGrath knew all was well.

The fallout from the Caulfield Cup was immense in the first few days. The Melbourne papers were quick to declare the failure of both Induna and Peter Pan, though Peter Pan had fared much better than Induna's tenth place. The Sydney papers, in contrast, were agog. 'How Peter Pan was robbed of a place,' sang the *Referee.* 'Peter Pan's Glory', shouted the *Sun* on page one. Each came back to a common conclusion. 'Peter Pan ran a remarkably good race,' said *Truth'* s racing correspondent. 'But I cannot understand why Knox allowed him to drop so far out of the race in the early part.' Said the *Sun'* s correspondent: 'In my opinion Knox rode the colt an atrocious race, and Phar Lap as a three-year-old might not have done much better.' 'Banjo' Paterson lent Peter Pan's effort a little more poetry. 'Not even the celestial horses ridden by the heavenly twins at the battle of Lake Regillus could have won from there,' he said.

The jockey had indeed judged a terrible race. Knox had given the leading division the best part of 20 lengths at the seven furlongs, and then asked Peter Pan to win the race inside the next two. Only a rare horse could have done that. Knox could only defend himself. 'From the time Peter Pan jumped away he was never going kindly,' he said after the race. 'He was always hanging, and didn't seem able to stretch out at all. The course didn't suit him, and he wasn't really doing his best at any part of the race.' McGrath responded, telling *Truth:* 'Knox did not ride him as I thought he would but a jockey cannot always carry out instructions to the letter. Once he [Peter Pan] did gather speed he went along as I know just how he can, but he is still only a baby and the effort to make up so much ground took toll of his stamina.' The old trainer's diplomacy was impressive. He was filthy over Knox's ride, but he wasn't about to let that go public.

The jockey went on after the Caulfield Cup oblivious to the rumblings of bad blood. McGrath had held his thunder, and had told Dangar to do the same. Spring carnival was no time to fire a jockey without first finding another, so they kept Knox in the dark. McGrath knew he now needed a rider with a stronger sense of judgement. If Peter Pan got into trouble in the two-mile Melbourne Cup, he would need a patient and confident jockey to coax him home, a task that had been beyond Andy Knox at Caulfield. When the newspapers asked, McGrath stated he would not be changing jockeys, and as no one asked Rodney Dangar about it, he didn't have to lie. The two men kept their cards close to their chests.

***

Routine began again on Monday. A little before dawn each morning, George Phillips would turn the latch on Peter Pan's stable and say good morning. He would straighten the box, brush the straw out of the colt's mane and tail, and rug, boot and tack him up. Then Phillips would jump aboard and take the colt for a walk, the old handler peering out beneath his weathered trilby and the young Peter Pan strolling like an old hack. Phillips would then lead him home to be dressed for the morning gallop. The rug was stripped, and a racing saddle replaced Phillips's riding seat, and the boots were carefully checked again before Peter Pan was led to the course proper.

He wasn't a pushy horse during trackwork. If his rider asked for it slow and steady, the colt didn't pull or fight the bit. When McGrath asked for a hot pace, Peter Pan settled into it beautifully, an effortless swing to his stride that devoured the distance. Following trackwork, the colt would be taken to the sand roll, one of the delights of every racehorse, and after a good brushing he was given his breakfast. He didn't fuss or play with his oats, taking the business of eating quite seriously, and he was left alone until noon, when he was fed again. More rest, then in the afternoon he was taken for a stroll for an hour or so, and fed again at five o'clock and eight o'clock. In between, Phillips doled out attention. He would wipe the horse's face with a damp cloth, brush his flaxen forelock out of his eyes and pick his feet for stones. It was routine, a handling so staid and sober that in jig time the over-thinking Peter Pan had become quite Amounis-like.

The Melbourne Stakes was less than two weeks away, a weight-for-age race over a mile and a quarter on 29 October. But it was at Flemington, and in that respect Peter Pan was halfway home. Most of the battle at Caulfield had been the track itself, and Peter Pan knew Flemington. He liked it, and it suited his way of going.

The Melbourne Stakes was due off on the first day of the Cup carnival, and Peter Pan needed to acquit himself if he was to remain in contention for the Tuesday. But McGrath had the colt in fine fettle. Peter Pan was working trials over Flemington early each morning. On Saturday, exactly a week to Cup carnival, the Moonee Valley meeting threw a new name into Cup contention. Yarramba, a five-year-old gelding, won the Moonee Valley Cup over a little more than 11 furlongs, and he won it in fine staying fashion. The horse had been a very average galloper so far, the winner of only two races in his career, but his win at Moonee Valley was a timely coming-good, for the Moonee Valley Cup was a great form race for the Melbourne Cup. Yarramba had earned only a 3lb penalty from it, and lightly weighted next Tuesday at 7st 3lb, he had to be given consideration.

Throughout the week, money continued to come in for the Melbourne Cup horses. Rogilla had earned many friends in Melbourne, people that didn't want to be caught out again by the rangy, white-faced chestnut charging home on his own. By Wednesday, he had narrowed into favouritism with Peter Pan and Middle Watch. Middle Watch had earned his price. A black son of The Night Patrol, he had won the AJC and VRC St Legers in 1932, two staying classics on the states' respective calendars, and his trainer was positive that if the first mile of the Cup went along at a good clip, his horse was impossible to beat. 'The parochial preferences of the Melbournites are strong,' teased the *Sydney Sportsman* in its discussions on the Melbourne Cup betting. 'They stick like chewing gum to their own, so Middle Watch may remain at the head of the market.' The horse was also engaged for the Melbourne Stakes.

McGrath, meanwhile, kept the dial turned up on Peter Pan's workouts. The colt mixed his short bursts at Flemington with short bursts at Williamstown, and the series of sharp gallops had him quivering fit. 'I'm not the least afraid that Peter will lose his steering apparatus at Flemington,' McGrath told the *Sportsman.* 'The long stretches there will give him the chance to settle down early in the race, and as regards him staying two miles, he'll do that alright.'

McGrath had also been fishing for a jockey, albeit quietly. As Saturday approached, he met with 32-year-old Billy Duncan, Victoria's champion race rider. Duncan was a cheerful, smooth-faced hoop. A natural lightweight, he was unsullied by excessive wasting. He had also got a good look at Peter Pan during the Caulfield Cup, especially in the last furlong when he had bored down on Top Hole, and Duncan liked what he saw – a masculine, tenacious fighter. Melbourne's leading hoop was usually disposed to the Mentone trainer Jack Holt, but this carnival had seen many of

Holt's first horses sidelined. Holt was, in fact, down to a small team of about six. So Duncan was free for the picking, and his loyalty would lie with whichever horse could win. Late on Friday night, too late for the Saturday-morning papers to sniff that something was afoot, Duncan agreed to pilot Peter Pan in the Melbourne Stakes the following day, and the Cup three days later.

***

Derby Day at Flemington, and the sun had woken from its stupor. For the first time in days, the grass was dry and the skies were clear, and Melbourne bristled with racing. Flemington began to spill with people by early morning, trains arriving from Bendigo and Ballarat, and trams from every suburb in between. By midday, the Members' driveway chugged steadily with motorcars, while others tramped along on foot. Thirty-seven thousand people were headed to Flemington, where the first race was due off at 1.30pm.

The Melbourne Stakes was the third event on the card, a weight-for-ager sandwiched between the Maribyrnong Plate for two-year-olds and the Victoria Derby. It wasn't an expensive race. The purse was worth only £750. In comparison, the Maribyrnong was worth £1500, and the Derby £4000. But it was a Melbourne Cup form-guide, much more so than the Derby because its entrants were not restricted by age. In the past, great horses such as Malua, Carbine and

Phar Lap had won the Melbourne Stakes and gone on to success in the Cup, and it was a race littered with first-class victors – Chester, Abercorn, Wakeful, Poseidon, Eurythmic, Gloaming and Manfred. On the other hand, the Melbourne Stakes placegetters had a history of upgrading their places. Lord Cardigan, Comedy King, Poitrel, Windbag and Nightmarch had all been minor placegetters, before thumping home in the Melbourne Cup three days later.

This year, there were nine horses entered, a small field but a good field. Peter Pan, Middle Watch and Rogilla topped the offering. Lough Neagh was also entered, the Queensland horse that had won the two-mile Randwick Plate a few weeks before, and Induna was back after his poor showing at Caulfield. Apart from these there was the Sydney horse Peter Jackson, along with Viol d'Amour and the outsiders Cimbrian and Compris.

Flemington was abuzz by lunchtime. There was an exceptional day's racing on the cards. Bar three horses, all entrants in Tuesday's Melbourne Cup were running that day, and all three-year-olds entered in it were running in the Derby, bar one of course. Peter Pan was taking the harder road through the Melbourne Stakes. The lawns and infield were packed to capacity, crowds that hadn't been seen since 1928. Racebooks had sold out by the second event. When the Wakeful Stakes kicked off at 1.30pm, each and every man was toasting spring racing.

Andy Knox made a rip-roaring start to day one. Devastated by the news that he had lost his ride on Peter Pan, the Sydney lightweight bounced back with a second-place finish in the Wakeful Stakes, and then drove Rapsonia home to win the Maribyrnong Plate. But there was hardly a pep in his step. McGrath had approached the jockey early in the morning, telling him of his dismissal from Peter. McGrath had stated that if Peter Pan won the Melbourne Stakes, Billy Duncan would remain engaged for the Cup. He added that it was nothing personal, and that if Peter Pan won the Melbourne Cup, Knox would be handsomely looked after. But Knox could only mumble in response. 'What's the use of that?' he replied, and the two men left it at that.

The horses were in the parade ring for the Melbourne Stakes shortly after the Maribyrnong. Rodney Dangar was there, dressed like a dandy and speaking with McGrath. The two discussed their horse's tactics in detail. After the bugle sounded, Billy Duncan crossed the paddock and jumped on Peter Pan. George Phillips led them down the lane that led to the course proper, flanked by thousands of cheering racegoers, and Duncan performed the preliminary gallop before reaching the mile-and-a-quarter start of the 63rd Melbourne Stakes.

Peter Pan had drawn postposition eight. Duncan had been drilled by Frank McGrath over where the colt should race, and his instructions were branded into the jockey's brain. Provided he rode as he was told, there was every chance they would demolish this field. The handicapper had given Peter Pan 7st 11lb, and he was the lightest-weighted horse going around. The closest to him were Peter Jackson and Lough Neagh, each with a full stone more.

Duncan was determined to squeeze every advantage out of Peter Pan's feathery weight. The race would start at the top of the river stretch, which began around the corner from the winning post and ran straight for nearly four furlongs, flanking the Maribyrnong River on the right. It then swept left-handed around 'the abattoirs' (a nickname for the stretch of Flemington Racecourse that ran past the old abattoir building on Smithfield Road, opposite the racecourse) and continued to bend until the home straight, where the field had just over two furlongs to run for home. As soon as Peter Pan had stepped onto the course, he knew where he was. Duncan would have no trouble at the barrier.

Rupert Greene, who acted as both VATC and VRC starter, called the field to attention. He had a sharp eye on the Sydney horses that had given him trouble at Caulfield. The jockeys made a semblance of a line, and walked their horses forward. Each could hear his own heart beat, feel the tension at the end of the rein. There was no sound but the procession of thoroughbreds, no breathing louder than their own, no horse in the world but the one they were sitting on. And then Rupert Greene raised his hand as they neared the barrier, and the starting tape flew up before them.

Peter Pan was like an electrical volt in water. In a matter of seconds, he had outjumped his rivals by a length and sprinted across to the running rail. Leaning slightly to the left to help him over, Duncan balanced himself immediately then eased off the pace, waiting for his rivals to come around him. Middle Watch and Viol d'Amour came, crossing his outside and moving onto the rails, and the pace slowed to a canter. Jim Munro on Middle Watch needed a strong tempo to give his mount a chance, and he had no option but to spurt around Viol d'Amour and run Middle Watch to the front.

Duncan had Peter Pan third on the rails, and the colt was cruising in mid-gear. Each time Duncan gave him a kick, the colt spurted forward, so enthusiastically that the jockey had to ease him to avoid the heels in front. Peter Pan had found his loping, elastic stride, and passing the mile-post, just two furlongs into the race, Duncan could feel the four-beat rhythm of the gallop, sweet and clean beneath him.

The field drummed down the backstretch, Middle Watch sidling along in front with Viol d'Amour just behind him. Peter Pan stuck to the rails. Lough Neagh had moved into fourth, and as they swung into the abattoirs, Rogilla was making a run on the outside. The Caulfield Cup winner had been squeezed out just after the jump, and his jockey Darby Munro was going wide. Gulping up the ground, Rogilla moved towards the leading division around Peter Pan, and at the seven-furlong pole Duncan found himself back a place or two. Middle Watch was still in the lead, trying to inject some tempo into the running, with Viol d'Amour behind him and Rogilla loping up the outside into third. Lough Neagh had also moved up, and Peter Pan had glued himself to the rails. In consequence, a number of horses had pushed ahead of him, and this was where Billy Duncan set himself apart from Andy Knox. Measuring the colt he had beneath him, and the pace they were dawdling along at, Duncan allowed Peter Pan to stay where he was. Better that than break the colt's stride, he thought, for it wasn't an easy one to find again when it was broken, such was its length.

The field approached the straight, and Rogilla was breathing all over Middle Watch. Quickly, the race upped its tempo, and the gap that Duncan was waiting for still hadn't appeared. But drawing on his patience for a moment longer, Duncan sat still on Peter Pan, and just before the field leaned into the home turn, he moved the colt off the rails. He shook the reins just a little. With an open plain of grass ahead of him, Peter Pan snatched the rein and took off, bolting down the centre of Flemington's straight with greyhound-like strides. In a moment, he was with the leaders.

Middle Watch and Rogilla were stride for stride on the rails, and the Pantheon colt ranged up to Rogilla's flank. For a stride or two, the three moved like a cavalry charge, 12 hooves carving the turf in crescendo. But then Rogilla and Peter Pan inched ahead of Middle Watch, and Rogilla was fighting hard. Duncan could see the older horse heaving, could hear the shouting of Darby Munro onboard. But Peter Pan was playing. Duncan flicked the reins and folded into his horse, pushing the colt into business, and they were gone from Rogilla in a second. The cheering fell down on top of them. It was the soundtrack of victory, the raucous, uncontrolled music of winning. And Peter Pan could hear it too. With his ears pinned and Duncan's hands against his neck, the silver-tailed chestnut sprinted past the winning post, a length and three-quarters in front. He had won the Melbourne Stakes, and it had been blissfully simple.

9

The longest two days in horse racing

Rodney Dangar stared absently from the rear seat of his hired motorcar as it wound its way through Melbourne's busy streets, ferrying him and Elsie back to the prestigious Menzies Hotel. He watched the last of the Saturday city-goers scurrying for evening trams, and the street merchants closing their newspaper stands, and he and Elsie were quiet. They were exhausted. Exhilarated. Their colt had won the Melbourne Stakes. The car paused briefly in Bourke Street traffic, idling outside the Salvation Army headquarters, when suddenly Dangar broke into laughter, his broad chuckles bursting the silence in the car. 'Beware the Gambling Cup,' read the Salvation Army's huge street poster. 'It speweth forth woe.'

Cup Week transformed Melbourne into a glorious city, a southern delight, but it also dragged out the puritans. The strict Sunday School had organised its annual picnic for the coming Tuesday, a deliberate ploy to keep its flock from the racetrack, but they must not have realised that the Melbourne Cup *was* a religion. There was little to be done about the hundreds of thousands of devotees that worshipped the first Tuesday in November. As the motorcar pulled away from Bourke Street, Dangar thought about the irony of the Salvation Army's little tout. Here he was, a clean-living, god-fearing citizen of Australia, a man that rarely bet and never forgot the charitable cause, and he was the owner of the Melbourne Cup favourite.

Peter Pan's triumph in the Melbourne Stakes that afternoon made him the first three-year-old winner in the history of that race. It had brought his winnings to £5699. It was the colt's fourth win in six starts, his first time around Flemington and his first race under Billy Duncan. He had downed the Caulfield Cup winner and the pre-post favourite for the Melbourne Cup, and he had done so by nearly two lengths. The public was impressed. Immediately after the race, Peter was backed into outright favouritism for Tuesday's big two-miler, while Middle Watch, a disappointing third behind Rogilla in the Melbourne Stakes, dropped out to 8/1.

Frank McGrath had spoken to *Truth* shortly after the Melbourne Stakes, and had little to say but I told you so. 'All along I've been telling you what a wonder colt he is, and his win in the Stakes this afternoon didn't surprise me in the least,' he told the newspaper. The patient training had turned Peter Pan into a fitness machine. The colt hadn't broken a sweat during the Melbourne Stakes, pulling up fresh and full after the mile and a quarter. The time wasn't anything to be impressed about – a dawdling 2:08 1/4 for the distance, a full five seconds over the course record – but the slow early pace accounted for it. In fact, a slow pace had often been the undoing of a true stayer like Peter Pan. It had unravelled Middle Watch, and even Rogilla had felt the sting in the final furlong. 'I've always harboured a 22-carat opinion of this leggy son of Pantheon,' quipped McGrath. 'I cannot see anything beating him on Tuesday.'

Billy Duncan was of a similar opinion: 'I was greatly impressed with Peter Pan. He has beautiful action, and to ride him is like sitting on a rocking horse.' Prior to the running of the Melbourne Stakes, Duncan had told Alec Hunter, owner of the three-year-old Victorian star Liberal, that he would ride his horse if Liberal won the Derby. Liberal did win the Derby, right after the Melbourne Stakes, but Duncan was too impressed with Peter Pan. Just before the last race on Saturday afternoon, he confirmed his ride on Peter for the Melbourne Cup, and Andy Knox was stricken. 'I should have been on him,' he told a friend after the Melbourne Stakes. 'Now he looks the really good thing I thought he was all along.'

Later that night, Dangar sent a telegram from Menzies Hotel to Baroona, to his manager Alec Young. 'SATURDAY'S RUN WOUND HIM UP. STABLE CONFIDENT. LOOKS GOOD THING. DANGAR.'

***

Frank McGrath had received words too, in a letter from Robert Wallace, the Irish owner of Denis Boy. Wallace and McGrath had struck a friendship years before, and when the Irishman had returned to his homeland he had sent McGrath Denis Boy to train. Now, Wallace had written to wish McGrath luck for the spring, and to hope for a few wins with his black horse in Melbourne. Since he'd penned his letter, Wallace had won the Metropolitan with Denis Boy, and on Saturday afternoon he had also won the Cantala Stakes, although news of the win would take a day or so to reach Ireland by cable. McGrath was thrilled. Robert Wallace had sent him a high-class racehorse in Denis Boy, a horse that without injury could have been a champion, and entrusted the trainer with absolute control of his career. The only way to return the favour was to win. But good as Denis Boy was, he was not Peter Pan.

Melbourne punters had backed Peter into favouritism on Saturday afternoon, even ahead of Victorian Middle Watch, but for the Cup no one was prepared to write off Rogilla. 'If gameness and grit will win a race, then Rogilla must be up to his eyeballs in Tuesday's mammoth affair,' said *Truth.* In his seven starts for the season, Rogilla had never been out of a place, competing in races from six to 13 furlongs against horses such as Chatham, Denis Boy and, of course, Peter Pan. Les Haigh, his affable Newcastle trainer, had hardly even noticed that his horse was beaten in the Melbourne Stakes. 'While I am afraid of McGrath's pair,' he told the press, 'Rogilla will go out fit to run for a kingdom, and he will be right there when the whips are cracking.'

With Saturday over, McGrath settled in for Tuesday, a waiting game that he'd never get used to. He'd been in this position in 1902, with Abundance when the colt had won the AJC Derby, then the VRC Derby, only to run third in the Melbourne Cup. He'd also been here with Prince Foote in 1909. The days between Saturday and Tuesday were the longest two days in horse racing. Every trainer and owner that ran his horse on Derby Day held his breath that his horse would stay fit and sound. It often happened that months of preparation would be destroyed in a second, with a horse falling in his box, striking himself in a gallop or taking a wrong step down the shed row. In 1931, Yarramba's connections ran foul of good luck when their horse, overreaching with his hind legs, gave himself a nasty wound on his near front fetlock the day before he was due for the Caulfield Cup. McGrath had had similar palpitations the previous week when Satmoth, joining Peter Pan on the gallops at Williamstown, fell in a heap just before they started. Though Satmoth was none the worse for his fall, McGrath aged a year just watching him. These types of things were all it took to spell the end of a Cup campaign.

Thankfully, the weather had cleared up. The Melbourne Stakes had been run under cloudy, windy conditions, but the rain had held. Sunday proved a scorcher. For the first time since McGrath had shipped his horses south, Peter Pan, Denis Boy, Satmoth and Lightning March felt the sun on their hides. They felt the sting of Victoria's insects, and breathed in the smell of drying turf, but on Monday it was gone again. A stiff southerly brought the temperatures back down, and the Commonwealth meteorologist saw rain for Tuesday racing. 'Umbrellas and galoshes are expected to play a prominent part at Flemington on Tuesday.' It was Melbourne to a season.

McGrath sent his horses on a steady round of Flemington on Monday morning, nothing searching for Peter Pan and Denis Boy, his two Cup chances. Satmoth was not racing until Saturday, and Lightning March's programme was undecided. Lining the running rails, the clockers watched each horse go by, and their information soaked through to the newspapers, the bookies and everyone in between them. 'The books are draping themselves with scowls at the thought of what is likely to happen them on Tuesday,' said *Truth.* 'Peter Pan, Rogilla, Oro and Lough Neagh are particularly bad horses in the doubles.'

McGrath had loaded up on the Rogilla–Peter Pan Cups double, which had laid off his loss on Peter Pan not winning the Caulfield Cup, but it was obvious that Sydney and Melbourne differed in their respective favourites. While Peter Pan was the unanimous selection of both cities, Sydney had backed its own horses into oblivion – Rogilla, Lough Neagh and Oro. Melbourne, on the other hand, had only gone after Rogilla since the Caulfield Cup, while Yarramba and Middle Watch, despite their dubious records, could be found in single figures. But even the enormous liabilities of Cup Week, even the fortunes that could be won on the doubles, were small change compared to the figures that came the way of Rodney Dangar. On Monday afternoon, the eve of the Melbourne Cup, he was approached by a gentleman, acting on behalf of an American client, who offered him £50,000 for Peter Pan.

It was a staggering amount of money. In 1932, £975 could buy a double-fronted brick cottage in Woollahra. Further into the city, on Goulburn Street, freehold premises had been sold for £10,500. In other words, £50,000 would set a man up for life, for a few lives in fact. But Rodney Dangar was no such man.

Dangar was already exceedingly wealthy, so he wasn't tempted by the money. Rather, there was one condition of the offer that made him refuse it point blank. It was that Peter Pan was to be scratched from the Cup. To Dangar, the very thought was sacrilege. He had no intention of burning the thousands of racegoers that had put their money where their faith was. He would not rip them off. He also knew that Peter Pan stood on the edge of greatness, this young horse he had bred himself and reared at Baroona. He knew that Americans were paying attention to Australian racing now, but he thought the offer crass. He refused it, and demanded that it remain an anonymous situation. News of it would smother all Cup coverage, and he didn't want that. He said he would never speak of the matter, and he was almost always good to his word.

As nightfall descended on Melbourne, on the eve of the 1932 Melbourne Cup, Peter Pan fell asleep, unaware that he was the hottest property in Sydney, that he was more valuable than a freehold block in downtown Sydney. Under the eye of George Phillips, and the occasional guard that strolled by, Dangar's super colt rested, nearly worth his weight in gold.

10

The 1932 Melbourne Cup

Tuesday morning broke cool and cloudy, just as the weatherman had said it would. A southerly had blown across Melbourne overnight, nudging the weekend's heatwave into distant memory, and as the city woke to early morning traffic, trench coats and ladies' furs were the order of the day. The first of the electric trains to Flemington left Spencer Street station just after nine o'clock, while the special tram services to the racecourse began from William Street at 9.15am. Thereafter, a steady stream of public transport ferried people to the Melbourne Cup, and by late morning the secretary of the VRC, Mr Arthur Kewney, wondered if they might break the Flemington record.

Kewney had been VRC secretary since 1925, and he had more optimism this day for the attendance than he had had in the last few years. Talk was of the passing of the Depression, and of good times again, and Flemington, at least, was on its way back to boom times in the hands of Kewney's bookkeeping. With the Depression had come a sharp drop in attendance, and Kewney had been forced to cut the Melbourne Cup purse to £7000. It hadn't affected his public profile, for everyone in the racing community was realistic about the hard times. In former years the Cup had been a £10,000 prize, along with a £2000 owners' sweepstakes, but this year even the sweepstakes was gone, leaving the winning horse with a £5000 share. It was scarcely more than the AJC Derby purse, only £580 more in fact, but the prestige was still there.

The lesser money hadn't dampened the Cup's distinction. Arthur Kewney was a patient, tactful secretary, and this year he was waiting for the turnout to tell him when he could reinstate the prizemoney. Nothing was worth more to him than the integrity of racing. He wasn't a betting man, just a clever accountant, and in his eight years of secretaryship he had coddled his club through the worst economy in history. But he wasn't a unique fixture at the VRC. The club had a history of excellent secretaries including its first one, the brilliant architect and surveyor Robert C. Bagot, who was instated in 1864 and never learned the difference between weight-for-age and handicap.

The first Melbourne Cup had been run in 1861, a two-mile handicap conceived by the then Victoria Turf Club (VTC). The VTC was one of two chief clubs hosting racing in Melbourne, the other being the Victoria Jockey Club (VJC). But the two clubs bickered endlessly, until both were disbanded. In 1864, they merged into a single entity, calling it the VRC. By then, the Melbourne Cup had been going at Flemington for three years, won first by Archer in 1861 and 1862, and by Banker in 1863. Quickly, the race became the greatest contest in the land, the unchallenged classic of the Australian turf. There was no bigger prize on the racing calendar. There was no other race that offered such sudden fortune, or called on more Spartan stamina. 'Its distance and its rigours call forth Homeric efforts from great-hearted horses,' wrote the *Sporting Globe.* Even Sydney was happy to play second fiddle to its southern rival for the duration of the spring carnival.

Flemington was thronged by lunchtime. The totalisator had opened for betting at eleven o'clock, and some 1500 staff were tending the bars and restaurants, selling entry tickets and keeping the gates. One hundred constables in uniform walked through the crowd, and there were 32 detectives from the criminal investigation branch working with 20 plain-clothed detectives. There were 377 licensed bookmakers, the largest of any racecourse in the world, so said the press. Melbourne's leading fielder, Mannie Lyons, operated from stand 47, and he could be heard above all voices in the paddock. Albert Sluice, at stand 78, was a well-liked identity in both Melbourne and Sydney, coming from a big bookmaking family. There was also Bert Levin, Gus Watson and Wallace Mitchell, all wrangling for the mug punter's money, and they usually got it. There was no other day when the average Australian felt more compelled to gamble than on Cup Day.

The celebrities of horse racing were also on hand with their picks. John Wren, Melbourne's famous and most adored back-alley entrepreneur, was putting his money on Denis Boy today. Harry Telford, the trainer of Phar Lap, had picked Induna. The VRC handicapper was on Lough Neagh or Liberal, while Walter Hickenbotham, trainer of Carbine, had selected Lough Neagh or Rogilla. But Peter Pan had his fans. His supporters included Sol Green, Eric Connolly and legendary trainer James Scobie, not to mention the entire team at *Truth* newspaper. Among the jockeys, Bobby Lewis, Harold Badger and even Andy Knox had claimed Peter Pan would win. But the overwhelming opinion was that a three-year-old would prevail this afternoon. 'To my mind, a good three-year-old should win the Cup,' wrote 'Musket' in the *Sporting Globe,* 'and Peter Pan is a good one.'

The Melbourne Cup had been won by three-year-olds on 20 occasions since 1861. The most recent was Trivalve in 1927. This year, there were nine of them contesting the two-mile contest, including Rodney Dangar's colt, who was just out of nappies. He was the most lightly raced horse in the field, and possibly the most inexperienced. If he won, at only his seventh start in a race, he would come close to Grand Flaneur, the unbeaten hero of 1880 who won the Cup at only his fourth start.

Racing kicked off at one o'clock with the Cup Hurdle, followed by a high-weight handicap, and the Mimosa Stakes, won by Billy Duncan, went off at 2.40pm. After that, there was no racing until 3.40pm, when the 72nd Melbourne Cup would go to post. There were 27 horses due to race, among them 1931's winner White Nose, along with two Caulfield Cup winners in Denis Boy and Rogilla, and a sprinkling of the classic winners from every state in Australia.

The betting rings were choking. More than 84,000 paying patrons had come to Flemington for the afternoon, not including the thousands who entered for free, and after the Mimosa was won most of them headed to the ring. Peter Pan, a precise favourite despite his Caulfield Cup loss, could not be found for better than 6/4. The books were taking no chances on the colt with the almost flawless three-year-old record. Rogilla was fetching 7/1, with Lough Neagh on 8s, and Liberal and Middle Watch were at 9s and 10s respectively. The weights had not affected the prices. Peter Pan was carrying his weight-for-age allocation of 7st 6lb, including his 3lb penalty for his AJC Derby win. Liberal, the Victoria Derby winner, had the same weight. Denis Boy was topweight with 9st 2lb, and Yarramba, the unlikely hero of the Moonee Valley Gold Cup, had 7st 3lb.

On the track, Peter Pan had drawn a respectable alley in 11. Cimbrian was on the rails. Denis Boy had drawn 12, and Liberal, unluckiest of all, was on the extreme outside. But the saddlecloth number – allocated by weight, with the heaviest-weighted horse number one – was also a moot point with punters. Since 1885, number four had been carried to victory six times. Peter Pan would carry saddlecloth number 18, and the only previous victor with that number had been Apologue back in 1907.

By 3.15pm, the horses were in the mounting yard. Dangar stood with McGrath, looking tall and distinguished. He was at ease being the best-dressed gentleman on course. In fact, he might have been the only man within miles wearing a dickie bow, and his white hair was combed and slicked. It was also his birthday, and he couldn't think of a better present than the £200 gold Melbourne Cup. A little way from him, his horse looked as sharp as he did. Peter Pan was in top order, a fit, sleek racing ship. For many huddled around the paddock fences, it was their first look at the Pantheon colt. Pretty and blond, he was a hit with the ladies.

Soon enough, 27 jockeys filed from their quarters, Duncan in the now familiar Dangar colours: orange with green hoops, orange cap. He ducked in towards McGrath for a brief second and last-minute instructions, then headed over to George Phillips and Peter Pan. Legging him up, Phillips slapped the jockey on the knee, wished him luck, and sent them on their way. As the horses headed out of the paddock and down the lane that led to the course proper, Dangar hurried to the stands to join Elsie. He was nervous, twittering with excitement.

Behind the grandstands, the betting ring was deserted. Only the fielders remained with their betting boards, smoking cigarettes or totting up their liabilities. The crowds had abandoned them to find their spots for the race, and without customers, the bookies had blown the odds out to attract any last passers-by. When the VRC official cruised past to record the starting prices for the Cup, he was surprised to find Peter Pan as long as 4/1, and so 4/1 was what he recorded, though next to no one had got such odds about the favourite. Out on the track, the horses milled at the two-mile mark, which was halfway down the straight-six chute. The Melbourne Cup would see them gallop a furlong onto the course proper, then pass the judge for the first time at the half-mile mark. They would then complete a full circuit of the course.

At a minute or two after 3.40pm, Rupert Greene called his horses into line. Peter Pan ducked in between his stablemate Denis Boy and Shadow King who, at his fourth attempt, was trying for a Cup win, and the 27 thoroughbreds stepped forward like the cavalry. Billy Duncan was calm. Harold Jones, on Denis Boy, was quietly confident. On Yarramba, Andy Knox stole a quick glance at Peter Pan, and his stomach sank. He turned back to face the barrier with the heavy lead of regret at how things had turned out. And as the field neared the starting tape, as Rupert Greene got ready to send them away, the sound went up in the grandstands. The swell of 90,000-odd cheers swept up from Flemington. At that moment the starting tape flew up and they were racing.

Billy Duncan hovered out of his saddle as he felt Peter Pan sit down on his hindquarters, the colt throwing his forefeet into mid-air and launching himself into stride. On either side of him, 26 horses did the same thing, and in seconds the straight line disintegrated and the field bunched towards the running rail. Peter Pan found his stride, and quickening into the leading bunch Duncan inched the horse onto the rail, finding luck between horses. Passing the judge for the first time, the colt was galloping ninth.

Induna led the field into the first turn, with Admiral Drake, Gaine Carrington and Liberal behind him. Next came Manawhenua and Rogilla, with Silent Bird and Havering in front of Peter. On the rails, Duncan couldn't believe his luck. Peter Pan, smooth as a rocking horse, was bounding along beautifully. His breathing was even, his neck was relaxed, and Duncan had plenty in reserve. At the back of the field, last of all, Andy Knox sat quietly on Yarramba.

The field galloped along the river, with Induna making no move to quicken. They ran the first half-mile in 52 seconds, and down the back they quickened by half a second. At the seven furlongs, turning into the abattoirs, Darby Munro moved Rogilla out. Much as he had done in the Caulfield Cup, he asked the gelding to go around the field, and Rogilla eased into second place. But behind him a wall of horses was coming, headed by Eastern Chief, and Duncan felt the tempo escalating. They were clipping along just short of 50 seconds now.

Peter Pan was cruising on the rails, feeling the light guidance of Duncan as he kept the colt off heels. Passing the six furlongs, the rail was clear, so Duncan flicked the reins and the colt surged forward. In a matter of strides Peter Pan had moved into fifth, with Manawhenua in front of him. Suddenly, though, Manawhenua moved off the rails. He opened a space large enough for Peter Pan to drift through. It was a rapid, unexpected gift, and Duncan snatched it. He drove Peter Pan into the hole, and the colt surged forward.

Duncan knew that in a field of 27 over two miles, in the nation's greatest handicap, gifts of this nature didn't occur often. A hole could mean the difference between winning and losing. The jockey was determined to use it before it expired, and Peter Pan bolted into the gap. But as he did, Manawhenua changed his mind and fell back towards the rails, slamming into Peter Pan's shoulder. Duncan's greatest gift suddenly became his worst nightmare.

As the field hurtled past the five-pole, Peter Pan was tossed onto the rails. Manawhenua had hit him so hard while he was travelling at speed that he found himself facing the infield, faltering, and Duncan could feel the colt going down. Peter's stride had been kicked from under him, the wind knocked clean out of him. He went up in the air, Duncan bouncing on him like a child's toy, and both saw the ground getting closer. Duncan's heart was in his mouth. He could hear a swamp of horseflesh behind him, and knew the awful moment that was coming. But suddenly, Peter Pan was jolted forward as another horse now barrelled into him from behind. Denis Boy had crashed into his hindquarters, propelling the young colt back onto his feet. The slap of the two horses rang in

Duncan's ears, but it slung Peter forward. Bobbing like a buoy in water, Peter Pan scrambled for a stride, but he was on his feet. He and Denis Boy fell back through the field like lead weights.

Billy Duncan thought his heart would fall through his teeth. His hands were trembling so hard that he could scarcely hold the reins. In one second they had been gunning for the lead, and the next they were nearly on the floor. He let the reins slip through his fingers, loosening his grip on the bewildered Peter Pan, coaxing the colt to settle down and find his stride again. At a point where every other runner was winding up for the dash for home, Peter Pan was calming down after nearly hitting the turf. He had lost six or seven lengths in the fracas, and had drifted into a dangerous spot in the field, nearing the back with a charge of horses in front of him. But Duncan was amazed as they ripped past the four-pole. Peter had loosened again and was running very well. He was neither distracted nor upset and had his mind on the task still. The scrimmage had knocked the bejesus out of his rider, much more than it had the colt.

The field swung off the half-mile post and ran down onto the turn for home. Some 12 lengths off the leaders, Duncan had a decision to make. He could run down the outside, but the extra ground was asking a lot of a young horse that had just had the stuffing knocked out of him. Peter didn't lack stamina, but after a bump such as he had received, reserves had been used. The jockey, therefore, opted for a rails run. He called on Peter Pan to thread his way to the front, and as the colt quickened, Duncan began to ride with his life. They picked off one horse after another as they bolted into the straight, winding in and out of runners, squeezing through the eye of a Melbourne Cup needle.

Induna had tired up front and dropped out, and on the outside, Yarramba had scrambled into the lead. Andy Knox had brought his gelding right around the outside, and there seemed no catching him. Yarramba was travelling strongly. But a wild cry came up from the crowds. 'Here comes Peter Pan!' Duncan and Peter had burst from the flock inside the two-furlong post, with electric speed. So quickly were they travelling that Knox didn't even see them coming, and the two horses leapt into the final furlong together, drawing away from the field.

Peter Pan was running like a horse possessed. His ears were pinned, his neck set with determination. He charged up to Yarramba's flanks. Then he was beside him, and in a kick he was ahead of the older horse. The crowd was screaming with excitement. Duncan was riding like a madman, nudging the colt forward into a narrow lead. He didn't know when the barrel would empty, or if it ever would, and Peter Pan stuck his neck in front. He didn't know how to give in, and refused to. 'No, Peter Pan will get there, Peter Pan will win it,' shouted the racecaller through the amplifiers, looking from one horse to another. 'Peter Pan wins it!' The colt burst over the line by a long neck, the winner.

Pandemonium ensued across Flemington Racecourse, a thousand trilbies sailing into the air. The shrieks were so loud that Duncan could hear nothing else, not even his horse's breaths as they slowed to a canter around the turn. The jockey shook his head slowly. He couldn't believe the race he had just had. Was he riding some sort of super horse, some colt the likes of which hadn't been known since Poseidon? Had everyone seen what had happened? He swung the colt around and cantered back to scale. There was a soundtrack of screams and cheers, and lining the rails the fans hooted and hollered at him for getting them home. He came to a walk at the lane, and smiled at Knox on Yarramba. Peter Pan, however, was in no mood for trivialities. The colt lashed out at his rival, sending the field scattering. Even the clerk of the course kept a wide berth, and Peter Pan trotted back to the mounting yard alone. The eruptions that met him were deafening as Duncan raised his whip to the crowd. Knox was devastated, deflated. He rode Yarramba back without a smile.

Peter Pan had run the two miles in 3.23 1/4. It was only half a second slower than Windbag's track record of 3.22 3/4, and the track today had been slowed by days of rain. The sectionals were good for the surface. The half-miles had been run in 51 seconds, 51 1/2, 49 3/4, and the final four furlongs in 50 3/4 seconds. The last six furlongs had been clocked in 1:15 flat, while the final mile had been run in 1.39 1/2. Considering that Yarramba had spotted Peter Pan so many lengths in the home straight, it was hard to imagine what the colt would have won by if he hadn't incurred such a clattering.

Rodney Dangar was waiting for his horse when he returned. He was overwhelmed, overpowered by pride and delight. McGrath was there too, a smile from ear to ear, mobbed by congratulatory handshakes. George Phillips was almost in tears. Each of them had played a critical part in shaping this moment, and Dangar, the man that he was, wouldn't forget it. Jumping to the ground, Billy Duncan's weathered visage was cracking with pride. The lines in his face were deep with joy, the type of joy that comes only from a Melbourne Cup victory. He slid his saddle from Peter's back, exclaimed his wonder to Phillips, then bounded over to McGrath and Dangar before weighing in. The race had left deep sweat around Peter's girth, but he was far from an exhausted horse. Standing in the paddock, he was alert and interested, his head up, his eyes large, the blood still bellowing through his veins. Governor-General Sir Isaac Isaacs presented the Melbourne Cup to Dangar, the trophy of the three-handled loving-cup design. Dangar accepted it with a broad smile, a strong handshake, and another hoorah from the crowd.

Frank McGrath watched on with a swollen heart. His bobby dazzler had won him his second Melbourne

Cup, and he was just about bursting at the sight of it. He had seen the crash at the five furlongs, and had dropped his glasses in disbelief and shock. It was over, he'd thought. He'd seen the colt disappear, seen him swallowed up. How he had come back to win he'd never know. In nearly 50 years of racing, McGrath had never seen anything like it.

A little way from the Peter Pan celebrations, Yarramba's connections were shattered. Knox couldn't conceal his dismay at the race's outcome, or his losing of the ride on Peter in the first place, and he sulked his way out of the paddock. The events of the past few days would stay with him for a long time. He had ridden a brave race on Yarramba, and had done everything right, but the colt he had feared all along had downed him good and proper.

The afternoon waned slowly into evening. The Cup Steeplechase took place, then the Yan Yean Stakes in which Billy Duncan rode his third winner for the day, and after that the trams began to ferry people from Flemington. They trundled along Epsom Road and back to William Street, and all across Melbourne that night, Cup balls and banquets had people partying into the night.

As had been tradition for 29 years, the Cup-winning jockey headed out to Wirth Bros. Circus to accept a gold-mounted whip. Standing in the circus ring, swarmed by goodwill, Duncan beamed as circus master Philip Wirth presented him with the crop. He recalled the night 14 years before when he had accepted it for riding Night Watch to victory. 'Peter Pan is the best horse I have ever ridden,' he told the delighted crowd, 'and I have ridden some good ones. Never had a horse to do what Peter Pan had today.' To squeals of delight, Duncan added, 'Phar Lap could not have recovered and won after the buffeting that Peter Pan received.'

***

The 1932 Melbourne Cup was lauded one of the best ever. No one could think of another Cup when a horse had been spread-eagled, then recovered enough to come back and win. What made it more remarkable was that Peter Pan was three years old. Starting for only the seventh time in a race, he had obviously learned one thing very clearly – how to be in front at the end.

Billy Duncan was wildly impressed with the horse. 'Such action I have never known before in a thoroughbred,' he said. Duncan hadn't known mid-race that it was Denis Boy, with Harold Jones up, who had slammed into him to set him right. Jones would remember the moment for a long time: 'For Peter Pan to win the Cup in such circumstances stamps him as a wonderful horse.' Maurice McCarten, who had been riding Lough Neagh close to Denis Boy when the incident occurred, was also astonished. 'I was amazed to learn that Peter Pan had won the race after having suffered such serious interference,' he told the

Sporting Globe. 'But my word, he must be a wonderfully good horse to have won after what I saw him get.' Jim Munro, also, had been coasting on Middle Watch behind Peter at the five-pole. 'I just missed the scramble,' he said, 'and I thought it impossible for Peter Pan to recover and win. It is the most miraculous recovery I have ever seen, but that a horse should win after it is beyond belief, except that I saw it with my own eyes.'

Veteran rider Bobby Lewis, who had ridden the three-year-old Phar Lap in his Melbourne Cup defeat of 1929, had approached Duncan after the race to marvel at the result. Lewis was a Cup master who had won the famous event four times in his career, and he had seen everything. But he hadn't seen anything like Peter Pan. 'Bill, I'll bet that was the roughest ride you ever had in your life,' he told his friend. 'I watched you the whole way and I thought you were down when you got that knock near the five furlongs post. He must be a wonderfully good horse to come through such a gruelling. He's one of the best I've ever seen.'

McGrath was in no doubt that Duncan had saved the day. Speaking to a posse of journalists in the mounting yard, the trainer had stated, 'The rider won it. No other jockey in Australia could have got him home in similar circumstances. When he got into trouble Duncan nursed him until he got into his stride again, instead of forcing him along when he was unbalanced.' McGrath was, sure as not, thinking of

Knox's Caulfield Cup effort. 'The Melbourne Cup is the foremost race in Australia, and it is every trainer's ambition to win it. I am the happiest man in Australia.' Dangar might have argued with that, however. 'I am exceedingly proud of Peter Pan,' he said. 'He is a marvellous colt, and I am doubly proud of his great success because of the fact that I bred him.'

In the hours after the Melbourne Cup, Peter Pan's win grew more extraordinary. Race analyses showed the horse was seventh at the five-furlong pole, then his collision sent him back to thirteenth, and within half a mile he had dashed back into contention. Third at the furlong pole, the colt had had only yards to catch Yarramba, but he had managed it, and was going away at the line. 'In all my Cup memories,' wrote Cliff J. Graves, the *Referee'* s leading turf journalist, 'I have never seen a horse take the Cup from behind a rival horse who had the lead Yarramba had set up, and for that reason one must take off his hat to an undoubted champion.'

In the hoopla that had followed the Cup finish, many had forgotten to glance at the rest of the field. That old plug Shadow King, running in his fourth Cup, had finished two lengths back in third, and it was his third minor placing in as many years. Manawhenua, who had given Peter Pan his awful bump, had driven on gamely into fourth, while Rogilla had faded hopelessly in the last three furlongs. Middle Watch had finished eighth, Lough Neagh tenth, and Denis Boy had been wiped out after crashing into Peter Pan.

He finished 13th, with Liberal, the other hot three-year-old in the race, just ahead of him. The stewards had conducted an enquiry into Peter's incident, but after hearing from Duncan, who stated that no rider, including himself, had meant to cause interference, they dropped the matter. It was what it was, they concluded – an accident.

Perhaps the most interesting of the post-race discussions were the ones that uttered Peter and Phar Lap in the same breath. 'Peter Pan in the eyes of the populace has filled the breach caused by the death of Phar Lap, and has become as much a national hero as the tragic Agua Caliente winner,' said the *Referee* a week after the race. Musing over Peter's rise in three months, 'Pilot' noted that 'Phar Lap's advance as a three-year-old was rapid, but that of Peter Pan has been even more marked.' As it stood, Dangar's colt had a far better record than the three-year-old Phar Lap had in November 1929. Phar Lap, at that stage, had been heavily raced by his trainer Harry Telford. He had started 15 times and meandered his way through obscure handicaps until his win in the 1929 AJC Derby, which was his 12th start. Peter Pan, at his third start, downed a Cup winner. At his fourth start he won a classic. At his sixth, he beat the Caulfield Cup winner. After his seventh, he was a champion.

Australia was caught quite off guard. No one expected the deeds of Phar Lap to be so quickly eclipsed, though Peter had a long way to travel before he would rival Phar Lap as a four-year-old. The colt had won the Melbourne Cup three-quarters of a second faster than any three-year-old in history, and this after almost coming down. Phar Lap had managed only third with the same weight, when the race had been run a full three-and-a-quarter seconds slower. 'Who would have thought that Australia would so soon have discovered a thoroughbred worthy to be classed with the mighty Phar Lap,' wrote the *Globe* on 2 November. Even 'Banjo' Paterson, not Peter Pan's greatest fan, had to admit the colt was superlative. 'Taking everything into consideration, it can be reasonably asserted that Peter Pan has eclipsed the performances of all previous Cup winners of his age,' he wrote in the *Mail.* 'The nearest approach to his Cup performance is that of Manfred in 1925, when the four-year-old Windbag had to establish the Flemington record to defeat the three-year-old by half a length.'

Not all of the general public were in agreement and a furore ensued in the newspapers after Cup Week. From Brisbane to Melbourne, readers had written in to defend their fallen idol Phar Lap, arguing there was no way the two horses were yet comparable. It was true. Phar Lap had been nigh invincible in his four-and five-year-old seasons, and Peter Pan had yet to prove he would be that. But on comparisons of age and performance, on comparisons of their three-year-old Cup efforts, there was good argument. 'Why one should regard as ridiculous the idea that Peter Pan can compare with Phar Lap is beyond comprehension,' Paterson stated. 'Up to date, he is immeasurably superior.'

The weekend after the big race, McGrath invited one of his old friends, the Victorian identity F.W. Purches, to come to look at the Pantheon colt. Purches had won the Cup of 1894 with Patron, and he was a brilliant judge of horse. 'Peter Pan impressed me as being much harder than Phar Lap was,' Purches said. 'If Phar Lap were alive today as a three-year-old and I had the choice between him and Peter Pan, I would take the Pantheon colt because of his being more robust.' Harry Telford, Phar Lap's embattled and somewhat bitter trainer, was less impressed. 'I will candidly admit that when I first saw Peter Pan I was a bit disappointed,' he told the *Globe.* 'He is a type different from Phar Lap. His washy appearance detracts from his looks.' Telford added that Peter was a great three-year-old, but only time would tell whether he was a great horse.

The bruising opinion from Telford was overlooked. It was natural that he wouldn't want another Phar Lap so very soon after the first, and McGrath could only shake his head that his old Randwick friend didn't see the things that he saw. The *Sporting Globe* surmised the situation perfectly. 'Phar Lap proved himself such a wonderful thoroughbred that there has been natural disinclination to depose him in favour of the recent find,' the paper stated. 'But it was admitted by almost everybody that there must be exceptional quality in a three-year-old that could overcome the setback that Peter Pan received in the Cup.'

Few were in doubt. If Dangar's chestnut came back in the autumn in similar style, there was nothing on Australian tracks to beat him.

***

Three days after Peter Pan's Cup, on Friday afternoon at 3.58pm, Bert 'Cardigan' Wolfe, racing reporter with the Sydney-based *Guardian,* received a telegram from Hollywood, California. It came from R.E. 'Lanny' Leighninger, chief publicity officer of the Agua Caliente Jockey Club (ACJC) in Mexico. Leighninger had his eyes on a new prize: 'GET BEST PROPOSITION PETER PAN. LANNY.'

Leighninger had coordinated the publicity during Phar Lap's visit to Agua Caliente in the early months of this year. He had milked the horse for all he was worth, and in doing so lifted the ACJC out of deep financial water. But Phar Lap's win at Caliente had also turned American racing on its head. Suddenly, American breeders and buyers were looking for Australian horses. It had all started with getting Phar Lap to Caliente, and Leighninger was vying to do it again for 1933. He would go via 'Cardigan', who had travelled with the Phar Lap team earlier in the year and was intimate with the Caliente operation.

The ACJC was ready to pay all expenses for Dangar's colt to travel. That included the ferrying of his owner, trainer, jockey and attendants. The club was also ready to host special races for Australian horses, in addition to the Agua Caliente Handicap that, in 1933, would be worth £18,000 to an Australian winner. 'I would emphasise the great opportunities for a first-class racehorse in America,' commented Billy Elliott, the young jockey who had steered Phar Lap to his Agua Caliente win in March. Elliott had just arrived back in Sydney after 10 months in America, and had barely stepped off the steamship *Mariposa* when he was collared about Peter Pan's future. 'If Peter Pan or Kuvera or any of our good 'uns popped across,' he said, 'those USA steeds would think a whirlwind had struck them.' Bert Wolfe was also in favour of the ploy. He believed there was a fortune to be made in Mexico, and if Peter Pan's people could be tempted, he could travel with them as he had done with Phar Lap. He telephoned Dangar about the cable.

Dangar had left Melbourne on Friday evening, boarding the Melbourne Express with Elsie at 5.30pm, and arriving into Central Station on Saturday morning at 10.45am. They were welcomed by their staff with armfuls of flowers, and driven back home to Arlington. Later that evening, the telephone rang.

Wolfe and Dangar discussed the merits of the Caliente offer but, try as he might, the reporter could not convince Dangar to agree to it. The lure of American fortune and glory, which had worked for Phar Lap's people, fell flat on Rodney Dangar. He was not interested. Wolfe was exasperated by the end of the telephone call. 'There is no hope of American racing men seeing Peter Pan unless they come here,' Dangar told Wolfe. 'He is a great colt and I am very proud to have bred him, and you can say definitely that he will do all his racing in Australia.' The story melted into the papers the following week. 'Mr Dangar is a sportsman to the fingertips,' wrote 'Musket' in the *Globe* on Wednesday, privately relieved that his fellow journalist had failed to lure away Australia's newest turf star. After all, it had not ended well for Phar Lap. 'He would rather see his great colt attain further honours at Flemington and Randwick than in a strange country.' 'Musket' was alluding to something that was surely on everyone's mind after Phar Lap's death. 'Mr Dangar does not intend to convert Peter Pan into a circus and hawk him over to Mexico.'

With the offer refused, Dangar sat in an armchair late on Saturday night in the lustrous surrounds of Arlington, swirling a cognac and thinking about all that had happened in a week. A £50,000 offer for Peter Pan, a Melbourne Cup, and a blank cheque from Mexico. He could have made an extraordinary amount of money from his horse. And the Americans were not the only ones trying to bait Peter Pan. Dangar's friend in England, a journalist named Albert Stewart Barrow who wrote as 'Sabretache' for London's *Tatler* magazine, had written to him to tell him to bring Peter Pan to

England for the Ascot Gold Cup. No Australian horse had ever attempted it.

Dangar had refused each offer unblinkingly, which masked how truly tempting they were. Prizemoney in Australia was deplorably low, and with it Peter would never reach the dizzy heights of all-time stakes winners. Even 'Musket' agreed with that: 'Now that stake money has been considerably reduced, Peter Pan cannot hope to win so much money as Phar Lap did.' But Dangar was extraordinarily rich. He wasn't racing his colt for the cash. He was racing for the glory, to say he had bred a classic winner that had reached the highest echelons. Much like the legacy of Carbine, Dangar saw Peter Pan leaving an imperishable mark on racing. But he also saw it as a duty to the Australian public to keep his colt in the country. Hundreds of thousands of people had paid the admission fees to Peter Pan's races, and gambled their shillings on him to come home first. Dangar believed he owed them for their loyalty, which could hardly be repaid by carting his horse to a desert track in Mexico. The 66-year-old reflected on the last couple of months. It was merely a year since the skittish Peter Pan had stepped off Baroona, and in seven months he had won five of seven starts. He had fought like a lion to win the greatest handicap in the world, and he had done it, and pulled up fresh as summer rain.

***

Frank McGrath slept a little easier the night of 1 November. When he woke the following morning, it wasn't with the same charge that he'd gotten used to. It was with relief, still and salient relief, and he was grateful for it. He kept his team in Melbourne for the remainder of the carnival, starting Satmoth, Denis Boy and Lightning March in various races. Denis Boy ran fourth in the C.B. Fisher Plate, while Satmoth finished third in the Final Handicap. On Saturday 12 November, plucky Satmoth ran Yarramba to within a length of winning the Williamstown Cup. Ridden by Andy Knox, Yarramba set a new course record for the race, cementing the form behind Peter Pan's win and clawing back some of the dignity the jockey had lost at Flemington.

For McGrath, 1932 was the year he was king. The 66-year-old trainer had topped the Sydney trainer's list and done it with a stable of brilliant chasers. Peter Pan had won £10,699 in stakes, Denis Boy £3092, and Satmoth had netted £1055. Between them, that was £14,846 – the price of a building downtown. McGrath had shown the same skill that had sewn him to horses such as Prince Foote, Abundance and Amounis. In 1932, he had brought his top three charges to a perfect pitch of condition, enabling them to snatch the biggest prizes in horse racing. But if asked about his success, old Macker remained reticent. He'd say he'd forgotten his secrets. He was ever humble.

Peter Pan left Melbourne on 7 November by the Express, late on a Monday night. McGrath saw no point in keeping the horse at Flemington, especially as he had no engagements lined up. He wanted the colt rested, so he sent George Phillips packing, and the horse and his attendant arrived into Sydney on Tuesday morning, a week after the great race. Peter Pan relaxed at Doncaster Avenue for several days, awaiting the return of Denis Boy, Satmoth and Lightning March. When the trio arrived, McGrath bundled them all off to Doonside, to a spelling property called Bungarribee owned by Thomas Russell Cleaver in Sydney's western district. For the first time in months, Peter Pan could feast on the grass between his feet. A few weeks of good pasture and summer sun, and the colt began to look like a robust three-year-old.

Sydney began to turn its face towards 1933. At the stroke of midnight on New Year's Eve, the GPO chimes burst into song, while on the harbour a medley of steam whistles blew through the night. The old year had been left behind, and good riddance. It had been the hardest, most savage that most could remember. Racing also said goodbye to an era. In the last few weeks of 1932, Carbine's last surviving son had died. Defence, a 22-year-old gelding who had won the Australian Cup of 1918, had been destroyed.

Over on Doncaster Avenue, back from Doonside a mere two days, Peter Pan chewed quietly on his hay. The ruckus of New Year's Eve had stirred him, but as all went still again he rested, waiting for the first light of 1933.

11

Horse racing changes overnight

On Saturday morning, 30 December, Sir James Joynton Smith, owner of Victoria Park Racing Club (and the magnate behind Smith's Newspapers), attended a meeting in Bligh Street, Sydney, along with his 39-year-old manager, William Donohue. They had applied for their pony track to come under AJC rules. To the other pony clubs, it seemed like a sell-out. One of Sydney's premier pony courses wanted to align itself with the AJC, to compete with Rosehill, Canterbury and Moorefield as a registered proprietary racetrack, to race under the Rules of Racing that governed Randwick and Warwick Farm. Victoria Park was abandoning the battling ranks of the ponies, or so it was felt.

But there was method to Joynton Smith's madness. Recent government legislation was about to restrict the number of race meetings held in metropolitan areas. Fearing their venue would be affected, Smith and Donohue foresaw the advantages of registering. They would be free to attract the weight-for-age titans such as Peter Pan, Rogilla and Chatham. They could host rich stakes races to get them. As the rules currently stood, no Randwick trainer could race his horse on an unregistered racetrack without getting disqualified. If Smith and Donohue could be allowed to continue to host pony races, and so were not abandoning their roots, then Victoria Park events would only get better.

The AJC granted Smith's application. Victoria Park would hold on to its 14 days of racing allocated for 1933, which included one Saturday and a bank holiday, and as such it emerged better off than the remaining proprietary pony clubs in Sydney. It was allowed to host one pony race per meeting, which exempted the club from certain items of the Rules of Racing, and moreover, any persons and horses that had previously been disqualified for taking part in an unregistered meeting were, from midnight on 4 January 1933, now free to race again. Suddenly, Victoria Park Racecourse was open for business to horses of the calibre of Peter Pan, and it was an historic day for 76-year-old Joynton Smith.

He welcomed in the New Year under AJC protection, and a resolve to start attracting the top-line horses to his racetrack. Within a few days, Kensington, Rosebery and Ascot clubs had also made applications for registration, and they too were granted. Racing in Sydney had changed overnight. After years of frowning upon the pony riffraff, after countless efforts to try to overthrow unregistered proprietary racing in Sydney, the AJC had finally taken control, and it hadn't even been their idea.

12

The glorious uncertainty of the turf

It was 11 January 1933, and the mercury crept idly towards record temperatures. Sydney was sweltering, sweating like a jockey in the hot box, and over on Doncaster Avenue Frank McGrath pushed his hat back and cursed. The heat was merciless. George Phillips had parked Peter Pan in the wash bay and was hosing the young horse down, and McGrath, leaning against the shed row with his arms folded, measured and mulled the colt over. It was two weeks since Peter had come back from Doonside, and he looked in splendid fettle.

McGrath had sent the colt out for six weeks, just long enough for him to rest. Peter had returned to Doncaster Avenue with weight, but he hadn't gone soft. He was still built like steel, still narrow and sleek, and it surprised McGrath that he hadn't filled out more. McGrath placed a measuring stick against Peter Pan's withers and found him to stand nearly 16.2 hands high. When he did fill out, the trainer thought, he'd be a monstrous stallion. As it was, he was a tall order for a three-year-old.

McGrath had started working Peter with easy gallops in January. For the first few weeks, the old trainer watched as his champion loped along the backstretch each morning, moving fluidly, gracefully, and pulling up fresh and limber. As January sidled into February, and Randwick welcomed back its top-notch horses, McGrath still took his time. There was no fast work on the agenda. One day he would send Peter out on a steady six furlongs, and the next the colt would go steady over a mile. By the second week of February, the press were asking questions. If Peter Pan wasn't galloping, then he wasn't ready to race. They wanted to know if McGrath was taking the colt to Melbourne for the autumn meetings.

These meetings began in late February, starting with the VATC Oakleigh Plate and Futurity Stakes, followed by the VRC's Newmarket Handicap and St Leger Stakes in early March. It was possible for a Sydney horse to run in these races, then return to Randwick for the AJC carnival in mid-April. Winooka and Chatham were doing it, and Denis Boy would likely do it, but McGrath had to decide if it was the right thing for Peter Pan. The colt was engaged in several events during the AJC meeting in April, most of them weight-for-age, but his biggest tests were the AJC St Leger and the Sydney Cup. The St Leger was a classic under set weights over a mile and three-quarters. The Sydney Cup, however, was another order. That was a handicap of two miles, and G.F. Wilson, the AJC handicapper, had given Peter Pan a whopping 9st. Under that weight, at his age, and against seasoned stayers, Peter could be easily undone.

McGrath and Dangar discussed the matters at length in early February. Both agreed that racing Peter Pan in Melbourne and Sydney was a trifle ambitious, so on 6 February they announced to the press that their colt would not travel south. Their sojourn in Melbourne during the spring had been easy because it was an extended stay. If they were to ship south for the VRC meeting this March, they'd have to sprint back to Sydney for April. They would miss the lead-up races they had planned for the colt, including the Rawson Stakes at Rosehill and the Chipping Norton Plate. So that left the matter of the Sydney Cup. McGrath was not keen to disclose his intentions on that race just yet, at least not to the public. He advised Dangar that the wise course of action was to monitor Peter Pan's progress, and agreeing, the two men mentioned nothing about their concerns. In turn, the press didn't suspect there were any. As far as the reporters believed, Peter Pan was a certainty for the Sydney Cup.

With Melbourne out of the picture, Peter Pan set to the tasks at hand. By the middle of February he was fit, though McGrath was still holding him to steady work. The colt was getting impatient. With fitness came impertinence, and each morning the son of Pantheon snatched harder on the bit, pulled heavier on the reins, craving to bounce along at his top. Still McGrath held him. He wanted no fast work just yet, and he watched each morning as Peter's track riders fought to keep their arms in their sockets.

The colt's reputation was the subject of much column space in the lead-up to autumn events. He was yet to prove that he could win after his rousing Melbourne Cup, but that didn't stop the press from their speculations. In February, Cliff Graves in the *Referee* lauded the victory of Melbourne's champion colt Liberal after he landed the C.F. Orr Stakes at Williamstown. Carrying 9st 1lb, Liberal had defeated no less than Chatham and Gaine Carrington. 'Peter Pan may be a champion,' said Alec Hunter, Liberal's owner, 'but he is not frightening me or my trainer.' As it turned out, though, the two three-year-olds would never meet again. Liberal snapped a fetlock in the St George Stakes at Caulfield and was ferried from racing forever. With him went a serious contender for Peter Pan's crown. Bronze Hawk had failed to train on, Gaine Carrington was looking average, and that left only the older horses to test Peter Pan's mettle.

McGrath announced Peter's first run would be in the Randwick Stakes, a one-mile weight-for-age event on the City Tattersall's card in mid-March. The race was being staged for the second time. In 1932 it had been an experimental addition, and had attracted a classy field. Such was its success, though, that it was back on the books, and apart from Peter Pan's autumn debut, Rogilla was running, as was Lough

Neagh, Johnnie Jason, Veilmond, Tregilla and Oro. McGrath had also entered Satmoth. Following this, Peter Pan was due to run in the Rawson Stakes at Rosehill on 1 April, then the Chipping Norton Plate at Warwick Farm on 8 April. The following week, the AJC autumn meeting would begin. Peter Pan would contest the St Leger classic on the Saturday, the Sydney Cup on the Monday, the Cumberland Plate on the Wednesday, and the AJC Plate the following Saturday. All up, it was just under eight miles of racing in five weeks. But the horse was fit. He had been raced lightly, rested well, and coddled from day one. As it was, he probably wouldn't run in the Sydney Cup anyway. McGrath couldn't shake the seriousness of Peter Pan's 9st over two miles. It might be asking a question too many.

By the end of the month, Peter Pan was flying. Early on the morning of Tuesday 28 February, with pony jockey J. Jewell aboard, he swallowed four furlongs of the Randwick's course proper in 51 3/4 seconds. The clockers hit their watches as the colt flashed past them, and then glanced at each other. It was the fastest time of the morning. Two days later, Peter bounded over seven furlongs, clipping the last four in the slightly eased time of 53 1/2. 'The Cup winner is going along excellently,' said the *Sportsman.* 'It looks as if the chestnut is going to be a real big noise again in the autumn.' As usual, 'Banjo' Paterson was guarded. 'It remains to be seen what he can do when he opposes the best of the older horses at weight-for-age,' wrote the famous poet in the *Sydney Mail* on 8 March.

As the final weeks of preparation neared, McGrath kept the dial turned up on Peter Pan. The colt was turning out half-mile workouts regularly in 51 and 52 seconds, rarely galloping more than seven furlongs, and usually alone. The Randwick Stakes was going to be a test of fitness. The first races of the season usually were, and it might have been the reason why the ring was taking risks with Peter Pan. On the eve of raceday, though many had seen the colt gallop strongly for many weeks, Rogilla and Veilmond were fancied over the Pantheon colt.

***

18 March broke beautifully over Randwick. The red warmth of dawn suggested high temperatures, and by afternoon it was a perfect, sunny day. Sydneyites poured through the Randwick turnstiles, replete in summer dresses and cotton shirts. They were coming for Peter Pan's weight-for-age race.

The Randwick Stakes was the third race on the card, due off at 2.35pm, and eight horses were due to line up. Peter Pan was a cautious favourite at 7/4, with Rogilla next at 3/1, and Veilmond was touching 7/2. At any time, Peter's favour rose and fell. He was carrying 8st 6lb against Rogilla's 8st 12lb, Tregilla and Veilmond's 9st 1lb, and Lough Neagh's 8st 11lb.

McGrath had had a job selecting a jockey for the Randwick ride. Jim Pike and Billy Duncan both had engagements in Melbourne for the weekend, and McGrath had dissolved associations with Andy Knox. Eventually, he secured Ted Bartle. Bartle was one of Sydney's most achieved, but least conspicuous, riders. He had risen to the top of the ranks the hard way, without lucky lifts or blares of publicity. He was not showy like Darby Munro, or cool and effective like Pike. He had had to prove he could ride, and it had taken many years to break into the peel of the top trainers. These days, Bartle hovered at the top by wins alone. He put in the hours, and was a hard man to beat on a horse, be it a sprint or over distance. This had something to do with his fitness. Bartle was always in shape, athletic and muscly, and McGrath was happy to have him.

The ring was buzzing like the old times. In fine sunshine, fielders were hollering their quotes as Peter Pan breezed steadily to the mile chute of the Randwick Stakes. There had been little rain in Sydney for weeks, so the track was perfect. The colt moved fluidly over the ground, elastically under Bartle's light seat, and the jockey was impressed. The starting tape was pulled low over the racetrack, and for a few moments the horses circled loosely. Then starter Jack Gaxieu called them to order at exactly 2.35pm, and Bartle turned Peter Pan around. Standing quietly in the field of eight, the colt waited for the jump. When it came, he bounded away with the field.

Tregilla missed the start by a length, and as the line of horses bunched onto the rails, Jim Munro took Lough Neagh to the front, heading Johnnie Jason for the early lead. In a tight bunch behind them, Bartle settled Peter Pan in third. The pace was searing. The field bellowed down on the six-furlong post in 23 seconds and, as was typical, Johnnie Jason swept past Lough Neagh to take the lead. Peter Pan, leaping over the turf, went with him, and passing the six furlongs he was poised in second place, with Satmoth and Lough Neagh behind him. The pressure was relentless from the leader. The field swept down on the half-mile in 49 seconds, drilling the next furlong in 12 seconds flat. On Rogilla, Darby Munro began to move from the back of the field, and he swung the white-faced chestnut around the outside until he was third, and they swung into the straight in that order – Johnnie Jason showing the way a length to Peter Pan, and Rogilla a half-length back in third.

Peter Pan was galloping with dizzy rhythm. They had covered five furlongs in 1:01, and thundering into the straight the field was quickening even further. These were sprint sectionals, not the sensible furlongs of seasoned stayers, and yet Bartle found his colt was tracking Johnnie Jason with ease, playing with the older horse, waiting for a cue to leap forward. It came as they passed the Leger stand. Easing off the rails, Bartle shook the reins at Peter Pan, and the colt bolted forward to run past Johnnie Jason. In a few strides he was clear, and though Rogilla tried to go with the younger horse, Peter Pan had gone like the clappers. He flashed over the line a length to the good of Rogilla, with Lough Neagh a length back in third, in the dazzling time of 1:36 1/4.

When Peter Pan pulled up, Bartle noticed the colt was blowing; not so much that it indicated an unfit horse, but enough to tell Bartle there was still some condition on him. With the veins standing in his neck, Peter Pan trotted back to a tumultuous reception. As he passed the grandstands, the crowd rose to its feet, cheering and clapping the local hero. 'And how did the public receive Peter's performance?' gushed *Truth.* 'They just rose en masse as he trotted back to the enclosure and let him have one long, big hand. It was a reception accorded only to the great.'

The Randwick Stakes had been run only a quarter of a second outside the Australasian mile record, set by Pavilion back in 1930 when he ran the Villiers in 1:36 flat. Peter Pan had run the last three furlongs of the Randwick Stakes in 35 1/4 seconds, the last half-mile in 47 1/4, and the mile had been run almost to perfection – 12 seconds to the furlong. It was Peter Pan's sixth win from eight starts, and brought his winnings to £11,088. It was a remarkable race, not only for time, and not only for the merit of beating the best weight-for-age horses in the country, but for the fact that Peter Pan was first up from a spell. Even 'Banjo' Paterson was impressed, albeit reluctantly. 'All great gallopers are freaks, and Peter Pan is no exception,' Paterson commented. 'He was long-legged and slabby-sided as an early three-year-old, and he is long-legged and slabby-sided still. Yet on Saturday he ran a mile within a fraction of the Randwick record and didn't appear to be hurrying himself at all. What a mover!'

The Randwick Stakes had cemented Peter's greatness, proving that he had trained on from his Melbourne Cup victory, but also that he could consistently tackle distances from a mile to two miles and it was all the same to him. The *Referee* lauded the race as interesting but unexciting. 'Peter Pan's superiority over the final furlong disposed of that possibility,' said 'Pilot'. The journalist also sought out McGrath after the race. 'A good colt, perhaps not quite a real champion yet, but a great stayer,' McGrath said.

McGrath's words seemed guarded and strange. In the spring, he had been convinced of Peter Pan's brilliance, and had not been shy about saying so. Had he noticed something about Peter Pan that the press hadn't? Had he grown less inclined to herald him? More likely, McGrath had tired of the comparisons Peter Pan was getting. Every time the newspapers wrote about the colt, somewhere appeared the name of Phar Lap. It had been relentless. Few were prepared to accept the horse on his merits, instead dropping him into the way of the Red Terror. Even Dangar was getting frustrated. The two men decided to tone down their press conferences. They would no longer tout their colt's abilities, as McGrath felt they were making matters worse for themselves. Peter Pan would have to speak for himself on the racetrack, and the newspapers would write what they wanted. But it was only the beginning, for Peter would never crawl out of the shadow of the dead hero.

***

After the Randwick Stakes, attention turned to the Sydney Cup and whether Peter Pan would start in it. Betting was yet to open on the big two-miler, but when it did Peter Pan, if he was declared, would be top of the market. For this reason, Dangar became anxious to make a decision. He didn't want to hoodwink the public into losing several thousands of pounds. The day after the Tattersall's meeting, he announced to the press that his decision about the Sydney Cup was forthcoming.

Dangar had no doubt his colt could go the two miles, but going the distance under 9st was an honest task. Peter Pan was still a three-year-old, and a slowly developing one too. The record of three-year-olds in the Sydney Cup wasn't strong. Fewer youngsters had won this race than its big Melbourne counterpart. Carbine had done it under 9st back in 1889, and his son Wallace did it with 2lb less in 1896, but Cup races were harder to win these days. Tracks were better, horses were faster, and there were more horses racing. At the scale weights, a three-year-old had a big advantage in the autumn, and if Dangar elected to keep his colt in weight-for-age events he could do very well. McGrath agreed with this. Peter Pan stood to earn around £4000 if he kept to his weight-for-age engagements, so Dangar could see no reason to risk his prized possession with the two miles. Peter had too many years of racing ahead, and he was too valuable a stud prospect. At 12.35pm on Monday afternoon, Dangar scratched Peter Pan from the Sydney Cup.

'Peter Pan was withdrawn from the Sydney Cup, and his owner deserves to be congratulated on his early decision,' wrote 'Pilot' in the *Referee.* 'If Peter Pan had remained in another week or two, a lot of money would have been lost on him in doubles, and those associated with him would have greatly suffered in popularity.' Dangar's sportsmanship was to be commended. Few racegoers had forgotten the betting fiascos that had circulated around Phar Lap when his connections had kept his racing schedule secret. Though the horse was a dear hero, the punting public had been badly burned by him. Phar Lap's people had wrung every penny they could out of their champion, racing him ceaselessly and guarding his program from the public to protect his odds, and they had sacrificed the horse on the altar of popularity. 'Mr Dangar is too good a sportsman to trifle with the public,' 'Pilot' stated, 'and Peter Pan is sure of an enthusiastic reception whenever he wins a race.'

With the Sydney Cup out, Peter Pan began to work towards the Rawson Stakes in two weeks' time. No one thought he could be beaten, and it began to affect the line-up for the St Leger. 'I don't think I'll take Peter Pan on in the St Leger,' commented the owner of Melbourne horse Metallurgy. 'What's the use of breaking my colt's heart chasing him?' Cimbrian, however, was up for the challenge. 'Cimbrian to take on Peter Pan, but we don't like his chances', scoffed the *Sportsman.* 'Peter Pan will engage in five races between April 1 and 22, and he looks a moral for the lot of them.'

By this time, McGrath had a full stable of charges. Denis Boy was back from Melbourne, Satmoth was clocking fair times, Lightning March was making friends, and Whittingham, the latest addition, was also a good prospect. McGrath had many other runners, drawing one of the biggest teams at Randwick in fact, but these were his top charges, and each morning they were clocked to the second.

The Rawson Stakes at Rosehill fell on April Fools' Day. It was a weight-for-age event over nine furlongs, and it had been the first weight-for-age event in Rosehill's history, begun in 1903. Poseidon, Malt King and Artilleryman had won it, and in recent times Limerick, Nightmarch and Waterline. Suffice it to say it was one of the best middle-distance races on the calendar, and was easy picking for Peter Pan if all went well. He was meeting Rogilla on 1lb better terms than in the Randwick Stakes, and it was supposed his run in that race had improved him.

The pair was running against familiar foes. Johnnie Jason, Oro and Lough Neagh were entered, as they had been in the Randwick Stakes, along with Kuvera, Dermid and Braeburn. McGrath had entered Denis Boy, too, hoping that the Irish import would strike his spring form. Peter Pan had already beaten each of the horses entered, and McGrath had brought the colt along perfectly. He wasn't at the pitch of condition, but he wouldn't be until the St Leger. If fitness failed him, talent would probably get him to the line.

The track at Rosehill was a little giving, as rain had dribbled over Sydney during the week. As Ted Bartle cantered Peter Pan to the start, he felt the squelch of the turf beneath him, but he wasn't alarmed. Conditions were not so bad that he needed to ride any differently. Peter Pan had been sent off just as the papers had said, at 3/1 odds-on favourite. The closest to him was Rogilla at 6/1, Kuvera at 7s, and Lough Neagh went out as deep at 12/1. As weight-for-age stipulated, Peter was carrying 8st 6lb again, with Rogilla 8st 13lb and Lough Neagh 8st 11lb. The whole of Rosehill was certain that Peter Pan would win. They believed it with their hearts, and they believed it with their pockets.

Jack Gaxieu called the field to attention, and Bartle swung Peter Pan to the outside. The colt had drawn the widest alley again, and he walked quietly up for Bartle until he was standing stock-still before the tape. Over on the inside, Rogilla was up to his antics. He was lunging away from the strands, Darby Munro fighting vigorously with the Newcastle horse to keep him in line. As the ruckus went on, Peter Pan, quite bored, reached forward and began to chew the bottom strand of the starting tape. 'Get your horse off the ropes!' boomed Gaxieu at Bartle. Immediately, Bartle backed Peter Pan off the barrier. Stepping back into the line, with all attention on the unhappy Rogilla, Peter Pan sidled up to the barrier again. The colt reached his neck out and nibbled on the last strand of the starting tape, and yet again the exasperated Gaxieu warned Bartle. Though the jockey corrected the colt once more, the distracted Peter Pan took a good hold of the bottom strand this time. Like a bored teenager, he chewed away and Bartle, when he should have been watching Peter Pan, was watching Rogilla. When Gaxieu's patience was drained and he threw the tapes into the air, Peter Pan was still hanging on to the webbing.

For a fraction of a second, the colt jumped with the rest of the field. But in a flash, that last strand in his mouth yanked his head skywards, and Bartle's reins flew into the air. The shock caused Peter Pan to rear, and he pivoted sideways to untangle himself from the starting tape, colliding with Denis Boy as he did. When the elastic strand flew out of his mouth, it catapulted into the air, just missing Lough Neagh's jockey, and on the outside Peter Pan was in an unholy mess.

Bartle gathered the colt up and urged him away. Ahead of them, the field had bolted off by at least six lengths, and up front, Dermid was cooking with gas.

The pacemaker had set off with such speed that he was settling his own chances, and behind him many of the others were scrambling to keep up. At the back, Peter Pan's situation was desperate.

An almighty roar went up from the grandstands when the favourite was spotted last. He was so far behind the rest of the field that he was unmistakeable, his silver hair streaming in the wind. Bartle was allowing him to bowl along, asking him to find his stride and catch up, and for the first three furlongs he was last. Bartle was starting to worry, trying not to panic, but there was nothing fluid in the way the colt was moving. He wasn't leaping over the turf the way he had at Randwick, and he seemed fractious that he was so far behind. Passing the five-pole, he had just managed to catch Braeburn at the back, and as Bartle began to ride a little more vigorously, he feared the champion was spent.

The speed of the first four furlongs had suited Lough Neagh to the ground, and the Queenslander had bounded into contention as Dermid fell from the front. Behind him, Kuvera was also travelling well, and a long way behind them the others came, Rogilla a tiring horse on the outside and Denis Boy not up to scratch. For a moment, it looked as if Peter Pan were coming. Bartle had shuffled the colt into that group, and into the straight they galloped. But Peter Pan had nothing to give. Straining to even keep with the losing horses, the colt was struggling. Bartle stopped riding him. The jockey sat up and lengthened his reins, and

Peter drifted back through the field until he was last again. Passing the judge, the pair cantered limply home, many seconds after Lough Neagh had bolted in.

The silence from the grandstands rolled over the racecourse. Not only had the public idol fallen, but he'd fallen so hard as to run last. The crowd couldn't believe it. 'If seven million volts had been turned on at Rosehill they wouldn't have provided a greater shock than that handed out by Peter Pan,' *Truth* exclaimed. Hurrying, Bartle brought the colt back to scale, ignoring the scowls that came his way. He knew that something terrible had happened at the barrier, but he didn't know exactly what. He did know there would be an inquiry, and he could picture it. How had he managed to ride a red-hot sure thing into so much trouble at the start?

Reaching George Phillips in the enclosure, Bartle jumped off the colt and noticed the trickle of blood that was oozing from Peter's mouth. He panicked a little, concerned about this reflection on his riding. Phillips was also concerned, but for very different reasons. Peter Pan had a young mouth. His teeth were still growing, his gums still developing and tender. Phillips had seen the bars of young horses' mouths broken during racing, and he was appalled that Peter Pan had come back to scale bloody. Within moments McGrath was on hand, however, and after a quick inspection of his star colt, he was satisfied that all looked okay. The trainer had seen the horse go in the air when the race started, and as he watched the dismal performance thereafter he became convinced that Peter Pan had wrenched himself. But striding back to the stalls, the colt didn't move like an injured horse. In fact, he looked quite perky, the incident forgotten in his mind.

The stewards hauled Bartle and Gaxieu into their rooms, and discussed the matter at length. Gaxieu stated he had warned Bartle twice about pulling his mount off the ropes. 'I did not see the horse with the webbing in his mouth, and I'm sure he didn't have it,' the starter argued bluntly. 'It would be extremely difficult to say just what was the cause of the incident.' Bartle could offer nothing conclusive. He thought that perhaps another horse had caught the tape and it had flicked back on Peter Pan, catching him under the chin. This, however, didn't concur with the blood in Peter Pan's mouth. In closing, the stewards took no action against any man, and the inquiry was written off. The incident was, quite simply, part of the glorious uncertainty of the turf.

McGrath drew consolation from the next race when he sent Whittingham out a 7/1 winner of the Railway Handicap, but he could feel it coming, the unkind, unrelenting wave of public criticism. 'To say the least of it, those who have placed Peter Pan on a pedestal may now feel inclined to recast their ideas,' spat *Truth* the following day. The same afternoon, the *Sun* newspaper hit the streets. 'Peter Pan last in the Rawson Stakes! It's almost unbelievable. In past years the Rawson Stakes has supplied many surprises, but it is safe to say that we'll have long beards before we see another champion like Peter Pan run last in that race.' Other journalists were less scathing. 'It was his babyishness that caused the trouble at the barrier,' stated 'Cardigan'. 'Musket' was also sympathetic. 'The pace was so solid from the start that poor Peter was not given breathing time once the race began. He may also have been thoroughly frightened, and that, naturally, would take a lot of fight out of him, for even a champion has to be at his best to concede a start to horses of class.'

McGrath and Dangar sat back and read it all. As had come the comparisons with Phar Lap, now came the comparisons with Manfred. Manfred had been left at the start of the 1925 AJC Derby by half a furlong, and he had fought back gallantly to win that race. Critics couldn't see why Peter Pan hadn't been able to do the same in the Rawson Stakes. But the public had forgotten the circumstances of 1925. Manfred's AJC Derby had been filled with moderate three-year-olds. Outside of the winner, Amounis and Vaals were the top horses, and neither of these was much good in their early years. Peter Pan was tussling with Derby winners and a Cantala winner. Also, when Manfred had been left at the start, the field had lumbered away from him at a canter. Peter Pan had had to chase a scalding pace. Everyone knew there was no way Manfred would have caught his leaders if they'd run like March hares. 'A field of weight-for-age horses travelling at their top takes a lot more catching than a field of moderate three-year-olds who are taking it easy,' reasoned 'Banjo' Paterson. 'The defeat should be wiped off the slate,' said 'Musket'.

In the days that followed, all the old criticisms of Peter Pan came back to the fray. There were the ones that claimed Peter Pan was a false alarm, and the ones that said he looked nothing like a champion. Dangar was exasperated. Did someone patent how a champion should look and not tell him? Didn't he hear only recently that Gloaming looked like a hurdle horse? Reading the *Referee* on Wednesday afternoon, Dangar slowly lost his wick. 'Peter Pan's effort was not worthy of a real champion ... The performance was not that of a superhorse ... His action was not impressive, either when parading or racing ... Between the spring and the autumn of his three-year-old career, Phar Lap had developed so tremendously that he was hardly recognisable as the same horse.'

There it was again, Dangar seethed. Phar Lap. He tossed the newspaper aside and got up and left the house.

13

'A horse can't do much more than win'

Alec Young was flummoxed. The manager of Baroona sat in Rodney Dangar's office, six floors above O'Connell Street, and put the newspapers down on the desk in front of him. There was only so much his patience could take. It was the week following the Rawson Stakes, and the criticisms of Peter Pan had come thick and furious. To Young, they were like hot coals. Each denigration burned him. He took a sheet of paper and penned a letter to 'Musket', one of the few journalists who had afforded Peter Pan a fair trial after the Rawson Stakes. 'Writing as one who has been closely associated with Peter Pan from his birth, and who naturally takes a very great interest in his welfare and doings generally, I just wish to express my appreciation of your remarks in this week's *Mail* in regard to Peter's poor showing at Rosehill last Saturday,' Young wrote. 'The horse was decidedly upset after his mishap at the barrier and, to any observant onlooker, was not going with his usual dash or style at any part of the journey thereafter.' 'Musket' ran the letter in the *Mail* the following week.

It was true that the *Sydney Mail* was one of few publications to give Peter Pan a fair go. *Smith's*

Weekly was another. ‘Such things should teach punters that laying odds on is a risky business,’ that paper had stated. ‘Odds-on chances are sometimes beaten on their merits.’ But, as Peter’s connections had found out, most of the media were only willing to recall Manfred’s Derby of 1925, and Peter’s failure to emulate it.

McGrath had tried to move on quickly. He’d been in the racing game long enough to ride the tides, and long enough to know the mob was fickle. He had more pressing matters right now. Lightning March was receiving veterinary attention at the moment because of bowel trouble, which was snatching much of McGrath’s time, and the old trainer was now in two minds about running Peter Pan in the Chipping Norton Plate. The colt himself was none the worse after Rosehill. The mouth wound had proved superficial, and he’d eaten up that night, but the trainer was worried about the horse’s fitness. If Peter Pan had been anywhere near his spring condition, he would have mowed into the leading division at Rosehill, as he had done in the Melbourne Cup. Even allowing for the fright he got, McGrath saw that Peter Pan had nothing in the tank to come home with. The fitness just wasn’t there yet. He telephoned Dangar on Tuesday night, and advised him to scratch Peter Pan from the Chipping Norton Plate.

It took Dangar a few days to withdraw his colt, and in those few days a wet-weather belt moved over Sydney and dumped barrels of rain on the city. It was clear that the Warwick Farm meeting would be one for the mudlarks, so when Dangar paid the forfeit fees to the AJC offices on Thursday, it came as little surprise. Some, however, were concerned with what the scratching really meant. 'Racing men will feel just a tinge of disappointment,' commented the *Telegraph,* which was enjoying a burst in readership since the *Arrow* went bust in March. 'It was thought that Peter Pan's form in that race would solve the mystery of the Rawson Stakes. However, racegoers will have to wait until the St Leger at Randwick to again see the chestnut in action.'

It was inevitable that Peter's scratching from the Chipping Norton would ignite gossip. By Friday morning, sensational rumours were flying around Randwick that the horse was not right. Professional punter and radio commentator Tom Ellis, speaking on radio station 2UE, stated that Peter Pan might not even run in the St Leger. McGrath, incensed by the misinformation, wrote to the Sunday papers to clarify that the rumours were furphies. 'Barring a breakdown,' the trainer stated, 'Peter Pan will certainly see the post for the Red Riband.' Tom Ellis hit back in the *Referee:* 'I did not say that Peter Pan definitely would not start in the Leger. I said that in my opinion the colt hadn't done well since his Rosehill mishap, and that was why he had been scratched from the Chipping Norton Plate. I added that unless Peter Pan did a little better during the forthcoming week, his connections might consider it risky to start him in a race unless they had definite evidence that he was thoroughly at his best. So you see, I was right on the mark.'

Ellis was actually right off the mark. No one knew Peter Pan better than Frank McGrath, and McGrath had no doubts about Peter's running in the St Leger. The horse was lacking only in fitness. But it didn't matter how many times he said so, because the scrutiny persisted. It was impossible to snatch the last word from these press fools.

On Saturday, the Warwick Farm meeting went off in fine style. The rain had stopped, but the track was a quagmire. Denis Boy started in the Chipping Norton Plate, and ran unplaced behind Lough Neagh, Kuvera and Rogilla. Whittingham was also unplaced in the Liverpool Handicap. McGrath was no stranger to form, but he was also a master tactician. It was no secret that he could fit a horse for a major plunge, so no one knew if his horses were off their game or readying for a major win next time out. Nonetheless, the trainer stepped up the acid on the morning tracks, particularly when it came to Peter Pan.

On Monday, the colt galloped with Denis Boy over a steady mile, but on Tuesday morning McGrath asked some questions of him. As Peter Pan and Denis Boy trotted to the mile start on the A grass, sunlight barely rising over the east, a score of eyes watched their every move. When the gallop began, the two horses set off in earnest. They clipped the first furlong in 12 seconds, the first two in 25, three in 37 1/4, and the first four furlongs in 49 3/4. The full mile took the pair 1:43 3/4, and as they dashed past the winning post, Peter Pan leading Denis Boy by three lengths, the stopwatches clicked and the clockers traded times. Respectable indeed. But as the horses pulled up, McGrath's face was stained with concern. The trainer suspected ligament trouble in Denis Boy, which could explain the cause behind the horse's loss of form. Denis Boy hadn't won a race this autumn, and though he'd been in and out of incident since he'd arrived from Ireland a few years before, McGrath was worried this time. He sidelined the horse for the rest of the week.

Peter Pan galloped over Randwick alone on the Wednesday, but on the Thursday McGrath took him to Rosebery where he was set a fetching task. The trainer sent the colt for nearly two circuits of the track, and with its rising straight, the distance was twice an uphill climb for Peter Pan. McGrath's hurdler Prismatic went with Peter for the first part of the trial, then Irish Blend, a speedster over a half-mile, joined in to bring him home. As Prismatic dropped out, Irish Blend put the sting into Peter Pan. Heavily shod, galloping 30 feet from the rails and twice up the hill, Peter Pan ran the six furlongs in 1:18 3/4, the seven in 1:31 1/4, and the full distance in 1:48 1/4. At the judge, Irish Blend was only a length to the good of Peter Pan. The clocks showed the seven-furlongs time was just three-quarters of a second outside the Rosebery track record.

On Friday 14 April, the final trials had wrapped up. Randwick was primed for the autumn carnival and, by nightfall, McGrath was sitting in his living room, mulling over proceedings. He felt tired. It had been a tough few weeks for him. Lightning March was sick, and scratched from all his autumn commitments. Denis Boy was possibly finished. Whittingham wasn't firing, and only a week before Satmoth's owners had moved their useful gelding to another stable. Where the spring had been an easy passage through success, the autumn was proving choppy and changeable. The criticisms about Peter Pan had continued relentlessly. McGrath was also quietly concerned that the St Leger was a stiff task for a three-year-old after a prep of only two races, one of which had to be discounted. Deep in his armchair, the trainer chewed the Leger possibilities over in his head.

With an ordinary racehorse, the Chipping Norton start would have been essential. But McGrath knew Peter Pan to possess tenacity in more doses than other horses he had dealt with. His grit would get him to the line, if nothing else. The St Leger was a tough task. It was a mile and three-quarters in classic company under set weights, and because of the Rawson Stakes, the competition had grown confident. After Peter's failure, six owners had paid up for their horses to run in the St Leger, a bigger field than most were expecting. There was the troublesome duo of Kuvera and Oro, and there was Braeburn, who had finished fourth in the Rawson Stakes. Metallurgy,

Eastern Chief, and the New Zealand filly La Moderne comprised the rest, and though Peter Pan was a cautious favourite, Braeburn had many fans. McGrath knew that the colt had won over all distances and that he was a first-class stayer. In any other year he would be the first-class three-year-old. Braeburn had also raced five times in the previous two months. Peter Pan was giving him lengths in terms of fitness.

The St Leger was Australia's oldest classic. First run in 1841, it predated the Melbourne Cup by 20 years. When the AJC moved in 1861 from its beginnings at Homebush, in Sydney's west, to the sandy knolls of Randwick, the St Leger moved with it to become a stalwart part of Randwick racing. To Dangar, though, it was more than this: it was an English institution, steeped with accolades and prestige. The Randwick version was modelled on the English St Leger, first run at Doncaster in 1776, and because Dangar was an Englishman to the core, a loyal subject of the mother country, winning the St Leger meant much more to him than it did to others.

The press was of the opinion that Peter Pan would win the race, but only if he was at his best. If he wasn't, the St Leger was wide open for Braeburn and Kuvera. McGrath, however, despite his concerns, knew that Peter Pan, even below par, was far better a racehorse than any of these other horses, but the doubts still clouded his mind. He was back under the same umbrella of pressure as when Peter had lost the Caulfield Cup, and he couldn't remember how he'd gotten here. The colt had only lost a race, a single event at Rosehill, but obviously loss sang louder than victory. McGrath knew, also, that Phar Lap had altered expectations of horses. If that was the case, nothing Peter did would ever be enough.

***

Saturday morning broke like a shepherd's warning. Streaks of pink lambasted the skies over Randwick, and at first light the last of the trackworkers left the racecourse, Peter Pan among them. The colt had breezed two furlongs with Whittingham in a spritely 25 seconds, and minutes later he was walking back to Doncaster Avenue. When he saw Randwick again that afternoon, there were 47,000 racegoers clamouring over his every step.

The weather preceding St Leger Day had been perfect. It had not rained on the Eastern Suburbs for over a week and, as a result, track conditions were ideal. George Law was Randwick's course overseer, and he expected the records to tumble today. He wasn't wrong. In the first race, Eatonwood set a world record for two miles over hurdles and, a few minutes after three o'clock, Winooka slashed the mile record at Randwick when he took the Doncaster Handicap with Jim Pike in 1:35 3/4. With the St Leger due off right after it, crowd expectations were high.

McGrath, under Dangar's request, had brought Jim Pike back to pilot Peter Pan, and 15 minutes before post time, the veteran jockey stood with the trainer and owner in the centre of the saddling paddock. It was a day for new procedures. For the sake of order and ease of identification, the AJC had just introduced a rule that stated all horses be paraded in order of saddlecloth number around the edge of the paddock, and horses were not to be called in for mounting until the jockeys had been given instructions. So, when orders were complete and Pike was mounted, Phillips walked Peter Pan around the edge of the paddock. He wore saddlecloth number one, and led Oro, Metallurgy, Eastern Chief, Kuvera and the filly La Moderne onto the course in that order.

Pike hadn't been up on the colt since the AJC Derby, but he marvelled that the horse felt quite himself, despite what the newspapers were saying. There was an educated energy to Peter Pan's step. Pike could see that racing, and experience, had stood the colt well. He cantered him through his preliminary and then to the mile-and-three-quarters start, which was on the straight. Easing him down, they mingled at the barrier for several moments. When Jack Gaxieu called for a line, Pike swivelled Peter Pan into place among horses, and all seven starters stood quietly. Ted Bartle was on Braeburn, Darby Munro was aboard the New Zealand filly. On Eastern Chief, Billy Duncan stole a glance at Jimmy Pike. He knew which horse to watch out for. Then the call went up, and they were off in the St Leger.

La Moderne was the quickest off her feet, and down the straight for the first time she led the field a giddy gallop, with Pike slotting Peter Pan in second. Beside him, Oro raced at his flank, with Metallurgy, Kuvera and Braeburn not far behind, and Eastern Chief bringing up the rear. But as soon as the order was set, the pace dropped off, and the field lumbered along. Aboard Oro, jockey Billy Cook took charge. Gathering his reins, he booted his horse away from Peter Pan and La Moderne, and as the field swung into the turn, he had raced the colt to a six-length lead.

La Moderne fell back through the field, and Pike sat quietly as Oro disappeared ahead of him. Peter Pan was bowling along, unconcerned by the daylight up front, and the veteran jockey wasn't about to charge into Oro's sudden sprint. If Cook wanted to exploit the rumours about Peter Pan's fitness, Pike thought, let him. Pike had plenty in tow. The crowds couldn't see the race order at this stage, but as the field lumbered into the far turn, eventually racing parallel to the grandstands, excited murmurs rose at Oro's lead. By the milepost, the horse had stolen 15 lengths on the field, and getting a little impatient, Pike let his reins out a touch. In response, the long-striding Peter Pan began to reach out, devouring the track between him and the horse in front.

Peter's strides were long and elastic as he dug into the turf. Pike was crouched over his neck, buried in the horse's blond mane, asking Peter Pan to get closer, and the pair began to bear down on Oro. Passing the six-post, they had dragged the field to within ten lengths of the frontrunner, and in the next two furlongs, Peter Pan was breathing on Oro. At the half-mile, he was at the leader's flanks, with Kuvera, Eastern Chief and Braeburn two lengths behind in his slipstream. As Oro and Peter galloped into the home turn, the battle cry ringing with glee from the grandstands, the war between the horses began.

Oro raced into the straight with Peter Pan on his outside. Hardridden, Oro was frantic, and Pike was urging Peter forward. Under hands and heels, the tall chestnut edged ahead, but the relentless Oro clung tight. Cook's mount was wavering, and for several strides he fell onto Peter Pan's shoulder. It looked to Pike like Cook's saddle had slipped. But Peter Pan shook off his rival in seconds. With Kuvera rallying on the rails behind Oro, Peter Pan began to run away from his adversary. Digging deeper and deeper, the colt moved away by a length, then another, until Pike could feel the breath of the others no more. Peter Pan dashed past the judge a length and a half to Oro, three-quarters back to Kuvera, eased at the line by the cool hands of Jim Pike.

Frank McGrath clapped his hands loudly, shaking his head at Peter Pan's class, at his obstinate refusal to lose. Not far away, Rodney and Elsie Dangar were hopping with delight. But down on the rails, few had noticed when Cliff Graves clicked his stopwatch to a halt, right at the moment when Peter Pan crossed the finishing line. The *Smith's Weekly* writer had started his watch as Peter Pan passed the judge the first time around, and now he stared at it with surprise. In his circuit of Randwick, exactly a mile and three furlongs around, Peter Pan had knocked a full second off the distance record set by Vaals in 1928. And this while he had towed the field back to the runaway Oro. 'Remarkable,' muttered the journalist.

Pike, as usual, looked underwhelmed. He trotted Peter Pan back to scale without a smile, stirring only when he touched his hat to the camera crew filming at the paddock gates, and when Peter Pan snapped at Oro. Not even the rapturous applause from the 47,000 patrons was enough to move him. But it moved Rodney Dangar. Peter Pan's owner was overcome with the thrill of winning the three-year-old classic, and he pumped the governor's hand as Sir Philip Game tied the red sash around his horse's neck. As the band spewed out renditions of Fantasia's *Gipsy Life,* and under balmy autumn sunshine, Dangar wished he could freeze the moment forever.

Peter Pan had run the St Leger in a time of 3:02. It was two and three-quarter seconds outside of Lady Valais's Leger record of 1924, but that grand mare hadn't had to run down a 15-length lead. Nor had the pace been a washout that year. The race had brought

Peter's tally to £12,668, and was his seventh win in 10 starts. He had started at 2/1 on, and repaid some of the losses after the Rawson Stakes fiasco. But more than all these things, more than the winnings or the sectionals or the repayments in the ring, Peter Pan had won a stern test with a less-than-ideal preparation. He had come into the mile and three-quarters with only two races in hand, one of which hadn't been a race at all, and he'd galloped against horses that had been racing for weeks. If the newspapers were right, and Peter wasn't at his best, then the St Leger proved he could beat horses at their top when he hadn't yet reached his.

Incredibly, the win wasn't enough for some. 'NOT THE HORSE HE WAS,' quipped *Truth.* 'It is clear now that Peter Pan, unless his lapse is only temporary, is hardly entitled to rank as Phar Lap's successor. In fact, on yesterday's display, he'll find the Red Terror's boots far too big for him.' The newspaper stated that only after Pike had cracked the whip did Peter Pan race on. It failed to mention the colt had run a blinder to catch the runaway Oro, or that he had run the circuit in record time. The paper had also forgotten that this was the second time Oro had fallen to Peter Pan – the first time was back in the Derby. Pike *had* drawn the whip on the colt, just as they'd entered the straight, but instead of the flaying that *Truth* had described, he had slapped the colt on his near-shoulder once, then driven him out for the final two furlongs. It was clear that *Truth* had expected nothing less than a procession from Peter Pan. The *Referee,* also, was in two minds about the colt: 'Peter Pan's time for the final mile was 1.37 which, with 8st 10lb, was sound travelling for a three-year-old after going three-quarters of a mile. But even making full allowance for the manner in which the race was won, Oro and Kuvera were a little too close to Peter Pan at the finish to suggest that he is yet another Phar Lap.'

Cliff Graves wasn't looking for another Phar Lap. Down on the rails that afternoon, he was the only turf journalist to clock the race with any accuracy, and from his unique angle, the St Leger had proved Peter Pan a champion. In his *Referee* column, he wrote, 'It seems that Peter Pan is the natural racing machine, needing little work or racing to prepare him for engagements, and clean-winded, he doesn't need the gruellingly fast gallops on the track to fit him for difficult races. The St Leger was a triumph of thoroughbred supremacy, and there can be no doubting now his complete staying superiority.'

The differences in opinion were extraordinary, and not just from one person to the next. Racing professionals couldn't agree on Peter Pan. Newspapers were running conflicting editorials, one writer proclaiming the horse a champion and the next a false alarm. It didn't help that Winooka had smashed the mile record just prior to the St Leger. After that, many were expecting a Pegasus-like performance from Peter Pan. But perhaps the worst words of all came from a letter to the *Telegraph* the following week. Writing to

'Cardigan', a Mr J.P. Walen from Leura, in the Blue Mountains, declared, 'I have never heard of a real good washy chestnut. They are never hardy and never last long. Anyway, he will never be a Phar Lap.'

***

At first light on Monday morning, as Peter Pan walked out for trackwork, a heavy ground fog settled over Randwick. The thick, misty blanket fell on the B grass, so that few could see the steady circuit that Peter Pan cantered with Whittingham. Under J. Jewell, the Pantheon colt felt perfect, fluid and flexible, but not wound up. It was Sydney Cup Day, and later that afternoon Rogilla won the big two-miler. Because he was also engaged for the Cumberland Plate with Peter Pan on Wednesday, a scintillating clash between the nation's top two stayers was expected ... until Monday afternoon, that is, when Winooka's trainer threw down the gauntlet for a match race with Peter Pan.

Trainer Mick Polson, high on his horse's record-setting Doncaster, approached the AJC secretary George Rowe with persuasions to bringing the horses together in Wednesday's All-Aged Plate. Recalling the matches between Gloaming and Beauford a decade before, and the outrageous response from the crowds in view of attendance, the trainer felt sure that a meeting of his superstar and Dangar's superstar would add 10,000 people to the grandstands on raceday. Rumours began to fly around Randwick that Polson had challenged Frank McGrath. Up and down Doncaster Avenue, racing folk leaned over their fences and discussed the race with their neighbours. Could Peter Pan beat Winooka over a mile?

If McGrath was considering the match, the conditions were grossly in Winooka's favour. The All-Aged Plate was a mile contest, and Peter Pan had been prepped for the staying races. Nothing on his card was less than a mile and three-quarters, so to bring Peter back to a lesser distance on Wednesday would mean certain defeat against a competitor that had been prepared for it. Winooka would have met a horse looking for an extra half-mile. McGrath thought the rumours ridiculous, and when declarations were made for the All-Aged Plate, Peter Pan's name was not among them. The colt would proceed as planned, with the Cumberland Plate on Wednesday afternoon and the AJC Plate on Saturday, and that brought attention back to Peter Pan and Rogilla.

'Peter Pan is not going to have an easy task in the Cumberland Plate,' stated 'Cardigan'. 'Rogilla, whether the race is run fast or slow, will shake the life out of the colt, and he will need to be right at his best to win.' Peter and Rogilla had met five times, Peter getting the upper hand on three occasions (Rogilla won the Caulfield Cup, and both had been unplaced in the Rawson Stakes). Speculation continued throughout the week.

By Wednesday morning, the day of the Cumberland Plate, the pleasing autumn temperatures of the week had deserted Sydney, and a stiff southerly sent chills around the racecourse. It did little to deter attendance. People spilled from the trams in their thousands, clutching racebooks and umbrellas and the form guide from the *Telegraph.* And they all had their opinions. Winooka for the All-Aged Plate early in the day, the crack two-year-old Hall Mark for the Champagne. But Peter Pan or Rogilla in the Cumberland? As it turned out, Les Haigh made the decision for them. Scratching Rogilla from the race that afternoon, he stated that his horse needed a rest, and it was a reasonable claim. Rogilla was a tough customer, but he had won the mile-and-a-half Autumn Plate on Saturday and the Sydney Cup on Monday. He was also due to run against Peter Pan in the two-and-a-quarter-mile AJC Plate on the coming Saturday. The Cumberland Plate, with its £775 purse, was small fish in the grander scheme of things.

With Rogilla's scratching, the field shrank to four. Outside of Peter Pan, there was only Johnnie Jason, Oro and Cimbrian, all of whom Peter had beaten on various occasions. As the race was a weight-for-age event, Oro carried 8st 4lb with Peter Pan, while Johnnie Jason was shouldering 8st 11lb to Cimbrian's 9st 3lb. Peter Pan was a long odds-on favourite. McGrath had brought Billy Duncan back for the ride, owing to Pike not being able to make the weight. Reunited for the first time since their Melbourne Cup triumph, Duncan and Peter Pan looked coolly confident as they trotted to the start at the top of the straight. In Duncan's mind, the race was in no doubt.

Jack Gaxieu had little trouble sending the four horses away. As they set off down the straight for the first time, with the cheers of the crowd in their ears, Johnnie Jason swept to the front as he always did, with Peter Pan in second and Oro and Cimbrian behind him. But from the get-go, Duncan had his hands full. A boisterous Peter Pan was full of running, and galloping out of the straight he was pulling like a steam train, trying to get around Johnnie Jason who was only cantering in front. With more than a mile to gallop, Duncan refused to let the colt lead the field, and he sat back in his stirrups, leaning against the weight of the thoroughbred beneath him, pleading with the colt to settle.

Johnnie Jason lumbered towards the mile-post, and sweeping around the turn there was no change to the order. Peter was still pulling his way through second place, with Oro and Cimbrian behind him, and as they ran towards the six-furlong post, Duncan finally settled Peter Pan. Finding a rhythm, the colt floated up to Johnnie Jason's flanks. At the half-mile, there was nothing between them.

The two horses swept into the home turn together, Johnnie Jason on the inside, Peter Pan on the outside, and for several strides they raced neck and neck. The short, burly Newcastle horse was digging deep, and a cheer rose up from the Flat at the tussle. Behind them, Cimbrian and Oro were three lengths away, racing hard to stay in touch. With two furlongs to go,

Duncan shortened his reins and waved his whip, shaking it at Peter's right eye. Immediately, the tussle was over. The tall chestnut sprung a new gear and began to eat up the turf. He drew away from Johnnie Jason by a length, then by two, and up in the stands and all across the Flat, Peter Pan's backers hollered for him to come home. There were thousands that had stalled their bets until this, the last big race of the day, and Peter Pan duly saluted. Galloping over the line alone, he won the Cumberland Plate by two-and-a-half lengths to the gallant Johnnie Jason, with Oro and Cimbrian nearly two lengths behind.

Billy Duncan savoured the claps and whistles as he brought Peter Pan back to scale. He was three from three on the Pantheon colt now, and he couldn't remember a grittier racehorse in all his years of riding. The crowd was on its feet for the colt, and as Duncan stripped the saddle from Peter Pan's back, the handshakes came from everywhere. None was stronger than Rodney Dangar's. The Cumberland Plate had now brought Peter's winnings to £13,443. In any other era, he would have surpassed the £20,000 mark by now. But it was the Depression, and the slashing of stakes was keeping the tally modest. Nonetheless, it was Peter's eighth win in 11 starts, and there was no doubt in Frank McGrath's mind: Peter Pan was a champion.

'A horse can't do more than win, and Peter did that alright,' wrote the *Sportsman.* Despite the outstanding effort, though, the same exhausted arguments prevailed: 'While he won with plenty up his sleeve, more than a few hard-headed turf students reckoned that he didn't gather Johnnie as quickly as he should have.' Even 'Cardigan' had run into writer's block, regurgitating the same words he had written over and over again. 'Without wishing for a moment to detract from Peter Pan's win, I still doubt whether he is as good as he was in the spring.' The media comments were becoming a joke around the McGrath yard. What exactly was expected of Peter Pan these days? A 10-lengths win, even 20 lengths? Was a win just not enough? McGrath was not about to ruin this new champion he had. He would not push Peter to win by ridiculous margins, no matter how much a few reporters demanded it. In a staying test like the Cumberland, Peter Pan would win as he liked. When he hit the front, no jockey was going to ask him to run away by a dozen lengths. As far as McGrath was concerned, two-and-a-half lengths were more than adequate.

McGrath didn't even read the papers. The morning after the race, it was business as usual for him. He sent Peter Pan a steady gallop over the tan track. Mick Polson, who had managed to win the All-Aged Plate with Winooka, had similar ideas for his charge, and the two trainers chatted idly as their turf stars drummed around Randwick. Like Peter Pan, Winooka was engaged to race on Saturday, and like Peter Pan he was unbeaten in the carnival so far. There was no doubting that Winooka was a brilliant miler, but the competition between the two horses was a newspaper myth. Winooka couldn't hold a candle to Pantheon's son over the true distances. Likewise, over the shorter courses Peter Pan would probably be beaten.

The AJC Plate was Peter Pan's final test, and it was going to be just that, a stern two and a quarter miles around Randwick against Rogilla, Lough Neagh and Johnnie Jason. La Moderne was also running again, as was an out-of-form galloper called Great Expectations, and at one stage Satmoth was entered, though by final declarations he was out. The field comprised the best staying horses in the land. There was no other group of thoroughbreds that between them had amassed so many Cups and sashes. There was Peter Pan, champion three-year-old and Melbourne Cup, St Leger and Derby winner. There was Rogilla, the Caulfield Cup and Sydney Cup winner that season. Lough Neagh had won the two-mile Randwick Plate in the spring and claimed the Chipping Norton two weeks earlier, and Johnnie Jason, though older now, had won the VRC Derby, the Sydney Cup and the Warwick Stakes (twice), all in the previous two years.

There was plenty of backing for the horses. Rogilla was getting to 2/1 in the ring, and was second favourite behind Peter Pan's 6/4 on. The fact that Lough Neagh was next at 14s gave some indication of the heat between the two favourites. Whatever the public thought, and most hearts fell on Dangar's colt, the newspapers were all over Rogilla. 'Peter Pan will need to beat a fast tattoo to keep with Rogilla down the straight this afternoon,' said the *Sportsman.*

The AJC Plate was due off at 3.45pm, and by the time Dangar, McGrath and Duncan stood huddled in the mounting yard, Winooka had already blitzed the C.W. Cropper Plate. Mick Polson's horse had wrapped up his autumn meeting unbeaten, and McGrath was anxious to do the same with Peter. The trainer instructed Duncan to make use of his light weight. Peter Pan was carrying nearly 1st less than Rogilla, and over two and a quarter miles that meant many lengths of an advantage. McGrath also stressed to Duncan, for the umpteenth time, not to let the colt get to the lead. It was almost impossible to bring a field home over the distance of the AJC Plate, he said, even with a pull in the weights. Though Duncan nodded to the trainer, in the jockey's mind it was easier said than done. There was not one horse in this field that was going to be willing to lead, not with Peter Pan in the wings.

Momentarily, McGrath and Duncan discussed the track conditions. Dangar hovered beside them, listening. Horses had been returning to scale all day with clods of mud caked to their shoulders and bellies, this in spite of it not raining for over a week. McGrath had heard a rumour that the AJC had accidentally left the water hoses turned on over the course all night, though George Law had refuted that claim quick smart. But the times turned in for the earlier races had been seconds outside those set during the week, so something was this day. McGrath told Duncan to be careful.

The Victorian jockey cantered Peter Pan down to the start with tactics in his head. He had already ridden twice that day, and the track, though not fast, had felt okay. He knew that Rogilla was a slow starter, and that even if they cantered home, the Newcastle horse would have enough sting to rush to the front and win. He also held Lough Neagh in high regard, for the Queenslander had been rested since the Sydney Cup. But as much as Duncan was calculating the chances of his rivals, so every other jockey was wondering something similar – how to beat Peter Pan.

Gaxieu called the jockeys to attention, and a cheer went up from the stands. The AJC Plate was the last of the big races for the autumn, and what a race to bring the curtain down. Some 25,000 people were yelling for the field to be on its way. Not more than a minute after 3.45pm, the starter's hand pressed the lever, the tape flew up, and they were off.

Great Expectations crossed to the rail first, and set off at a pace that surprised the rest of the field. Moving into the straight and past the judge for the first time, he clipped the first half-mile in 53 seconds, with Johnnie Jason galloping behind him and Peter Pan running third. Duncan had taken a firm hold of the colt, and as they loped out of the straight he had settled well. He was running with rhythm, shadowing Johnnie Jason's every stride, while at the tail end of everything Rogilla had dropped right out. Some 15 lengths spread the field before him, but his jockey sat quietly, watching the procession in front.

Peter Pan was galloping on the rails, relishing the good tempo for a change. He stretched out with big, loose strides, and as they shot past the nine furlongs, Great Expectations was spent. Johnnie Jason, hoping to get a break on Peter Pan, bounded to the lead and galloped away, but Duncan had expected as much. Letting his reins out, he asked Peter Pan to pick up, and the chestnut galloped after Johnnie Jason, refusing to let the Newcastle horse get away. Before the rest of the field had a chance to shake up and follow, the two frontrunners had left the field for dust.

Down the backstretch they ran, the two leaders broken from the field, Johnnie Jason trying to drop Peter Pan but the colt tracking his every move. Lengths behind, Rogilla was shaken up, and given his head the big horse lumbered from the rear towards the leaders. By the five-pole he was within a length of Peter Pan. Up in the stands an almighty roar went up. Rogilla had moved to Peter Pan's flank. Duncan could feel the breath from the horse's white face, could see the battle was nigh, and when they passed the half-mile before the turn, he ended it before it began. He looked towards Johnnie Jason, who was still carving up the sectionals ahead of him, and he asked Peter Pan to go on.

The son of Pantheon responded with a tremendous leap, bursting away from Rogilla. In less than a furlong he ranged up to Johnnie Jason and, as in the

Cumberland Plate, the two horses thundered into the straight together, Johnnie Jason on the inside and Peter Pan on the outside, four lengths clear of Rogilla and two long furlongs to go. Duncan could feel Peter Pan inching forward, gaining the upper hand without so much as an effort. He edged ahead of Johnnie Jason into daylight. The crowd was getting louder, getting frantic, and when that happened it meant only one thing. Duncan glanced over his left shoulder and saw it – Lough Neagh closing like a steam train, bearing down on Peter Pan with every stride. He began to ride the colt furiously.

Lough Neagh's withering run ate into Peter Pan's lead, and Rogilla had come too. Inside the final furlong there was a flurry of heaving horses and pumping jockeys. Peter Pan was fighting for his position in front, with Lough Neagh on his outside. Johnnie Jason still had a run on the rails, with Rogilla behind him, and less than two lengths separated the four horses. From the stands it looked as if Lough Neagh would get there, but Peter Pan would not be denied. The colt dug furiously with every stride, heaving under Billy Duncan's urgings, bursting his heart to be in front at the line, and Lough Neagh couldn't get past him. The winning post came in a flash, and Peter Pan prevailed by a neck.

From various standpoints around Randwick, the race was so close it looked as if Lough Neagh had caused an upset. The cheers and bellows went mute for a moment as everyone stared at the semaphore board. When Peter Pan's number came up, an almighty roar broke over the racecourse: the people's favourite was home once more, breaking the ring at 6/4 on. No one was cheering louder than Rodney Rouse Dangar. Once again, Peter Pan had defied his critics and won. Once again, he had shown remarkable resilience to win. Dangar could have cried with pride. As Peter Pan trotted back to scale, the ovations surrounding him were momentous. At this moment, the crowd didn't care how he had won, or by how many lengths. He had won, and that was all that mattered. Peter Pan had repaid their faith and filled their pockets, and the newspapers could say what they wanted. Today he was a champion again.

The AJC Plate brought Peter Pan's winnings to £14,218. He had tallied the entire amount in his three-year-old season, with nine wins (including his dead-heat) in 11 starts, or 12 starts if his two-year-old race was included. He had beaten every cup, sash and plate winner of merit, every top weight-for-age stayer. He had won from a mile to two and a quarter miles, and he had done so through inexperience, interference and mishap. 'To hell with the newspapers,' thought Dangar, giddy as he bounded down the Members' stairs to his racehorse. 'Let achievement speak for itself.'

***

On the still, autumnal afternoon of Tuesday 9 May, over two weeks after Peter Pan's unbeaten run at Randwick, Frank McGrath stood in his yard and listened to the silence. Instead of wheelbarrows and horses' hooves, there were swallows chattering loudly. He could hear them for the first time in months. Peter had gone off to Doonside that morning, and with him some of McGrath's other charges. Whittingham had also gone from the yard, but not for a spell. His owner had transferred him to the Melbourne stables of Jack Holt, and with Satmoth's move earlier in the year and Prismatic's recent move to the rival yard of Fred Foulsham, the three horses were a tough loss for McGrath. But even these were simple headaches compared to Denis Boy's breaking down. McGrath had laboured over the Irish horse's injury since that morning of trackwork back in April. Denis Boy had problems with his suspensory ligament, and just after the Cumberland Plate McGrath had cabled Robert Wallace in Ireland with advice to retire the stallion. Though the horse wasn't lame, the trainer knew another race would certainly ruin him, and the big black beast deserved better than that. There were stud prospects to consider. Shortly after, Wallace had wired his response to put the horse up for sale, and 'Denny Boy', as McGrath called him, was due for the Inglis yards on 4 July.

Down the shed row, the trainer had at least one new horse. It was a little bay two-year-old by Heroic, a son of his own mare Fair Rosaleen, who had won him the Wagga Wagga Cup back in 1925. McGrath had named the colt Australia Fair, and he had private hopes for the youngster. He was even more excited when the colt won a Nursery Handicap at Randwick a few weeks later.

But miles away, in the fattening pastures around Thomas Cleaver's property at Doonside, Peter Pan grew into his skin. Strong and robust, the flaxen-haired chestnut waited for the horse float to take him back to Randwick, and it ambled up Cleaver's driveway on a wintry Tuesday afternoon, 20 June.

14

'He's only a four-year-old, and a young one at that'

George Phillips combed the straw around stable number six, pushing it high into the corners to stop the draughts and spreading it thin and loose in the middle, then he stuffed the manger with hay and hauled the water bucket back in. When he heard the heavy chug of the motor float out front, he stood up, brushed off his trousers and went outside to meet it.

Peter Pan was returning from Doonside on a typical winter's day. A drizzle dampened the air, hardly heavy enough to be called rain. Stepping off the float, the colt stopped for a moment to check where he was, breathing in the familiar whiffs of Doncaster Avenue, then he followed George Phillips into the yard and into box number six. McGrath had reshuffled the accommodation with the departure of several horses, and Peter was resuming the stable that had belonged to Amounis. Number six was a little further into the yard, but it was all the same to Peter Pan. He snatched at the freshly stuffed manger while Phillips removed his rugs and travelling boots.

The colt had put on weight during the six-week break, though he was still light in frame. He was at least 16.3 hands high now, and his four spindles looked even longer and straighter. But he had musculature where he hadn't had it the prevous spring. He was less of the kid who was all elbows and more of the brutish athlete, and even now, though his coat was thick with winter, he was a paler chestnut. Even his mane was whiter.

For the next few weeks of late June and early July, Peter and Phillips were inseparable. It was the time that the strapper loved the most, because Peter Pan was at his most relaxed. He wasn't wired with racing, or distracted with fast work. At these times, Phillips could enjoy him without press intrusion. Frank McGrath was holidaying in north Queensland until the last week of July, and overseen by his brother, yard foreman Maurice McGrath, the horse and strapper stepped onto the racetrack each morning after breakfast, trotting and cantering in steady bouts and chiselling off the colt's pasture fat. By the time McGrath returned, Peter Pan was in trim order, and he'd hardly made a newspaper headline.

The VRC handicapper, J.H. Davis, had released the first weights for the 1933 Melbourne and Caulfield cups, and with 9st 7lb for the Flemington event, Peter Pan had topped the weight-carrying list. Rogilla was next with 9st 4lb. Davis had rated Peter Pan, who would be a four-year-old by the time November rolled around, 8lb worse than Phar Lap in 1930, and most thought it a fair assessment. Though the AJC handicapper had rated Peter Pan much more highly with his 9st allocation for the Sydney Cup the previous

April, it was likely the autumn results had influenced Davis's decision. Peter Pan had won his races, but not by crazy margins, so he wasn't about to shelf Peter Pan with the same 9st 12lb that he had given Phar Lap.

McGrath, when he learned of the allocation, was happy. It mattered little to him that only once had a four-year-old carried such weight to victory in the big two-miler, and that was of course Telford's Red Terror. He didn't question for a second that Peter Pan could do it. Though the colt hadn't carried more than 8st 10lb to victory in all his starts, his three-year-old tasks were over now. When he began racing again in the spring, it would be under four-year-old rules. The press wasn't as hopeful as the trainer. 'Peter Pan is a great horse, but he has a great horse's weight,' quipped the *Telegraph.* 'Although he may be able to hold those near him, his trouble may come from a good three-year-old who will carry weight-for-age or less.' To McGrath, that good three-year-old looked like the Jack Holt – trained Hall Mark, the two-year-old that had swept the Sires' Produce and Champagne Stakes at Randwick the previous autumn. He had slipped in to the Melbourne Cup with 7st 8lb, or 2lb over weight-for-age. Peter Pan would be giving him nearly 2st.

The moment the weights were released, Dangar's colt was installed as favourite for the Melbourne Cup. On 29 June, the bookies posted their first charts for the race, with Peter Pan heading the quotations, followed by the two-year-olds Hall Mark and Blixten, both of whom would be three-year-olds by Cup time. Rogilla was grouped with Kuvera, Lough Neagh and Braeburn as a fighting chance, and popping into contention was a New Zealand filly called Silver Scorn, an unflashy but brilliant daughter of English sire Silverado.

Silver Scorn had been brought to Australia by the Randwick trainer Fred Cush. Cush had paid a pretty penny for the filly, for prior to her purchase she had won 13 of 14 starts in New Zealand, a record unequalled by any recent champion on either side of the Tasman. She had arrived in Sydney at the end of autumn racing, and by the spring, like Peter Pan, she would be a four-year-old. The meeting of the two horses was eagerly awaited. Two weeks after the declaration of weights, however, Cush scratched his star filly from the Caulfield Cup, believing her unfairly treated by the handicapper, and he further declared that Silver Scorn's entire spring itinerary was unclear. It was two weeks after pre-post betting had begun on the cups, and two weeks after some serious cash had floated into the ring on doubles betting. The *Telegraph* spoke for all. 'CONNECTIONS OF SILVER SCORN INVITE PUBLIC CONDEMNATION,' the headline stated on 27 July. McGrath knew too well that no horse was safe from the press.

Peter Pan remained in light work until the end of July, and by 1 August McGrath was back on deck. It was also Peter Pan's official birthday that day, along with every racehorse in Australia, but it was a very happy celebration for Peter. He was among a select number of racehorses remembered by the Melbourne Hospital Birthday League. The Birthday League celebrated the generosity of racehorse owners who had donated heavily to the hospital after an important race win. In Dangar's case, it had been after Peter's Melbourne Cup victory, so on 1 August he received a birthday card from the league, as did Liberal and Windbag, VRC chairman Lachlan Mackinnon's Star d'Or, and five other horses.

Peter Pan began to work before breakfast in August. McGrath was noticing improved fitness each day. As soon as the colt was trotted onto the track each morning for work, he pranced and squealed beneath his track rider, pigrooting when he felt like it and gambolling about. It did little good to scold him. Peter Pan wasn't a horse that liked to be told what to do. 'You can coax him, but you can't bluff him,' Phillips would tell the riders each morning, and most of them listened. When they didn't, they found themselves aboard an uncooperative handful. By the second week of August, McGrath had his clock out. In a chilly ground frost, the colt galloped a mile in 1.58 1/2, and two days later he went over 10 furlongs, the last four in 58 seconds. On 15 August, Peter Pan galloped another 10 furlongs on the course proper in 2.29, the last half-mile in 57 1/2 seconds.

On Saturday 19 August, McGrath floated the horse to Moorefield Racecourse for an exhibition gallop between races. Ridden by Ted Bartle, Peter Pan trotted a circuit of the popular Kogarah course, then began to stretch out. Reaching the half-mile, Bartle gave the colt his head and the pair clocked the four furlongs in 51 3/4 seconds. Up in the stands, Dangar was watching. Like the clockers, he was tracking his colt's every progress. He followed Peter to trackwork and to exhibition gallops like these. He was devoted to his horse, and without a job to hold down he was free to go everywhere with his horse. That afternoon, he could see that McGrath's long, steady drills for Peter Pan were in aid of a second Melbourne Cup.

On paper, Peter Pan's campaign was due to start at Warwick Farm on 26 August, in the seven-furlong Warwick Stakes. The line-up was delirious. Silver Scorn was at last making her debut, running against Rogilla, Kuvera, Lough Neagh and Braeburn. That grandson of Windbag, Chatham, was also returning to racing. He had been written off in the autumn with broken wind, but a blood drain had cleared him of infirmity and he was back. Dangar was a little worried about starting Peter Pan too soon. In the autumn, he had watched the colt win the Randwick Stakes first up after a spell when he wasn't quite fit, and he suspected the effort had taken its toll on the rest of the season. He would prefer to stall his colt's debut if it meant a fitter racehorse for November. McGrath agreed, so by the middle of the week Peter Pan was out of the Warwick Stakes. In the AJC's first ever meeting broadcast by amplifiers across the course,

Chatham made a mockery of the Warwick Stakes field, running Kuvera and Rogilla into a new course record, and in his wake choked the much vaunted Silver Scorn, seventh of nine horses.

Dangar showed up to trackwork early the next morning, weathering the cold when most men of leisure were still tucked into bed. He watched as Peter Pan worked an easy mile around Randwick. As the colt lumbered past, a handful of journalists pressed him for comments about Peter's progress. 'He's better than ever, don't you think?' Dangar said. He enjoyed his little speeches to the press. He could talk about his colt all day long. 'He didn't race yesterday because we felt a stern race just now would probably do him no good.' Someone pressed him on Peter Pan's autumn form. 'There is not the slightest doubt in my mind that Peter Pan did not show to advantage in the autumn because of his race in the Randwick Stakes,' Dangar said. 'He won it, but it knocked him about. More than likely he was affected for the remainder of the campaign.' Half a dozen voices interjected, and Dangar raised his hands to calm his audience. 'I am fairly confident that Peter Pan is now a better horse than ever.'

By the middle of the following week, however, Frank McGrath was not sure. On the Thursday morning, through a heavy ground fog and temperatures that would put the chill up anyone, Peter Pan worked a mile on the course proper in 1:46, brought home over the last six furlongs by Ptolemy in 1:20 flat.

Something was wrong. Through the fog, McGrath could see the colt overcompensating in his gallop. Moving to the rails, the trainer listened as Peter Pan approached. The stride was awful. It wasn't fluid or rhythmical. The one-two-three-four beat was more like one-two-three, then a hesitant four. As he ran past, McGrath could see the colt looked stiff. He yelled at track jockey George Pownall to pull up straight away.

The colt wasn't lame, and he looked sound, but he wasn't the same horse either. After track gallops, Peter Pan would walk home full of being, but on this Thursday morning, with the ground fog clinging to Randwick until well after seven o'clock, Peter wasn't himself. Back at the yard, McGrath went over the horse from poll to tail, sliding his hands down the horse's legs, searching for heat. He checked his hips, his back and neck, then settled on his shoulders. Moving across the shoulder blades, he found nothing on the offside, but pressing hard on the muscles on the nearside, McGrath stopped in his tracks. Peter Pan was tied up in his left shoulder.[1] George Phillips, standing at Peter's head, could see that McGrath

---

1 All accounts of Peter Pan's life have described him as suffering from rheumatism, and in his lifetime this was upheld as the diagnosis for his troubled shoulder. However, modern veterinary practice does not recognise rheumatism in horses, and it is almost certain the trouble was due to tying-up.

had found a problem. He didn't need to be told what was wrong. He shivered in the cold chill of the morning, panicked on the inside about what might be in store for Peter Pan. The trainer was labouring on Peter's nearside, rubbing his hands around the base of the horse's neck and down into the pocket around his elbows. He kept coming back to the same spot. When he stopped, McGrath looked grave and issued Phillips a series of quick instructions. Leading the horse into his stall, the strapper flipped a rug onto Peter Pan, then went off to fetch another. Returning with two more rugs, he dressed the colt in them before bringing another straw bale into the stable and packing the walls tight to stop the draughts. Then he disappeared to prepare a hot fomentation.

McGrath had gone inside to telephone Dangar. The news wasn't good. Tying-up was a serious condition for a racehorse, a muscular disorder that presented itself as mere stiffness after exercise. But at its worst, tying-up could be so painful that a horse could barely stand, let alone take weight. McGrath had seen horses that couldn't even move with it, so wracked with pain they appeared paralysed. In Peter's case, McGrath hoped it was an ugly complaint brought about by the chilly temperatures, and that with adequate treatment he could ward it off. But if it were more than that, if the muscles were so stiff that the horse couldn't gallop cleanly, then the damage would wipe Peter Pan from racing that year.

As McGrath broke the news to Peter Pan's owner, back at the yard George Phillips applied his fomentation. Intended to relax and soften the shoulder muscles, the fomentation was a heated concoction of camphor blocks dissolved in methylated spirits and spirits of ammonia, and to apply it, Phillips soaked large flannel cloths in the hot mixture, laying them over the horse's near-shoulder. Draping the first cloth over the withers, he laid the others on top of it, pressing them into the shoulder until they cooled and no longer stuck together. Peter relaxed as the heat furrowed into his tight muscles. Heating the fomentation again, he reapplied the cloths for half-an-hour until McGrath returned to the stable. Taking over, the trainer instructed Phillips to make another mix, and between them the two men worked on Peter Pan throughout the day.

The following morning, Dangar arrived at the yard before dawn and travelled with McGrath to Rosebery Racecourse, to which Peter Pan had been floated for trackwork. The two men stood gingerly by as the horse trotted a circuit of the track, but before he could go up a gear the trainer called a halt to the workout. Peter Pan was sore, visibly sore, and they shipped him back to the yard straight away. Stripping the colt of his travelling gear, Phillips got to work with the fomentation again, McGrath and Dangar watching, though in stern conversation. Dangar was in a mind to scratch his beloved horse from all proceedings there and then. Even he could see the fire was gone from his colt. But McGrath steadied the nervous owner with his optimism. They would see how Peter fared the following day. Muscle soreness was a sporadic complaint, McGrath explained. It might go away of its own accord.

At Rosebery the next morning, McGrath was grateful for his cool head. He stood by the rails opposite the winning post, with a loose collection of watchers around him, and saw Peter Pan trot a smooth circuit of the racecourse. The horse looked in stronger trim. McGrath gave the signal for Pownall to step it up, and breaking into a slow canter Peter Pan moved into low gear. Beyond the three furlongs, he was allowed to go a little faster, and though he wasn't clocked, he passed his audience at the winning post in splendid order. To anyone not in the know, he appeared as fit as ever.

Peter Pan returned to Doncaster Avenue in high spirits. He stepped off the horse float in little leaps, skidding onto the concrete outside the yard with a noisy clatter. Nearby, Dangar had arrived to see his horse, and he looked relieved, renewed even. Today Peter Pan was okay. 'I don't want you to jump from one extreme to the other,' he told the waiting folds of the press later that morning. 'Yesterday I was anything but enamoured of the position with Peter Pan. But today I am much more hopeful.' He recalled the morning's workout, as reported to him by McGrath, reiterating his pleasure that the horse had moved freely, but also clarifying something the press already suspected: 'Although I am looking to the future with a little more confidence today, it is safe to say that Peter Pan will not run in the Chelmsford Stakes.' Dangar had confirmed this with McGrath earlier in the morning.

The Chelmsford Stakes was on Saturday week at Randwick, and traditionally it was a race that reintroduced champions to the public after the winter months. It was also a prelude to the bigger AJC spring carnival that occurred in October. After Peter's scratching from the Warwick Stakes, the Chelmsford had been their next target, but given that the colt hadn't worked solidly for days now, it came as no surprise to the racegoing public that Peter Pan had been scratched from this event too. 'We are still hopeful of being able to run him in one of the weight-for-age races before the AJC spring meeting,' the owner told the reporters. 'And, of course, if he progresses satisfactorily he will contest the Randwick weight-for-age attractions, after which he will go south.'

Before the journalists dispersed that morning, one of them suggested to Dangar that Peter Pan's troubles had amounted from his hard Melbourne Cup run the previous November. 'I cannot agree with that contention, gentlemen,' Dangar said calmly, for he had heard this suggested before, 'even allowing for the fact that a preparation for the Melbourne Cup is most rigorous. Peter Pan has not been over-raced and he was treated kindly after the Cup. You will realise that he is also flesh and bone, and subject to the ails we are heir to. He is perfectly sound in the bone, though. His present trouble is a muscular one.'

The journalist's assertion lingered with Dangar as he drove back to Arlington that morning. When Manawhenua had slammed Peter Pan into the running rail, had it caused the damage that was now presenting itself? Was it coincidence that it was the same shoulder? McGrath had stressed to Dangar that it was. The two had already discussed the matter when the shoulder problem had first appeared. Peter Pan had been spelled immediately after the Melbourne Cup, so any stress on the colt's physicality at that time had dissolved with rest. Peter also had not shown any signs of unsoundness during the autumn. If he had, he would have been scratched immediately, as neither Dangar nor McGrath was willing to take risks with him. They were both rich men who didn't need the money, and they were good horsemen. The colt's welfare would always be foremost.

In the days that ensued, reports of sore horses came thick and fast from Randwick. Outside of McGrath's yard, Fred Cush had found Silver Scorn with similar muscular troubles in her shoulder, while nearby, the gallopers Jacko and Mince Pie were also struck down. Rumours of a rheumatic virus abounded around the racecourse, but sensible men like Frank McGrath knew the absurdity of the suggestion. Muscular problems were not something that could be caught in the wind. They were problems associated with fitness and condition, possibly even with weather, and if the latter wasn't a cause, it certainly wasn't helping. Early mornings at Randwick remained bitterly cold into September, and walking onto the track each morning, Peter Pan was rugged to the hilt.

By the Monday, things were looking positive. Peter was again floated to Rosebery, where he worked a circuit of the course in a smart trot before breezing the last three furlongs in 49 1/4. Immediately after the gallop, veterinarian Roy Stewart inspected the horse and could find little wrong with him. Just to be careful, McGrath reapplied the hot fomentation again that afternoon, and he wondered if he were out of the woods. There was no sign of cramping or scratchiness in Peter's movement, and the horse was his usual aloof self in the stable. McGrath allowed his confidence to grow. He entered Peter Pan in the Spring Stakes, to be run at Rosebery on Wednesday week.

Down in Melbourne, the good news about Peter's improvement was not as quick to travel as the bad news. Peter Pan had been solidly backed in Caulfield Cup – Melbourne Cup doubles for weeks now, thousands of pounds exchanging hands in backdoor betting shops and offcourse outfits, and a nervousness had swept through pockets at word of his woes. One bookmaker held more than £1000 on combinations beginning with the colt, and if it eventuated that Peter didn't run in the Cup, the bookies would reap a rare harvest. It was also emerging that Peter's possible absence from the AJC spring meeting was enticing other weight-for-age horses to compete. Ammon Ra, the 1931 AJC Derby winner, had been almost on his way to Melbourne to tackle the early spring races down there, but his owners were having second thoughts about that plan. Without Peter Pan, the weight-for-age events in Sydney were wide open.

The week progressed much as it had started, and McGrath refused to ask any fast work of Peter Pan. He sent the colt to the track each morning with several rugs on, only taking them off when the horse went off to gallop, and throwing them back on immediately afterwards. He watched every step Peter took, listened to every beat, and back at the yards each morning he ran his hands over every inch of the chestnut's frame. Phillips, working tirelessly in aid of Peter's welfare, kept the stable bedded deep with straw, checked the rugs each night and changed them in the morning, and between them, the two men felt as if they'd beaten the trouble away. When the trainer's Australia Fair pulled up muscle-sore that week, McGrath was forgiven for thinking a hex had befallen his yard.

That weekend, Dangar took his family to Rotherwood, but each morning he telephoned McGrath to enquire of Peter's progress. The trainer had the same report for him each morning: the horse was fine, though he hadn't done any fast work, and he would telephone if anything were amiss. By Monday night, however, McGrath was wracked with worry. He was heading into a Cup campaign with a horse that hadn't yet galloped at his top. There was no way of telling if Peter Pan were fit, though he wasn't racing fit. And it was out of the question that he could take the horse to Melbourne without prior racing, for the travel would chip away at him. There was little else to be done. He had to up the ante with Peter's morning work.

The following morning, on Tuesday 12 September, McGrath floated Peter Pan to Rosebery with George Phillips, veterinarian Roy Stewart, and track jockey George Pownall, who had been riding most of Peter's work for the previous few weeks. The weather was clear as a bell. Though nippy, the temperature that morning was actually a touch warmer than it had been for weeks, and under blue skies, McGrath legged Pownall into the saddle. 'Warm him up a circuit,' the trainer instructed his jockey, 'then bring him back the last six at his top. I think he's ready.' With a sharp nod, Pownall trotted Peter Pan on to the course proper.

McGrath, Stewart and Phillips waited by the rails, the trainer hoisting his binoculars to watch the disappearing racehorse. So far, Peter Pan looked smooth and untroubled. As he lumbered in a steady canter around the course, nothing looked amiss. As he passed the mile-post, still nothing was amiss. Nearing the six-furlong post, Pownall shortened his reins and stepped things up, and Peter Pan responded. When they passed the six-post, McGrath clicked his stopwatch and held his breath.

The smooth drum of Peter Pan's stride was music to Pownall's ears. The colt was reaching out with reckless abandon, eating up the turf, elated to be finally running. He swept around the home turn in mere seconds, carrying the jockey closer to the little crowd at the winning post. Leaning deep into the flying blond hair, Pownall clicked to the colt for more effort. Peter Pan surged forward, charging into the empty straight like there was no tomorrow, and as he burst across the finishing line, Frank McGrath clicked his stopwatch again. It read 1:19, a very decent effort for an unfit racehorse.

Peter Pan began to wind down from his gallop, but the oxygen in his blood, and consequently his muscles, was running low. He had expended most of it boxing out the six furlongs. As he pulled up, the muscles in his troubled shoulder began to contract. By the time he had slowed to a walk, the shoulder was so cramped he could barely move it. Peter bobbed unsteadily, trying to shift the weight somewhere else, anywhere else but on to the side that was painful. In alarm, Pownall jumped off the horse and looked around for Frank McGrath.

As soon as the track jockey had started to pull up, McGrath had seen the terrible action in Peter Pan's gait, and his heart sank. Yelling to an equally panicked Phillips, he sprinted towards the troubled horse, pulling the saddle off as soon as he reached the colt, with Phillips throwing the rugs on. Together, they led the horse to the stalls where veterinarian

Roy Stewart waited. There was little that could be done right then. Stewart advised that the trouble was no different to that which McGrath had been fending off for weeks now. Peter Pan was tied-up in that shoulder, but this morning the condition was so acute that the horse was horribly lame. He had hobbled to the stalls like a tired hack. Stewart advised the trainer to float Peter Pan back to Randwick and get started with the fomentation once again. He would call to the yard in the afternoon, and if the horse was no better, they would physic him.

The short drive back to Randwick felt like years as McGrath measured the weight of the morning's events. In his mind, there was no chance of Peter Pan defending his Cup title this year. There was little chance of the horse racing at all. They could fend away the problems in that shoulder with foments and blankets, but without rest the problem would always be there, badgering the horse's fitness and interrupting his training. With a long spell, Peter stood a better chance as a five-year-old than he did right now. When McGrath telephoned Dangar at Rotherwood later that morning, he advised the owner to withdraw his horse from all spring engagements. Though shattered with disappointment, Dangar had been ready for such news. McGrath had prepared him well enough for it.

Peter Pan spent the rest of Tuesday morning bathed in hot fomentation, and by late afternoon McGrath had him out of his box and walking. The horse appeared quite recovered. He wasn't showing any signs of soreness, and his action wasn't cramped, but it was a false prophecy. McGrath knew well that if he sent the chestnut out for a dash the following day, he would come back as lame as this morning. Dangar was due back to Sydney in the next two days, and McGrath decided to postpone all decisions until then. But it wasn't long before the story hit the wrong ears, and 36-year-old 'Cardigan' presented himself at the yard. Because McGrath was resigned to Peter Pan's grave situation, he had no secrets to keep from the reporter. 'It's not much use going on with him if he is constantly lame after galloping,' the old trainer told the journalist. 'If he was a moderate horse, or even a six-year-old, it might be wise to keep him going, but it can't be forgotten that he is only a four-year-old, and a young one at that. With a good spell, he might come back brand new.'

'Cardigan' telephoned Dangar that night at Rotherwood. This was the biggest story in racing, and he wanted the scoop from all corners. 'No risks will be taken with Peter Pan,' Dangar confirmed. 'When I see McGrath in two or three days I will then decide what is to be done, but I'm not the least hopeful that Peter will start this spring.' Ultimately, the decision was with Dangar. McGrath could advise all he wanted, and Dangar would listen, but it was Dangar who would make the final call. 'Cardigan' asked him about the repercussions of scratching the hot favourite from the Cup when early doubles had amounted to several thousands of pounds. Dangar was silent for a moment, for this was a sore point with him. 'I am sorry that racegoers throughout Australia should lose their money on my horse. But early backers take that risk,' Dangar said. 'And I am sure that they will agree with me when I say that the horse must be the first considered.'

'Cardigan' hung up the telephone. It was clear to him that owner and trainer were on the same page: Peter Pan would not race this season if he were at risk. The journalist thought back to 1931. In that year, he had made many calls like the one he had just made to Dangar, but back then they were to the connections of Phar Lap, venturing guesses as to whether the Red Terror would start in the Cup that year. Phar Lap had been allotted a massive 10st 10lb and no horse had carried that weight to victory over two miles. To 'Cardigan', it had seemed the owners had had little option but to run their horse, for responsibility to the public had completely taken over. Dangar, with his comparatively young colt, wasn't faced with such debts yet.

Peter Pan's immediate future was on ice throughout that Wednesday as McGrath waited for the owner to return from Rotherwood. Early on Thursday morning, Dangar left Sutton Forest in his Packard motorcar, arriving at his trainer's yard by eleven o'clock, and the two men spoke at length. Without rest, McGrath feared, Peter Pan was in danger of permanent muscle damage. As a five-year-old, he could come back and still reach the heights expected of him. As it had been all along with this colt, patience would be the key to his programme. Dangar agreed with that summation. His faith in his trainer was never better. At 12.35pm that afternoon, on Thursday 14 September, Rodney Dangar strode into the AJC offices at 6 Bligh Street, Sydney, and scratched his horse from all Sydney and Melbourne engagements that spring.

Down the length of the east coast, bookies celebrated. It was the biggest reap for the bag swingers in recent memory. At a conservative guess, some £7500 had gone into the ring on pre-post backing, about £5000 of that on Peter Pan alone. McGrath, like Dangar, was conscious of the public's disappointment. Peter Pan was the nation's favourite racehorse. The blond Adonis had oozed into the void left by Phar Lap the previous year, racegoers yearning to see him. He spiked attendance, thrilled the ladies, and to boot he was a brilliant racehorse. It was a huge disappointment to learn that he was out of all spring racing.

In the days that followed, McGrath made preparations for Peter's holiday. Dangar had wondered if the colt should return to Baroona, but in the end he would go back to Doonside. McGrath wished to visit the horse to check on his condition occasionally, and Baroona was too far away to do that with any frequency. For a week or two, Peter Pan was rested at Doncaster Avenue, until the float chugged up one morning to take him west. With a heavy heart, McGrath loaded the colt into the float, watched it trundle away, then counted down the days until 1934.

15

The rest of 1933

Late in October, on a still and stifling afternoon, three men sat on the verandah of the Bungarribee homestead at Doonside, where Peter Pan was spelling. They were Bungarribee master Thomas Russell Cleaver, the journalist 'Banjo' Paterson and Rodney Rouse Dangar. They sat clouded in cigarette smog. Without a breath of wind, the smell of smoke, sweat and livestock fouled the air.

'It was the wrong spot for them,' Dangar stated, dragging on his cigarette. 'It's too busy down there for such an experiment.' He was referring to Sydney's first traffic lights. The city's Transport Commission had installed the first 'electromatic vehicle-actuated street traffic controllers' at the intersection of Kent and Market streets, and at eleven o'clock on the Friday morning of 13 October 1933, the 'thinking machines', as the *Herald* had dubbed them, were switched on. Traffic jams had followed. 'All the traffic around there is deliveries between the docks,' Dangar added. Cleaver believed that was why it was a good spot for them. 'Banjo' Paterson said it was progress.

Australia had been inching away from the Depression since the turn of the year. By the last quarter of 1933, the number of unemployed unionists had fallen to 23 per cent, down from 26 per cent in the first quarter. In the coming November, the federal budget was being touted as the 'restoration budget', with Prime Minister Joseph Lyons even quoting the number of new telephone connections as proof of the buds of recovery. Yet nowhere was the advent of the good times more obvious than at the racetrack. The betting ring was alight with huge wagers and £100 notes, and happy days in the ring meant happy days in the stands. As long as there was money to bet, and people could bet it freely, the grandstands would fill, and fill they did. On 30 September, a week after Peter Pan had left for Doonside, an enormous crowd had flocked to Randwick for the first day of the AJC spring carnival to see Chatham win the Epsom again, Hall Mark the Derby, and Rogilla the weight-for-age Spring Stakes.

'I hear that Deputy Ruler might be coming your way,' Paterson said to Cleaver. There was little that occurred in racing that didn't get past Paterson's ears.

'I heard that too,' Cleaver replied dryly. Bungarribee was the most popular thoroughbred spelling property in Sydney, so Cleaver was well abreast of who was coming his way. Deputy Ruler, who had run second to Hall Mark in the Derby a few weeks prior, had been sold to Frank McGrath's friend Bill Pearson, and was due at Bungarribee soon.

'How much did Bill pay for him?' Cleaver asked. Dangar knew the answer, for McGrath had told him all about the transaction, but he didn't interject.

'Two thousand guineas,' Paterson responded, 'and he's worth every penny.'

Paterson was of the old-school type of racing man. He liked a well-bred three-year-old to be classically conformed, with a deep girth, broad hindquarters and a handsome head. He didn't think Peter Pan was nearly handsome enough. Dangar's colt was so different to every thoroughbred that had come before him it was almost disconcerting, especially because he was a winner. Though Paterson had vilified the colt often in his editorials, Dangar didn't hold it against him. The two men had long associations in horse racing, and anyway, the sport was full of opinions. Deputy Ruler, on the other hand, was Paterson's classic thoroughbred. He was a New Zealand colt by the upcoming English sire Chief Ruler, a son of The Tetrarch, and had the dam of an English Derby winner in his pedigree. He was also smooth-looking, the type of horse that Paterson enjoyed.

Thomas Cleaver's mind strayed through the past few months as the three men sat shrouded in the clinging heat and smoke, none of them speaking. He thought of the new young blood emerging in racing, like Deputy Ruler, and the blood that had passed, like Denis Boy. The Irish horse had visited Doonside on and off for many seasons. 'I suppose Denny Boy is getting along alright,' he said to Paterson and Dangar, not sure which one would have the more information on the horse. Denis Boy, when he had gone to auction in July, had been sold as a sire for 725 guineas. It was a mediocre price for such a horse. Top stallion prospects usually sold for at least a few thousand.

'I should suppose he's getting good mares,' Paterson said. He knew the stud where Denis Boy had gone to, and knew there was a fine band of broodmares there. The horse had joined two other imported stallions at Tatyoon Stud, the property of Sydney racing trainer William Booth, out west.

'Wasn't your trainer cut up about losing him Rodney?' Cleaver ventured.

'He was,' Dangar replied, nodding slowly. 'McGrath was very attached to that horse. I should say he expected more money for him in the sale ring.'

The three men chatted away, and the heat of the afternoon clung tight to Bungarribee. The oak, hibiscus and pine trees were still, and most of the horses dozed motionless. From the wide, round verandah of the homestead, Cleaver, Dangar and Paterson could see them, the Bungarribee paddocks falling away from the house before them. Peter Pan, easily spotted by his pale blond hair, rested in the shade, a statue but for the idle swish of his tail. The heat was working wonders for his joints, and there were no signs of scratchiness about him. Cleaver had noticed that even after gambolling around his paddock, lately the colt wasn't tentative on that near-shoulder. Dangar had visited on and off with his veterinarian Dr Stuart C. Pottie. Pottie came from one of the oldest animal practices in Sydney. His father had begun a veterinary clinic in Castlereagh Street mid-way through the last century, treating working horses and ponies. The family name was a deeply respected one around the city, and his services didn't come cheap, not that that mattered to Dangar. Pottie had checked Peter Pan's liver and kidney for damage, but the vet wasn't concerned at all. Come December, when McGrath proposed to bring Peter Pan back in, Pottie was convinced the colt would be right as rain.

The sun began to stretch away towards the Blue Mountains, and the city, to the east, beckoned Dangar and Paterson away from Doonside. They shook hands with Thomas Cleaver late in the afternoon, then left the western district in their motorcars, Dangar bound for Arlington. Not a week later, Rogilla won the Cox Plate, and after that, during Cup Week, that ominous three-year-old Hall Mark won the Melbourne Cup by a neck. The brilliant little son of Heroic had added the great two-miler to his Sires' Produce, Champagne, AJC and VRC Derby wins, and he joined the list of titans to be toppled next autumn.

The end of 1933 came quickly after that. The new year settled on Australia. Down in Melbourne, the *Argus* was still waiting for prosperity, which it claimed had been just around the corner this time the previous year. In the picture houses, a Jean Harlow film began to screen. *Blond Bombshell,* the story of a sexpot film star, had nothing to do with Peter Pan, but in a few decades time, the nickname would be bestowed upon him.

16

'Peter Pan is only one horse, not two or three'

The rain began to fall on the last day of January, lazy at first, in slow, straight tumbles. By 2 February 1934 it was cyclonic, thumping Sydney with a fury not seen in years. All around the city and its suburbs, motorcars lay strewn by the kerbsides, flooded and abandoned. In the harbour, ships were dragging their anchors out of cove, and in Randwick, the Chisholm stables on King Street, where Peter Pan's mother had been sold to Dangar in 1925, were hit with winds so severe they were partly demolished. The company could be forgiven for thinking the gods were against it. H. Chisholm & Co. had suffered during the Depression. Competition from Inglis had been relentless. Averages were down, costs were up, and top prices were significantly lower than those on Inglis's block. A few days after the storm, as H. Chisholm & Co. picked up its fallen bits of building and its dignity, R.M. Chisholm, the company's principal, announced that Inglis had purchased his business. The 1934 yearling sales would be the last time young thoroughbreds would sell at King Street, Randwick.

Not so far away, on Doncaster Avenue, Peter Pan was back in work after nearly 10 months since his last race start. McGrath had brought him in from Doonside at the beginning of December, and when he'd stepped off the float the trainer was agape at how much the horse had filled out. Gone were the traces of boyhood, replaced instead with the masculine lines of a mature racehorse. He had smooth, solid shoulders and a short, muscly neck. His barrel was a perfect, rounded engine, and his hindquarters, though not mammoth like Phar Lap's had been, fit him perfectly. He was as straight as organ flutes, 'a magnificent stamp of the thoroughbred', so said the *Sydney Morning Herald.*

McGrath kept him off the early tracks until well into February, so for the first two months Peter cantered after breakfast, usually unhurried and usually rugged. McGrath was taking no chances with him. He wasn't about to rush. The trainer wanted to strum the benefits of seven months at grass, and so Peter sauntered around Randwick until the day after the big February storm, when he was floated to Rosebery and sent against the clock for the first time. The result wasn't a quick one, but the horse pulled up sound, and that was all McGrath was looking for right now.

Peter Pan had returned to racing halfway through his four-year-old year, for the autumn season. As was usual, the programmes ahead of the best horses were a constant point of discussion. Dangar had declared his horse would not start in the Sydney Cup, and also that Peter would not head south for the autumn events in Melbourne. He would concentrate, as he had done in 1933, on the Sydney purses. But McGrath was sending instead his three-year-olds Deputy Ruler and Australia Fair, and in the first week of February, following Peter Pan's Rosebery trial, McGrath shuttled south for a few weeks, leaving his champion's preparation in Maurice McGrath's hands.

Peter was progressing nicely. He had shown only a little trouble since coming back from Doonside, and that was late in January when signs of the muscular issues sprang up one morning. Dangar had immediately called in Dr Stuart Pottie, who diagnosed the horse with too liberal a supply of uric acid in his blood. Pottie declared that aside from this minor incident the horse was quite well, and he was right. The following day, Peter Pan was lumbering around the cinder track after breakfast, not a care in the world. The press was watching his every step. In early February, with Rogilla, Silver Scorn, Chatham and Kuvera back on the tracks, scrutiny came thick, fast and often. 'Many at Randwick are definite in their opinion that Mr Dangar's horse won't be any devastating force this autumn,' said the *Sportsman*. 'Some go as far as to say that the mighty blond will never survive another preparation.' After such a long absence, probability was stacked against a return to form.

With McGrath still in Melbourne by the second week of February, Peter Pan's work was stepped up. Having furnished into a massive racehorse, fully 17 hands, Peter Pan was carving the turf as he had never done before. Though he was an elastic galloper, his size now meant he hit the track harder and deeper, much more than half a tonne of horseflesh digging with every stride, and for a horse with muscular troubles, there was always the worry he would jar himself. Each morning after track gallops, George Phillips rubbed a camphor-block solution into Peter Pan's near shoulder, and he was endlessly rugged. McGrath was far from thinking that his horse was a spent force, but his team worked ceaselessly to make sure he wouldn't be.

After the wet start to the month, showers began again on 18 February. The following day, a Monday, they were twice as heavy, and on Tuesday, when the McGrath team stepped onto the track before breakfast, a gale was blowing down the home straight, sending everything in its path sideways. On Wednesday conditions were torrential, and on Thursday every track on Randwick Racecourse was waterlogged. Over four-and-a-half inches of rain sat like an inland sea on the course proper, and McGrath, learning of all this from Melbourne, was worried. It was damp, miserable spells like this that leaked into Peter Pan's muscles and ruined him. He was sent to Rosebery's famous holding track for the rest of the week as McGrath made his way back to Sydney.

Dangar and McGrath had already conferred on Peter's programme for the season, and as the St Leger had been their task last autumn, so this year it would be the King's Cup, due to be run on the last Saturday of the AJC meeting, on 7 April. Upheld as one of the plums of the turf calendar, the King's Cup was held in a different capital city every year, with a £2000 purse and a £100 gold cup, the latter a personal gift from the affable King George V. The race was run over a mile and a half, with conditions stating that the highest weight be 9st 5lb and the lowest not less than 7st. Since its inauguration in 1927, when it was run at Flemington, the King's Cup had been staged at Randwick, Eagle Farm (in Brisbane), Perth, Morphetville (in South Australia) and Hobart. It had also been won by such names as Limerick, Valparaiso, Phar Lap, Second Wind and, in 1933, Kuvera.

The attraction of the race was not just its illustrious sponsorship. Once the weights were declared, no horse could be penalised thereafter, which meant that if an entrant were to win the Doncaster or the Sydney Cup between the declaration of weights and raceday, there would be no penalty. The horse would run with the weight it had been allotted, making the contest an appealing proposition, even for the horses less fit to win it. For Rodney Dangar, the King's Cup was a jewel in the racing crown. Its very name bespoke English significance, and it was, being a gift from the very King himself. Peter pan's owner wanted the trophy more than anything, to look at it at Arlington, to say his homebred racehorse was recognised by king and country.

Peter's path to the King's Cup would begin with the City Tattersall's Club Randwick Stakes on 3 March, the race he had won when first up the previous year.

Two weeks later, he would contest the Rawson Stakes at Rosehill, in which he had gotten tangled in the strands in 1933, and then he would race in the Chipping Norton Plate at Warwick Farm on 24 March. These three lead-in races were the ideal prep for the AJC autumn carnival, in which Peter was due to contest the Autumn Plate on 31 March, the Cumberland Plate four days later, and the King's Cup on the final day, 7 April. All in all, McGrath had engaged his champion in six races, or just under eight and a half miles in five weeks.

By the end of February, the rain had cleared and March approached with the promise of balmy weather. On the last Saturday in February, both Peter Pan and Chatham ran exhibition gallops between races at Rosebery, both running six furlongs unextended, with Peter shading half a second off Chatham's time. Though Chatham was slower, comments suggested the champion miler was a little more forward in condition than Peter Pan. 'Both are good first up,' suggested 'Pilot', 'but this time Chatham may be a little better than Peter Pan.' The two horses would meet for the first time in the Randwick Stakes.

***

A little after 2.20pm on Saturday 3 March, Peter Pan strode into the mounting yard for the Randwick Stakes like he'd never left it. His aloof character had only grown to support his size, and the hundreds of racegoers that clamoured around the rails were agog, wondering how a horse could grow so much in a year. Peter Pan had always been tall, but had he been quite so massive? He would have been the centre of attention were it not for the other horses parading with him. The Randwick Stakes had attracted a small but stellar line-up. Chatham was top weight with 9st 1lb; Peter Pan was next with 1lb less; Lough Neagh, with a few races already into him, had 8st 12lb; Silver Scorn was next with 8st 11lb; and Blixten, a three-year-old and winner of the Batman Stakes at Flemington the prevous spring, had 8st 1lb. 'There are only five acceptors,' wrote the *Telegraph,* 'but what a field.'

Nearly all the Sydney newspapers had tipped Chatham to win. He had the advantage of running over his ideal distance of a mile, he was a brilliant horse first up, and he wasn't battling with an 11-month absence, as was Peter Pan. The ring agreed in theory, but the money still came for Peter Pan. Though Chatham was favourite at 5/4 on, Peter Pan had been backed into 3s, with Lough Neagh touching 7/2. No one wanted anything to do with Silver Scorn, the once-touted champion of New Zealand, and Blixten could be had at 20/1.

McGrath wasn't sure what to expect of Peter Pan. He was just such a horse that could surprise everyone, but the trainer wasn't hopeful. He told Dangar that his only expectations should be that Peter pulls up sound. McGrath had engaged Darcy Webb for the ride, owing to all the top Sydney jockeys being in Melbourne. Webb was an ex-Queensland hoop, and on moving south many years before had been connected to Mick Polson, Jim Pike's golfing companion, for a time. He had ridden Lough Neagh to several wins over the preceding few years, and was a capable horseman. McGrath instructed the jockey not to push Peter Pan out during the Randwick Stakes. He was more interested in how the horse would pull up than how he would run.

A little before 2.40pm, Phillips legged Darcy Webb into the saddle and the pair cantered to the mile start of the weight-for-age event. In the grandstands, 24,000 racegoers bubbled, waiting for the amplifiers to come to life to tell them the story of the race. The five horses walked in a line towards Jack Gaxieu's tape, and halted momentarily before it. Peter Pan, having not lined up since his AJC Plate victory the previous April, was shuffled forward by Darcy Webb, the jockey ever ready for a lazy start. But when the tape sprang up, the son of Pantheon leaped away, and the 1934 Randwick Stakes was on.

After the initial scurry of the jump the five horses settled into a slow lumbering stride. For a length or two out of the mile chute they moved in slow unison, until jockey Stan Davidson sent Chatham forward, and the crack miler lunged ahead from the pack, with Lough Neagh urged to go with him. By the time the field had run a furlong, Chatham had shot away with Lough Neagh on his heels, and several lengths separated the two leaders from Peter Pan, Silver Scorn and Blixten.

Darcy Webb sat quietly on Peter Pan, heeding McGrath's words not to bustle the four-year-old. Peter Pan was bowling along easily, perhaps not as fit or free as Webb would like him to be racing against Chatham, but he wasn't tardy. They tracked the leaders into the first turn, with Lough Neagh getting to within a neck of the sprinting Chatham. As they passed the half-mile, Chatham was getting faster, inching away from the persistent Lough Neagh, and three lengths back came Peter Pan, with Blixten close by and Silver Scorn last of all. Approaching the home turn, the race was in no doubt. Chatham was running a merry mile, galloping down the straight all on his own. Several lengths behind, Lough Neagh was furiously ridden, with Peter Pan breathing down his neck and Blixten not far behind.

Webb had shortened his reins and asked for some effort from Peter, and for several strides the horse obliged. His great elastic bounds carried him up to Lough Neagh, and he was within a breath of second place. But Chatham was destroying the last four furlongs in 47 seconds, and the sting was too much for the unfit Peter Pan. He faded, and Webb didn't push him as Lough Neagh plugged on into second place. As Chatham bolted over the line, a dazzling four lengths to Lough Neagh, Blixten shaved a length off Peter Pan's best effort and ran into third, with

Peter a close fourth, and Silver Scorn a bedraggled last.

The cheers around Randwick were wondrous. The great Chatham had run within a quarter of a second of Winooka's mile record, and it was his eighth win of the 1933–34 season, his sixteenth overall. He had cost 650 guineas as a yearling back in 1929, and this afternoon was just shy of £12,000 in winnings. He deserved every cheer and accolade that came his way. As Peter Pan returned to scale, McGrath was waiting with Dangar and Phillips. The little group hardly looked deflated. None had been interested in winning the race, as McGrath had made it very clear that the Randwick Stakes was simply a stern test of soundness. If Peter Pan returned from the race clean, if there were no sign of tension or soreness in that shoulder, it would be cause for cheer. So when Darcy Webb stripped the saddle from Peter's back, and McGrath ran his hands all over the big chestnut and emerged smiling, the little group congratulated itself. Their racehorse was on song again.

This time, the majority of the newspapers seemed to understand the wisdom of Peter Pan's loss, and they spared him the whipping they had dished out the previous year. But a few hardnoses still managed to decry the effort. Words to the effect of 'the passing of a great racehorse' were heard in abject circles, but surprisingly, the usually tepid 'Banjo' Paterson, so far pleased to jump on the wagon of criticism, leapt to Peter's defence. 'Peter Pan is only one horse, not two or three,' he wrote in the *Sydney Mail,* 'and yet, after proving himself a stayer in his last Melbourne Cup, etc, he is expected to come out as another horse altogether and beat Australia's best miler over a mile when half fit.' Paterson's colleague 'Musket' thought similarly: 'Peter Pan is essentially a stayer and, even when thoroughly wound up, too lazy to have any prospects of success against Chatham over a mile. But when the distance is two miles, Peter Pan will be seen to more advantage.'

Down in Melbourne, Jim Pike learned of the result and was both vindicated and surprised. The veteran hoop had known that Chatham would make a good show, and had said so all along. But of Peter Pan, he was a little startled the champion had been beaten so conclusively. 'I was surprised at that,' he told the *Sportsman,* 'though I didn't give him much chance of beating Chatham. I didn't think he was quite forward enough to win at a mile just yet.' Responding to rumours that Darcy Webb was to replace Pike as Peter's regular pilot, a confusion that had arisen in the wake of Pike's commitment to Chatham, the jockey was his usual candid self. 'I'll ride Peter Pan in all of his races, even if he and Chatham meet,' he stated. 'But in any race where Chatham is engaged and Peter Pan is not running, I'll be on Chatham.'

The confusion concerning the jockeys was only just beginning, but immediately after the Randwick Stakes, at least, there was no unrest between the camps. Both Chatham and Peter Pan returned to work, with McGrath stepping up the ante. The test of soundness was now behind Peter, and the trainer wanted the puppy fat off his horse by the running of the Rawson Stakes in two Saturdays' time.

The following week, Dangar stood with McGrath nearly every morning, watching his horse rehabilitate into a dashing thoroughbred. The two men saw him wind up seven furlongs in 1.33, then six furlongs the following morning in 1.17 1/4, the best time of the morning. Peter Pan had worked solid, grinding drills for two weeks straight now. He was on his toes, sharp and athletic though not entirely fit, and McGrath was confident that in the Rawson Stakes, Peter Pan would make a better fight of things.

The race was emerging into a finer battle than the Randwick Stakes had been. Again the field was small, with only five acceptors. But along with Peter Pan, Chatham, Lough Neagh and Blixten, Rogilla had thrown his name into the fray, and the nine-furlong weight-for-age event was fast becoming the showdown of the year. Far from Peter Pan being considered, it was the meeting of Rogilla and Chatham that was causing all the spin, though most considered Chatham a sure thing. None thought that Peter Pan would factor, let alone win. 'The Melbourne Cup winner is not regarded as a danger,' stated the *Sportsman.* 'Still, he's a lazy sort of codger who can always shape a ton better with the colours up than in private.'

The *Sportsman* was more correct than it knew. Peter Pan, a true staying type, preferred not to set the tracks alight during trackwork. Nor did he need to. From day one, McGrath had learned the horse appreciated short, sharp work often. He was not an Amounis who would work all day long, so it helped that he was a light horse that never carried much fat. In addition, Peter Pan was opinionated. If he disapproved of how he was being handled, he was quick to let everyone know. When Peter Pan was stroppy, man and beast alike knew it, or whichever one was nearer at the time. Only George Phillips seemed to avoid the five-year-old's temper.

By the end of the week, the jockey debacle was just beginning. Though Jim Pike had stated he would ride Peter Pan in any race in which Chatham was also engaged, by Thursday he had changed his mind. Sydney's top hoop was as sure as everyone that Chatham had a chance where Peter Pan had none, and Pike approached Dangar to be relieved of his commitment. Any man of sound mind would agree that Chatham had a better chance than Peter Pan right now, Dangar thought. This was sport, and Pike made his living from it. Dangar would not stand in his favourite rider's way. So, disappointed but gracious, Dangar wished Pike the best of luck with Chatham. Within hours, Webb was reinstated for Peter Pan.

Pike's switch fell right onto the betting ring. Chatham was installed an odds-on favourite for the Rawson Stakes, with Rogilla fetching 3/1, and incredibly, Peter Pan and Lough Neagh could be found at

20s. But a few punters with good memories were wary. They recalled that the Rawson was typically a graveyard for favourites. Such had been the case the previous year with Peter Pan, and they wondered if such would be the case with Chatham. But neither Pike, nor Chatham's trainer Fred Williams, nor many others, were concerned, and the money kept coming. Chatham was carrying all the coin at 9/2 on, and there wasn't a soul in the state that thought he didn't deserve it.

***

Saturday was St Patrick's Day in Sydney, and the Rawson Stakes was due off at 3.10pm. It was a perfect autumn day, the kind that made the harbour city famous. Judging by the weather, racegoers would be out en masse this afternoon, eager to witness the clash of the weight-for-agers. Chatham had the heaviest burden of 9st 2lb. Peter Pan was next with 9st, with Rogilla and Lough Neagh both shouldering 8st 13lb, and Blixten, the youngest, with 8st 4lb. With Darcy Webb on Peter, and Pike piloting Chatham, Rogilla had his usual steely partner in Darby Munro, with Edwin Tanwan on Lough Neagh, and Maurice McCarten riding Blixten. There was no other race on the card that had attracted such stout competition.

McGrath had floated Peter Pan and Deputy Ruler to Rosehill in the morning. His other entrants that day, Cid and Confab, were in tow. Deputy Ruler was contesting the Three-Year-Old Handicap at 1.40pm, the first race on the card, and when Dangar called on his trainer shortly after arriving, McGrath was preparing the Kiwi colt in the stalls. Beside him, Peter Pan chewed on his lead shank. Dangar noticed that McGrath was a little on edge. The trainer was fussing with tack, and wasn't much interested in his top owner's presence. There was much significance tied to Peter and Deputy today, as both had something to prove – Peter Pan that he was back to form, and Deputy Ruler that he had form at all. Dangar decided to leave the trainer to his business, and returned to the saddling paddock where a large crowd was milling in the sunshine.

The Rosehill Racing Club had attracted 8000 guests, not including the jockeys, trainers, press and members who had strolled in for free. It was the largest attendance the club could boast in years, for this was a small, independent racetrack that didn't have the bankroll of the AJC. The fact that it was surviving the Depression at all was a minor miracle. At 1.40pm, Frank McGrath could only watch as Deputy Ruler ran fourth in the Three-Year-Old Handicap, and it aggravated the trainer's concerns that the horse was a lot of hot air.

Cid also finished out of the placings, and as the Rawson Stakes approached, McGrath got to wondering if today would be Peter Pan's day. He knew the horse was fit enough to win, but it might take more than one race to bring him back after almost a year off.

There was also the small mountain of Chatham and Rogilla. McGrath sent Peter into the saddling paddock shortly before three o'clock. The horse looked well, and vastly fitter since the City Tattersall's meeting. Chatham, with his brawny, sprinter-like brown frame, attracted many compliments, and the big, rangy gelding, Rogilla, looked racing fit. Lough Neagh, also, looked hard as tack. They left the paddock in that order of fancy – Chatham was 3/1 odds on, Rogilla 3/1 against, and 20 bar those.

Pike drew Chatham to the rails for the jump. On the outside of him was Rogilla, with the remaining three on his outside. The nine-furlong start meant the field had a short run into the first turn, but Webb wasn't worried about his outside draw. The field was small, and he thought the tactics for each horse obvious – Rogilla would come from behind, Chatham would go to the front, and the others would be somewhere in between. The five horses walked to the barrier and halted before it, Rogilla making his usual fuss before deciding to behave. Then the tape went up and the Rawson Stakes began.

Chatham and Rogilla were the fastest away from the line, and the two horses took the lead in the early stages. But before they had run a furlong, Munro took a hold of Rogilla, and the big gelding fell back through the field to second-last. With a furlong travelled, Chatham was leading with Lough Neagh on his flanks, and four lengths back Peter Pan led the trailing division, with Rogilla close by and Blixten last.

Webb could feel Peter galloping smoothly, and the big chestnut took the first turn with easy strides. Ahead of them, the gap was opening up as Lough Neagh drew away with Chatham, and down the back-stretch the two horses were six lengths clear of Peter Pan, Rogilla and Blixten, and neither was letting up. Lough Neagh was out to crack the champion miler, and he was doing a good job. They blazed out of the backstretch together, but Peter Pan began to close the daylight. With four furlongs to go, he had moved to within four lengths, with Rogilla in his slipstream. Peter had his eye on the leaders now, and was reaching into the turf to close the gap. With every stride he carried Darcy Webb closer, and as they approached the home turn they heard the crowds hollering for competition. Jim Pike heard it too, and he asked Chatham to go on.

Webb saw Pike start to ride, and expected the dark bay Chatham to streak away into the sunset. For a moment he was worried, for the leaders still had a good three lengths on the field, but to his surprise Chatham had nothing. Though Pike was asking, his mount could not shake Lough Neagh, and cheers mellowed into confusion. The odds-on favourite looked beaten.

Lough Neagh belted into the home turn a clear neck in front of Chatham, and still three lengths away, Webb was winding up Peter Pan. The big chestnut had begun to fly by the time he hit the turn, and Webb expected a clear run to the leaders. But as Peter

Pan leaned into the home turn, Rogilla came around him, and Munro was riding the gelding so close that suddenly Peter was pocketed. Webb had no room to ride his horse out, and Rogilla slammed right into Peter Pan, knocking the chestnut onto the running rail for the third time in his life. The collision wheeled Peter Pan sideways. For an ugly moment, he spun around to face the grandstands. But Rogilla had shot away and left him some room to right himself, and Webb stood in his irons to help his horse, balancing them both with some quick horsemanship. Ahead of him, Rogilla was punching away from Lough Neagh and Chatham.

The scrimmage had knocked the whip out of Webb's hand, and now he was left with a big, unbalanced racehorse and nothing but hands, heels and hope. But Webb knew that Peter Pan was a monster in a finish, and he began to ride for his life, urging and hollering the horse forward. Peter Pan had lost many lengths, and only Blixten was behind him, but the big chestnut roared to life. He began to work those long, elastic legs, and within a furlong he had passed Chatham and was half a length past Lough Neagh. Rogilla was only ahead by another length, and Peter Pan was just getting into top gear. He inched into the gelding's lead, breathing on his hindquarters, then his flanks. The winning post came too soon. Rogilla flashed past the judge three-quarters of a length ahead of Peter Pan, in the trackrecord time of 1:50 1/2.

Everyone at Rosehill was on their feet. The gallant Rogilla had lifted Chatham's crown, and once again the Rawson Stakes had dealt its expensive hand. The big bettors that had lain at odds-on fell around the racecourse like men without legs, and Fred Williams, Chatham's trainer, looked more than disappointed when he greeted his horse back to the paddock. Jim Pike, who had deserted Peter to ride Chatham, was stone-faced. Frank McGrath and Rodney Dangar were ecstatic. McGrath, not a man to give smiles away, was beaming. He had seen the buffeting in the home turn, and was convinced that without it, Peter would have beaten Rogilla. There was no doubt in his mind now that the son of Pantheon was back to form.

The horses trotted back to scale, and though Webb hadn't lodged any protest, most racegoers at Rosehill waited for the flags to be hoisted. There was no doubt that the bump Peter received on the home turn had cost him many lengths; more lengths, in fact, than he had lost by. There was also no doubt that if Webb so desired one, a protest would be well warranted. Rogilla had served Peter Pan serious interference, and to prove it, Peter had come back to scale with a huge white stain on his offside, just above his stifle. He had given the running rail enough of a greeting to peel its paint.

The stewards questioned Webb about the incident. 'Darby Munro had me pocketed, and I couldn't get out,' he responded to the inquiry. 'Otherwise I think Peter Pan would have won it.' He was right. Peter was travelling much faster than Rogilla when they crossed the line, and only for the interference would have won easily. But Dangar wouldn't hear of an objection. He was not the sort of sportsman to win a race on protest, preferring to win without favours. When the weight flag went up and the result was official, there was no quibble to be heard over his horse's second place.

For half an hour after the race, McGrath and Dangar watched Peter Pan closely for any signs that the run had undone him. On the contrary, the horse cooled off fresh as cut grass, and by the time McGrath was readying Confab for the last race of the day, Peter Pan was in splendid order, relaxed and supple and grappling with his hay. 'Those proposing to hold a wake over Peter Pan had better put it off, hadn't they,' McGrath told a small posse of journalists. That was all the scribes needed for their stories the following day.

McGrath packed up his horses and sent them back to Kensington, and the weight-for-age order had been reinstated in Sydney. Rogilla and Peter Pan were back at the top of reckoning. Rogilla's victory had been a popular one. The white-faced gelding was a likeable, honest racehorse that had known adversity. During his summer spell, he had had surgery on his right eye that had rendered him half blind. Left in a stall in a veterinary hospital for weeks, he had been unable to lie down, move around or exercise for fear of knocking the stitches, so his return to form was all the more impressive. In fact, there were no two horses more closely matched in heart than Rogilla and Peter Pan. They were fast becoming horse racing's greatest rivalry.

***

Rogilla had met Peter Pan on several occasions now, but while his record at the middle distances was good, he had never beaten the Pantheon horse when they had travelled over two miles or more. Peter Pan was an immensely superior stayer, but Les Haigh, lessee-trainer of Rogilla, was emphatic that over a mile and a half there was nothing between the two horses. He blurted it to anyone who would listen. Nevertheless, Cliff Graves stated the obvious. 'At three years, Peter Pan was Rogilla's complete master,' he wrote in the *Referee.* 'Following last Saturday's contest when Rogilla, after impeding Peter Pan's progress, beat him by only three-quarters of a length, there would be many punters who would turn eagerly to Peter Pan even if Rogilla opposed him.'

Truth had telephoned Dangar on Saturday night to gather his feelings on Peter Pan's effort. 'It was a splendid performance in my opinion, in view of the fact that, the Randwick Stakes aside, he had not had a run for practically 12 months.' Dangar confirmed that Peter would run in the Chipping Norton Plate the following week, and said that with ordinary luck the champion would win the King's Cup on 7 April. 'The bookmakers are hardly likely to be as liberal as they were today,' he added. 'They laid a remarkable price about a horse who might have won the Rawson Stakes but for being pocketed.' Though Dangar wasn't a betting man, as many of the respectable squattocracy weren't, the absurdity of Peter's 20/1 price hadn't escaped even him.

The Rawson Stakes had netted Peter Pan £80, which pushed his winnings to £14,298. It was impossible not to imagine what he would have won by now if he'd raced outside of the Depression, or if he hadn't been sidelined the previous spring. Even with stakes improving in response to the slow climb out of recession, prizes were still a shadow of what Pantheon, Spearfelt and Windbag had competed for through the 1920s. Nevertheless, it wasn't about the money for Rodney Dangar. Peter Pan's career wasn't about toppling Phar Lap as the highest money-earner. Dangar was selecting races for their integrity and prestige. These were the prizes he wanted on his mantelpiece. The St Leger had been one, and the King's Cup was another. The biggest one – the Melbourne Cup – was already in the bag, but would it be a wild dream to chase another?

Entries for the 1934 Melbourne Cup were due on 5 June. With each nomination came a £2 fee. Not only had the VRC returned the Cup to its pre-Depression value of £10,000, but this year the Cup was a centenary celebration. Melbourne was recognising its 100th year of settlement, and the Duke of Gloucester – the very single, very likeable Prince Henry, third son of the King – was due to share in the festivities. Word was out that the Duke would present the Melbourne Cup trophy to the winning owner, and that a number of races were to be staged in his honour at Flemington and Randwick alike. The Duke's involvement made the Cup all the more enticing for Rodney Dangar.

With fewer and fewer concerns that Peter Pan would succumb to soreness, McGrath set about with fast work for the Chipping Norton the following week. His goal was to have Peter rippling by the start of the AJC meeting. On Monday morning, in showery conditions, he sent the chestnut seven furlongs around the course proper at Randwick, and on Tuesday morning a similar task. With the flags out 50 feet and a strong wind pushing him home, Peter Pan ran the seven furlongs in 1:33. On Thursday, he bettered that by four seconds. Galloping with Deputy Ruler, Peter Pan clocked 1.29 3/4 for the distance, powering so far clear of his companion that the Deputy was eased up. Peter had run sectionals of 24 seconds, 36 1/2 seconds, 49 1/2, 1:03, and 1:15 3/4, which wasn't far off the perfect 12 seconds to the furlong. 'Peter Pan stretched out in great style,' commented the *Sportsman.* 'He is now not far from his absolute best.'

With his Rawson Stakes effort, and the fetching track times during the week, Peter Pan was installed as favourite for the Chipping Norton Plate. Privately, Dangar held concerns that the short straight at Warwick Farm would work against him, but there was nothing to suggest the horse couldn't overcome that. Peter Pan had opened his winning account at the Farm back in 1932, and the Chipping Norton was a good race to continue on his way. It was a weight-for-age contest over a mile and a quarter, and a real notch in the belt of racing folk, but this time Chatham and Rogilla would be absent. Chatham was being rested for the Doncaster the following Saturday, and Rogilla was in the shorter, easier Liverpool Handicap.

Nevertheless, the Chipping Norton had attracted an impressive roster. Outside of Peter Pan there was Lough Neagh, Oro, Silver Scorn and Peter Jackson. Blixten was also trying his luck again. 'The hero of the 1932 Melbourne Cup should return to the list of winners at Warwick Farm,' predicted the *Telegraph.* But should and would were two very different matters.

***

On the Saturday morning McGrath floated four horses to Warwick Farm – Peter Pan, Lightning March, Confab and Australia Fair. In an effort to attract bigger fields, the AJC had announced free float-transport to the Farm, which didn't affect Frank McGrath so much, but for the smaller trainers it was welcome news. The fields at the western track had always been small, due to the expense of shipping three and four horses nearly 20 miles out of Sydney and back. Traditionally, the smaller trainers had only sent the better members of their teams, but now they could afford to send more. As a result, the fields for Chipping Norton Plate Day were swollen.

Peter Pan's race was due off at 3.15pm, and just before three o'clock he stepped into the saddling paddock. The AJC farrier, Ted McClenahan, came over to check his shoes. A loaded shoe, which resembled a regular racing plate except that it contained fillings of lead, had been found at Moorefield racetrack earlier in the week. Loaded shoes were used to 'pull' a horse in a race, or slow him down to prevent him winning, and it was a serious find. The AJC had since introduced a mandatory inspection of all horses' shoes before going to post. It was a small step to reducing the skulduggery that was rampant in horse racing, and the few seconds of inspection were a welcome inconvenience. Racing would be cleaner for it, so no one complained.

Jim Pike was back on board for the Chipping Norton Plate, and he and Peter Pan were equal second in the weights with Oro at 9st. Closing Time, a five-year-old, carried top weight of 9st 3lb, while Silver Scorn and Lough Neagh each had 8st 13lb. 'Keep up with Closing Time,' McGrath instructed Pike as he legged the jockey into the saddle. 'He could steal a real big break in the early part. Stay within three or four lengths of him when you settle down.' Pike nodded, and they strode away from the trainer.

As George Phillips led Peter Pan out of the enclosure and towards the course proper, there was nothing to suggest the ring was wrong in quoting the chestnut at even money. He cantered down to the start in his usual relaxed state of mind. He looked fit and athletic, and the only concern was the track itself. Warwick Farm, with its egg-shaped circumference and short straight, was not ideal for a long striding, dyed-in-the-wool stayer like Peter Pan.

There were no shenanigans as the horses waited for the barrier to rise, and when it did they set off in smart order. Closing Time, the little horse with the big turn of foot, jumped fastest, and he led the field out of the straight. The horses ran into the first turn at an almighty clip, Closing Time ensuring there was no loafing to be had. For a moment, Lough Neagh was galloping next, but almost immediately, Peter Pan barged his way into second. The big chestnut had no patience today, and he hauled Jim Pike into the leading division, testing the old jockey's shoulders. Unable to hold him back, and reasoning this was how McGrath wanted it, Pike let him have his way, and they bounded past the mile-post in that order – Closing Time two lengths ahead, Peter Pan second, with Silver Scorn a neck away in third. Lough Neagh was leading the trailers.

Up in the grandstand, Frank McGrath yelled out in temper that Peter Pan was so far up on the pace. On a small, tight-turning track like the Farm, a big stayer had to be ridden right if he was to sustain a run, and at the moment Peter Pan was too close to the front. Yes, McGrath had told Pike to ride him three or four off Closing Time, but here was Closing Time bleating out the sectionals, and in the lead. What was Pike doing? But the jockey was as surprised as anyone to find himself on Closing Time's heels, and Peter Pan was not in a negotiating mood. The big chestnut had wrestled for his head since the jump, so Pike decided to let Peter Pan run his own race.

The field belted past the half-mile, and Peter had climbed to within half a length of Closing Time, while Lough Neagh crept past Silver Scorn into third, and the Kiwi mare galloped on in fourth. Closing Time had scorched the sectionals, but at the turn for home Silver Scorn came around Peter Pan and went after Lough Neagh and the leader. When Pike asked Peter Pan to go too, the chestnut came up empty. He had wasted precious fitness in the furious opening stages. Silver Scorn had run past him like he was standing still. In a matter of strides, she picked off Closing Time and galloped into the straight by herself.

In the short run for home, Closing Time managed to stick into second, with the plucky Blixten running third, and then a sorry line of superior racehorses followed, Peter Pan ambling home in sixth, Oro seventh, and Lough Neagh – the second-best horse in the race after Peter – landing the booby prize. As the horses passed the judge one after another, the jeers, hoots and whistles of an angry mob erupted. Pike couldn't remember a more hostile crowd as he trotted Peter Pan back to scale, and it was all directed at the winner. Racegoers waved their arms at Silver Scorn and launched their ticket stubs over the rails at the mare that had reversed her form so miraculously. She had cost punters thousands, and the Warwick Farm patrons felt cheated.

Pike couldn't explain Peter Pan's terrible showing, but he knew that he should have ridden the horse a better race. It was a big mistake allowing him to bowl along on top of the hot pace, despite the trainer's orders, for Peter Pan didn't have a sprinter's turn of foot. After searing through the first seven furlongs, he'd had nothing in the tank for the final three, and that was typical for a true stayer like Peter. Thankfully, the big chestnut wasn't the only failure. Lough Neagh had run dead last, and there was no explaining that. But in the minutes after the Chipping Norton Plate, the crowd had words only for Silver Scorn, and they weren't kind.

George Phillips, embarrassed, led Peter Pan out of the paddock as quickly as he could. The jeers and hollers continued, and back at the stalls McGrath vetted his charge for any signs of soreness or weakness. He was looking for anything physical that could explain Peter's performance, but he knew well that he would find nothing. It was as simple as sin what had happened: Peter Pan had been too close to the pace to win. Pike had followed McGrath's orders without interpreting the variables, and had reasoned that even so far in front in the early stages he would have steam enough to come home. It was a rare error for both trainer and jockey to make.

By the end of the day, when the crowd had settled down and remembered that Peter Pan hadn't won, rumours began to drip that McGrath's moke was lame. Racegoers seemed unable to believe that the horse who had shown such promise in the Rawson Stakes had finished no better than sixth, and the press hovered over McGrath, waiting for an explanation. The trainer wasn't about to lambast Pike, for he knew that Peter had done himself no favours in the way he had pulled. Anyway, Pike had been following orders. McGrath was also not a man to savage the good name of another, so he merely stated that Peter's plans to run in the Autumn Plate the following Saturday still stood, and he left it at that. The big fish were waiting next weekend.

17

A week in 1934

It was Tuesday morning, 27 March, three days after the Chipping Norton. Frank McGrath stood by the rails at Rosebery, his overcoat buttoned up and a stopwatch in his right hand. The racecourse was quiet, local strings not due for another 20 minutes or so, and the old trainer peered into the grey light of morning. Somewhere behind him he could hear the trundle of delivery trucks on Gardeners Road. The coolness of the night stuck close to the track, and rain since yesterday had left it squelching. Still, it was in better tick than Randwick, although the two racehorses that had shot off from the seven furlongs didn't seem to notice. They were Deputy Ruler and Peter Pan.

McGrath held up his field glasses and watched them run. They were two streaking figures at the other end of the track, wide out on the course proper and running around the hurdles. Deputy Ruler was on the inside of Peter Pan, who was heavily shod and carrying a heavier rider, and they mowed into the sectionals, disappearing around the bends like two mad hares. Before McGrath knew it, they had burst into earshot. The two horses shattered the morning silence with their breaths and hooves, puncturing the air that hung over the home straight.

McGrath dropped his glasses to watch the last two furlongs up the straight, and Peter Pan spurted into view. The blond champion had left the Deputy trailing, and with big, clean, beautiful gulps of wind he plundered the straight with reckless abandon. Click. McGrath snapped his watch to a stop as Peter shot past him, and he let out a breath. One minute and 30 seconds, or the best damn seven furlongs that had been seen at Rosebery for years.

Uneasiness had settled on McGrath since Peter Pan's Chipping Norton. 'I don't want to think about it anymore, thank you gentlemen,' he'd said to a posse of reporters on Sunday morning, waving them away with a frosty sweep of his hand. In less than a week the AJC meeting was to begin, and it was crunch time for Peter. After Saturday, McGrath wasn't even sure if the chestnut was hardened for battle. The Chipping Norton had been Peter's first unexplained loss. In every other loss, excuses had been at the ready. But at Warwick Farm the horse had been fit, he wasn't left at the start, nor was he hampered in running. Even with ill-judged tactics, he should have been able to place better than sixth. So, after the atrocious affairs of the Chipping Norton, Peter Pan was heading into the AJC races without a win, and without any promising form to lead the way.

McGrath had spent Sunday and Monday grasping to understand things, to find out if Saturday's race had been a signal that all was not well. Was it possible that Peter Pan was finished with racing? Had the big chestnut detached himself from the driving career of competition? If he had, then he had only done it recently. He had run Rogilla to a half-length in the Rawson Stakes a week ago, and his morning work had been excellent. It was with such concerns that McGrath had shipped Peter Pan to Rosebery on Tuesday. With the scintillating results of that work, the old trainer came to two conclusions: the moody Peter hadn't felt like fighting at Warwick Farm last weekend, and his staying constitution had developed immeasurably. Over the shorter courses, and with the top weights he was bound to get, Peter Pan needed to be ridden perfectly to be within an ounce of winning.

Buoyed by Tuesday's Rosebery work, McGrath attacked the rest of the week with salt. On Wednesday, he sent Peter Pan to Rosebery again as the rain splashed on and on, and on Thursday he kept the chestnut at home, sending Peter a stiff mile over Randwick's course proper. Clock-watchers couldn't believe their eyes. The big, tall Peter Pan clipped the first three furlongs in 38 seconds, four furlongs in a tick over 50, and they expected that the final four furlongs, and the slop, would wind the horse down. But bouncing into the straight Peter Pan was still going like the clappers. He tossed away the final three furlongs in 38 1/2, leaving his watchers in a puddle of discontent. These were more like the times of a speed horse, not the sectionals of a horse born to stay.

By Friday night, McGrath had his steel back. His faith was restored and he looked to the AJC meeting with zeal. He had a horse that, in less than two years of racing, had been to the brink and back again more times than he could remember. The last week of March slipped away quickly.

18

'Why is this horse so good?'

Ride the race as you see it, Jim,' McGrath said, as he legged the jockey into the saddle. Pike nodded. Beneath him, Peter Pan fidgeted to be on his way. It was Saturday 31 March, a little after 1.30 in the afternoon and the first day of the AJC autumn meeting. The horses for the Autumn Plate, all seven of them, were about to leave the paddock, deserting an enclosure that bobbled with black umbrellas. Rain was bothering Sydney again, and only the brave and boisterous had come out. Though 44,500 people were packing the grandstands, it was short of what the AJC had expected.

Pike trotted Peter Pan to the starting tape, which was stretched across the track once the horses were behind it. The Autumn Plate was a mile-and-a-half contest, so the jump would occur in front of the grandstands. As Peter Pan circled, some of his rivals became agitated at the swell of human voices, and as usual Peter pinned his ears at any horse that came too close. Pike didn't rebuke him, instead ignoring his mount's temper. The jockey hoped, in fact, that such spirit would return him to the winner's circle.

The Autumn Plate was the second race of the day, and the AJC's first big weight-for-age event. It was also being touted as the rematch of the season, with Silver Scorn lining up against Peter Pan once again, only this time the Kiwi mare was favoured to win. Every single sporting paper had dropped her into the top spot. It was an extraordinary situation, and one that Pike couldn't quite grasp. One good win at the Farm didn't qualify a horse for favouritism in a field like this. Privately, confidently, Pike felt that this day Peter Pan had the goods.

The field was called to order some seconds before 1.45pm, and Jack Gaxieu, barking orders at the jockeys, tidied a loose lot of horses into a neat string. Lough Neagh stood on the rail, with Oro next to him. Peter Jackson was next, with Heroic Prince and Miss Nottava between horses. Silver Scorn came then, and Peter Pan had drawn the outside position. It was yet another race where the son of Pantheon had picked the shortest straw. Pike wound the reins into his fingers, and his worn, gnarly face looked up at Gaxieu. Peter Pan stood stock-still, as ready for the jump as his jockey, while beside him the chomping and restless steps of six horses broke the tension. They were all carrying 9st bar Silver Scorn, who had 8st 13lb. The tape flew up, and in a clean, brisk charge, the seven-horse field was off and running.

Peter Pan leaped away like a gentleman. On this day he was in no hurry, and as the field crowded ahead of him, he settled at the back with Heroic Prince, six or seven lengths off the pace. Up front, Lough Neagh had kicked to the lead, and as they swung out of the straight and into the first bend, Oro was second, Silver Scorn was next, with Miss Nottava and Peter Jackson behind them, and then a gap to Heroic Prince and Peter Pan. Pike could feel the steady, ambling strides of his chestnut, and knew that, up front, Lough Neagh was in no great hurry either.

The field swung into the back stretch in that order, and it wasn't until the six-pole that Edwin Tanwan got busy up front. He pushed Lough Neagh into a new gear, and the tempo lifted, with Oro closing the gap on the leader to half a length, and the rest of the horses moving closer. At the back, Pike clapped his eyes on the five-furlong pole, and as he neared it he drew Peter Pan to the outside. He was sending the big chestnut around the entire field, and Peter, with seven-league strides, swallowed the competition in a heartbeat. He ranged up to Lough Neagh with four furlongs to go, and the two horses leaned into the home turn together. For a second, Peter Pan fell onto the smaller horse, forgetting there wasn't room for two, but Pike shifted the chestnut back to his course and they entered the straight just ahead. Lough Neagh, Peter's valiant chaser of nearly two years, was spent. He had nothing to throw at his old foe, and

Pike gave his horse one slap of the whip. Peter Pan charged down the Randwick straight on his own. One, two, two-and-a-half lengths clear. He bolted past the judges.

As was his wont, Pike showed nothing of elation, or even mild bemusement. He simply stood in his stirrups and sent Peter Pan back to scale. As he approached the gate, he heard the odd cry of frustration from the odd frustrated punter who had lost money on Peter in the Chipping Norton. But the jubilance of the crowd soaked up the unhappy callers, and Pike, high on Peter Pan, felt Randwick's affection for a returning champion. 'You'll do us, Pikey,' called one fan as the pair trotted in. 'Good on yer,' another said, and it went as such until Pike was on the ground and had slipped the saddle from Peter Pan's back. He pumped Dangar's hand, and slapped McGrath on the back, then strode into the jockeys' room to weigh in. When the flag went up for correct weights, a grand cheer rang out across the racecourse. Peter Pan was back on top. 'Well, well,' said McGrath. 'If all goes well, Mr Dangar here will be having a drink out of the King's Cup this time next Saturday.'

The Autumn Plate had been won in a time of 2:38 1/2, and the official margins were two-and-a-half lengths and three-quarters of a length, with Peter Jackson staying well for third. It brought Peter's winnings to £15,298, and was his tenth victory from 16 starts. Down in the ring, the bookies were licking their wounds. The coins had come for Peter Pan late, and he had closed at 6/4 after opening at 3/1. Leading fielder Jim Hackett had laid at 3s, taking £300 to £100 on two occasions, while Fred Vockler at the other end had taken 5/2 and 2/1 about £50. Nevertheless, Silver Scorn had started official favourite, and her 10 to 9 now looked a ridiculous swindle, even if she had run second.

Pike peeled off Dangar's orange and green colours back in the jockey room, and later that afternoon he stripped for the Doncaster aboard Chatham. With the steadier weight of 10st 4lb, and Rogilla carrying nearly 1st less, Chatham broke the hearts of the Doncaster field and ran away with the records. Rogilla faded into seventh place. As Pike returned to scale after the race, he cracked a smile for the first and only time that day.

***

The newspapers were in full throttle by Sunday afternoon, starting with the garrulous tabloid *Truth.* 'Peter Pan, by his runaway victory in yesterday's Autumn Plate, has proved that he has come back, and has come back to stay,' wrote the newspaper, underneath a headline that read 'PETER PAN PLAYED 'EM IN THE PLATE'. On Monday, the *Telegraph* was emphatic. 'Peter Pan of old,' spoke its banners. 'Had opponents beaten at the turn.' In the *Mail,* 'Musket' was proud: 'Peter Pan's victory on clearly demonstrates that the big chestnut is as good as ever he was, and that is saying a deal.' But his colleague 'Banjo' Paterson was back to his scintillating, scathing best: 'The dictum that they run in all shapes was never better exemplified than in the case of Peter Pan, and his appearance raises the eternal question: why is this horse so good? Is it his action, or his heart, or his pedigree? It certainly is not his appearance, for few would pick him for the champion that he is.'

Paterson was so far off the mark it was risible. Nearly every newspaper in Sydneytown had declared Peter Pan a dashing racehorse that season. Only his flaxen hair remained the oddity. In every other way he was a dream staying-machine, a horse with light lines, powerful shoulders, and the length to run all day. He was loose-limbed, clean-winded, and a brash competitor. Paterson's words were redundant.

***

AJC proceedings kicked off again on Monday, and with better weather, 53,000 racegoers turned up for Sydney Cup Day, its best crowd since 1930. By Wednesday, the third day of the carnival, the rain had disappeared altogether, and late in the morning more than 26,000 people were filing through the turnstiles on Alison Road. On the Flat, queues of people stood across the course proper, waiting their turn to file into the Leger reserve. The bookies were already under the pump. Hundreds clamoured around their white umbrellas, and the tote counters were clogged.

The Sport of Kings had bucked Old Man Depression. According to the *Referee,* the £1 punters of 1932 were now betting fivers, and if that ratio was representative, then at least five times as much money was pouring into Randwick. People poured into the racecourse with an optimism that hadn't been seen since the good times, and Colin Stephen, chairman of the AJC, knew the steady climb out of the Depression was over. Racegoers were back to enjoy racing for racing's sake.

The Cumberland Plate had been increased to two miles from its mile and three-quarters when Peter won it the previous year. In an effort to encourage a truly run race, the AJC had imposed a curious condition that stated the two miles had to be completed in three minutes and 35 seconds or better, else the total stake would be cut in half. As it stood, the race was worth £1000, but at worst, the winner would take £387. With only five horses engaged, no one knew how the race would be run.

The field was almost identical to that of the Autumn Plate. Lough Neagh and Heroic Prince were heaviest in the weights with 9st 1lb, with Peter Pan and Oro carrying 1lb less, and Silver Scorn was in with 8st 12lb. The ring had Peter leading the betting at 9/4 on, with 11/2 against Silver Scorn, and the others started at 15s. There was little room for doubt concerning Peter Pan. Every newspaper in the land had tipped him to win this time, and Silver Scorn, who had failed miserably in the Sydney Cup on the Monday, was touted to chase him home.

The five horses went to the post a little before 3.50pm. When Jack Gaxieu sent them off, they lumbered away in slow motion, no horse ready to dash to the front. By mischance, Oro found himself in the lead, and he led the field out of the straight for the first time, cantering the opening batch of furlongs in 16 and 17 seconds. It was a shambolic pace. The field travelled the first five furlongs in 1:17 3/4, and at that pace it was slower than the hurdle race earlier on the card. Back in the field, Pike was having a hard time of it with Peter Pan. The long-striding, loose-limbed chestnut had no room to stretch out, and Pike wasn't about to take him to the lead just for leg room. Instead, he checked the big horse several times in running, and until well into the back straight, Peter Pan was galloping with his head in the air and his mouth open. On Silver Scorn, Sid Cracknell wasn't faring much better.

As they moved towards the six-pole, jockey Jack Pratt gave Oro his head, and in less than a furlong the white-faced leader had sprinted to a 12-length lead. It was a sensational burst from Oro that left the other horses flat-footed and, at the back, Pike and Cracknell grew concerned. The two jockeys urged their horses forward, Peter beginning to eat into the turf, carrying Pike towards Oro. He moved around the outside of Heroic Prince and Lough Neagh, and before they had even reached the home turn he was racing second. Silver Scorn, who had tried to go with him, was spent after a furlong.

Oro thundered into the straight three lengths ahead of Peter, and Pratt was still holding his mount. Pike could see the leader had plenty in reserve, and he began to ride Peter Pan out, entreating the big chestnut to close the gap on the leader. Feeling Peter Pan coming, Pratt began to pound on Oro, but the gap was closing. No horse was more in his element at this distance than Peter Pan. With his big heart singing and his legs keeping on, the son of Pantheon ground his way onto Oro's flanks. At the two-furlong pole they were stride for stride, eyeing each other, neither horse giving in. But then the furlong pole flashed past and Oro cracked. Peter Pan, savage in victory, found a new gear, and he kicked away from Oro with a brazen burst of speed. In three strides he was out by a length, and he shot past the winning post in Spartan fashion. No horse in the land had a patch on him at two miles.

The official time for the race read 3:39 1/4, which cut the total stake to £500. After the dawdling pace in the opening stages, Peter Pan had run the last mile in 1.37 3/4, and the last half-mile in 48 seconds exactly. That was a near-perfect effort for a horse that had already gone a mile and a half. There was just no limit to Peter's stamina. As Pike brought him back to scale, the thousands of punters that had laid at odds-on cheered the pair. They didn't care that the race had been embarrassingly long. They cared that they could now ride a cab home instead of a tram, and the only ones left lamenting the race were the AJC officials, whose time limit had failed miserably. The Cumberland lifted Peter's tally to £15,685 and 10 shillings. It was his eleventh victory from 17 starts, and over two miles he remained unbeaten.

The race was a terrific result for Peter Pan, but it was labelled a farce in the newspapers and Dangar was bothered that his horse had been part of a poor spectacle. He loathed the idea that Peter Pan was associated with anything unsporting, but the reality was that it was Peter's usual tactics to sit off the pace, so the goings-on up front were out of Pike's control. McGrath, on the other hand, took different consolations. The Cumberland had thrown up Peter Pan's versatility. Back in 1932, when Peter had won the Melbourne Cup, he ran a swift, near-record time for the two miles, in spite of his bump at the five-furlong pole. In 1933 he had taken the two-and-a-quarter-mile AJC Plate in stern fashion. Now he had taken the Cumberland in altogether different circumstances. Speed, interference, slowness – they were all the same to Peter Pan, and after the Cumberland there remained only one cherry left to pick that season.

***

The King's Cup approached with awful weather, the clear skies that had graced the carnival the previous few days growing thick with purple clouds. Showers began to drench Randwick again on Thursday, and throughout the night and into Friday morning buckets of water toppled onto the racecourse, leaving it deep and squashy and a woe for many trainers. By raceday morning, enough prayers had been said around Randwick that the parish had skated into God's good books overnight.

McGrath worried about the weather for one reason: Peter Pan's shoulder problems could recur. With damp walls and drafts whistling up and down Doncaster Avenue, he took to double-rugging his champion yet again, and he piled the straw high in Peter's box, driving out his own concerns that the horse would go amiss again. He hadn't forgotten that it was weather like this that had started the muscular problems in the first place. When it came to the King's Cup itself, though, McGrath wasn't concerned about Peter handling the going. He worried only that Peter's top weight would be all the heavier in sticky footing.

Peter Pan was carrying 9st 5lb, which was the maximum condition for the King's Cup. Rogilla had slipped in with 2lb less, with Lough Neagh carrying 8st 11lb, while Kuvera, Silver Scorn and Melbourne Cup-winner Hall Mark had all been allotted 8st 9lb. Next in the weights was Oro with 8st 6lb, then Limarch, who had won the St Leger a week earlier, had 8st and then came the 7st squadron of Heroic Prince, Miss Nottava, First Balloon and Mr Kerry.

Such were the weight conditions of the annual King's Cup that a fair-handicap horse, and one kept fresh for the race, could win it easily. With Peter Pan giving away 31lb, Mr Kerry, with 7st, seemed just such a horse.

Opinions were divided on the calibre of the field. No one questioned the quality of Peter Pan and Rogilla, but many argued that stalling the race until the last day of the carnival had resulted in a tired batch of horses far from their best. There was credence to that argument. Lough Neagh had been beaten in each of his starts during the meeting, while Silver Scorn had tackled two two-mile events in as many days of racing. Rogilla, also, had not won a race during the meeting, running into Chatham in both his outings, and it could be said that Kuvera and Hall Mark were not on song. Hall Mark had been beaten in the St Leger days before, and as had been said of Peter Pan this time the previous year, the three-year-old was not as good as when he won his Cup the previous spring. But on the other hand, many applauded the AJC for delaying the star event until the final day of the meeting. If nothing else, it was holding public interest right up to the carnival's conclusion, and the merits of the field were inarguable. Every horse bar First Balloon had won a principal race, and between the runners there were two Melbourne Cups, a Sydney and Caulfield Cup, a few St Legers, a Dunedin Cup, an Australian Cup, an AJC Plate, a Summer Cup, and two Tattersall's

Cups. Kuvera was also the defending King's Cup victor.

By the morning of the race, the rain was still pattering down and Lough Neagh was withdrawn. People began to arrive at the racecourse under black umbrellas, or were dashing about under newspapers. It hardly dented the mood; racegoers milled about the paddocks and betting rings with their usual fervour, and for their defiance, by the time the first race kicked off at one o'clock, the drizzle had stopped. Little clouds of steam rose from the footpaths with the afternoon mercury, and quickly the cloakrooms filled with furs and overcoats.

The field for the King's Cup was parading by three o'clock. Peter Pan, in saddlecloth number 1, looked big and leggy and viciously fit. He was also rather full of himself. Behind him, Rogilla looked lighter for his defeats by Chatham. Peter had opened at very short odds. There was little better than 2/1 to be had on him to win but throughout the afternoon support had come for various horses, affecting his price. Mr Kerry was gaining friends due to his feathery weight, and Hall Mark's odds were also narrowing as his Victorian owner, Charlie Kellow, attempted to square his losses on the St Leger. But a seasoned few had not given up on Rogilla either, and despite his lack of form during the week, money fell into the ring for the white-faced gelding. It sent Peter's price to 9/4 at one stage, and just before betting closed he had drifted to 3/1. Rogilla was starting at 4/1, Limarch at

7s, Mr Kerry was fetching 8s, and Kuvera and Hall Mark could be had at 10/1.

Up in the Members' stand, Rodney Dangar sat with Elsie as she twitched and fiddled with her gloves. Peter Pan's owner, too, was barely able to contain his nervousness. He hoped beyond all hopes that today was Peter's day. 'I'm not interested in the prize-money,' he had been heard to say in the paddock, 'I just want the trophy.'

Post time was delayed at 3.15pm when Mr Kerry was trotted back to the saddling paddock, leaving the other 10 horses pacing in loose circles on the course proper. Confused mumbles ran over the crowd, in particular on the Flat, and were only quieted when it was seen that Mr Kerry had thrown a shoe and was being re-plated in the paddock. Out on the track, Jim Pike was irritated. With 9st 5lb on Peter Pan's back, he had to keep the horse moving, and it was a full 10 minutes before Mr Kerry returned. That was 10 minutes longer than Peter should have had to carry his top weight, and Pike was worried that it would tell on his mount when it counted.

Mr Kerry had hardly touched the track when Jack Gaxieu called the 11 horses to order. Silver Scorn lined up against the rails, with Peter Pan drawing a good position next to her. The troublesome Mr Kerry was on the outside. With the clerk of the course mounted behind it, the field stood quietly, ready to be on its way. Gaxieu pressed the lever and they were off.

Silver Scorn leaped hard on the inside, and as the bigger Peter Pan heaved himself into stride, the New Zealand mare dashed to an early lead. Oro, breaking almost as well, quickened away from his outside spot and crossed to the rails. As the field settled down the straight, these two led from Peter Pan, Kuvera and Mr Kerry, who were galloping three across the track. Behind him, Pike could sense the bobbing white face of Rogilla, who was tracked by First Balloon and Limarch, and at the back came Hall Mark, Miss Nottava and Heroic Prince, nearly eight lengths spreading the field from first to last.

They fell out of the straight in that order, but passing the nine-furlong pole Mr Kerry moved up, and he and Oro went past Silver Scorn, both horses hoping to set an honest speed and wear down the champions behind them. Pike was not worried, allowing Peter Pan a long rein to bowl along in the lead division. The big chestnut was running beautifully, his long legs consuming the ground without effort. If the going was sticky, Peter hadn't noticed, and he ambled along the rails with Silver Scorn, Kuvera now behind him. Rogilla's white face had disappeared back in the field.

Oro and Mr Kerry stretched their lead to two-and-some lengths, and down the back stretch Pike watched as the two leaders burned themselves out, sweeping into the far turn with the rest of the field in tow. It wasn't until the half-mile that Pike decided to move. As he asked Peter Pan to hurry along, the closing wall of horses behind him got louder. Peter began to stretch out, chasing down the distance in front of him, sensing the game was on. He burst into that powerful, staying stride of his, and within a click or two he had carried Pike to the leaders. Switching to the outside, Pike brought his horse around them, and as they converged into the home turn, Mr Kerry's nose was just in front on the rails, with Oro in the middle and Peter Pan belting around them on the outside. The grandstands erupted.

For a few strides, Mr Kerry plugged on with his feather weight, but Peter Pan was all over him. The chestnut disposed of the two horses in a heartbeat, and Pike rode for home. Sending Peter towards the rail, the veteran jockey lowered himself onto Peter Pan's neck and pushed his every stride. For a moment, the race looked all over, but on the outside, the brown ball of Kuvera was drawing alongside. The little horse had exploded down the home straight, and he threw everything he had at Peter Pan. The two horses ran stride for stride, Peter's head going up as Kuvera's came back down, and they were galloping so close their jockeys' irons were clinking. Behind Peter Pan, Darby Munro on Rogilla was waiting desperately for a hole on the rails. But there was no room. The big frame of Peter Pan crowded the rails, and Kuvera had left him no space to go anywhere. And then it happened.

Peter Pan had had enough of Kuvera. With only a furlong to race, the tetchy, territorial chestnut reached out and took a savage snap at his rival, telling the littler horse in no uncertain terms to back off. As he did, his big body followed the direction of his neck, and he leaned on Kuvera for a fraction of a stride, creating a hole for Munro to squeeze through. Rogilla charged into it without a thought, but there wasn't enough room for him. Munro yanked Rogilla into the hedge that was planted under the running rail, just to have enough room. It was bullish riding on Munro's part, but he knew opportunity when he saw it. Suddenly there were three horses battling for the race, and crazed cheers erupted at the spectacle.

Pike found himself the ham in a sandwich. Rogilla and Kuvera were galloping so close on either side that he couldn't even crouch in his stirrups, let alone flail his whip. In the line of three horses, Pike's head was stuck highest – he was almost standing in his irons – and his chestnut was fighting and fighting to get clear of the other two horses. But as the winning post loomed closer, Rogilla's head bobbed in front. He had that much more room than Peter Pan to get out of his pocket. Pike could do nothing. He despaired as they dashed past the judge, for he knew that the Newcastle gelding had prevailed by a nose.

Dangar was on his feet, his hands to his face, as he watched Rogilla down Peter Pan by a breath. He didn't see the rest of the field pass the judge, though he watched them, and for a moment he was paralysed by disappointment. He couldn't believe that the King's Cup had been teased from him so sneakily. But his sporting nature got the better of him quickly, and he tucked his grief aside. He joined Frank McGrath in the paddock, and waited for Peter to return to scale.

The cheers were almost hysterical as Rogilla, Peter Pan and Kuvera trotted home. While Munro wore a grin that would break glass, Pike was austere, and immediately he expressed his sorrow to Dangar and McGrath. Both men, however, were racing gentlemen. They had seen the closing stages almost as well as Pike had, and neither was annoyed at the jockey. On the contrary, Dangar shook Pike's hand vigorously, and commended him for riding so well. 'That's racing,' Dangar said, shrugging. 'My horse ran a marvellous race.'

As Pike moved towards the scales, he was crowded by journalists waiting to get his story. 'Peter Pan was a moral of morals licked,' he told them, edging past the throng to the scales. When correct weight was declared, he stopped to talk some more. 'I was hampered and wedged in over the final half-furlong, and could positively do nothing to assist Peter,' he said. 'Over the last bit I was right up in the air throwing anything at him in an endeavour to get the last bit out of him. I'm certain that one cut of my whip would have meant the difference between winning and losing.'

***

'The best horse didn't win the King's Cup,' announced *Truth* the following day. 'There's not the slightest doubt that Peter Pan should have won the race and Mr Dangar, who had his heart on winning this prize of prizes, is to be commiserated with.' The newspaper further stated that Pike should not have allowed Munro to come up on his inside, but it also conceded that Munro quite bullied his way into contention.

Munro was adamant that Rogilla's winning was never in question. He stated that even if the race had gone another half a furlong, Rogilla would still have won. Pike disagreed, declaring Peter was only beaten in the last stride or two. That opinion was supported by Cliff Graves, who wrote in the *Referee,* 'In a finish like Saturday's the slightest factor can tell, and perhaps, with the luck to get an inside run instead of having to go around, Peter Pan would have returned the winner of this year's King's Cup.'

With such a tight loss, it was impossible for Peter's connections to ignore the 'what ifs'. For example, what if Pike hadn't had to run three wide on the home turn? What if Mr Kerry had not thrown a shoe and left Peter Pan with his big weight for 10 minutes more than was necessary? What if Kuvera had given him more space to gallop in the dying stages? There were so many 'what ifs' they were driving Macker mad. The old trainer knew that it was better to go down by a length than by a nose. There was no room for retrospection then.

Peter Pan's second place earned him £300. The race had been run in the smart time of 2:32, which was two seconds outside the record for the distance, but the going accounted for that. The King's Cup was also the seventh time Peter Pan had met Rogilla. Since their first meeting in the Caulfield Cup back in 1932, the two horses had raced each other over distances from a mile to two and a quarter miles, and Peter Pan was ahead with four wins. From a mile to a mile and a half, the pair was two wins apiece. But twice they had met over two miles or more, and twice Peter Pan had vanquished the Newcastle horse. More and more Les Haigh's opinion – that there was nothing between the two horses over middle distances – grew into solid fact.

King's Cup Day was the last of the AJC carnival, and over the four days of racing 157,500 racegoers had turned out to watch the spectacles. Sydney Cup Day had produced the greatest crowd, and the greatest turnover on the tote. Some £66,300 was invested, which was a 17 per cent increase on investments for the same day in 1933. Overall, tote betting throughout the carnival was up nearly 13 per cent on the previous year, this in spite of some wicked weather. They were figures that proved conclusively to the AJC, and the racegoing public, that the Depression had been left behind, at least at the racecourse.

***

A few mornings later, under dark umbrellas and darker clouds, for the rain had kept coming after the carnival, Leslie Fraser, chief steward of the AJC, stood in the middle of Randwick's home straight with his assistant stewards and George Law, keeper of the track. The men were keen to be off the grass and out of the rain, but there was the business of this hedge to attend to first. Its presence under the running rail had enabled Rogilla to find room where there wasn't any on Saturday, for the hedge stuck out a little less than a foot underneath the rail. The gelding had simply run through it without scraping the fence. Fraser was arguing for its removal. There should be no ambiguity in the dying stages of a big race, he was saying, ducking from driblets of water that were falling off the edge of his umbrella. Law saw his point. Spurred by the weather, the group of men agreed that the hedge was to be removed before spring racing, and hastily they shuffled into the Members' bar, out of the rain.

On the other side of Alison Road, opposite the racecourse, on King Street and behind the tram depot, the H. Chisholm & Co. sale ring, and parts of its stables, lay smouldering in an ashen heap. In the early hours of the Friday morning before Peter Pan's King's Cup, a cigarette butt had ignited some coir matting, and within minutes the sale ring was in flames. Tossing its sparks high and wide, the fire had swept through a stable block filled with yearlings, for it was Easter sale time, and three of the youngsters had burned to death. Now, several days after the dreadful incident, the charred remains of Harry

Chisholm's dynasty were a problem for William Inglis & Co.

As Inglis had purchased the goodwill of the Chisholm company back in February, the site was their responsibility. They had no intention of restoring it back to stables. From 1935 onwards all thoroughbreds sold in Randwick would be sold at their facility in Young Street. Therefore, they were left with little option now but to raze the entire Chisholm site to the ground. They set about with subdividing the block, and by October, the divisions would be auctioned for up to £14 a foot, and apartments would soon follow. The footfall of horses was starting to disappear around Randwick.

19

'Gentlemen like you'

Rodney Dangar glanced out the window of his office. It was Monday morning, 16 April, and O'Connell Street was spotted with black umbrellas and little figures dashing for cover. It was still raining in Sydney. The pavements had been damp for weeks, the lawns in Hyde Park were waterlogged, and the city felt smaller, danker, dirtier. Thick, depressing mats of cloud hung low and loaded over the city. Dangar was glad that Peter Pan was finished for the season; ever since the shoulder problem had cropped up, bad weather made him nervous. He picked up the morning's mail off the desk in front of him. There was an invoice for the hot water system at Baroona, and a statement of returns from Australian Mutual Provident, but he selected first an envelope addressed from 39 Robertson Road, Centennial Park. He recognised the handwriting. It was a letter from Jim Pike.

Dangar had sent a letter to Pike on 10 April, thanking him for his riding of Peter Pan during the autumn carnival. He was anxious to express his admiration of the jockey, his riding as well as his manner, and the best way to do so was financially. He had enclosed a generous cheque with the letter, and he suspected the letter now in his hands was an acknowledgement.

Dear Mr Dangar,

Received your letter of the 10th inst, also cheque, and thank you very much for same. It is very seldom owners show their appreciation of my services in this manner, and it is a pleasure to ride for gentlemen like you. Let us hope your horse comes back better than ever in the spring, and be able to show how great he really is.

Yours sincerely,

J. Pike

Pike's handwriting was quite different to Dangar's. It was not the script of an educated man, but the scribe of one who wrote only when he had to. His letter to Dangar was as brief as Pike was reticent, but it was polite and grateful, and expressive of the type of man that Dangar enjoyed – a humble character whose nature belied his success. Dangar knew that his financial generosity towards the jockey was a good call, as Pike was never wont to take advantage of it. Dangar had also never heard Pike utter a negative word about Peter Pan, even after the disastrous Chipping Norton Plate.

Alec Young interrupted his thoughts. Tapping lightly on the glass panels of Dangar's door, the Baroona manager stepped inside with a bundle of papers sheltered under his overcoat. Young was down from Whittingham for a few days to catch up with the boss. Dangar informed Young that Peter Pan had gone to Doonside over the weekend. The horse was in wonderful order, and McGrath expected him to be there for six weeks. They were still deliberating the spring programme, as Peter hadn't raced in the spring since his three-year-old days. McGrath had mentioned that a sharp bout of mile races might be just the prep for the Melbourne Cup, but they hadn't indulged in the wisdom of that yet. There were plenty of winter afternoons for doing so.

But the King's Cup had barely been run when chatter had started on the Melbourne Cup. After the AJC meeting, there was no doubt that Peter Pan was an invincible staying force. His wins in the Autumn Plate, and particularly the Cumberland, showed him to have lost none of his two-mile form. But McGrath knew there was half a season of racing between now and November. He, for one, wasn't going to get cocky and elect his racehorse a Centenary Cup certainty. It would be nice to think that Peter Pan would win another Melbourne Cup, but no horse had done it in 72 years.

Dangar and Young talked long into the morning, and many miles west of them, Peter Pan stood under a pine tree at Doonside, sheltering from the rain. The water had turned his winter coat a shabby shade of ginger, and his blond hair was matted against his neck. To any passer-by he was just a wet nag under a tree. But that was a fiction spun by the fickle hands of weather.

20

Brilliant things

At the end of July 1934, a birthday card left Melbourne Hospital, bound for 4 O'Connell Street, Sydney. It rode the mail train across the Victorian border into New South Wales, reaching Sydney's Central Station late in the evening. Eventually it was stuffed into a postman's knapsack. On 1 August 1934, it was delivered to Rodney Dangar, right in time for Peter Pan's fifth birthday.

The Melbourne Hospital Birthday League had a few more names on its list this year. In addition to Peter Pan, and the stars Windbag, Liberal, Star d'Or, and a few others, the league was also celebrating Gaine Carrington, who had been admitted for his Caulfield Cup win in 1933, Prismatic, McGrath's ex-hurdler who had won the Grand National Hurdle Race only weeks before, and recent Cup winner Hall Mark. The respective owners had each paid £25 to the Melbourne Hospital, which invested the money and reaped the interest, and the horses became part of a fashionable little club.

At five, and now a stallion, Peter Pan had been racing for two years. His record stood at 18 starts for 11 wins (including his dead-heat), two seconds and five unplaced efforts. Of the latter, he had twice run a close fourth, and of the remaining three unplaced runs, only the Chipping Norton was inexplicable. It was a record that, at the quickest glance, spelled dogged consistency. Here was a horse that had finished in the first four horses 15 out of 18 times, a horse that might never have won again after 1933 were it not for his owner and trainer. In the principled and patient hands of Dangar and McGrath, Peter Pan had breached the fences of breakdown.

The nation was similarly invigorated. Electricity and telephones were tramped into homes in their thousands, buoyed by government enthusiasm and a public hunger for progress. Standing on the cusp of the 1934–35 racing season, expectations of Peter Pan had changed too. Australians no longer needed heroes. They no longer needed a horse to supplant Phar Lap. Instead, Australians craved the bright spectacle of brilliance. So that was how the new turf season arrived on 1 August 1934 ... expectant of brilliant things.

***

As with the seasons that had come before it, the spring of 1934 had a target for Peter Pan. It was the Centenary Melbourne Cup, due to be raced on 6 November at Flemington. The odds of winning a second Melbourne Cup were slim. No horse had done it since Archer in 1862, and he had accomplished it in the race's first two runnings, when it had been little more than an ambitious two-mile handicap. Now it attracted the best horses in the country. Already Hall Mark would be out to defend his crown. Rogilla would likely run, as would the latest Sydney Cup winner Broad Arrow, and a glut of three-year-olds would be snapping at Peter Pan's heels. It didn't bode well for the horse that would certainly carry top weight.

When Peter Pan last raced in the spring, it was in his three-year-old year of 1932, and the spring races were a different challenge then. They were derbies leading into St Legers, not weight-for-age battles against seasoned fighters. McGrath proposed that to have Peter Pan set for November, and to not burn him out in the months between, he would start him in the shorter, sharper races this spring: the nine-furlong Chelmsford Stakes, the one-mile Hill Stakes, and gradually progressing to the AJC spring meeting, where he would run in the Spring Stakes and the Craven Plate, both weight-for-age AJC classics. McGrath had also not ruled out the Cox Plate at Moonee Valley which, in theory, could be a fine start to Peter Pan's Victorian visit. But the old trainer wasn't decided on that one yet.

With the horses back in from Doonside, the key players in Peter Pan's life mustered on Doncaster Avenue. There was Rodney Dangar, 61 years old, and Frank McGrath, who was almost 68. The dependable George Phillips was there, along with John Tyler, a pony hoop who was now Peter's regular morning rider, and up and down the shed row, McGrath's other charges waited. There was Deputy Ruler, Australia

Fair, Cid, Highboy, Master Brierly and Peter Pan. There were about 15 others too, but these six were McGrath's spring guns.

***

Peter Pan had been back in from Doonside since early winter, but McGrath was bringing him along slowly – very slowly. The trainer had two reasons for this. The first was that he didn't plan to start Peter Pan racing until 8 September, in the Chelmsford Stakes at the Tattersall's Club meeting at Randwick. It was at least a week after most of Peter's rivals would debut, and they would therefore meet him with a race or two in hand. The other reason was that McGrath was readying Peter for months of racing. If all went well, the horse would finish his campaign in late November, when the Centenary celebrations would migrate from Melbourne to Sydney. So, to the tune of being in for the long haul, McGrath was sparing his horse unnecessary labour.

With easy tasks being asked of him in the mornings, Peter Pan grew easily bored. He was not an unquestioning thoroughbred. Rather, he demanded stimulation, so McGrath took him all over the Eastern Suburbs for trackwork. He varied the routine between Randwick and the pony tracks of Rosebery, Kensington and Victoria Park. The latter was a little way west of Randwick, and it was on this course that Peter Pan started to work against the clock.

Victoria Park was just a tick from Randwick, and fringed the inner-west industrial suburbs of Zetland and Waterloo. It was a lovely racetrack, built with iron-lace charm, and for trackwork it was much loved, even by Randwick's residents. The course proper was kikuyu grass, a spongy, traffic-resistant and self-repairing turf. To boot, the entire racecourse was built on a drained swamp, meaning that on any given day, but especially during spells of dry weather, there was always good give in the going. McGrath maintained a stout affection for the pony courses, no doubt the early roots of his training days, but he also knew them to often outweigh Randwick in their assets. Rosebery, for example, was the finest wet-weather track in metropolitan Sydney, and in McGrath's opinion, it was impossible to better Victoria Park for fast work. It proved wisdom. On 21 August, a snappy winter's day, the rain began to fall in Sydney, and it didn't look like stopping.

McGrath had had no luck with Peter Pan's weather. In each of his preparations this year, drizzle and dampness had overridden the seasons. Peter's shoulder problem had not cropped up for some time, but the trainer feared it would always be present, lurking on the edge of the horse's soundness. Wet tracks and sodden turf had meant extra rugs and extra precautions, especially for a slender thoroughbred that was apt to feeling the cold. It looked to McGrath like the spring of 1934 would be no different. Dodging the downpours as much as possible, he ferried Peter Pan to Rosebery on the very wet mornings, and it wasn't until the end of August that the chestnut began to record any noticeable times.

In the Les Haigh camp, Rogilla was firing on all cylinders. The Newcastle gelding was now eight years old, but there was no sign of him being spent. He had begun the season in a Flying Handicap over Rosebery's six-furlong distance, and carried 10st up the rise to win by a neck. On 25 August at Warwick Farm, he ran in the Warwick Stakes, and though running unplaced, Haigh was not disappointed. The Warwick Stakes was no slouch contest. Chatham was the winner at 11/8 on and, first up, he was impressive. Rogilla, Kuvera, Silver Scorn, Oro and Closing Time hadn't managed to get within clicks of the Windbag horse. Now crowned Australia's greatest miler, and many concluded the greatest miler ever, Chatham was proving absolutely ageless.

The rain continued into the first days of September, and each morning an army of horses, trainers, riders and grooms trudged through the slosh on Randwick Racecourse. The course proper had been closed for nigh on a month due to repairs, and in fact the only grass track available was the inner B grass, which was small, had no straights and tended to cut up quickly. Exasperated, trainers such as McGrath deserted for Victoria Park, next-door Kensington and Rosebery, all of which enjoyed a spike in visiting training fees. But increasingly, McGrath grew uneasy about the Chelmsford Stakes at Randwick. Though he had declared his horse a certainty to run, he was worried about the going, which would certainly be heavy. Peter Pan was not known for being a mudlark, and in the Chelmsford he would carry 9st 11lb. Rogilla had 3lb less.

On Friday afternoon, the day before raceday, the heavens opened again and dumped an inch of water over the Eastern Suburbs with a brilliant electrical storm. It was the sixteenth straight day of storms and rain in Sydney, which was soaking the racing industry. Canterbury Park Racecourse had had to postpone its meeting the previous Saturday because of the weather, and deferring it until Thursday, two days before the Chelmsford, had an immediate impact on Peter Pan. Chatham, who was due to run at Canterbury, would honour his commitment to the western Sydney club. In so doing, he would forgo his appearance in the Chelmsford Stakes, for two races in three days were too much even for him. Even without Chatham, the Chelmsford had attracted a strong contingent. Rogilla's entry stood, along with Peter Pan's, and Nightly, a New Zealand visitor who had run second to Chatham in the Warwick Stakes a fortnight earlier, made up this trio of top weights. A host of three-year-olds comprised the rest of the field, including Derby aspirant Theo, and Gladswood, Duke Caledon and a few others.

Before retiring that Friday night prior to the Chelmsford, McGrath was wracked with questions about the wisdom of starting Peter Pan. The trainer was anxious about the going, because under penalty conditions Peter Pan would not be suited. He was giving Rogilla 3lb, but if he didn't run he would be starting his season very late. He decided to make an inspection of the track at first light before deciding on Peter's entry.

***

The storm clouds moved away throughout the night, so that by the time McGrath awoke, Randwick's course proper had had a little time to dry. Upon inspection, McGrath found it to be holding, and the trainer made the decision to start Peter Pan. His other charges Deputy Ruler and Nekarbo would also start that afternoon, along with Cid and Highboy in the Tramway Handicap.

The Chelmsford was the feature race of the Tattersall's Club meeting, and its value had climbed back to its pre-Depression days of £1000. It was the first big event of the spring, and as it had done since its inception in 1895, it was attracting major attention. This year it was being touted as the King's Cup rematch. The race had a winners' list of enviable proportions; in fact, it was doubtful if any single race was more associated with champions. Heroic, Windbag, Limerick (three times), Phar Lap and Gaine Carrington had all won the Chelmsford in the preceding 10 years. Gloaming had debuted in this race in 1918 and won it. Rogilla was defending champ this year, and if he won again he would draw even with Peter Pan on the tally board. He would have beaten Dangar's chestnut home as many times as Peter had beaten him.

The Chelmsford was due off at 3.20pm, and was a nine-furlongs weight-for-age event. McGrath had had the same headaches with Jim Pike once again, the top jockey having declared his loyalty to Chatham for the Chelmsford. The old trainer was getting a little tired of this, but Dangar was insistent: Pike was to be retained if at all possible, regardless of his loyalties to other camps. Though Chatham was now not running, McGrath had sought another rider by the time Chatham was scratched, and Jim Munro was to pilot Peter Pan. He would ride against his brother on Rogilla. Though Pike was free on Saturday morning, and Dangar had ventured that the top hoop should be engaged, McGrath had no intention of ejecting Munro from the ride. Darby's older brother was a capable, top-tier, accomplished horseman, and the trainer also knew that Peter Pan would clash with Chatham again soon. Rather than scratch around for a new jockey every few weeks, he thought he would stick with Jim Munro for the time being. Part of him felt that Pike didn't deserve the ride. Munro would be Peter Pan's seventh jockey, but the horse would probably not notice the difference. He was that sort of animal: aloof and arrogant enough not to care who was on his back.

In the ring, the money had come for Rogilla. By the start of racing he was 11/8 on. Nightly, the New Zealander, was 9/2 against, and Peter Pan was way out at 7s. Apparently there was little faith in his making a good showing. Every single newspaper had tipped Rogilla to win. Most of them thought Peter Pan would do not better than third, and Nightly and Duke Caledon were being supported above him. 'Rogilla looks a moral if he leaves the post,' wrote the *Telegraph,* referring to the Newcastle gelding's misbehaviours at the barrier. When the horses stripped for the pre-post parade, however, many were surprised at Peter's showing. He looked fit and muscular, while Rogilla moped around the enclosure with his head almost between his front knees.

When the bugle sounded, McGrath legged Jim Munro into the saddle. The jockey had turned 28 the day before, and was hoping to make his Peter Pan debut an extension of his birthday celebrations. McGrath told him to stay off the pace, but to otherwise ride the race as he saw it. Jim, older than brother Darby by six years, nodded and headed towards the track. He was reputed for his tactful riding, a jockey who could change his style and methods to suit the horse he was steering. He had been in many a race when Peter Pan had swooped from the back to win, and he had a feeling he would figure this big chestnut out. He was a personality horse, the type of animal that Munro enjoyed.

The nine-horse field gathered at the start, which was just around the bend from the mile chute. Jack Gaxieu began to shuffle them about, as if arranging a deck of cards on a neat, green poker table of turf. First this horse came in, then Rogilla jumped out. By the time he was sent back in, some other horse had backed out of the line. Gaxieu's temperature rose steadily. There was no job in Sydney that demanded patience like this one. Eventually, the horses for the Chelmsford Stakes were lined up. In the tiny second they stood still, Jack Gaxieu snatched his opportunity and sent them on their way. With the whoosh of the tape, the field of nine sprang to life, and Nightly outsprinted his rivals to the front. Inside half a furlong he dashed away, with three-year-old The Marne close behind.

As they approached the mile-post, The Marne galloped past the leader into a pacemaking position, and he led the field into the back stretch, a length and a bit to Gladswood and Nightly, with Duke Caledon, Peter Pan, The Raider and Marcus Cicero next. Theo was just behind them, and Darby Munro had dragged Rogilla back to last. The odds-on favourite was up to his usual tactics. On Peter Pan, Jim Munro grew acquainted with the chestnut's strides. Bowling along in the middle division, Peter was galloping sweetly, stretching his long legs for the first time in months. The Marne was making a good race of it. He was clipping the sectionals in quick time for a damp track, and that suited the long-striding Peter Pan.

The field barrelled down onto the six-furlong post. Jim Munro knew that by the five-furlong mark, his brother would start making tracks on Rogilla. Easing Peter Pan out a touch, he gave the horse some rein and allowed him to move forward, and Peter strode closer to Duke Caledon. Nightly and Gladswood were still ahead of him, and The Marne was tiring up front. Munro could feel a whole lot of horse beneath him, and he knew he had it under him to get to the front and stay there. But he'd been right about his brother's tactics: Darby had sent Rogilla around the tail of the field at the five-pole, and had dispensed of Theo and Marcus Cicero in a heartbeat. He was coming, watching Peter Pan's every move.

The Marne hit the home turn a length in front of Gladswood. Peter Pan was pressing Nightly, and as they leaned into the bend, he ran past the New Zealand horse, edging to the outside to get around the group in front. Behind him, the white face of Rogilla bobbed ominously, and the Randwick crowd was on its feet, yelling for another King's Cup finish. Before the straight, The Marne was spent, and for a stride or two Gladswood was gallant in the lead. But the older, bigger Peter Pan swept around the younger horse and plunged into the lead. Then, forgetting himself, he skewed his neck towards the grandstands. Jim Munro, who had been resting his hands on Peter Pan's neck as he pushed him along, stood off the horse and straightened him out, and Peter responded immediately. He ate into the home stretch with giddy ease, and for a moment it looked all over.

But the younger Darby was riding like the 'Demon Darb' he was known as, and he flailed and drove Rogilla down onto Peter Pan's lead. Inside the last half-furlong, the two horses were neck for neck, but Jim Munro was under orders not to kill Peter Pan at the finish. The horse was first up from rest. The jockey rode him out, but he didn't raise the whip. A few strides from the line and Rogilla edged in front; they dashed past the post in that order, Rogilla prevailing by half a length.

The cheers from the grandstands were momentous, from the Leger to the Paddock and across to the Flat. But they weren't for the valiant Rogilla downing Peter Pan. They were for the spectacle that these two horses insisted on serving each and every time they met at weight-forage. When the pair trotted back to scale, only moderate applause was afforded the winner. Rogilla had swung in and out of form too often for Randwick punters to adore him like they did Peter Pan.

With £750 going to Rogilla, Peter Pan's share of the Chelmsford purse was £150. It brought his winnings to £16,135 (plus the 10 shillings he had won in the Cumberland), and Rogilla had levelled the scoreboard. Of the eight races in which they had met since 1932, they had led each other home four times respectively. Today, however, even in second place,

Peter Pan had been impressive. Conceding the winner 3lb in weight, and first up to Rogilla's two starts, he had bounced into racing in solid form, so solid, in fact, that Perce Miller and George Tancred strolled straight to the bag swingers after the race.

Miller and Tancred were huge punters, the kind of men who were trailed by hacks at every meeting they went to. Following the Chelmsford Stakes, the two men cornered bookie Frank Alldritt, hoping to get a price about Sir Simper and Peter Pan for the Caulfield–Melbourne Cup double. Sir Simper had won at Epsom the day before. 'Nothin' doing,' drawled Alldritt, 'someone has had a decent serving already. I laid £5000 to £50 about it not so very long ago.' Hardly disheartened, Miller and Tancred knew they would get their price with an SP bookie later on.

Across the board, everyone thought that Peter Pan's effort boded well for the Melbourne Cup, and that was reflected in doubles betting. Before the afternoon was out, the price on the Rogilla–Peter Pan Cups double had shortened several points, and thousands had floated around the country in other combinations. It was also no secret that Haigh was priming Rogilla for the Caulfield Cup, so the doubles pickings look fruitful.

Having acquainted himself with Peter Pan, Jim Munro returned to scale with an odd idea in his head. It had sprouted as soon as he had stood off Peter in the home straight, when the horse had been running like a corkscrew. As soon as Munro had come off his neck, Peter began to run honestly. Was it possible, the jockey wondered, that the horse resented contact? It wasn't a ridiculous suggestion. Peter Pan had savaged other horses that had come too close, even at the most unsuitable moments like in the King's Cup when he had snatched at Kuvera. He was also wont to kick the daylights out of any horse that infringed his space as he returned to scale. That had happened after the Melbourne Cup of '32 when poor Yarramba had been too eager to enter the lane. Munro had enjoyed his ride on Peter Pan, had found him to be tractable and classy. But there was intelligence about this stallion, and independence that demanded careful handling. Munro was amazed that Peter hadn't complained more about the constant varying of pilot. He couldn't wait to jump onboard again.

The Chelmsford was heralded a great success, in particular by the AJC, which had come under fire from certain owners and trainers for not altering the conditions of the race. As it stood, the Chelmsford was a weight-for-age event with penalties and allowances, so it didn't suit some horses, but the handicapper had stood fast on the issue. The AJC refused to amend the conditions, and each year the results explained why. Rogilla's win was the thirteenth straight year that a penalised horse had won the race. Moreover, the two older horses had made a mockery of the three-year-olds. Also, throughout the day Oro had trounced his rivals in the Spring Handicap by five lengths, and Lough Neagh had fallen short by a head in the Tramway. It was conclusive proof that among this year's batch of youngsters there was no child prodigy, due wholly to 'Old Man Depression'.

Peter Pan had been bred before the 1929 stock market crash, as had Oro, Chatham, Rogilla and Lough Neagh. They were products of the roaring twenties, a time of flagrancy and indulgence, and when arguably the classiest tract of stallions was getting going – Heroic, Windbag and Magpie. When the Depression hit, it sideswiped the breeding industry. The small producer just didn't have the money to breed or race. When typically he would be discarding average mares, now he was keeping them, sending them to cheaper stallions. When typically he would be sending his poorer racehorses to the paddock, now he was racing them for longer, squeezing the last bit of juice from them because he couldn't afford a better one. In 1933, 'Cardigan' had exclaimed that he had never seen so many over-raced and over-aged racehorses at an autumn carnival. Though the Depression, officially, was over, only now were the weaker products arriving on the track. The 1934 three-year-olds were all bred around 1930, smack in the middle of the hard times, and their lack of class was showing. None had managed to defeat Peter Pan and his cohorts.

***

In America, the Los Angeles Turf Club was chasing. It had released its racing schedule, featuring the inaugural $100,000 Santa Anita Handicap, and acting as an emissary to the club, Mr H.A. Buck, a New Yorker, was travelling the world, enticing the big horses and their owners into the world's richest handicap. Though the English horses were the prime targets, an American newspaper expressed its hope that Peter Pan might come. It was as likely as Rodney Dangar going broke.

21

The Sir Herbert Maitland Stakes

It was a curious day on 19 September when Dangar found himself at Victoria Park. Not usually disposed to the riffraff of the pony tracks, he wandered around the paddock lawn, a little less dandy than usual, a little less bourgeois. The racecourse was filled with the colourful characters of mid-week racing. It was a Wednesday, so those that spilled into the racetrack were unbound by nine-to-five hours. Some of them were shift workers, others unemployed, and some were simply diehards on a lunchbreak. Either way, they were quite distinct from the gentlemen's quarter at Randwick.

Dangar was surprised by Victoria Park, its attention to detail and its intimacy. It was classy, almost like Randwick's little brother, and the stand was more like a grand house than the host of a few hundred people. To the east were the cottage roofs of Kensington; to the north, beyond the factories and vacant land, the GPO clock tower. Though only a few skips from Randwick, Victoria Park had a whole different feel. It was lovelier than Dangar was expecting. He found the whole place rather charming.

Frank McGrath was quite at home in it all. He had started on the pony circuit, and he knew its faces, knew its characters and colours like the lines on his hand. When Victoria Park had defected to AJC control the previous year, he had been thrilled to bring his thoroughbreds back here for racing. Today, he was elated to bring Peter Pan. McGrath had selected for the horse the fourth race on the card, the weight-for-age Sir Herbert Maitland Stakes, and he had scratched Peter from the previous Saturday's Hill Stakes just to be here. The original plan was to migrate from the Chelmsford on to the Hill Stakes, which Peter Pan had won at only his third start, but this year's prep was open plan. McGrath was happy to detour from what they had done before. Peter Pan was familiar with Victoria Park, he galloped on it several times a week, and this day's race was worth £400 to the winner. It was only £50 less than what the Hill Stakes was offering, and it was many kilometres of a float ride shorter.

The Sir Herbert Maitland Stakes had been running for several years, at least since 1923. It was named in honour of Sydney Hospital's late director, a friend of Joynton Smith, the owner of the track. When Victoria Park fell into AJC regulation, the race was hoisted onto a weight-for-age platform, with allowances in an effort to attract the thoroughbred stars. It worked. In its first weight-forage running in 1933, the Maitland Stakes pulled some impressive gallopers, but the winner was the then little heard of Deputy Ruler. The race was a seven-furlong contest, so fell into the domain of the sprinting contingent. It was an unusual option for Peter Pan. He hadn't run over less than a mile since his very first start, and it seemed out of kilter to ask him to sprint this day. McGrath's wisdom grew even stranger in light of Chatham's entry in the Herbert Maitland. No one, not the newspapers, the punters or the milkman, thought Peter Pan would beat Chatham over Chatham's favourite journey.

In addition to these two, the Maitland Stakes had attracted Lough Neagh, Silver Scorn and Silver Ring. Duke Caledon was also trying again, and there was Golden Wings, Neat Star and Rustler. They made up a nine-horse field, which was the surviving lot of more than 30 nominations. Peter Pan and Chatham were equal in the weights with 9st 3lb. Golden Wings, Lough Neagh and Silver Ring had 9st. Silver Scorn was next with 8st 12lb, and the others varied between 7st 2lb and 6st 13lb. Chatham was a raw favourite at 4/1 on, and Peter Pan was in the parking lot at 7s. Lough Neagh was next at 8/1, then 25s for Silver Scorn and 33/1 bar the field. The result, to most, was a no-brainer.

'The shortness of the race mitigates very badly against Peter Pan,' the *Telegraph* had stated during the week, 'and Chatham should score his sixth successive victory.' Chatham had won the Hill Stakes at Rosehill the previous Saturday, albeit without Peter and Rogilla to beat home. His form was so lethal right now that in the sprinting division he was nigh unbeatable. 'A horse who will be an everlasting memory to present day racing enthusiasts,' *Truth* had commented after the Hill Stakes. Chatham was a thick, burly horse of chocolate colouring, a strong and set six-year-old. He had the smallest feet of any racehorse galloping, or 'goat feet' as Jim Pike called them, but they hardly stopped the horse from winning. Chatham possessed a Cox Plate, two Craven Plates, two Epsoms, three Linlithgow Stakes and a Tramway in his cupboard. He looked especially well today.

At 2.15pm, Phillips led Peter Pan from the race stalls along the horse path, pausing for a moment to allow the horse's shoes to be examined before entering the paddock. Chatham was already there, in saddlecloth number three, sweating in the heat of the afternoon. Phillips slipped Peter Pan ahead of him as number one saddlecloth, and with Closing Time scratched, the two champions followed each other in the parade. They were so physically different it was amusing. Pike, as was his wont, was aboard Chatham, and Jim Munro was told to keep a handy position, to not let Chatham steal an early break. Though McGrath was hopeful, he really didn't think Peter Pan would defeat Chatham. Another furlong, then maybe.

With the jockeys up, the horses filed out of the paddock and onto the course proper. Cantering to the seven-furlong mark, which was halfway down the back straight, Peter Pan took a good look around him. A solitary grey horse was grazing in the infield pastures, and the grandstands were hazy in the afternoon heat. Bubbles of sweat rested on Peter Pan's neck and behind his elbows, but he moved through the oily heat like he relished it. It was a change from sloshing through the mud. As the horses mingled at the start, the totalisator bell rang for three minutes. This was the last signal for punters to get their shillings on, and a flurry of bodies darted from the tote building back to the track to watch the race. With Jack Gaxieu calling them to order, the horses for the Sir Herbert Maitland Stakes lined up. The tapes flew up, and they were racing.

Chatham, breaking fastest, dashed to an early lead down the back straight, and on Peter Pan, Jim Munro watched the familiar sight of the chocolate-brown haunches pull away. He allowed Peter Pan to relax into the straight but, with Lough Neagh, the pair was running last. In front of them, a wall of horses clamoured the rails, with Silver Scorn leading them behind Chatham, and no horse breaking from the pack to chase the leader. Peter Pan had settled like a professional; with a little room he was stretching out in style. Munro sat still on his mount, watching the cottages on Dowling Street disappear one by one on his left, and as the nine horses swung into the far turn there was no change to the order. Chatham had shaken off Silver Scorn, and had dashed to a two-length lead. The rest of the pack was chasing, with Lough Neagh and Peter Pan bringing up the rear.

The bend into the home turn was big and broad, so that once the field was out of the backstretch it was a continual turn into the home straight. Arcing around it, Munro niggled Peter Pan away from Lough Neagh, and he guided the chestnut around the bunched field, covering many feet of extra ground. Behind him, Lough Neagh followed. As the horses thundered around the turn, Chatham was two lengths ahead of Silver Scorn, with another two lengths to Silver Ring and Golden Wings. Munro, midfield, had a lot of work to do, but he had Peter Pan wound tight. When he hit the straight, with less than three furlongs to catch Chatham, Munro unleashed unholy mayhem.

Peter Pan sprung away from the pack like a startled deer. In a blink, he had carried Munro around the chasing pack, and his giant strides belted him past Silver Scorn with insulting ease. A roar sang up from the Leger stand. Chatham had already passed the packed grandstand, but Peter Pan was leaping along. The thousands that thronged the Leger could see it with their own eyes. They hadn't seen a horse move so quickly in years. 'Here comes Peter Pan!' they hollered. 'Here he comes!' Flat to the boards, Chatham could go no faster. Pike, stealing a glance over his shoulder, could see Peter Pan charging down the centre of the straight, but he knew that Chatham had nothing left to give. He drove the horse out but he didn't hit him. He didn't need to. Peter Pan came like a comet plane. Within 20 yards of the judge, he drew even with Chatham, then Munro shook his whip and the son of Pantheon burst away. He crossed the line a neck ahead of Chatham, three lengths back to Duke Caledon. Peter had run the last half-mile in 47 seconds and broken the track record – 1:24 1/2 for the seven.

Munro was hauling on the reins to slow the big racehorse down. It was an incredible effort, and the jockey could only marvel at how Australia's greatest stayer had flogged Australia's greatest sprinter. In the grandstand, Dangar was clapping his palms off. Below him, thousands of ordinary racing patrons had been treated to a rare spectacle. They whooped and whistled their appreciation, for David had surely toppled Goliath, and at 7/1 to boot. As the horses filed back into the enclosure, Frank McGrath stood shaking his head. He was staggered that his horse had run so quickly, bewildered that he had shaken Chatham senseless. He greeted Jim Munro with animated applause, and as they stripped the saddle from Peter's back, a swarm of reporters surrounded the group. Peter, antsy at their clamouring, swung himself away from the scale and sent them scattering. A few panicky murmurs flew into the air. 'He's one of the greatest horses I have ridden,' declared Munro to the reporters, who all shuffled back in as soon as Peter Pan was backed away. 'Only an out-and-out champion could have conceded Chatham such a start.'

Munro was right on the money. Chatham had clapped on the pace from the barrier rise, and at the three furlongs he had a six-length advantage over

Peter Pan. Even with a furlong-and-a-half to race, he was three lengths to the good of Dangar's horse, which gave some idea of how quickly Peter Pan was travelling down the straight. He had shaved three-quarters of a second off Deputy Ruler's 1933 course record. Pike, a little confounded by the result, could offer no explanation for Chatham's defeat. 'Near the Leger I glanced back and saw Peter Pan closing on me rapidly. Chatham was fully extended, and it was impossible to get another ounce from him,' the jockey stated, a little dry from the disappointment. 'To have come from so far back to win at such a distance as seven furlongs gives Peter Pan's form a new significance,' the *Referee* commented. 'He is far more brilliant than we thought he was.'

McGrath followed his horse back to the stalls, still amazed at the state of play just gone. He told himself he shouldn't be surprised. Peter Pan had been stunning him since his arrival at Doncaster Avenue more than two years before. Anything that he had asked of the horse, Peter had delivered. His brilliance was more raw than Amounis's had been, and more electric than Phar Lap's. He was aloof, slightly arrogant, but a classy, heaven-sent racehorse. Today, all of Australia had learned it. But the victory had also proven the wisdom of McGrath's preparation. The short, sharp workouts had fitted Peter Pan for the Sir Herbert Maitland Stakes. He hadn't been drilled or pressed in the weeks preceding, for there was a long road to travel before Cup Day, but by God was he fit. Chatham wouldn't forget this day in a hurry.

The race brought Peter's tally to £16,535 and 10 shillings. From 20 starts, he had 12 wins and three seconds, but the Maitland Stakes signalled a milestone in his career because he had stepped back from the staying division to tackle the best sprinter seen in years. And he had won, leaving the track record in his wake. There was now no horse of worth racing in Australia, no champion in either the staying or sprinting divisions, that Peter had not beat home. He deserved the accolades that would follow the race, and they came. 'No horse in Australia could have lived with him in that great final furlong dash,' the *Sportsman* declared. 'What miracle had happened for Pete to down Australia's greatest sprinter over such a short course?'

That evening, still abuzz with Peter Pan's brilliance, Dangar thought about penning a letter to the *Tatler* journalist 'Sabretache' in London. The pair had become good friends on paper, with letters over and back across the oceans, and he knew the English writer would enjoy news of the Sir Herbert Maitland Stakes. On 25 September, he took a neat sheet of cotton paper and wrote to his friend. 'He is a superhorse, a stone-and-a-half better now than he was at four years old. A wonderful attribute, his possessing this sprinting ability as well as staying power.' Dangar included with his letter clippings of the press commentary. 'May the luck be with me on Melbourne Cup Day. Think of me!'

'Sabretache' did. Writing in *Tatler* after reading Dangar's letter, he declared, 'I hope, when I get the result, the owner's and my own hopes will have been realised.'

22

'Not one horse sweeping the stakes races, but two or three'

There was a smoky sign of daylight when Randwick came to life the morning after the Maitland Stakes, a slow creeping light in the east that, in an hour or so, would wash the grandstands with brilliant sunshine. McGrath, in rolled sleeves and thick woollen trousers, could feel that it was going to be hot again. There wasn't a breath of wind on the racetrack and even now, at first light, the air was raspy. The morning riders were just arriving, parking their sedans behind the grandstands. Darby Munro was there, dressed in beige and chocolate, a sweater and cravat to match. Billy Cook, who had ridden Amounis years back, had his hair plastered and parted and smelled like a perfumery. Jim Pike was demure in brown, though neat. In fact, as they passed McGrath, nodding good morning to the old trainer, he remembered that the days of riding hacks to trackwork were over. Back then, the jocks arrived dishevelled and rosy cheeked. These days, they looked like Mark Foy mannequins.

McGrath leaned off the running rail when he saw John Tyler arrive. Tyler was Peter Pan's trackwork rider, and he was an ageing fellow, a tough-as-boots ex-pony hoop who had defaulted to the AJC in August '33. He'd been race riding at least since 1921. Tyler and Peter Pan clicked during trackwork. The horse, with all his opinions and attitude, was rarely a handful for Tyler, and Tyler was little. His riding weight hovered at 7st 3lb, so at any time Peter Pan could have had his merry way. Instead, the chestnut was polite and agreeable in Tyler's leathery hands. This morning, the jockey was fresh and wide eyed. He had walked from his house on Duke Street, on the far western side of Kensington, and unlike Munro, Cook and Pike, Tyler couldn't afford a fancy motorcar. He was dour in riding slacks and scuffed boots.

McGrath and Tyler strode off to meet the team, which had been walked and loosened up in the half hour before. As they approached, George Phillips pulled the rug off Peter Pan, tightened the girth and the surcingle, and slipped the horse the end of a carrot. As Peter chewed, distracted by the sweet juice of his treat, McGrath legged Tyler into the saddle and asked for a steady mile. He wanted no fast work after the mad dash of the day before.

Trotting away from the group, Tyler made his way to the course proper, then turned towards the mile-pole and began lumbering along. Gathering his reins, the jockey clucked to Peter Pan to hurry up, and the chestnut began to stride out. With the flags out 40 feet and the track fast, Peter Pan sprung along. Tyler marvelled out how limber he felt, how unjaded he was after the Maitland Stakes. He lifted his forelegs with sprite-like vigour, and as they entered the straight he did what he usually did and stared into the grandstands. McGrath had not managed to shake that obstinate habit out of him. Urging him a little faster, Tyler churned out the last half-mile in 52 seconds. As they pulled up, the sweat that dampened Peter's neck played tricks. He wasn't an unfit horse. The heat of the morning had caught up to him.

Coming to a stop before McGrath, Tyler jumped off Peter Pan and gave him a hearty pat. Phillips slipped Peter the other end of his carrot, and threw a rug over his back. McGrath looked him over for scrapes and knocks, checking a scratch on one of his pasterns that had occurred during the Chelmsford. The trainer noticed Peter was hardly blowing, then he sent Phillips away with him and directed Tyler to Deputy Ruler. Cid, Highboy and King Charles were waiting too, and Australia Fair was being rested. He hadn't the same constitution as Peter Pan, but not one of McGrath's other charges did.

McGrath left his position on the rail by mid-morning, and strolled back to Doncaster Avenue. It was hot. Just after eight o'clock, the eastern sun was in full boast already. McGrath felt sticky in his shoes and woollen pants, and prayed for a southerly that would blow the high pressure away. As it happened, he got one. Later that evening, a front moved in from the Pacific and sent the heat on its way. For the rest of the week, Sydney shivered in the high teens.

***

After the Maitland Stakes, the AJC spring meeting was next on McGrath's agenda. None of the weight-for-age races, the ones that Peter Pan was aimed at, were the carnival highlights. The premier events were the AJC Derby and the Epsom and Metropolitan handicaps. Peter Pan was prepped for the Spring Stakes on the first day, the Craven Plate on the third day, and possibly the two-mile Randwick Plate on the last day. The latter race was a wavering option. McGrath was inclined to think it unwise to run Peter Pan over two miles before sending him to Melbourne, and the trainer was almost sure that Peter would only run twice during the meeting – on Saturday 29 September and Wednesday 3 October. The Spring Stakes was already being touted as another titan rematch between Peter and Rogilla, and the Craven Plate was even better. Chatham would join them in that race.

The build-up to the Spring Stakes began in earnest. 'Desert Gold and Poitrel; Gloaming and Beauford; Spearfelt and Windbag ... many great thoroughbred pairs have helped to make the Spring Stakes famous for mighty struggles,' said the *Referee* in the week leading up to the carnival. 'I feel sure that the hard-headed form men will switch off Rogilla this year to back Peter Pan,' added 'Pilot'. That consensus ran deep around Randwick. 'Which of the mighty chestnuts will win when they lock horns in Saturday's Spring Stakes at standard weight-for-age?'

wondered the *Sportsman.* 'Peter Pan we think.' 'Peter Pan, an idol with the public, is likely to start favourite,' the *Telegraph* added. 'He should justify the confidence reposed in him.' Indeed, Peter Pan had been backed into oblivion. He would reach 6/4 on by flag fall.

The Spring Stakes would see Peter and Rogilla clash for the ninth time, and the fifth time at weight-for-age, of which Peter Pan was leading three to two. It was a mile-and-a-half contest worth £1000 to the winner, and three horses carried the top weight of 9st 5lb. They were the five-year-olds: Peter Pan, Oro and Braeburn. Rogilla was in receipt of 2lb, as were Topical and Gippsland, and the remaining three – Nightly, Limarch and Waikare (pronounced Whycar-ee) – had 9st. From a Cups point-of-view, it was a scintillating race. Peter Pan was favourite for the Melbourne Cup, and Rogilla for the Caulfield. Nightly was also gaining friends for Flemington's two-miler, and Gippsland had been graced a feathery weight for it. Oro, though not in Cups contention, had broken track records during the week, and had won his last two races. He had never beaten Peter Pan home, but if he were going to do it, it would be this weekend.

***

29 September dawned still and stale. The trams behind Randwick Racecourse were spilling sweaty, disagreeable racegoers onto the platforms, and jackets and hats lay limp on nearby fence posts. It was too

hot to carry them, much less wear them. The entire personnel of the city's tram and bus networks were on the job today, nearly 5000 workers. Tram services had started from Central Station at ten o'clock that morning, and the first-class tram had pulled out of Bridge Street in the city at 11.30am. Buses were running from Bondi Junction and Kings Cross, charging nine pence each way. There was even a service from Manly, on the other side of the harbour.

Since the crack of dawn, the racecourse had been bustling. Lorries had ambled in and out all morning, delivering 12,000 pies, 3000 frankfurt sausages, 1300 loaves of bread, and many more thousands of rolls. Five hundred turkeys had lost their lives to feed the Derby Day crowd. Miss Bishop, the firm that held the catering contract for all AJC enclosures, including Warwick Farm, had 500 employees on the roster this day, and a few of them had been baking 12,000 scones since early morning. The AJC itself had 420 employees in various roles for the first day of the meeting, and it was warranted. Some 60,000 people crammed the Paddock, the Leger and the Flat by noon.

A slight northeasterly was ruffling summer frocks when racing kicked off at 12.30pm. Though the AJC Derby was the expensive event of the day, every racebook was folded to the Epsom pages. Not only was the Epsom the first of the doubles-betting races, coupled with the Metropolitan on Monday, it was also Chatham's third Epsom, and he was vying to win it with 10st 9lb. No handicap in Australia had ever been won with more than 10st 5lb (Carbine's 1890 Cup record), but the coins were coming for Chatham. Fortunes had been laid on the Windbag wonder, and McGrath thought it ludicrous. Carbine was the most lethal horse he had seen on a track in all his years with horses, and McGrath knew that Chatham was a street away. He won't be seen at the finish, the trainer predicted. At about 2.35pm, Theo struggled home to win the Derby, and a little after that, McGrath's guess ran true. Chatham was crushed with his big weight in the Epsom and finished 11th in a field of 20. Pike was shattered, though he concealed it. He was very fond of Chatham. Australia Fair, McGrath's own little battler, ran third.

At 3.30pm, the horses emerged into the paddock for the Spring Stakes, and right away there was trouble afoot. Peter Pan wanted to be nowhere near the racetrack. A sullen, swollen stream of clouds had moved in over Randwick, and the frivolity of the afternoon's racing had been tempered. Where the trees had been still all day, now they rocked in warning. A change was coming, and Peter Pan was in a terrible mood. He had snapped at George Phillips earlier, and though Phillips ignored it, he knew it was a bad sign for Peter. When any horse came near the son of Pantheon, he flattened his ears and scowled. McGrath had checked the horse for any illness or discomfort and Peter Pan had eaten up the previous night, and again this morning. He had cantered well at dawn. There was nothing amiss, so McGrath put it down to moodiness, and the burgeoning hormones of a five-year-old stallion.

In the betting ring, Jim Hackett was shouting his odds from stand F8. There was a clamour of people around him, and further away, Jack Shaw was similarly crowded. 'Twos against Rogilla,' Shaw was yelling, 'I'll give you that, sir,' and he handed over a stub. Jim Pike was back aboard Peter Pan, so money was coming for the pair. 'Seven to two, yessir,' Shaw boomed. When the tote alarm sounded that the horses were at the post, a final scramble for bargains began, and then the betting ring emptied like a raided bar in Darlinghurst. Hackett, Shaw and the other bookies waited for Peter Pan or Rogilla to send them broke.

At the post, Jim Pike, reinstated for the carnival, knew that Peter was sour. He kept the horse on the fringe of the others, but there was no avoiding them when Jack Gaxieu called the line. It took only a few seconds for Peter Pan to kick the horse beside him, and not once. When he missed Braeburn the first time, he tried again, and Gaxieu's line fell into disarray as Braeburn lurched away. 'Keep your horse under control, Mr Pike,' the starter yelled. 'Heaven save me,' he muttered under his breath. With Pike distracting Peter Pan away from savagery and back to the bridle, the other eight horses stepped back into line. Gaxieu sent the tapes into the air.

Oro broke fastest, and cutting over to the rails he led Limarch, Nightly and Waikare past the stands. Gippsland was just ahead of Peter Pan, with Rogilla and Braeburn behind him, and Topical brought up the rear. Though the weather was changing, and the big events were already decided, the crowds sent the field out of the straight with a roar.

Oro had kicked to nearly two lengths of a lead when they rounded the turn into the backstretch. Midfield, Peter Pan was finding the pace a little lazy, and Pike was worried as they galloped down the back. If it stayed this way, he would have to pull the big fella out, which was better than checking him off the heels of the horse in front, but was still not ideal running. With Oro in no great hurry, and Nightly, Limarch and Waikare packed behind him, Pike waited, and Rogilla drew along his inside.

Both Pike and Darby Munro were watching each other. They knew they were the only two in the race, and up to this stage they'd been playing identical twins. With Pike eyeing Munro, and Munro eyeing Pike, neither of their horses had gone after the lead. But Peter Pan had a much bigger stride than Rogilla, and he was stuck for room, so nearing the six-pole Pike moved Peter Pan out. Sending the big chestnut around the pack, Peter was galloping three wide. Passing the five-furlong pole, he was covering 25 feet of ground more than the horses on his inside, and as he went around them, they went too. Pike had no option but to stay wide. Behind him, Rogilla was hugging the rails, waiting.

With four furlongs to go, Oro and Waikare were fighting for the lead, but Peter Pan had gone after them. He was a length behind as they entered the straight. On his inside, Limarch was on the rails. Pike got ready to send his horse to the lead, and he crouched low and raised his whip in his left hand. Waikare was dropping out, and Oro was left on his own. Peter Pan drew alongside him, ready to burst down the last bit by himself.

The whip came down on Peter's quarters a furlong from home as Rogilla ranged up on his outside. It might have been surprise, but more than likely it was temper, because Peter Pan veered away from the sting and crashed into Oro's little frame. Keith Cook, who was riding Oro, felt his mount lurch then fall sideways, smacking into Limarch who had dived into Waikare's pocket at just the wrong moment. Falling onto the running rail, Limarch baulked under jockey Ted Bartle, and he fell back through the field like an anvil, injured and startled. Oro hadn't time to right himself.

Peter Pan, however, had dashed into the lead and crossed to the rails, and he was in full flight towards the judge. Pike stole a glance over his left shoulder. In the muddle of swerving into Oro, he had allowed Rogilla to make ground on his outside. Darby Munro was aiming the last run at Peter Pan, and he came with every stride. Once again, the two horses were fighting it out down Randwick straight's final yards.

The Leger crowd rose with excitement, and the Flat patrons were hysterical on the fence. On the outside, Munro was riding for all he was worth; on the inside, Pike had a different battle. Peter Pan had his face turned towards his bitter rival, and at any moment Pike expected the horse to take a piece out of Rogilla's neck. He leaned heavy on his inside rein, yanking Peter's head back into place, but the horse wouldn't come. His head was almost under Rogilla's neck. With an impossible situation, the jockey drove Peter as best he could, and even in his ill temper, the horse kept stride with Rogilla. Their heads bobbed together, their knees rose as one. In the stands, racegoers couldn't separate them, and the shrill cheers were deafening around the racecourse. But Peter Pan's distraction was Rogilla's game-set-match. The Newcastle gelding burst over the line a head in front, and Frank McGrath couldn't believe it.

Jim Pike's face was ashen as he pulled up Peter Pan. But he didn't shake his head, or drop it between his shoulders. He reined his horse in and followed Rogilla back to scale. Though he expected them, very few catcalls came his way, even when most of the racecourse had backed his mount to odds-on. Staying clear of Peter Pan, the rest of the field followed him back to the paddock. Oro had clung tight to his wits and run into third place two lengths behind, and a bewildered Keith Cook knew that troubles were ahead. The incident at the top of the straight had occurred in full view of the stewards, and Limarch had struggled home in sixth. There was no need for either Cook or Bartle to lodge a protest. The result would have been no different, but the stewards were waiting for Pike when he stripped Peter's saddle.

J.E. Pike was a taciturn fellow at the best of times, but now he could only repeat what had happened in the straight. 'As Peter Pan was going past Oro, Rogilla rushed up on the outside. Realising that the latter is a more solid horse in a tight finish, I drew the whip on Peter Pan,' he told the stewards. 'As I hit him, he veered into the rails so quickly that it was impossible to pull him off the horses alongside me. The thing was over in a second, and the damage done.' The stewards knew Pike was an honourable horseman. He had the best reputation of any jockey riding, but he wasn't immune from responsibility. The stipes kept him in their room for several minutes.

In the saddling paddock, emotions were taut, stretched thin like a trip wire. 'It's a wonder your horse isn't badly crippled,' Ted Bartle was saying to Limarch's trainer, the New Zealander J.T. Jamieson. Jamieson was running a temperature. 'It is a deplorable state of affairs,' he boomed. Limarch had run into interference in three of his last four starts. The horse had been floated back to his stable, but within an hour word would reach the racecourse that he was sore and lame. His trainer had every right to be upset. The horse had come from New Zealand to tackle the Metropolitan, and due to Peter Pan's temper, that plan was out the window. But Keith Cook at least knew there was nothing Pike could have done. Oro's jockey told reporters that Pike could not very well have avoided the trouble. The steward's report stated otherwise. Their inquisition concluded that Pike was at fault for not exercising greater control over Peter Pan. As a result, serious interference had occurred and a horse was hurt. They suspended Sydney's top rider for two months. In one fell swoop, Pike lost his mounts for the Melbourne Cup carnival.

Peter Pan's posse was confounded, stunned at the severity of the penalty. Frank McGrath, given the chance, would have testified that Peter Pan was in an antsy state prior to running. Rodney Dangar was horrified. At the worst possible time he had lost the best possible jockey. He was struggling with diplomacy down in the paddock, but nonetheless expressed his regret to J.T. Jamieson. Everyone waited for Pike to emerge. 'Peter Pan has had an off day,' he said. 'I've never known him to be so sour and only once before have I known him to kick at the barrier.'

'Could you have won, Pikey?' a journalist asked from the middle of the group.

'Well, Peter Pan had only to keep his head straight to win,' Pike replied. 'He was going better than Rogilla, but he was paying more attention to his rival than to his race.' As an afterthought, the jockey added, 'He was a certainty beaten.'

The clouds overhead had turned a dark, bruising colour, and in the excitement of the Spring Stakes, racegoers had forgotten to look up. Now, many of them opted for the trams. Babbling about the day's events, they joined in a steady stream out of the racecourse. Some recalled that Peter Pan had lunged for Kuvera in the King's Cup. Others remembered that Pike had been similarly suspended for the 1932 Melbourne carnivals.

Jim Pike, however, refused to wallow in his bad luck. He had elected to sit out the Derby this year, refusing to waste to 8st 10lb, but now he wished he had acted differently. With Chatham's loss in the Epsom, and Peter Pan's mid-race fiasco, the day had been expensive. Moreover, he was back to the spring of two years ago. Peter Pan was the best chance in the Centenary Melbourne Cup and, as in '32, he was forbidden to ride him. Chatham looked a good thing in the Cox Plate, and again, as in '32, he was also forbidden to ride *him.* It was a ridiculous situation, but the jockey decided there was no point appealing it.

***

The change that was blowing in over the Eastern Suburbs, and the close of racing, emptied the racecourse in an hour. An army of AJC workers moved in to straighten the place for Monday. There were millions of ticket stubs strewn about, and the bins were overflowing. Racebooks lay abandoned on the lawns and under seats, and the odd jacket hung here and there. Not all of them made it to lost property. George Law, Randwick's groundskeeper, wandered around the

Leger lawn with a sack in his hand. He was picking up rubbish, and his old grey pony followed, pulling a little cart behind him. There was no lead rope attached to the pony. The pair had worked like this for years. Right now, if anyone had seen them that didn't know them, they would have been stupefied. The ageing grey pony was picking up strewn garbage with his mouth, twisting his neck around and dumping it in the cart. Together, he and Law worked the Leger reserve for more than an hour.

The rain that had threatened didn't fall until late in the night. By then, McGrath had had time to digest the Spring Stakes. Peter Pan was without a jockey now for the remainder of the season, but that wasn't a problem outright. Jim Munro could probably ride when Pike was unavailable. McGrath was a little more worried about Peter Pan's temperament. It was true that a strapping stallion of five years could have his mind on things other than racing. But McGrath wasn't convinced that was Peter's problem today. The horse's moodiness wasn't a daily issue. It wasn't even a weekly issue. In fact, in any other stallion it would have proved no problem at all. In a horse like Peter Pan, however, a character that broadcast his opinions, it had proved a problem. McGrath decided that the horse, as he had done with the Chipping Norton in the autumn, just hadn't felt like running. On learning that he had had to run anyway, Peter Pan had revolted as best he could. It was as simple as that.

The Spring Stakes had been run in 2:32, which was three-quarters of a second faster than the three-year-olds had run in the Derby. It was also the same time they had run in the King's Cup back in April. Peter's share of the prize brought his winnings to £16,735 and 10 shillings, and the weight-for-age duel between him and Rogilla was even. For six meetings on the scale, they had won three apiece, but Rogilla had now beaten Peter Pan in their last three outings. The Spring Stakes was Peter's 21st start, and his third race for the season. McGrath was very satisfied with the progress. Peter had a win and two seconds on the board, and he had lost by no further than a head each time. There was no disgrace in today's performance, although McGrath would prefer it if his horse didn't savage those around him.

***

Craven Plate Day was dry and grey. The clouds were low, and a rousing breeze was whipping around the corners of the grandstands. Though the third day of the carnival was not traditionally a huge day for attendance, being a Wednesday, AJC secretary George Rowe was hopeful of a good turnout. The first two days of the carnival had improved on the previous year's attendance, and if today exceeded 20,000 people, it would be more than what he had got in 1933. As it turned out, he would get 27,000.

The Craven Plate was due off at two o'clock, and only five horses were engaged. Peter Pan and Chatham led the field with 9st 4lb, Rogilla and Lough Neagh had 9st 1lb, and Nightly, now an up-and-coming stayer, had 9st. The race was a mile and a quarter, and Chatham was vying for his third successive win, something only Phar Lap had ever done before in that event.

When the horses came in to parade, McGrath was standing with Dangar in the centre of the saddling paddock. A little while later, jockey Jim Munro appeared, sporting Dangar's orange and green silks, and he joined the two men in their huddle. With his arms folded around his narrow little frame, Munro listened to McGrath's instructions. The trainer looked intense, peering through his glasses at the jockey and nodding his head, his hands going this way and that. McGrath had spent the previous night reviewing his tactics to defeat Rogilla. In their last three meetings, Rogilla had come at Peter Pan from behind, and he had won each time. In the Melbourne Cup of '32, Peter Pan had come from behind. He had also snatched the Maitland Stakes when he had come at Chatham from the back. 'Sit off the pace, sit right at the back if you have to,' he told Munro. 'He has enough dash to get to the front down the straight.' Munro nodded, but McGrath pressed his arm. 'Let Rogilla go before you.'

Peter Pan stepped into the middle of the ring, and McGrath tossed Munro into the saddle. The jockey eyed the other runners. His wily brother, the Demon

Darb, was on Rogilla, and Stan Davidson had scooped the ride on Chatham in Pike's absence, while Maurice McCarten was piloting Nightly. The books had kept a lid on Peter Pan, and it was hard to get anything better than 10/9 against him. Rogilla was better at 6/4, and Chatham, who had lost his last two outings, was friendless at 8/1. Most considered the race a contest between Peter and Rogilla, because it was getting to look that way every time the pair met. Across the racecourse, loyalties were split. Peter Pan was a public favourite, but he was yet to beat Rogilla that season.

Munro circled Peter Pan at the start, knowing well that McGrath was desperate to turn the tables on Rogilla. The trainer had been earnest in his instructions, and without the handicap of a filthy temper, Peter would be pliable to Munro's riding. Without much delay, the five horses were assembled into a line.

In this small field, the jump was civilised. As the five horses lurched into stride, Munro took a hold on Peter, and he let the others dash ahead of him. Inside the first furlong, though Chatham and Lough Neagh had broken fastest, Nightly led the field, and he ran the first two furlongs on his own. In the middle, Rogilla was hugging the rails, and Peter Pan was last of all. Some five lengths spread the field.

The horses swung into the first turn in no great hurry. Nightly had run the first two furlongs in 28 seconds, but as they bowled along the backstretch, Chatham came around him to take the lead, and the

Windbag horse opened up more than a length. Stan Davidson, not wanting to interfere with his mount, let him stretch out, and they ran past the six-furlong pole nearly two lengths ahead. Nightly was next, then a length to Rogilla on the rail. Lough Neagh was after him, and Peter Pan was last, loping easily in Munro's control.

Out of the far turn they galloped, and at the half-mile they began to bunch up. Chatham had been given a breather, and had come back to the field for a moment. Nightly had run up to his flanks, and Rogilla was close too. Darby Munro had given his horse a dream run on the rails, and at the back, brother Jim knew he would have to go around to get Peter Pan close. But he had a tight hold on Peter still, for he wasn't about to go too early.

The horses galloped into the home turn, and Davidson let Chatham go. He charged the bay horse into the straight, and he didn't stop driving. Chatham leaped ahead by two lengths to Nightly, Rogilla was a length back and Lough Neagh and Peter Pan were winding up together. Jim Munro let his reins out. He urged Peter to go when they straightened, and the big chestnut took off underneath him. He motored down the straight with monstrous strides, picking off his rivals one by one. Rogilla, under furious riding from Darby Munro, was coming up empty, and Peter Pan dashed past him, eating into Chatham's lead.

Within 100 yards of the post, Peter had come to the leader's flanks. Munro raised his whip and hit the horse, and Peter Pan fell away from it. Switching the stick to his inside hand, Munro rode with all his heart to get Peter Pan home. But Chatham was relentless, and his break in the straight had been too much. He won his third Craven Plate by three-quarters of a length to Peter Pan, and Rogilla was a length and a half away third. They were a second outside Phar Lap's record, running the 10 furlongs in 2:03 1/2.

In the ring, the bag swingers let out a cheerful shout. They would take home every penny laid on Peter Pan and Rogilla, but their high spirits were drowned by the ovation afforded Chatham, for the gallant miler had turned the tables on Dangar's horse. As he trotted back to scale, with Peter Pan and Rogilla in tow, the racecourse stood and cheered. Even Dangar and McGrath clapped, knowing this was what racing needed – not one horse sweeping the stakes races, but two or three.

Jim Munro was pleased with Peter Pan's run. As he slipped the saddle from the horse's back he told McGrath so. But he had overdone the waiting tactics, albeit following the trainer's orders, though he had beaten Rogilla home. Munro was annoyed that he had given Chatham such a start. At the distance, Peter Pan had four lengths to make on the leader, and no one could give Chatham that when he was in form, not even Peter Pan.

After the Craven Plate, Peter's winnings climbed to £16,985 and 10 shillings. His share of the prize was £250. More importantly, he had finished ahead of Rogilla, which was almost as necessary to the public as the race result itself. McGrath was not unhappy with the result. If he'd ever thought there were two great horses in Sydney with nothing between them at the middle distances, now he was positive there were three.

***

In early October in Sydney, the sun falls behind the Blue Mountains at about six o'clock, but long shadows have already swallowed Randwick Racecourse. Under the grandstands, the air is crisp and cool, and on this evening, Thursday 4 October, the day after the Craven Plate, McGrath knew it. He shivered, and hurried along to the AJC office. The racecourse was spotless and entirely silent. McGrath's footfalls climbed all the way to the roof. When he swung open the door to the office, he was glad of human company – and electric heating.

The clerk behind the counter knew why McGrath had come. He presented a thick journal in front of the trainer, with a pen and a ruler, and McGrath drew a line through Peter Pan's name. He was scratching his horse from Saturday's Randwick Plate, and Les Haigh had been in before him. Rogilla was out already, and that left the race to Oro, Lough Neagh or Nightly. McGrath paid the forfeit fee to the clerk, then left the office.

He'd been inside only minutes, but twilight had paled into nightfall. McGrath strode away from the racetrack and towards the cottage lights of Doncaster Avenue. His mind was busy. He was sending horses to Melbourne, but which horses to send, and for which races? The options swam in his head. This week, more than any other week of the year, McGrath felt older, nearly all of his 67 years. But the smell of home cooking wafted out of the windows on Doncaster Avenue, smeared with the scent of horses and sweet hay, and he forgot his troubles and followed his stomach inside.

23

The men who saw Archer

In October 1934, there were a few men with long memories. Behind their glassy eyes and mottled complexions, their white wispy hair and whiskers, they had long tunnels that went back through time, to the sight of Archer winning the first two Melbourne Cups. They were more than 80 years old now, and if they weren't, they were close. They shuffled around these modern times like pebbles caught in spokes, wary of engines, grieving for hansom cabs, and every so often they had cause to think back. In the spring of '34, they had cause enough.

The minds of these old men fell backwards to Archer. They remembered a masculine stallion, a huge horse, similar to Phar Lap in proportions but bay. They recalled the first afternoon they saw him in Melbourne. It was Thursday 7 November 1861, and a mild day with a light southerly wind and only a spatter of rain in the morning. They thought Archer too gross and clumsy to cover two miles, and they pleaded with the gods of the colony that the New South Wales horse would fail in Victorian company. But Archer didn't, and the first Melbourne Cup went north, along with the sweepstakes of 20 sovereigns and £610.

Flemington was not spectacular then. It was a callow racecourse, finding its feet and plying its trade without starting strands or amplifiers or racecourse keepers. Its grandstand was a flimsy scaffold, and its turf studded with tufts and holes and mowed by sheep. But this Melbourne Cup race, this great handicap, it changed Flemington that day. New South Wales and South Australia sent representatives, and 22 owners paid up the full amount of the sweepstakes, though only 17 competed. Two horses were killed during running, and Twilight, an unruly brown mare, bolted the circuit of the track before agreeing to start. In neighbouring states, the newspapers awaited the race report by steamship.

The old men of Melbourne remembered everything about that day. Their memories had photographed the ladies' tidy bonnets and bold crinolines, and the cravats and beaver hats of the gentlemen in the paddock. There were games of skill and chance on the lawns that robbed the unwary, and little bars of rum and canteens with lemonade. There were four-in-hand carriages, the hansom cabs they missed so much, and the horse-drawn buses that glutted the entrance to the racecourse. The old boys could see these images clearly, not in black and white, or fuzzy and quick like the old silent films. They were real and reachable, and in 1934 they were dusted off and recalled.

Peter Pan's entry in the Centenary Melbourne Cup was an effort to up-end the horse they had seen that day. No horse had won two Cups for 72 years, and the old men thought they might die before it happened. They recalled that The Grafter had come the closest, losing the 1897 Cup by a head and then winning the following year, but neither Carbine nor Phar Lap, the yardsticks in the minds of racing men, had won twice, and both were entered multiple times. There were great ones in between, of course. The Barb, or the 'Black Demon' as he was coined, was peerless, a monstrous dark horse that could stir the stout heart of a man. It was hard to forget Malua also, a horse that won the Newmarket sprint, the Australian and Melbourne cups, and the Grand National Hurdle Race all in the same season. There was Chester, and unbeaten Grand Flaneur, and the speedy Newhaven who, up to 10 furlongs, was as ruthless as Carbine. In their minds, the old men saw these horses flying down the Flemington straight before the turn of the century, their jockeys' legs hugging their horses' bellies and clods of turf billowing.

Things changed after that. Though there was Poseidon, Prince Foote and Comedy King, there was Federation, motorcars and Tod Sloan's miniature stirrups. There was industry and commercialism. Some of the goldfields had become ghost towns. Was life any better? The old fellows couldn't decide. They didn't need to remember now, because there were photographs and telephones, and the race reports were overnight. Instead of 4000 faces at the Melbourne Cup, there were 104,000, and the newspapers devoted 32 columns to rehashing the race, not the column-and-a-bit of 1861. But the crash of '29 brought everything down like a house of cards. The old men, and they were very old now, were reminded of the hard times of the 1890s – lines on the streets, poverty, sad and tired horses on the racetrack.

But the wheel of time had kept rolling, and the 74th Melbourne Cup was here. It was plump with hope and celebration, just like it had been in the old days, and Peter Pan had stepped off the Melbourne Express at St Albans, in pursuit of Archer's scalp.

24

The battle for Darby Munro

It was a warm Wednesday evening on 10 October, a week since the Craven Plate, and Tom Breen sat in a folding chair, his hat tipped and a shotgun limp in his lap. He was a big fellow, not especially young, the sort of man not easily crossed. He was also a friend of Frank McGrath. The two had met, ironically, at their Catholic church in Kensington, and so had begun a long association. Still but watchful now, not two feet from Peter Pan's box, Breen was the horse's appointed bodyguard at the Mackinnon & Cox yards at Flemington.

Peter Pan had arrived from Sydney that morning, listless and tired from the 16-hour trip south. With Australia Fair and Master Brierly, he had been settled in down the shed row from Chatham and Theo, and Flemington's sounds and scents were old news again. There was the smell of cut grass from the straight six, the odour of paddock roses that travelled on the breeze, and the sight of the steely Tom Breen. Peter had reacquainted himself with Melbourne's dry winds, its cooler nights, so that by sunfall he was quite at home. Breen kept his vigil into the night.

The deployment of a guard had been Rodney Dangar's idea. It wasn't because there had been rumours of malice, or even malcontent. It was rather that Dangar would sleep better knowing his horse was protected. Money had been shovelled into the Melbourne Cup markets since June, much of it on Peter, and if the right horses came off in the Caulfield Cup, doubles backers would be right on song. It was scenarios like these that brought the worst out in the wrong types of people, and McGrath knew it. In his 30 or so years at Randwick, he had seen everything from knobbling to thistling and loading. He had gone looking for Breen right away.

The Melbourne Cup was more than three weeks away, and Peter Pan's schedule was set. He would race in the Melbourne Stakes on Saturday 3 November, then the Cup three days later. He would also contest the Duke of Gloucester Cup the following Saturday, a race on Dangar's radar because it was being specially hosted for the visiting royals, but McGrath was in grey territory about the weeks preceding these races. He didn't want to start Peter in the Melbourne Stakes without a prep race, but there was only one prep race that fitted Peter Pan's profile. It was the weight-for-age W.S. Cox Plate, due off on 27 October, the Saturday between the Caulfield and Melbourne cups meetings, and already Chatham, Rogilla and Hall Mark were contenders.

McGrath had chewed over the options. Peter Pan had been given 9st 10lb for the Melbourne Cup, a great horse's weight, and he would need to be at the peak of fitness to win with that burden. It was 9lb over weight-for-age. If McGrath didn't start the horse in the Cox Plate, Peter would start in the Cup off the back of only a single run in five weeks, in the Melbourne Stakes three days beforehand. The trainer didn't doubt the task was doable, but it wasn't ideal. On Tuesday morning, 16 October, McGrath made a late nomination for the Cox Plate.

***

The first few days in Melbourne were easy streets for Peter Pan. It wasn't because he was finding his Flemington feet, or even because McGrath was delayed in Sydney. It had more to do with the rain that, not even 24 hours after Peter's arrival, began to tumble like judgement day. The morning following his arrival, the grass tracks at Caulfield were flooded and closed, and no fast work could be done at Flemington. It also became very cold.

With the tracks soft underfoot, Peter Pan did just enough to stay fit. McGrath's orders were clear. There would be no fast galloping until the ground allowed it. If Peter slipped in the wet, overexertion in righting himself could render him unfit to race, and so George Phillips cantered him for days. But with McGrath's arrival to Melbourne around 15 October, and an ease in rainfall, Peter's programme was stepped up. He began to work the short, sharp bursts that had seen him through the AJC carnival, and on Tuesday 16 October he worked six furlongs on Flemington's course proper in 1:29, the first three in 39 seconds. For many of Melbourne's clockers, it was the first time they'd seen the chestnut since 1932. 'Racegoers will see quite a different Peter Pan to the one they saw two years ago. He has made up wonderfully,' commented the Melbourne-based *Sporting Globe.* 'Always a tall horse, Peter Pan has developed into a most powerful animal. Frank McGrath must certainly feel proud of his condition.'

He was. With the benefit of AJC racing, Peter Pan needed little to keep him in tune. On Thursday 18 October, though the course proper was soft after yet more rain, Peter turned out a smart mile gallop with two other Sydney candidates, Sarcherie and Journal. Sarcherie belonged to J.J. Leahy, a broad, boisterous cattleman and horse breeder. She was a kind, honest filly, though she was yet to win anything big. Journal, on the other hand, was a Caulfield Cup fancy. McGrath had backed this brown gelding into Peter Pan for the Cups double, and on this Thursday morning, with an unforgiving bite in the breeze, the three horses turned the mile over in 1:47 3/4. With Journal on the inside, Sarcherie in the middle and Peter Pan on the outside, the three horses clocked the first half-mile in 52 seconds, and the six in 1:20. They were 30 feet out with the flags and in heavy going, so the time was respectable. In the straight, Sarcherie was left by her rivals, and at the finish, Peter Pan was ahead by half a length, but neither Andy Knox on Journal, nor Clarrie Scahill on Peter, asked much from their mounts. When they pulled up, McGrath was satisfied.

Scahill had come with the team from Sydney, along with McGrath, his brother Maurice, a cool but excited George Phillips, and the grooms for Australia Fair and Master Brierly. Scahill was a regular rider for McGrath's morning gallops, and had worked and lived closely with the trainer since 1928. He resided only a few doors up from McGrath these days, and was an efficient, reliable rider. Though he didn't have the same relationship with Peter that John Tyler had, Scahill could handle the temperamental stallion, could coax him to behave during trackwork. That was just as well, because shortly after the Thursday-morning gallop with Sarcherie and Journal, trouble reared its ugly head.

After a solitary workout on Friday morning, nothing exerting or expeditious about it, Peter Pan pulled up lame. His action was unmistakable to Scahill. The near shoulder, having been right for some months now, was tied up again. Looking anxiously around for McGrath, Scahill jumped off and waited, and with the trainer came a posse of concerned onlookers. Peter Pan stood favouring his near side, and walking him forward, McGrath found his action scratchy and brittle. Dismayed, he called for the horse float and spirited Peter Pan back to the yard.

The old trainer was crestfallen. His best laid plans had unravelled in the blink of a moment. Peter Pan stood on the fringe of history, of a rare Melbourne Cup double, and suddenly he might not run at all. McGrath felt like some giant hand of bad luck was pressing down on his chest. The news reached the bookies even before it reached Rodney Dangar. Peter's price for the Cup blew out instantly. Rumours about his condition spread like locusts around Melbourne, while at the Mackinnon & Cox yards, McGrath swore at the overcast skies. In the week and a bit that Peter Pan had been at Flemington, the weather couldn't have been more damp, dismal or hungover. The wet tracks, the draughts and the unseasonably cold spring had brought them back to the same problem – that near shoulder was cramped.

McGrath ordered Phillips to get busy with the fomentation, and the two men worked on the horse throughout the morning. The camphor blocks and ammonia were soaked into washcloths, and hot towels were laid over Peter Pan's shoulder for hours. It was painstaking, tiresome labour, but McGrath wanted to see if their efforts were effective. In the afternoon, he walked Peter Pan out of his box, finding the horse smooth in his action and sound in his walk. He sent him on his usual afternoon exercise, relief etched all over his face.

In the days that followed, McGrath woke with the birds to tend to his horse, checking him for ailments and fending off his own panic at the slightest hint of lameness. It helped on Saturday 20 October when Journal, piloted by Andy Knox, won the Caulfield Cup at 7/1. McGrath's lucrative double was alive, but it was a long two weeks to Cup Day. On 22 October, Peter Pan galloped soundly with Clarrie Scahill, and the following day he ran a solitary mile in 1:46 1/2. On pulling up, he showed no distress in either temperament or action, and walking back to the sheds he was free-moving and confident. Though the time was nothing special, Chatham had taken 1:33 to clear seven furlongs that morning with the help of Vista over the final four, so all up Peter's effort was rather a good one. McGrath wondered if the worst was behind them.

It wasn't. On Wednesday morning, Peter Pan was scratchy again after his work, but by the afternoon he was crystal clear of his ailment. 'Peter Pan's shoulder trouble is as puzzling as it is worrying to his trainer,' reported the *Telegraph* back in Sydney. 'It appears and disappears unexpectedly.' While it was a troubling problem, McGrath recognised that they weren't in dire straits. The shoulder was responding to attention, and Peter Pan was sound more than he was lame, but the Cox Plate was four days away. McGrath telephoned Dangar about their options.

Dangar wasn't due to Melbourne until 30 October, some four days before the Melbourne Stakes. The news of Peter Pan's shoulder recurrence was about as welcome to him as cholera. But, like the trainer, he had suspected the problem was dormant, not cured, and so he tuned his mind to optimism. He suggested to McGrath that he could send veterinarian Stuart Pottie down on the overnight, but McGrath felt the trouble was not yet serious enough for that. Their attention right now was whether to start Peter Pan in the Cox Plate, and as things stood, McGrath felt that it would adversely affect their Cup chances if they did. Dangar agreed. Peter Pan would not start in the Cox Plate.

The scratching ignited rumours all over again, but McGrath had long learned to ignore them. When reporters asked him about Peter Pan's condition, he told them there were no problems, but the gossip persisted. Peter eased in Melbourne Cup betting again, with AJC Derby–winner Theo heading the market, helped by his victory in the Caulfield Guineas. The New Zealand raider Sir Simper had run a cracker in the Caulfield Cup and had gone into second favouritism, while Peter Pan sat with Hall Mark, Nightly and now Journal in the betting – not quite favourite, but within the top six contenders. It was reasonable. Backers would not see Peter Pan race until the Melbourne Stakes, three days before Cup Day, and that wasn't ideal for anyone. It wasn't ideal for the punter with coin in his pocket, and it certainly wasn't ideal for Frank McGrath.

On Saturday 27 October, Chatham won the Cox Plate, his second, and in his wake trailed Hall Mark and Rogilla. It was an illustrious win for the Sydney star, proving, if it still needed to be proved, that he was Australia's most decorated middle-distance racehorse. Watching from the sidelines, McGrath swelled at the significance of the Sir Herbert Maitland Stakes not two months before. Peter Pan had beaten a horse that day with form enough to go on and win the Cox Plate. The trainer grew confident, and more so in the days that followed. Though the drizzle kept on, Peter Pan began to sparkle. On the Monday after the Cox Plate, he ran nine furlongs in 1:58 1/2, an exceptional time given Flemington was sodden. The first four furlongs took him 54 seconds, the six in 1:19, and the mile took 1:45 flat. The following morning, he worked the smartest eight furlongs of the day in 1:46. 'His effort was a gem,' commented Melbourne's *Truth.* McGrath rubbished rumours that Peter Pan wasn't right. 'He is as fit as hands can make him,' the trainer said. 'He will strip one of the fittest horses in the Cup.'

***

Peter Pan's prospects were looking bright, but despite his own confidence now, McGrath had a practical dilemma: which jockey was going to pilot Peter Pan for his three Flemington races? Without the grace of timing, Jim Munro had announced he was deserting Australia for India, and was sailing on the P&O liner *Mooltan* from Sydney on 22 October. With Pike suspended, and the older Munro somewhere on the skirt of the Pacific, Dangar and McGrath had no jockey, and pickings were thin. Most, if not all, of the top riders were tied to mounts already.

Rodney Dangar resisted being angry with Jim Munro. It was offensive timing for the rider to make such a decision, but the owner erred towards frustration, not anger. There was just no point to the latter. As jockeys were wont to do, Munro had gone where the cash was, to a rich retainer in India riding for Alec Higgins. Jim Munro's side of the story was, in fact, a little more complicated. The 28-year-old had had an uneasy relationship with Sydney. Several years before he had left to ride in Germany, and met with wild success there, but upon his return home he had found himself disinherited by the owners and trainers he longed to ride for. Perhaps there was a bout of begrudging in that, but more likely the Sydney racing fraternity, opinionated and difficult to infiltrate, was chilly towards the lad that country-hopped at his leisure. Better to reward the boys that stayed at home. So Jim Munro found himself in the shadows of Pike, brother Darb and Billy Duncan, though he was equal to their tasks. Right in time for the Centenary Melbourne Cup, Munro had had enough and, as if by magic, his offer had appeared from India.

The Peter Pan camp urgently needed a top jockey, and one who could handle the tenacious horse over two miles. Both Dangar and McGrath agreed that Darby Munro was the only man for the task. The problem was, Demon Darb was tied to Rogilla, as he had been for years, and that was how the war began.

McGrath made representations to Darby before Jim had even booked passage on the *Mooltan.* The old trainer was positive that the younger Munro would see the situation for what it was, a lucrative opportunity, and Munro did see it that way. He told McGrath he would request a release from Rogilla, but the fate of that request would rest in the hands of Rogilla's lessee-trainer Les Haigh. As it transpired, Haigh was less than enamoured about losing his regular rider. It was delicate turf to be treading, but McGrath suspected that Rogilla was not the horse he had been in Sydney. When the old warrior managed only sixth in the Caulfield Cup and third in the Cox Plate, his suspicions were confirmed. Thus, McGrath's representations to Darby Munro were based on the premise that it wasn't certain Rogilla would even proceed to the Melbourne Cup. In McGrath's eyes, Munro was within his riding rights to seek the mount with the best chance of winning, especially if his regular ride might not even start. Dangar, in Sydney, was content to let his trainer navigate this one.

Haigh had different ideas to McGrath. He was repulsed by the situation facing him. Two days after the Caulfield Cup he stated, unequivocally, that his gelding would take his place in the Melbourne Cup, and Haigh's word was his bond. He refused to accept any suggestion that Rogilla was spent or out of form. He declared he had no intention of releasing Darby Munro, and the Peter Pan camp fell into despair. Haigh was entitled to dig his heels in. He had had first rights to Darby Munro since 1932 and, up until now, McGrath had never come calling with Peter Pan. Now, for the most important race of the year, a race that had eluded Rogilla each time he had competed in it, the Peter Pan camp had come running. It was unfair, but that was racing, and all parties simply wanted the best shot at victory.

The dispute spilled into the newspapers. Dangar, though publicly silent on the matter, was privately mortified. It was more regrettable for Frank McGrath, however, for he loathed falling out with a fellow trainer. Les Haigh was a pleasant, and more than reasonable, fellow. He was also a neighbour these days, having relocated his yard from Newcastle to Bowral Street, Kensington. Neither McGrath nor Haigh was the kind of man who craved confrontation, but the Rogilla–Peter Pan rivalry was a public headline now, and neither party was backing down.

Darby himself possessed no confusion about which way he was swinging. Seeking out McGrath, he found the trainer at the Victoria Hotel in the city. The jockey explained that he wanted to ride Peter Pan, and that Haigh had engaged him for the Caulfield Cup only. 'That being the case,' McGrath replied, 'you can ride him.' But the trainer advised that the engagement included the Melbourne Stakes and the Duke of Gloucester Cup, and when Munro agreed, McGrath thought that was that. To his surprise then, on Wednesday 23 October, Les Haigh informed McGrath that it was news to him that Munro had been engaged for only one race on Rogilla. They were back to square one, and with no white flag in sight, the stewards at the VRC threatened to intervene.

McGrath and Dangar could have elected the easier route and engaged a less prolific, less problematic jockey for Peter Pan. But the reality was that as Peter got older and stronger, and more inclined to let his opinions get the better of him, he needed an experienced, rigorous rider who wouldn't accept his sourness. In the Melbourne Cup, over two miles and under 9st 10lb, Peter Pan would have to run very truly to win, and show none of the moodiness that had settled him in the Spring Stakes. Responding to that analysis before sailing off to India, Jim Munro revealed, 'Peter Pan is a peculiar horse, for the easier his task the less he likes it. When he has something very definite to accomplish, as in the Sir Herbert Maitland Stakes, he gets down to his job like a Phar Lap, and it will probably be the same in the Melbourne Cup.' For good measure, though, Jim Munro took his little brother aside before he left Sydney, confident that Darby would be piloting Peter Pan in his absence. He told his sibling about the chestnut's foibles, about his aversion to being crowded by horse and rider. 'When you ride him, sit up in the saddle,' he said to Darby, 'and be vigorous. He'll finish like a train for you.'

Darby Munro almost didn't need to be told. He'd ridden Rogilla to enough close finishes with Peter Pan to know what the big chestnut was like. The younger Munro was an observant rider, in and out of the saddle. He was known for tipping horses that he had ridden against and appraising their future chances though he'd never ridden them. But the part of him that interested McGrath the most was the rigour in his riding. Munro would sit poised on a horse until the moment was ready to finish big. He could push a horse through the eye of a needle, and when he dashed through the hedge on Rogilla to snatch the King's Cup in the autumn, everyone knew it. He was also a one-cut jockey, a man who could achieve with one sting of the whip what other jockeys achieved in several. In his riding style, he was no quiet commander like Jim Pike, but it didn't matter to Demon Darb how he won. What mattered was that he won.

By Tuesday 30 October, a week to Cup Day, there was no end in sight for the battle over Darby Munro. When asked by the *Telegraph* about the fiasco, McGrath stated that not only was the jockey engaged for the Melbourne Cup, he would also ride Peter Pan in the Melbourne Stakes on Saturday, whether Rogilla raced or not. Rogilla *was* racing, in both contests, and in defiance of McGrath's confidence Haigh retorted that he would go to the stewards if he had to. The stewards, in fact, were quite busy. They were dealing with quibbles over Andy Knox's engagements, and Harold Skidmore's too, and with four days left before the start of the carnival, punters deserved to know the fate of their fancies. In the hands of the stipes, Haigh was positive he would win the war, and that possibility weighed heavily on Frank McGrath's mind. In preparation for it, he told Sydney jockey Keith Cook to be on hand. Cook had never piloted Peter Pan, but he was McGrath's stable jockey at the moment, lately riding Cid and Highboy to good wins. It was a worst-case scenario for McGrath, but he had little confidence the stewards would award him Darby Munro.

On Wednesday, the parties were still no closer to agreement. Dangar arrived by the Melbourne Express that morning, and went straight to the yard to confer with McGrath on the matter. Dangar, reasonable and businesslike, thought it absurd that a compromise hadn't yet been reached. He suggested to McGrath that both trainers and jockey sit down together to discuss the matter. McGrath organised the meeting, which would occur the following day, but Haigh was still defiant. Commenting to the press late on Wednesday night, he said, 'Munro will ride my horse, and that is all I know about it.'

The conference took place the following morning, and Dangar stayed away. In civil but terse tones McGrath told Haigh that it was never his intention to impinge on Rogilla's chances, but Munro had expressed his commitment to ride Peter Pan, and no trainer within his right mind would reject the services of a leading jockey when he didn't already have one. Sheepishly, Munro confirmed that he had made himself available to Peter Pan without a release from Haigh. But he declared that he wanted to ride Peter Pan, telling Haigh that, with respect, Peter had a better chance of winning than Rogilla. McGrath also stated that Haigh could employ Stan Davidson, who had as much of a record with Rogilla as Munro had, while McGrath had no such option.

Haigh was within his bounds to send the two men packing. It was an affront to his integrity that he was here at all, fighting with another trainer over a jockey that was rightfully his. But it was impossible to ignore the fact that Munro didn't want to ride Rogilla. Haigh found it almost insulting. Munro had had splendid wins aboard his gutsy gelding – the Cox Plate and King's Cup to name two – but he had so easily switched teams. Haigh knew it was all in the spirit of business for the rider, but that was little solace right now. McGrath also wasn't backing down. He was one of the biggest trainers at Randwick, and was used to getting his own way. Though he was trying to act with decorum and respect, he was making it clear he would go to the stewards if required. And Haigh was suddenly tired of the affair. Munro wanted out, and the Newcastle trainer relented. He released his jockey from Rogilla.

Haigh knew there should be nothing personal in this mess, though it was hard to see it that way. Each of the men simply wanted to further their chances of Melbourne Cup success, and if there was injury there Haigh wanted no part of it any longer. He lit a cigarette, took a long drag and wished his opposition luck. Then he left them to telephone Stan Davidson.

The anvil that had been hanging over Frank McGrath's head was gone. He could breathe again. Darby Munro would ride Peter Pan, and not just in the Cup. He would pilot Peter through the Melbourne Stakes, the Duke of Gloucester Cup and, if all went well, the

Randwick race meeting hosted in honour of the Duke on 22 November. But as this good news made the McGrath camp sleep easier in their beds those two days before the Melbourne Stakes, the rain began to fall in miserable torrents over Flemington.

25

Whose turn is it this time?

The Birdcage was full of colour. Ladies in rayon pleats and neat wool folds milled on the lawn in their finery, nursing racebooks and purses, babbling excitedly about Derby Day. They wore chiffon, silk and gabardine, and French-inspired frocks from the house of Madeleine Vionnet. Around them, young gentlemen shifted as they approached, the sexy pulse of femininity alive and high on raceday. Though the rain had tumbled all night, and for two days before that, the first day of the Cup carnival was bright and dry, and 40,000 people had arrived at Flemington that morning. Outside Peter Pan's race stall, half an hour before the Melbourne Stakes, hundreds of them were crammed three deep, hoping to fetch a peek at the 1932 Cup winner.

McGrath stripped his horse's rugs before the little crowd, and took his time saddling. He marvelled at the slope of Peter Pan's shoulder, at the deep incline at the base of his neck, the solid, muscular lines of his barrel. He flattened the hair under the saddle, brushed tufts of straw from his tail, then stood back while George Phillips led him out of the stall. When Peter Pan emerged, the onlookers gasped at the horse they hadn't seen for two years. He was enormous, fully 17.1 hands high.

Stepping into the paddock, Peter Pan paraded for the Melbourne Stakes under saddlecloth number four. Around him were Chatham, then Hall Mark, Rogilla, Sir Simper, Heroic Prince and Nightly. With the lightest weight, Journal brought up the procession, and the eight horses comprised the most competitive field of weight-foragers seen at Flemington for years. While the merits of Peter Pan, Chatham, Hall Mark and Rogilla needed no iteration, Nightly had won the two-mile Randwick Plate a few weeks earlier, and the Moonee Valley Cup the previous weekend. Sir Simper had won the Toorak Handicap and run third in the Caulfield Cup. These two alone were competing favourites for the Melbourne Cup. Heroic Prince had won the Australian Cup in 1933, and Journal was the recent winner of the Caulfield Cup. The line-up was luscious, and even though Peter Pan hadn't won a race since the Sir Herbert Maitland Stakes on 19 September, he was pre-post favourite at 5/2.

On the face of it, he deserved that price. From four starts that spring he had won once and run second every other time, and his biggest losing margin was less than a length. But the quandary was that he had shared the spoils with Chatham and Rogilla all the way through, and no one was quite sure whose turn it was in the Melbourne Stakes. Add into the mix that Hall Mark had beaten Chatham and Rogilla in the Caulfield Stakes three weeks earlier, only to lose to Chatham in the Cox Plate the previous week, and punters and bookies were facing a quartet of confusion. Cautiously, they sent Chatham in at 3/1, Hall Mark at 9/2, Rogilla at 5s, and 14/1 the rest.

McGrath had secured better odds in Sydney, the only bonus to come from the rumours of crippling that had circled Peter Pan's name. The old trainer was bubbling with confidence at his horse's chance. He knew that the lameness of three weeks ago had been brief and intermittent, and he knew the Pantheon horse was in good form, settled and confident. In fact, he was almost irritated that the press hadn't bothered to report Peter Pan as fit as he was. Right up to this morning, maddening stories had appeared that the horse was scratchy.

The Melbourne Stakes was a unique contest for the eight horses that day. It was not a staying test, being only a mile and a quarter, but the straights of Flemington were a challenge like no other, and the race demanded stamina in equal measure to speed. Because the track was soft after weeks of rain, mudlark Chatham looked the winner on paper, but the fact was that he had never beaten Peter Pan down the imposing home straight of Flemington. Of the ten furlongs that comprised the Melbourne Stakes, nearly seven were straight running: almost four down the backstretch and three down the straight. The tiring finish at the end would suit the stayers in the race, and it was predicted a contest to determine thoroughbred superiority. But while Peter Pan, Chatham, Hall Mark and Rogilla had all proved their thoroughbred superiority before, together they were a racing student's delight. The Stakes wasn't so much a Melbourne Cup trial as a battle for middle-distance weight-for-age supremacy.

In the centre of proceedings, Rodney Dangar, Frank McGrath and brother Maurice stood with Darby Munro, the dark-haired, poker-faced jockey decked out in the Dangar colours. Though few realised it that day, Peter Pan's silks had changed since he last raced. Dangar had inverted his colours to green, orange hoops and green cap, instead of orange, green hoops and orange cap. The difference was so subtle as to be almost unnoticeable. McGrath gave his final instructions to his rider, and Munro strode over to Peter Pan when George Phillips brought him in. Legging him up, McGrath wished the Demon Darb luck, and told him to be confident of the ride he had beneath him.

Every horse feels different to a rider, and under Darby Munro, Peter Pan felt loose and athletic. He was nothing like Rogilla, who would canter to the post with his nose in the air, the muscles in his neck inverted and tight. Munro would never get over the withering finish of Rogilla in a race, but he was impressed by Peter's velveteen stride, his light mouth and buoyant energy. He was just as Billy Duncan had described him in '32 – a rocking horse – and Munro knew that a canter as smooth and as long as Peter's would transpire to a beautiful gallop. When he reached the barrier, he pulled Peter Pan up, pacing around with the other seven horses while starter Rupert Greene readied himself. Stan Davidson was piloting

Chatham in Pike's absence, so Les Haigh had had to opt for the New Zealand jockey Turoa Webster for Rogilla. Maurice McCarten was on Nightly, Frank Dempsey on Hall Mark, and Andy Knox was on Journal. Though Knox had long moved on from his Peter Pan days, he harboured great fears about the chestnut whenever he rode against him.

The eight horses jumped in a smart line. When they pulled away from the starting post, Nightly, drawn on the inside, dashed to take the early lead. On the outside, Stan Davidson kept a tight hold of Chatham but crossed to take second place, and on Peter Pan, Darby Munro could see that the Sydney sprinter wasn't about to dash off as he usually did. Munro slotted Peter Pan about third on the rails, and as the field thundered through the first two furlongs, Nightly held a narrow lead over Chatham, Peter Pan was galloping with Sir Simper on his outside, with Hall Mark and Journal behind them, and Rogilla and Heroic Prince bringing up the rear.

Chatham made a move to take the lead. Munro asked Peter Pan to quicken. The horse ran with Nightly and Sir Simper, and Munro knew that any point he could kick to the lead. With Chatham bowling along in front down the riverside and past the abattoirs, the field remained bunched behind him. With the soft track, no one was in search of time records, but they weren't dawdling either. They had gone a decent pace in the first half, and as they ran past the half-mile Chatham raised the tempo. He drew clear of Nightly by two lengths, with Peter Pan coasting along in third. Hall Mark had zipped into contention from the back, tracking Peter's heels.

As they entered the straight, Munro saw Davidson go for Chatham, and he wondered if the star sprinter would rip away from the pack. Lengthening his reins, Munro clicked Peter Pan into a higher gear, sending the horse down the middle of the straight in pursuit of Chatham's lead. Stan Davidson began to ride furiously, sensing the approach of the trailing horses. Glancing behind him, he saw Peter Pan plunging into his lead, and he pushed and hollered at Chatham to gallop faster. But there was no getting away from Peter Pan today. Munro was simply cruising, edging his big horse along with hands and heels. With two furlongs to go, he had passed Nightly and drawn alongside Chatham, with Hall Mark in his slipstream. A few strides later, he had burst into a solitary lead, and Munro lost sight of the others.

Peter Pan was out by two lengths, and as he usually did when he found himself alone in front, he turned his head to see who was coming, his attention wavering towards the fans that hollered his name. But Munro was having none of that. With a slap on the shoulder, he straightened Peter Pan and sent the chestnut for home. With ease, with ridiculous ease, the son of Pantheon held off a late challenge from Hall Mark to win the Melbourne Stakes by a length, with Nightly winning a third-place tussle with Chatham, and Rogilla a distant fifth. Journal, the Caulfield Cup winner, ran last.

In the grandstands and in the bustling infield, the crowd shrieked with appreciation. The Melbourne Cup winner of two years ago had upheld his unbeaten Flemington record, and had done so with merit and conviction. In fact, the Cup winners of the last two years had run the quinella. Peter Pan had proved himself a weight-for-age champion. Two Cox Plate winners, two Caulfield Cup winners, and the various other performers that the Melbourne Stakes had churned out had had no response to Rodney Dangar's stallion. He had won pulling up. Standing in his stirrups after the judge, Darby Munro counted his lucky stars that he had fought so hard for the ride.

Dangar was beaming up in his owner's box, and Elsie was hopping with delight. They watched as their grand racehorse trotted down the lane and back to scale, cheered and clapped by thousands of racegoers that lined the fences. Dangar slipped downstairs to welcome him back to the saddling paddock. Munro's face was cracked with a giant, devilish smile. Unlike Pike, the Demon Darb wore his elation on his sleeve. Jumping off, Munro gave Peter a hearty slap on the neck, then saluted the crowd, a sportsman through to his bones. Nudging through the congratulations and handshakes, he made his way to the jockeys' room, but not before he told McGrath and Dangar that it was one of the easiest races he had ever ridden. 'He's a lovely horse to ride,' he said to the two men, and McGrath nodded in agreement, while Dangar's face popped with pride. 'He'll follow any pace and take any openings offered,' Munro added. In the centre of the fuss, with his veins standing in his neck and his nostrils flared, Peter Pan looked about with indignant nobility.

George Phillips, animated and proud, led the horse back to the Birdcage with Frank and Maurice McGrath in tow. The trainer searched for signs of lameness, but there were none to be found. Not only was Peter Pan sound, he was a freak of fitness. Apart from the sweat around his girth and the mud under his belly, it was impossible to tell that the horse had been around the course at all. Leaving Phillips and Maurice to escort Peter to the yard, McGrath headed back to the enclosure, where the atmosphere bristled with celebration.

'Did you think he'd win, Macker?' yelled a reporter as the trainer walked by.

'I knew he would win,' McGrath replied. 'Haven't I been saying it for weeks?'

'Is he sound though?' the reporter asked.

'I wish you boys would report the right story,' the old trainer said as he walked away. 'I'm getting tired of reading that my horse is all cut and broke in the press.'

Peter Pan had won the Melbourne Stakes in 2:05 3/4, a respectable time given the state of the track. The record for the distance was only two-and-a-half seconds faster. It was Peter's 13th win in 23 starts, and had proven him a versatile, superior galloper who had the measure of any weight-for-ager in the land. The £700 purse lifted his winnings to £17,685, and though Munro was Peter Pan's eighth different jockey, he had travelled as sweetly as if it were Jim Pike riding. His 9st 3lb had been an afterthought, and he had given 3lb to Hall Mark and Nightly in second and third. In the Melbourne Cup, Peter would give Hall Mark 8lb, and Nightly 6lb, but if today's performance stood for anything, the extra weight would not trouble him. Provided the rain stayed away, and there were no disasters in between, he might run off with his second Cup in three days' time.

The Sydney press was full of praise for Peter Pan's win, stating he was the horse of old, but the Melbourne boys refused to acknowledge it as one of merit. Instead, they credited their own Hall Mark, stating that Hall Mark's pull in the weights made him a better pick for the Cup. Everyone knew the gulf between Sydney and Melbourne was never greater than in the first week of November. Not only this, but Cup Week was also a time for self-proclaimed, outlandishly confident racing experts, and in the two days between Derby Day and Cup Day of 1934, as Peter Pan stood at Archer's tail, poised to join him in legendry, one of these experts stepped out in fine form.

26

'A horse will not win the Cup a second time'

William John Stewart McKay was 66 years old during Cup Week of 1934. He was a retired doctor of gynaecology, an esteemed one, at Lewisham Hospital in Sydney's west, and he was also a writer. Since 1888, he had published *The History of Ancient Gynaecology* and *Operations Up the Uterus.* He had also released research on the death adder, and anatomy and poisons of the dog tick, but in recent years he had turned his attention to racehorses. His 1933 book, *Staying Power of the Racehorse,* was a heralded volume that had taken years to complete. In it, he purported his own theories about that which makes a thoroughbred a stayer, and it was the greatest cheerleader for Phar Lap that had ever graced a bookshelf.

McKay was a confident man, and he found himself in the newspapers in the weeks before each Melbourne Cup, gracing their columns with his predictions and analyses, touting his latest fancy or stripping the dignity from a horse he didn't like. In 1934, when the *Australasian* came calling, McKay obliged the newspaper with his forecasts as he did every year, and they were published on Monday 5 November 1934.

He began by selecting 16 horses with chances, based on the premise that each must possess what he had coined over 10 years 'a staying heart', or a constitution of power enough to pump blood around a horse that is travelling two miles in time somewhere about 3:25. 'I always have in mind,' McKay began, 'that each horse selected must have as his first credential a sire that possessed a staying heart.' After this prerequisite, he worked off two beliefs: that a horse will not win the Cup a second time, and that the Cup is a race for the lightly weighted galloper.

McKay's selections for 1934 were discussed in order of their allotted weights, and because Peter Pan carried top weight of 9st 10lb, he came first. Explicitly, as if spiriting 'Banjo' Paterson, McKay wrote the horse off in a matter of sentences. 'That Peter Pan can go two miles in weight-for-age company is true. That he can win his second Melbourne Cup with 9st 10lb on board is, to my mind, impossible. The overexertion necessary to achieve his first mighty victory must have affected him, and must have diminished his reserve of force. And so, if Peter Pan starts he will run against me, good horse though he may be up to 12 furlongs, or up to two miles at weight-for-age.'

Stewart McKay had forgotten that Peter Pan was undefeated over two miles or more, be it in handicap or weight-for-age company. The prediction was a vast insult to his record, and a wild underestimation of the horse's constitution. But in the last two years, like 'Banjo' Paterson, McKay had been confounded by Peter Pan. The son of Pantheon didn't fit the physical perimeters of the classic racehorse, especially those that filled *Staying Power of the Racehorse,* and rather than embrace the achievements of this marvellous thoroughbred, McKay had instead berated Dangar's horse. Like Paterson, he was waiting for Peter Pan to fold under pressure, and he was convinced that the 1934 Melbourne Cup was the ticket.

'I know there are many who hold that Peter Pan is Rogilla's master over two miles,' McKay continued for the *Australasian* readers. 'This is one of those popular mistakes that the approaching Cup race will smash once and for all. Rogilla is the greatest horse in Australasia, one of the very few true stayers we possess. Twill be a glad hour for his breeder, Mr Hunter White, when he sees his great horse pressed by Nightly, yet winning.' There was no halting McKay's confidence, or his page-21 tirade.

The doctor claimed that Nightly was Rogilla's greatest danger. It was his fancy that these two horses, which Peter Pan had spanked in the Melbourne Stakes, would fly down the Flemington straight together. McKay also stated that game though Hall Mark was, he was not a two-mile handicapper, albeit last year's Cup winner, and he had already fouled the horse's owner Charles B. Kellow with this opinion. Summing up, McKay pronounced Rogilla the winner. 'If the going is good, I expect Rogilla to just beat Nightly, with Broad Arrow and Farndale close up. Should it be a wet day and the going heavy, then I expect Broad Arrow to win, but Nightly will not be far away and may even win, as he likes the wet.'

McKay's analysis of the Cup field was a half-page tally of self-deduced facts, and its author was positive that these facts were authority. But McKay had also been positive in 1933 that Rogilla would fight out the finish of the Cup and prevail. He didn't. McKay had also had that opinion in 1932. In 1931, he had stated that Phar Lap's burden of 10st 10lb would not affect him, though it did, terribly. Actually, McKay's theories had been crazily wide of the mark in recent years, and yet each year he flung them into the *Australasian,* convinced that they were expert.

Like its upmarket contemporary, the *Sporting Globe* newspaper also went in search of specialist opinion. It landed on Billy Duncan, and Peter Pan's former jockey, now retired after a race fall, looked the field over and landed on Sir Simper. 'Frankly, I would say that if I were given my choice of mounts in the Melbourne Cup, it would be Sir Simper,' he stated. 'He is a horse with plenty of courage, and he is sure to run out the two miles.' Like McKay, Duncan filed through the merits of the other runners, but from the perspective of a former rider. 'Jockeys are considered bad judges,' he wrote, 'but, seeing that I have been out of the saddle for so long, perhaps I can claim to take an unbiased view of things.'

Duncan felt Peter Pan's task hopeless, which even he conceded was an extraordinary verdict for the horse that won him the Cup so sensationally two years earlier. 'I like him tremendously as a horse, but I somehow don't think he can win the Cup,' the ex-hoop wrote. 'He is good, but he can't give the weight to good horses like Sir Simper and Theo.' Duncan further recalled Peter Pan's inclination to slow down when he hit the front, and to look around for another horse, but he embellished this recollection with an odd detail. 'When he hits the front he wants to stop and savage anything that comes along. Because of my fall I have not seen much of him lately, but from what I have heard I believe he is now a bigger "savager" than he used to be.'

Peter Pan had never actually stopped while he was in the lead to savage anyone. The incident Duncan had likely heard about was the King's Cup when Peter Pan had cracked a temper at being sandwiched and expressed it on Kuvera. In the Spring Stakes, his sourness had sent him onto Limarch, but he hadn't savaged that horse, and even in the closing stages of the race, when he and Rogilla were like one, he hadn't bared his teeth at his rival, though he probably wanted to. He had simply raced with his head under Rogilla's neck. Duncan's accusations came back to a simple premise – Peter Pan had been accused over the last few years of everything from robbery to manslaughter.

The *Globe* listed Billy Duncan's selections in order – Sir Simper, followed home by Theo, Nightly and Farndale. The jockey's dismissal of Peter Pan was disappointing. Duncan was four for four on Peter Pan, unbeaten on him from distances of a mile and a quarter to two and a quarter miles, but his wasn't a unique opinion on the eve of the 1934 Melbourne Cup. 'Banjo' Paterson, as usual, had his stick to throw on the fire. 'Neither weight nor distance would trouble Peter Pan so much as the fact that he is a five-year-old stallion and may be developing a will of his own. He may give way to the temptation to have a mouthful of a rival.' The prince of punters, Eric Connolly, had selected Nightly as his choice. He likened the New Zealand horse to Windbag, who could 'go at both ends', he said. Percy Miller, stud master of Kia Ora Stud, had also selected Nightly, though a son of Pantheon would be good for business for Pantheon now stood at Kia Ora. Sydney trainer William Kelso was going with Sir Simper, along with AJC secretary George Rowe. Harry Telford, Phar Lap's former trainer, had selected Theo, saying that he couldn't go past a good three-year-old in the Cup (though he hadn't had that opinion in 1932). Few of racing's major names had thrown support to Peter Pan. Sydney bookmakers Arthur Matthews and Wallace Mitchell were exceptions, both thinking Peter a horse great enough to accomplish a second win. 'To my mind, Peter Pan is a certainty,' Matthews commented.

Truth went in search of a statement from Andy Knox, the Sydney lightweight and former pilot of Peter Pan in 1932. Knox was very confident about Journal's Cup chances, but he had a surprising amount to say about Peter Pan. 'All the hoops that rode in the Melbourne Stakes on Saturday reckoned Peter Pan never went better in his life,' the jockey said, recalling how he had tracked Peter throughout the race on Journal, only to see his former flame dash away in the straight. 'When I saw him running fourth going along the back pulling Darby out of the saddle, I knew there would be only one in it at the finish. Peter, in my opinion – and don't forget I've ridden him in many races and understand him – is as well this spring as when he beat me on Yarramba just two years ago. Will I ever forget that day?'

That day, the Cup of '32, had proved the biggest shock for young Andy Knox in the years that had spanned his riding career. He was haunted by it, the sweeping feeling of victory he'd had a furlong from home, when he'd peeped over his shoulder and there wasn't a horse in sight of his. 'Imagine my surprise when we got to within 100 yards of the peg,' he recalled, 'and I spotted Peter's silver mane flashing up like one of those comet planes on the inside of me.' Knox still held Peter in high regard. 'He has a crushing weight this year, but he is just the boy that can hump it. Without a doubt he is the greatest stayer in the land, and only stayers win Melbourne Cups.'

Knox felt that Peter Pan would have to get a saloon passage throughout the Cup to win, because he knew that when a horse receives a few bumps with nearly 10st on his back, no matter the greatness of the animal, he takes some holding together. But Peter, in Knox's eyes, was a rare one, even with his mighty weight. 'If Journal is beaten on Tuesday,' the jockey said, 'I hope it is Peter Pan that leathers him. He looks certain to fill a place, and I am only hoping that if I am in front on Journal with 50 yards to go, that Peter isn't too handy.'

Buller Franklin was hoping that Peter Pan would be very handy at that point on Tuesday. One of Sydney's biggest punters, Franklin had backed Peter at 5/2 in all parts of the ring for the Melbourne Stakes on Saturday, and had shovelled his winnings into the Cup result, praying and pleading that Peter would prevail a little after 3.50pm on Tuesday. But Franklin had also set £500 to £400 on Theo winning the Derby, which that horse did, so Sydney's prolific punter, who was also a prolific fisherman, had faith in both Sydney runners. However, his common sense told him that Theo hadn't convinced by his narrow victory on Saturday, while Peter Pan had romped home as he pleased. Buller Franklin set about with topping up his tickets on the seasoned Peter Pan.

Around Melbourne, everyday citizens were also choosing their favourites, and their choices were reflected in the ring. Reasoning that the track might be heavy, punters had steered away from betting on Peter Pan, despite the result of the Melbourne Stakes, because as much as the weight might not bother the champion, it would bother him much more in heavy going. In response, money had come for Theo and Nightly, and it began to come for Sir Simper in the two days after Derby Day. These three remained in the forefront of public favouritism, though Peter Pan was held in much esteem sentimentally. Then the society ladies stepped forward with a different set in their minds. They were supporting Sarcherie, J.J. Leahy's little mare. 'Not that Sarcherie looks a winner on paper, or anything like that,' wrote the quirky, female social writer for *Truth* newspaper, 'but because Sarcherie is the only one of us down-trodden sex that is in the jolly old race.'

History was giving its own tips to the punters of 1934. For example, only Archer had won a Melbourne Cup twice, and that was way back in the woods of old men's minds. If this suggested anything, it was that Peter Pan and Hall Mark didn't have much of a chance. As history stood, only one stallion had sired three Melbourne Cup winners, and that was Positano, who had got Lord Cardigan, Piastre and Poseidon. But if Nightly could win this year, he would propel Night Raid into a similar standing, as Nightly would join Nightmarch and Phar Lap as sons of the New Zealand sire on the winners list.

And history wasn't forgetting the age factor. There were 22 three-year-olds that had won the Cup since its inception in 1861, while 17 four-year-olds had scored. The five-year-olds held the greatest record with 19 wins, while six-year-olds had 10 victories and the aged horses had prevailed five times. It wasn't forbidden to race two-year-olds in the Melbourne Cup, and they had contested it before, but none had won it. In other words, the Cup was not a good race for the very young or the very old.

Up in Sydney, the *Referee* fell onto the streets on Cup eve, and within its large, imposing pages, amid Cup predictions and forecasts, Rodney Dangar had written on his beloved Peter Pan. 'Today, perhaps, now that Peter Pan is all ready for his second attempt to win the Cup, you will want to know what I think about his chances,' he wrote. 'Well, every owner thinks well of his horse or the animal would not be in the race. Whether he wins or not is not the real point, though I certainly should be a proud owner to win the greatest Cup race in our history, the Centenary Cup. But the mere winning of a race is not the be-all and end-all of the game. A man can take a pride in the horse himself, and I know that, win or lose, Peter Pan will always remain a joy and a delight to us who have seen him grow up from a skittish colt and watched him through all his triumphs and disappointments.'

It was a testament to Dangar's reputation that the newspaper had come knocking, but he was a celebrity in Sydney society at a time when celebrity was an elusive, noble thing. His *Referee* article was an affectionate, nostalgic representation of his feelings on the eve of Peter's Melbourne Cup, and it revealed that here was one man, of all the experts, that knew the value of his horse no matter the result. 'Surely to be the owner and breeder of a young colt like him, born and bred up on the homestead where I myself first saw the light of day, is an excuse not only for feeling a thrill of pleasure and joy, but also for a little pardonable pride.'

So with these thoughts in their minds, and drunk full of opinions from experts, Australians everywhere prepared for Tuesday 6 November. They flooded the department stores, snatching suits, frocks and millinery for raceday, and bleating about the only event in Australia that brought everything to a halt. For the mug punter, the tote odds would do on Cup Day, but the true gambler had been skulking between the SP bookies since June, out the back of milk bars and barber shops and down sultry alleyways. Yet in the bleak, breaking hours of Tuesday morning in Melbourne, everyone, everywhere, began to revise their options. The rain that was falling was murderous and nothing could escape it, especially the deep, deified turf of Flemington Racecourse.

27

The 1934 Melbourne Cup

Hours before the gates had opened to the madding crowds of Cup Day, the Centenary Cup racebook awaited dispersal. In neat, decorous bundles around Flemington, at the ticket offices and inside the turnstiles, it waited, priced at a shilling and, for the first time in years, sporting a new front cover. The ornate, monochrome design of years past was gone, replaced by a single illustration of a rangy, reddish-bay racehorse, replete with jockey and saddlecloth number one. If the VRC was trying to give punters a subtle Melbourne Cup tip, the effect was lost on most who paid over their shilling. Peter Pan, bearing saddlecloth number one, had drawn the extreme outside barrier in the Cup field of 25, and this disastrous marble, coupled with nearly 10st on a heavy track, dissolved much belief that the 1932 hero would be the hero again today.

Under a steady stream of black umbrellas, racegoers began to pour into Flemington, from trains that had left Spencer Street Station and trams that had rattled along Racecourse Road. It had been raining for hours, well since the night before, and deep puddles of water were everywhere. There were women in pale leghorn hats and thin shoes, leaping and diving over potholes, and others that took shelter under plaid rugs and flimsy umbrellas. Gallant gentlemen in top hats and tails were spattered before the running of the first race, and the Centenary Cup racebook, with its crisp new pages, was foxed and soiled within hours as the rain pelted down upon Flemington. It was a sorry affair. Within an hour of arriving at the course, many turned on their heels and headed for home.

For those that stayed, despair gradually mutated into jollity. They settled down to make a joke of the weather, especially those in the stands. There was fun to be had in watching the antics of the folk stuck out in the open, and by the running of the Mimosa Stakes at 2.20pm, no one expected the weather to break. It was what it was: a sodden, sorry Melbourne Cup washout.

The vice-regal party arrived after luncheon, announcing the presence of the Duke of Gloucester. But though the carriages trotted down the course proper with their usual pageantry, they were empty, and the confounded public realised that the Duke and his party had gone straight to the Members' stand by motorcar. A surge of disappointment rippled through the crowd, especially from those who had braved the rain to stand unprotected, waiting for a glimpse of the Duke. Now too dishevelled to dash for cover, and too wet to care, they stood out in the rain waiting for the Cup. A little after three o'clock, with the weather still pelting them, they expected the first of the runners into the saddling paddock.

In the Birdcage, Frank McGrath stood out of the rain next to Peter Pan, sheltered in race stall number 60. Hall Mark was tethered a few stalls up in 64. McGrath watched as George Phillips carefully plaited Peter's tail and wound it up into a tight knot. The five-year-old stallion chomped idly on his bit, nonplussed about the weather or the sudden stumpy tail he found himself with, and around him, trainers and strappers readied their horses for a run through the mud. The course proper was waterlogged, and the Cup already had its casualties. Miramond, Spearflash and Iolaus had been scratched, bringing the field down to 22 runners, and the going was so bad that the stewards had contemplated postponing the race altogether. After an inspection of the track, proceedings were declared on, and one by one, the 1934 Centenary Cup runners left the sanctum of the Birdcage and headed to the saddling paddock.

Peter Pan's coat turned a deep, brassy red as he made his way through the rain, his number-one saddlecloth growing grey and shabby and his blond mane clinging to his neck. Everywhere, the Melbourne Cup horses arched their necks away from the rain, and McGrath couldn't remember, in all his years of coming to Flemington, a wetter, more miserable afternoon. The mottled, thick clouds above him were chipping away at his confidence, and he knew that the best preparation, the most brilliant Cup campaign, could be undone in conditions like this.

Peter's price had drifted in the ring from fours to about nines, due largely to his weight, his draw, and now the mudbath he would have to run through. In isolation, any one of these handicaps would be enough to a blow a horse's price. Together, they produced an almost insurmountable hurdle. As Darby Munro strolled towards McGrath and Dangar, the ring was hollering odds of 14/1 about Peter Pan. Nightly and Sir Simper were 9/2 against, with Theo and Broad Arrow at 10s, and Rogilla and Hall Mark were out with Peter Pan, somewhere in the twilight of public favouritism.

Dangar didn't look confident standing in the rain in the paddock. Phillips, sensing that he was looking for reassurance, piped up. 'Look here, Mr Dangar, the others have to go through it too.' Munro had gone around in the Railway Highweight already, the second race of the day, on a horse that had drawn alley 26, and as he greeted McGrath, his expression was confident. Munro knew that he was piloting the best horse in the race. His ride aboard Peter in Saturday's Melbourne Stakes had been an education for this event. Munro had found the horse's action effortless, and he suspected that on the firmer outside going, Peter Pan's weight would mean less than it would if he had drawn near the rails. Since the Highweight, the going on the inside had become furrowed and deep, and completely unsuited to a horse with a ton on his back. Munro was anxious to make a mockery of all these obstacles put before Peter Pan, and he said so to

McGrath. 'I'm glad I'm not going around,' McGrath responded.

Munro told the trainer that he wasn't going to look for a position amid the field, that it would be silly not to make use of the outside draw. Neither trainer nor jockey was concerned about Peter covering the extra ground, as he would have to do travelling three or four horses deep. It was already fact that Peter Pan would run all day if he had to, so the only question was whether he could run the extra distance with all the extra weight. The closest Peter had yet carried to 9st 10lb was the pound more he had lumped in the Chelmsford in early September. But that race had been only nine furlongs, nearly a mile less than this day's contest, and Randwick was a different ball game to Flemington. Two miles on the Melbourne track was a test more severe than two miles at Randwick, so McGrath could only conclude that Peter Pan's task was monumental. If any horse could do it, he was sure it was this one.

'He's all yours,' the trainer said as he swung Darby Munro into the saddle.

The Demon Darb grinned, gathered up his reins and said, 'Watch us win this.'

***

Nearly 700 miles north, at the very same moment in the dockside Sydney suburb of Ultimo, 24-year-old Percival John Galea was huddled around a wireless set. He was a milk-truck driver for the Fresh Food and Ice Company, whose factory sat down on the Ultimo docks, and his milk route saw him run about the opulent suburbs of Woollahra and Edgecliff. Not so many days ago, Galea had made his usual drop to Arlington, meeting the master of that house, as he often did. Galea had tipped his hat and smiled to the good sir, and Rodney Rouse Dangar had bid him good day. Galea knew well that Mr Dangar was Peter Pan's owner, as did everyone who dropped to Arlington, but on this particular morning, with the harbour glittering away behind the mansion, the wealthy esquire had chatted to the milk boy about the pending Melbourne Cup.

It was no secret that Perce Galea liked to bet. He had been dabbling with SP bookies since the age of 14, but they were shillings bets here and there, nothing that could be called a serious punt. On this morning, however, Mr Dangar was about to change Galea's life. He told the fresh-faced delivery boy to muster every shilling he had and place it on the peerless Peter Pan. He told Galea that his horse was as close to a certainty as existed, and the milk boy had driven away from Arlington that morning with plans aplenty.

Galea now huddled around the wireless set at work with his ticket hot in his pocket, listening as the radio caller announced that the horses were at the post. There were a dozen fellows around him, each with their own little wagers, their own tips. They jostled closer to the set as the time neared 3.50pm. None had any idea of the weather conditions down in Melbourne. But Perce Galea knew one thing: if Peter Pan came in, he would have money like he'd never had it before. More than that, Galea suspected his milk days would be over.

***

Andrew Mitchelson was also listening to the Cup, but from the comfort of the grandstand at Flemington. At 85 years old, this wiry ex-jockey was getting on these days, but he could see and hear perfectly well, and he could remember better. In fact, Mitchelson could recall his ride in the 1865 Melbourne Cup like it had happened last night, could remember the big, brash winner Toryboy as if he were down on the lawn in front of him. A little unsteady on his feet now, and about as light as he was 69 years earlier, Mitchelson watched and listened as Peter Pan bid for history. He was one of the old men who had seen Archer and, having seldom missed a Cup meeting since 1861, he appreciated the significance of the moment.

Mitchelson hadn't ridden Toryboy in 1865. He had piloted Frolic, in days when the Cup was run on the Tuesday and the Derby the following Thursday. Frolic was killed in the Derby that year, but that was another story. The young Mitchelson came to be the foreman for trainer Walter S. Hickenbotham, and in that role he had attended to Carbine. But time hadn't spun tall tales in this old fellow's mind. Legendry had little place in his memory. He was still undecided as to whether Carbine was quite as brilliant as Hickenbotham's later champion, Newhaven. Mitchelson could recall the trainer telling him that he'd never found out just how fast Newhaven could travel, and so the horse lingered in the ex-jockey's mind as one of the best equines he had ever seen.

Mitchelson had moved to Melbourne at the age of nine, when the city itself was not much older than him. Within four years, Archer had won the first Melbourne Cup, and three years after that, the young jockey was getting rides at Flemington, at a time when Gladstone was causing a stir and the roads were lined with fortune seekers plying their fates at the goldfields. He regretted, though only a little, that he had never ridden a Cup winner, and as he watched now the 22 starters for the 1934 event, that regret was sharper. Even through the rain, through the gloom that shrouded Flemington, the Cup was a magnificent event, and he hoped for a little history this year. Subtly, not wanting to draw attention onto himself, Andy Mitchelson cheered for Peter Pan.

***

Across Flemington at 3.50pm, controlled hysteria simmered in every racegoer that had stayed to witness the big race. There were thousands of jostling bodies crammed into the Flat, men and women who had pressed themselves into special trains that morning and who clamoured now for a glimpse of the winning post. And they were a cheerful lot, though saturated. They didn't yearn to trade places with the better classes across the track. Rather, they looked up at the frenzied crowds in the Hill stand and were glad they were among the gypsies. It occurred to them that they wouldn't mind having, with which to wager, what it cost those flash people over there to buy their spots on the Lawn. Across the track, on those very lawns, the wealthy were thinking similar things. They were grateful they would not be among the sorry lot in the infield, even if that unkempt crowd seemed to be enjoying itself more. It was a Cup Day game: everyone pleased to be there, no matter the class or category.

In the dying minutes before the jump, the clouds over Melbourne split and sunshine burst onto Flemington. Across the racecourse, umbrellas disappeared and the crackling roar of the people grew louder, as if the sun had turned up their dials. It was an incredible weather situation that the Cup would be run in full sunshine after such misery the past 24 hours, but no one was complaining, least of all the 22 jockeys sitting aboard the Melbourne Cup runners. Their horses had picked up their heads, and though nothing could be done about the squelch underfoot, none of them would have to run through driving rain.

Rupert Greene began to call the field to order. Panto stepped up on the inside, having drawn the box seat on the rails, and Sydney Cup winner and renowned mudlark Broad Arrow was on his outside. Then came Theo, Marabou, Sir Simper, Farndale and Hall Mark in that order. Rogilla stepped midfield in 13. In 19, Nightly behaved under jockey Maurice McCarten, and Sarcherie had drawn 24 on Peter Pan's inside. But Greene was having all sorts of trouble with the field. The horses, especially those near the rails, were up to their fetlocks in mud, and they lurched and danced out of the puddles, sending Rupert Greene's walk-up start into chaos. Journal was floundering badly, wobbling on his feet like he was about to faint. Andy Knox was pale with worry, convinced his horse had been 'got at'. The VRC starter swung the 22 horses around several times, hollering at the jockeys to take control of their mounts.

On the outside, Darby Munro's thick, dark eyebrows were pinched into a frown, and with an eye on the field and another on the long straight ahead of him, he was ready, his heart thumping against his ribcage, his weight eased off Peter Pan's back. Many minutes later, Greene assembled the field into an order, and the horses stepped forward in situ – 22 beautiful, breathing beasts set for two miles through the mud. It was 3.57pm.

***

Nearly 90,000 voices lifted Flemington when the 1934 Cup field was sent on its way. Peter Pan, under the lead weights in his saddle, was a little slow off the line, but the 21 horses on his inside were anchored by the slush. As a result, the field broke evenly, surging into a gallop in slow motion. As they lumbered away from the barrier, many tripping through the going underfoot, Gladswood snatched an early lead, with Flail just behind him. Peter Pan wasn't far off, trailing the leaders though running in the middle of the track.

The crowd hollered as the 22 horses lumbered past the stands for the first time, a wave of voices that rose through the Birdcage, the Lawn and the Flat. Flail had ducked across Gladswood to take up the running, and passing the judge's box, these two were clear of Panto, Nightly and St Valorey. Sir Simper had opted for the rails run, with Broad Arrow on his outside, and Darby Munro had tucked in Peter Pan beside the Sydney Cup winner. He was three deep on the track, and behind him a struggling string of horses ploughed through the wet. Hall Mark was midfield on the rail, and Nightly was travelling well. Rogilla was behind them, with Stan Davidson at the controls, and they picked their way out of the straight in that order. The going was too heavy for any time records today.

Munro was giving Peter Pan plenty of time to settle, and the big chestnut was coasting along in his outside spot, finding his feet without trouble through the difficult going. On his inside, clods of turf were flying in all directions, pelting the horses in their chests and bellies and clouding the jockeys' sights.

By the time the field was galloping down the river side, most of the silks had turned a greasy, muddy brown in colour, and the horses at the back could hardly see where they were headed. Still, Peter Pan cruised three horses wide, bouncing through the mud, Munro not asking him for a thing.

They galloped past the halfway mark and Rogilla, having slipped through the field in search of less traffic, joined Flail in the lead. Race favourites Nightly and Sir Simper had moved into a forward position behind them, and though Munro couldn't make out the silks anymore, he could see that Sir Simper was in trouble. The 9/2 shot was struggling through the ground, and Harold Badger was riding for his life. As they ran past the six-furlong post, Nightly was also dropping back. Maurice McCarten had found the New Zealand favourite wanting, and the two horses fell from their perches like shot quarry. Still, Peter Pan ambled along untroubled, covering 45 feet more from his outside position.

As Flail led the field into the home turn, Munro heard the swell of the crowd rising in his ears. He clucked to Peter Pan to pick up his game, and the Pantheon stallion moved towards the leaders without changing gear. On his inside, Sarcherie went with him. Flail had little left, and entering the straight, Panto was on the rails, with Rogilla slashing into the turf beside him. Theo was there too, with Sarcherie leaping around all of them. But widest of all, Peter Pan was simply playing. With monstrous strides he gathered up the leading division, and at the top of the straight, Munro rode for home. He let out his reins and slid his face into Peter's mane, and he booted the chestnut down the Flemington straight as only the Demon Darb could.

Peter Pan responded like a steam train. He shot away from the field, his response so effortless and easy that Munro had no idea how far in front he had gone. Daring not to look back, the jockey didn't stop riding. Peter drew away by a length. Two lengths. Three lengths. Munro couldn't hear the slosh of the field anymore, just the rhythmical, billowing breaths from Peter Pan's nostrils. But the crowd was deafening, cheering and stomping at this marvellous horse out in front. The Flat patrons were ready to knock the fences down. They screamed as Sarcherie chased bravely, but the little mare couldn't breach Peter's three-length lead. The son of Pantheon was magnificent, straight as a gun barrel and peerless. He galloped over the line three lengths clear of Sarcherie. Conquering.

***

Next to that wireless set in Ultimo, Perce Galea had ridden Peter Pan over the finish line with Munro, hollering and punching out at the radio box as if the stallion could very well hear him. Now, he was cheering wildly, leaping and bouncing like a schoolboy. His ticket had won him £170, or more than 42 weeks of wages.

***

Andy Mitchelson was cheering too, as buoyantly as his little old frame would allow. Peter Pan, the leggy Sydney racehorse, had shattered a 72-year hoodoo, and the ex-hoop was overcome – with history, and memories of all the steeds that had tried before and failed. Leaning against the grandstand railing, he stroked his thick white beard and looked over the Flemington crowd. He was glad he had lived so long to see such a day.

***

Munro stood in his irons after the winning post and looked up to the skies. He was bursting with some kind of inexplicable joy, the ecstasy of a jockey who has just won his first Melbourne Cup. He thought of Jim in India, and praised the gods he had fought so hard for this mount. His green and orange silks glittered in the sunshine. He was clean, bar a spattering of mud around his knees, and Peter Pan wasn't too shabby either. He was beady with sweat, his veins standing on end, but he wasn't soiled and bruised. His belly and legs were caked with mud; otherwise his coat was still a pale chestnut. As Munro had suspected, their saving grace had been their number 25 marble.

There was no question about the result, but when the judges raised the numbers another cheer broke out across Flemington. Peter Pan, in saddlecloth number one, had won by an official margin of three lengths to Sarcherie. La Trobe, the lightest weighted runner with 6st 10lb, was a neck away third. Hall Mark had finished sixth in the field, and Rogilla had done no better than 12th. Meanwhile, the pre-post favourites Nightly and Sir Simper, both backed wildly into 9/2 before running, had run last and dead last together.

It turned out that Sydney horses had run first and second in the Centenary Cup, and around the race-course, New South Welshmen were giddy. Colin Stephen, chairman of the AJC, was bloated with pride up in the Members', and he pumped the hands of his committeemen Anthony Thompson and Patrick Osborne. Buller Franklin was already on his way to the ring, his Melbourne Stakes– Melbourne Cup double ticket cradled in his hot little hands.

The rumbustious ovations grew again as Peter Pan trotted down the lane. Darby Munro tipped his hat to the cheers, and the crowd saluted the horse that so few had backed. The pair entered the paddock as indisputable champions, and now it was the Duke of Gloucester's turn to applaud. Flanked by VRC men Lachlan Mackinnon and Arthur Kewney, and standing before a little mahogany table cradling the Cup trophy, the Prince welcomed Peter Pan back to scale. He wasn't an Australian, but he was a horseman, and the moment was not beyond him.

Munro slid off Peter Pan at the winner's peg, and was overwhelmed by Dangar and McGrath, then brother Maurice and George Phillips, emotional, slapped him on the back before taking charge of Peter. The horse was listless, though not distressed. Phillips led him to the middle of the paddock where there was space, and Peter shifted on his feet, dancing against the reins looped through his strapper's hands. The run had looked easy, and Peter Pan was machine fit, but he had galloped much further than two miles from his outside spot, and through mud that had sunk him to his fetlocks. Every horse had come back filthy and exhausted from the ordeal, none more so than Sir Simper who looked fit to collapse. Peter Pan shifted restlessly in the paddock, and a large circle of people, in awe, gathered around Dangar's champion to breathe in his iron nature, to stand in the shadow of this great giant.

Dangar removed his hat and stepped into the presentation ceremony. He looked tall and splendid, neat in a dickie bow, his pale brown overcoat buttoned up and his face smooth and smiling. He could hardly stand still with the honour. Surely the Centenary Cup trophy was more than compensation for the loss of the King's Cup the previous April, and he'd rather a hundred moments like this, waiting for the King's son to shake his hand. The Duke stood chatting with

Darby Munro, the Demon Darb regaling His Highness with a short history of the Melbourne Cup. Every so often, the jockey raised his hands to emphasise some point, and the Duke glanced over at Peter Pan, for he was a man who appreciated a good horse. Then he stepped forward to congratulate Rodney Dangar, and the thousands of people who packed the racecourse cheered again for this likeable Sydney owner.

'He is a very fine thoroughbred,' the Duke said to Dangar after the 18-carat gold, three-handled Melbourne Cup trophy, the second for Dangar's collection, was in the owner's hands.

'A typically English one, I should say,' Dangar responded. It wasn't quite true, but the owner was childlike with delight.

The Duke asked to learn a little of Peter Pan's first victory two years ago, and Dangar lovingly recollected, as if a father speaking of his son, Peter's charge down the straight after falling back on his haunches at the five-furlong pole.

'He is a gallant horse, and well deserves his second victory,' the Duke responded politely, and then a wave of chanting grew up through the crowd and drowned the two men's words.

'Where's Frank?' the people called. 'Where's McGrath?' The old trainer had remained with his racehorse, but he stepped forward when he heard the cries, and it was almost too much for him to bear. He was received by the Duke and the throngs of cheering racegoers, surely one of the best days of his life.

The Duke departed the paddock after that, mingled with the racegoers on the Lawn, then strolled down the lane where the horses came on and off the course. Dangar and McGrath remained with Darby Munro in the paddock, flashbulbs going off around them while reporters pressed for comment. 'When I sat down and rode him, it was remarkable the way he responded,' Munro told them, describing Peter Pan's surge down the home straight. 'Halfway down I knew he would win, but I made sure, and kept him going to the post.' In fact, the jockey explained, he was sure he'd been out by only a length or so, not three. The reporters asked him what sort of a horse Peter was. 'There is no doubt that he has splendid action,' the jockey replied. 'It appears to be effortless for him. It is a treat to ride him.'

Munro returned with correct weight for his win, as had Sarcherie, though La Trobe had weighed in 6lb overweight. One by the one, the horses left the paddock for the Birdcage, an elated McGrath and his brother following George Phillips and Peter Pan back to the stalls. The horse was still toey, still wound tight from his run, and McGrath wondered at the sight of the spent and sorry rivals that had tried to chase him home. He wondered how many would line up on Saturday for the Duke of Gloucester Cup. In the stall, Phillips got to work unwinding Peter Pan's tail and scratching the mud off his skin. A large crowd had gathered to look at the champion, to cheer him again. At the racket, Peter raised his head and stared at them. McGrath stepped out to talk to the reporters among the onlookers. 'Well, what could anyone wish for more,' the old trainer said. 'Isn't it a wonderful double? He's a real champion. He did all that was asked of him and then a lot more.'

A few stalls away, Sir Simper's trainer was trying to stave off the criticism. 'The heavy going might have suited him and it might not,' he told his own gathering of journalists. 'He has never had a go in it before.' La Trobe's trainer simply said what he thought. 'The best horse won,' he declared. Back in the jockeys' room, La Trobe's rider was as candid as the trainer. 'He was not a good enough match for Peter Pan.' All in all, the old adage had rung true: mud levels all racehorses. But in 1934, there was a single exception to the rule.

***

The Melbourne Cup had been run in 3:40 1/2, the slowest time since Glencoe's win in 1868, and almost a replica of the time run by The Assyrian in 1882. It was a reflection on the appalling state of the track, and the riders who had sloshed through it that afternoon couldn't remember it in worse condition. The first mile of the Cup had been covered in 1:50 1/2, the next half-mile in 56 1/2 seconds, and the last half in a slightly faster 53 1/4. Three lengths separated first from second and third, then another two back to fourth, a further two to fifth, and nearly three back to the chasing pack. Peter Pan had spread-eagled the field. The win was worth £8000 to him, plus the £200 gold cup, and it shot his winnings to £25,685 and 10 shillings, not including the £400 value of both Cup trophies.

On analysis, Peter Pan's victory grew more extraordinary. Sarcherie, in second place, had carried 7st 2lb, or more than 2 1/2st less than Peter Pan. In third, La Trobe had been the featherweight, assigned a full 3st less than Peter. Only these two had managed to get near him, and they hadn't managed it very well. Of the heavy weights, Rogilla had failed in 12th, and Nightly, with 9st 4lb, had been a spectacular flop. In fact, the conditions on Cup Day had suited only the lightly weighted horses, and aside from Peter Pan, that was how the race transpired. Of the first five home, only the winner carried more than 8st.

These things signified not only Peter Pan's brilliance as a galloper; they also proved he was nigh unbeatable over two miles, regardless of conditions. He had started four times over the marathon distance now, and was unbeaten each time out. He had won in the wet, the dry, and the downright disastrous. He was also unbeaten at Flemington, four for four now, and was the only horse in racing history to win the Melbourne Stakes–Melbourne Cup double twice. And if his record required any further evaluation, it was that only four horses in 74 years had carried more weight to victory in a Melbourne Cup. They were

Archer, Carbine, Poitrel and Phar Lap – a constellation of racing immortals.

'Warrawee', who wrote the breeding pages of the *Referee,* said in his post-mortem, 'When year after year I see horses which are not bred to stay being confidently backed into top line positions for the Cup, I feel that I have lived and written in vain, since a large army of people do not appear to learn anything from their past experiences. All through, my first pick for the Cup was Peter Pan, primarily because he is bred to stay, has proved himself over a distance, and because he has great speed as well as great stamina.' 'Warrawee', a romantic, had lost a potential small fortune on Peter Pan's Melbourne Cup, for his bank manager had refused to overdraw his account by £100 so that he might lay heavily on the Journal–Peter Pan double.

The *Sporting Globe* stated, 'To use an expression, Peter Pan put one over the gallery of experts.' And so he had. 'Banjo' Paterson was rewriting his column up in Sydney, and Billy Duncan was wishing he could rewrite his of the week before. Peter Pan had made a mockery of W.J. Stewart McKay, as had Rogilla and Nightly in their failures, but the humblest pie of all sat waiting for J.P. Walen, the man who had written to the *Telegraph* in 1933 with these words: 'I have never heard of a real good washy chestnut. They are never hardy and never last long. Anyway, he will never be a Phar Lap.'

Walen had been right about the last bit. Peter Pan was no Phar Lap. This day, he was better.

28

'This is becoming a habit'

It was easy to forget, amid the spoils of that week's Melbourne Cup, that life had gone on as it always had. The slow wheel of everyday had kept turning. Grass had grown a little longer, faces a little older. People had died, and among them was Joseph E. Brien, the man who had gone to England in 1924 and returned with Pantheon. Brien had been ill for many years, and the old master of Kingsfield Stud hadn't clapped eyes on Pantheon for a long time. He had died on 17 October in his Sydney home, about the same time as spring racing was gathering gears, but his obscurity lately, and the Centenary Melbourne Cup, had left few remembering him. 'Cardigan' wasn't one of them.

'The late Mr J.E. Brien did a service to Australian bloodstock when he imported Pantheon to Australia,' the journalist pointed out in the *Telegraph,* only hours after Peter Pan had made turf history. 'Theorists may write about the inferiority of our horses and the manner in which they have deteriorated, but when we can still breed horses like Peter Pan, there is not much wrong with Australian bloodstock.'

Back in Melbourne, Sydney trainers were preparing to leave with their charges, and Chatham and Theo departed the Mackinnon & Cox yards a day or so after the Cup, bound for the Melbourne Express. Chatham had presented lame, so lame that it was suspected his racing career was over, and he was spirited back to Randwick. Peter Pan wasn't going anywhere, having a race yet to contest at Flemington, and by Thursday morning he was back on the training tracks. McGrath sent him on a useful circuit of the sand track, and rider Clarrie Scahill didn't ask much of the champion. The big chestnut moved sweetly, none the worse for his epic through the mud on Tuesday. He was a wonder to McGrath. Here was a horse whose joints reacted sourly to bad weather, but the same horse had powered through a brutal two miles of mud and swamp better than any that week. Rodney Dangar suspected that Peter Pan simply preferred the climate in Melbourne, though since they'd arrived over three weeks ago the weather had been atrocious, worse than anything they'd seen in Sydney in years. None of it had mattered to Peter Pan.

After the morning gallops on Thursday, the clouds stuck overhead and sunshine was patchy for racing that day, Oaks Day. There was a constant dribble of rain throughout the afternoon, so the course proper had little time to dry out, despite a whipping southerly wind. The Lawn was still a quagmire. The VRC had closed access to it to allow the grass time to recover for Saturday's racing, and straw and ashes were strewn everywhere. The VRC had worked overtime to restore its racecourse after the woes of Cup Day, but the state of the course proper was telling on race fields. That afternoon, the C.B. Fisher Plate, a popular post-Cup contest, had only three starters, while the Oaks could drum up only eight. Both races were over a mile and a half, and each took a little over 2:53 and 2:52 to complete. The course record for the distance was 2:29 1/2.

***

Flemington arose early for its final day of racing. It was Saturday 10 November, and the rain was spilling again, although it was light and the cloud cover thin. This time, racegoers dressed accordingly: chiffon, silk and rayon were nowhere to be seen, with the more dour tones of felt and fur taking their place, the wealthy in top hats and tails. Though the first race was scheduled for one o'clock, Flemington was packed by midday.

The Duke of Gloucester was again the honoured visitor for this final day, with the Duke of Gloucester Cup due off at 2.15pm. It was the second race on the card, a handicap without penalties over a mile and three-quarters, and the maximum weight – declared when the race was announced many weeks prior – was 9st 7lb, which Peter Pan would carry. The previous week, declarations for the race had included Rogilla, also with top weight, and Hall Mark and Nightly, each with 1lb less. In fact, there were 67 horses still nominated by Derby Day, and they included Sir Simper, Kuvera, Oro, Lough Neagh and Theo.

By final declarations that morning, however, only nine remained. The Melbourne Cup, and the track, had taken its toll. Rogilla was out, having showed poor form during the carnival, as was Hall Mark. Most of the top Sydney names were also gone. Sir Simper and the four-year-old Burlesque were late-morning scratchings, so the seven-horse field comprised Peter Pan, Nightly, Broad Arrow, Flail, Hyperion, Curator and Wallopian.

The race looked a moral for Peter Pan. He was carrying three less pounds today over a course that was two furlongs shorter. The track was improved and the field smaller, and with Darby Munro aboard, the odds were in his favour. The best that could be had about him was 9/4 on, with Nightly next at 9/2 against, and Hyperion, a three-year-old, at 10s. Next in favour was Broad Arrow at 20/1. 'Who's to beat him?' quipped *Truth* of Peter Pan. 'Conditions of the race give the mighty chestnut such a pull in the weights that he will be home and hosed while some of the others are still dragging their anchors at the top of the straight.'

The VRC had allowed an hour between races to launch the Duke of Gloucester Cup. By 1.30pm, the horses were leaving the Birdcage for the saddling paddock, and the pomp and ceremony attached to the race had begun. The Duke had arrived, electing to view the race from the middle-class surrounds of the Hill stand, and when the hysteria surrounding His Majesty had subsided, most eyes fell onto the horses racing in his honour.

Nightly, a son of Night Raid, was not a robust horse, and the four-year-old entirely lacked lustre. The New Zealand visitor had started on each of the four days of the meeting, and unless he was Phar Lap (the Cup had proved that he wasn't), he wouldn't withstand the vigours of a further race. In saddlecloth number three, Sydney Cup-winner Broad Arrow looked very well. McGrath thought it no fluke that this seven-year-old gelding, a robust chestnut, had run fourth in Tuesday's Cup. The horse liked a soft track, was a proven stayer, and he looked strong this afternoon. McGrath couldn't believe the odds about him, either; Broad Arrow was paying 20/1 in the ring. McGrath knew that if any of these horses were going to follow Peter home, it was this one.

The 68-year-old trainer was in good form. He could hardly hide his humour. Peter Pan had clinched both his races and was on song for the third. McGrath's Journal–Peter Pan double had also netted him a small fortune back in Sydney. Additionally, he had won on Peter Pan with double-figure odds here in Melbourne, and had a tidy sum on the result of the next race.

The jockeys began to mount for the Duke of Gloucester Cup, and McGrath gave few instructions to Darby Munro, trusting him to ride the race as he saw fit, and to produce Peter Pan in front at the end. The Demon Darb saw no obstacles to that.

The field was a second-rate one compared to the Melbourne Stakes and the Cup, with only two real dangers in the way of competition. Munro wasn't even worried about the going. Peter Pan had proved his steel in that respect, not to mention the course was much improved since Tuesday. It was still heavy, but only the hurdle race had been over it so far this day, so it wouldn't be too cut up. Munro reasoned that if he played a similar hand to Tuesday, the result would be the same.

He trotted Peter Pan down the lane that led to the track, following the clerk of the course and his grey pony. The pair swung to the left and cantered down to the mile-and-three-quarter start, which was close to where the straight six met the course proper. The crowd cheered and hollered at them as they passed, for this elegant son of Pantheon had become the people's champion. They hadn't idolised a horse since Phar Lap, and now Peter had supplanted the dead hero. It was a marvellous feeling for Munro. The Sydney jockey had ridden champions, for Rogilla was a champion, but he had never felt such public adulation for a horse. He wanted desperately to win, to keep the glory train on its tracks. His concentration peaked as he reached the start.

Rupert Greene called the seven horses to order. Flail was on the rails, with Hyperion on his outside. Wallopian came next, then Nightly. Broad Arrow was on his outside, with Peter Pan in postposition eight, and Curator, who belonged to VRC chairman Lachlan

Mackinnon, was on the extreme outside. Munro took care not to get too close to Curator, who was often left at the post due to his obstinate, uncontrollable behaviour. Peter Pan wasn't in the humour for the three-year-old on his outside. He let fly at the youngster more than once, his heels missing their target each time. Munro steadied the champion, readying to make full use of the outside draw, and when Greene threw the tapes up, he was in no great hurry to scurry away.

Curator dashed across Peter Pan within strides of the break and joined Wallopian in the lead as the seven-horse field thundered down the straight for the first time. Broad Arrow sat behind them, closely packed with Hyperion, Nightly and Flail. Out the back, Peter Pan loped along last. Munro was keeping him off the rails and away from the sticky ground, worrying odds-on backers as he swung out of the straight. No one enjoyed seeing a favourite hang off the tail of the field.

Commencing to run along the river, Wallopian pulled away from Curator by two lengths. Another two lengths away, Broad Arrow lumbered along under Harold Skidmore. Peter Pan had drawn alongside Flail. His easy, effortless strides were carrying him into the field, and Munro sat still on the champion, easing him out of the cut just a little. The chestnut's clean wind and beautiful action still surprised the jockey. It was like Peter didn't even notice the ground he ran across, Munro thought.

Without urging, the horse began to circle the field, bounding around the outside of every runner. By the seven-furlong pole, he had passed Nightly too. Curator had snatched the lead from Wallopian again, and Munro kept an eye on proceedings up front. The second-favourite was behind him now, but there was still Broad Arrow. He waited a little longer.

The field thundered past the half-mile pole, Peter Pan ranging up on the outside, five horses wide. In a cluster, Wallopian, Curator, Broad Arrow and Hyperion were on his inside, and at a position this far wide he was running yards more than his rivals. Swinging into the straight, Broad Arrow nudged ahead of Wallopian by half a length, and the others fell away. In a moment, Wallopian was gone too. Down the straight the two leaders went, Broad Arrow flat-out on the rails, Peter Pan wide and in full flight. Until the furlong post there was nothing between them, then Munro drove Peter Pan to a half-length lead. The Demon Darb began to ride for his worth, hands and heels all the way, and Peter reached out for his jockey, digging for that reserve of stamina, lifting his 9st 7lb for that last little bit. This furlong, the last of 40 furlongs over three races that week, was hurting him. Munro could feel it. There wasn't the same boundless joy in his finish, the same effortlessness. But Peter was still relentless, refusing to let Broad Arrow get any closer. Munro thought he might burst before the finish line.

Broad Arrow had 12lb less than the champion, but he could not breach the lead, and the two horses punched out the finish in a titan battle. They flashed past the judge together, but Peter Pan prevailed by a decisive half-length. They had leathered the other five horses. Hyperion was two lengths back in third, with Wallopian another three away, pressed by Nightly in fourth. The time was 3:04 3/4.

Frank McGrath's face was etched with relief as the horses crossed the line and disappeared out of the straight. He knew that courage alone had brought victory to Peter Pan, for the Duke of Gloucester Cup had been more of a challenge than anyone had anticipated. The old trainer looked around for Rodney Dangar, and spotted him making his way out of the stands to the paddock. Dangar was jubilant, giddy almost, for the royal trophy was another cherished prize. Already the Duke was on his way from the Hill stand to present it, and the crowds were gathering around the paddock. When the horses trotted in, Peter Pan looked alert and toey.

The jockeys hopped off their mounts, one by one disappearing from the paddock until only Peter Pan remained, flanked by George Phillips, Dangar, McGrath and a vice-regal party. The tall stallion bowed his head when VRC secretary Arthur Kewney gave him a scratch on the nose. When the time came for Dangar to receive the trophy, he stepped up in a grey top hat and smart black tails. The Duke laughed that their meeting was becoming a habit. 'My word he is a superhorse,' he told Dangar as he handed over the ornate little two-handled gold trophy. Dangar looked humbled, radiant too that the King's son should think so highly of the thoroughbred he had bred in his own fair pastures. Dangar felt he was exactly where he should be; he wanted this Royal stamp more than anyone else. He chatted with Arthur Kewney and Lachlan Mackinnon as the Duke shook hands with Darby Munro. Nearby, Frank McGrath stood with the Governor of Victoria, the recently appointed Lord Huntingfield, and their conversation was animated and friendly. Flashbulbs snapped all around the little group, and the applause for them was heartfelt.

Peter Pan was led away from the racecourse, his last start at Flemington a complete success. The rain had held, and as he was taken back to the Birdcage, he was clapped and cheered by crowds of people who lined the fences to call his name. Children reached out to touch his coat, and small-time punters saluted the horse, a few quid better off for him. At the stalls, there was no peace from fans; it wasn't until George Phillips brought him back to the Mackinnon & Cox yards later on that Peter Pan was able to rest. He ate well that night, and slept better, and the following day he was given light exercise around Flemington. On Monday afternoon, 12 November, with the rain finally spent and a hint of summer in the air, Peter Pan was rugged up and readied for the Melbourne

Express. He slipped out of the city a little before nightfall.

***

The Duke of Gloucester Cup was worth the world to Rodney Dangar, but in stakes value it was worth £1400, plus the £100 gold cup. Peter Pan had now earned £27,085, and trophies to the value of £500. He sat fourteenth on the ladder of all-time highest earners in Australia, pressing Spearfelt, Trivalve and Manfred's records. The Duke of Gloucester Cup had been his 25th race and his 15th win, with five seconds and five unplaced runs. He was undefeated over two miles or more, and he was undefeated at Flemington. He had started five times at Melbourne's premier racecourse, over distances from a mile and a quarter to two miles, and he had registered five wins. It was an enviable record for a horse that was only five years old.

McGrath had worked some genius this spring, fitting his horse for a gruelling campaign that had climaxed with three races in one week. The method behind the preparation had been outstanding. He had primed Peter Pan with sprint lessons, and the plan had been so successful that the son of Pantheon had beaten the nation's greatest sprinter at his own game in track-record time. Peter had peaked for the Melbourne Cup, and over seven days he raced three times – on Saturday, Tuesday and the following Saturday – or five miles of galloping all up. Neither weight, nor distance nor weather nor a change of jockey had stopped him on his merry way, and he was the greatest horse in Australasia right now.

But the cynics crawled out of the woodwork after Peter Pan left Flemington. 'Is he on the down grade?' asked the *Sporting Globe.* 'The fact that it took him longer than usual to beat off Broad Arrow in the Duke of Gloucester Cup on Saturday has caused racing men to wonder if the son of Pantheon is feeling the effects of his racing.' It was like the autumn of 1933 all over again, when winning had simply not been enough for the press.

Even Jim Pike threw caution to the wind for he was sceptical, even a little worried, that a new super-horse had arrived so soon. 'Great as Peter Pan has proved himself, he has a long way to go before attaining the standard of Phar Lap,' the veteran jockey commented. To Peter's fans, it was a bruising insult. It was very memorable to them that Phar Lap had failed in two of his three Melbourne Cup efforts, so Peter's record in the great race was infinitely better. It was also clear that like Phar Lap, Peter Pan could go seven furlongs or 18 furlongs, so the standard that Pike was referring to was a very grey area. Perhaps startled by his own disrespect, Pike attempted to rectify his comments. 'Peter Pan still has a bright future. I cannot praise him too highly. He is the best stayer, next to Phar Lap, I have been associated with.'

If Dangar read the comments, his generosity disguised it. He sent Pike a massive cheque when he returned to Sydney, to recognise the old jockey's part in Peter Pan's spring success and compensate him for being sidelined due to the horse's misbehaviour. It was a magnificent gesture. Jim Pike had jilted Peter Pan in favour of Chatham all spring. He had talked down Dangar's horse to the press, and reneged on riding commitments. Still Dangar favoured him. The owner liked Pike, thought him a professional, honest rider. The decisions he had made had not been personal, but proficient. Danger wanted the partnership to continue, even if it looked like Pike didn't deserve it. The jockey was grateful. Phar Lap's connections, unlike Peter Pan's, had never given Pike a shilling outside of his riding fees.

After their return to Sydney, Rodney and Elsie Dangar celebrated their horse's success in fine style. They invited 250 distinguished guests to a reception at the Royal Sydney Golf Club, and amid white hydrangeas and golden gladiolas, the 1932 and 1934 Melbourne Cups sat, with the Duke of Gloucester Cup, on the mantelpiece of the main reception room.

***

With the Flemington meeting over, Peter Pan had one more race before he retired for the summer. It was the Duke of Gloucester Plate, due to be run over a mile and a half at Randwick on Thursday 22

November. Like the Duke of Gloucester Cup, it was a handicap event without penalties, with the maximum weight being 9st 5lb and the minimum 7st. As expected, Peter Pan was allotted the highest burden, but this time the next horse in the weights was Kuvera with 8st 1lb, a full 18lb less than Peter.

The field for the race was going to be large, and it would consist of very useful middle-distance horses with little racing behind them. Oro would be the greatest danger, for he was always there in Peter Pan's wake. He would have been a top horse in another era, and he was carrying only 7st 13lb. He hadn't travelled to Melbourne, and he was ideal over the distance. Nightly was also nominated, as was the Metropolitan winner Waikare. There was also Broad Arrow again, and the AJC handicapper had given him a mere 7st 9lb. Granted, the weights had been declared before the VRC meeting, but Broad Arrow was a Sydney Cup winner. Allotting him less than 8st seemed a wild injustice.

The press knew that the race would be no easy task for Peter Pan. Analysis of the weights showed that the Melbourne Cup winner would have to improve his game from his last outing to give such weight away. Still, he was the early odds-on favourite, but with many of the Plate contestants competing in the Williamstown Cup in Victoria in the interim, serious betting on the race was postponed. In the shade of this temporary peace, McGrath concentrated on relaxing Peter Pan back into Doncaster Avenue.

The champion had travelled well, losing no condition on the return journey from Melbourne. McGrath's goal was to keep him fit and refreshed for the Plate, and each morning Peter Pan breezed six and seven furlongs around Randwick, nothing strenuous or labouring. But it was the longest stretch of racing Peter had endured in his career. His season had begun on 8 September with the Chelmsford Stakes, and the Duke of Gloucester Plate would be his eighth race in a row. He had travelled to Melbourne and back in the middle of it, and one could hardly say his races hadn't been challenging. His momentous effort in the Melbourne Cup conditions would affect any horse, even one with a constitution like his.

As the Thursday meeting approached, the going promised to be good. The course proper at Randwick looked lush and spongy. The city was also preparing for the Duke of Gloucester himself, who would arrive through Sydney Heads in the royal yacht the morning of raceday. City streets were awash with flags, and a holiday had been declared for 22 November. If there was anything that Sydney could do, it was upstage its interstate rivals.

On 17 November, five days before the Randwick meeting, the Williamstown Cup made a mockery of the form. Broad Arrow and Nightly were beaten into eighth and ninth places, and no Melbourne Cup runner finished in the first seven. It opened up the Duke of Gloucester Plate market, with Peter Pan staying safe at even money, and a horse called Senior creeping into contention. Senior was no principal galloper, but his form in Sydney races over the previous few weeks had been consistent. He was a useful off-season performer, winning races during the Christmas and New Year meetings, and at 7st 7lb he was favourably weighted. He opened at 10s in the betting, but 24 hours before the big race he was 8/1. Mr Kerry was touching 16s, Oro was at 20/1 and 25/1 the field. No one, not the punters or the bookies, or most of the loyal local newspapers, could see Peter Pan getting beaten.

***

Sydney turned on one of its perfect, glittering welcomes as the Duke's yacht came through the heads under splendid sunshine. Harbour ferries sat waiting in the water, crowded with cheering passengers, and hundreds of vessels followed the royal procession, tooting their whistles and angling for better views. As the Duke made his way up the harbour, he waved to the masses of people who packed the prominent headlands and coves. As the marvellous, imposing arches of the bridge appeared, the crowds grew thicker.

The royal yacht eased into Farm Cove, where the reception was tremendous. In Perth, Melbourne and Hobart, the Duke had received a rapturous welcome, but nothing like what he saw now as he stepped off in Sydney. The Royal Botanic Gardens flanked the thousands that greeted him, while behind him the Harbour Bridge, only two years old, was steely and magnificent. The city was a vision, and as the Duke shook hands with the Governor of New South Wales, Sir Philip Game, Premier Bertram Stevens and prominent politician Earle Page, he told them so. Delighted, the city's leaders led the Duke through the streets towards Randwick.

The vice-regal party arrived at the racecourse after the first race. In the state carriage, the Duke of Gloucester was trotted down the straight before a packed house. Long after his arrival, the trams and buses kept arriving, spilling racegoers into the course. Amid the payouts for the first race and the calls for the second, thousands of people mingled in the sunshine, resplendent in summer frocks and light shirts. In the Leger and on the Flat, they sat on picnic blankets and toasted the state holiday, and around them, colourful blooms fell over the fences. It was Sydney racing at its finest.

The Duke of Gloucester Plate was the third race on the card. It was the final leg of a trifecta of royal races this spring, and Peter Pan had clinched the first two. Dangar really wanted the third. His horse led the parade around the saddling paddock. Thirteen horses had survived the final cut, with Peter top weight, then Kuvera. These were the only entrants in the field above the 8st mark. Peter Pan had receded from odds-on to even money, with only Senior attracting much attention. He was still paying 8/1, and the next closest were Braeburn, Upoko Ariki and Broad Arrow, all at 15s. The race was worth £1500 to the winner, plus a £100 gold cup. But Peter Pan's connections were more interested now in keeping their winning streak unbroken, though Frank McGrath was dubious about that when he legged Darby Munro into the saddle. Peter Pan was in a mood, and it was usually his undoing.

Before Jack Gaxieu sent the 13 horses on their way, Munro had his hands full trying to steer Peter's heels away from horses. The big chestnut was ready to kick the stuffing out of his rivals, which wasn't new behaviour, but in a standstill start it was inconvenient. When the tapes flew up, Peter Pan had his thoughts on something other than running, and all but Mr Kerry leaped away from him. As he lurched into stride, Munro drew him over to the running rail; they galloped out of the straight almost last.

Lancaster King had taken the early lead, and as the field swung away from the stands he led at a blistering clip from Oro, Brown Force, Miss Nottava and Kuvera. Out the back, Munro was taking his time on Peter Pan. He kept him on the rails, so as the field swung into the back stretch, Peter was still second last. But he was lumbering along without effort, his big fluid strides finding plenty of room, even with the hot pace. Before they passed the six-pole, Peter Pan had moved towards the leaders, but the pack was tightly bunched. At the five-furlong pole, Munro had to check his horse to prevent him running onto heels, and the interruption burst Peter Pan's rhythm. Though Munro should have steered his ride to the outside, he insisted on making an inside run.

The leading division passed the four-furlong post and sprinted towards the home turn, Magnitas, Miss Nottava and Braeburn all in a line. Oro was out in the middle of the track, and each horse was fighting for the lead. Behind them, Peter Pan had weaved into contention, and all he needed now was a hole to open up among the leaders. By sticking to the rails, Munro had ensured the shortest possible passage with his big weight, but it was also the most limiting. If a hole didn't appear, there would be nowhere to go.

The searing pace put paid to Miss Nottava, who fell from the leaders as they entered the straight. Oro, with jockey Jack Pratt, surged ahead, and with less than two furlongs to go, Munro could feel Peter Pan opening up. The chestnut was eating up the going, ready to take the lead when he got some room. As Braeburn fell away, the hole he needed appeared and Munro went for it, riding as if it was the King's Cup all over again. The crowd was on its feet, calling for Peter Pan to take the lead. It looked like he would. In mere strides he had leaped into contention, ready to pick off Oro's great surge. But on his outside, Magnitas suddenly shifted over into his path. Munro had to haul on the reins to stop Peter Pan from careening into him. Peter fell against the rail for a moment, long enough to poach the very breath he needed. Oro dashed away, as did Magnitas. With only a furlong to run, Munro knew he couldn't balance his horse in time enough to make a second charge. He eased Peter Pan right down, and passing the judge they were sixth. Oro had claimed the Duke of Gloucester Plate in track-record time.

Disappointment overwhelmed Darby Munro as he returned Peter Pan to scale. The horse had done nothing wrong. He hadn't been sour in his running or lacklustre in his effort, and without Magnitas shifting over, Munro was positive Peter Pan would have won. But criticism would come his way through the papers. He had ridden the horse very differently from each of the three wins he had scored in Melbourne. Peter Pan was a long-striding, easy-moving thoroughbred. It suited him to be on the outside where he wouldn't get into trouble, and that had proved a useful formula down south. Also, it was easier to push smaller horses through tight holes on the rails. Peter Pan wasn't a small horse.

Dangar, though a little empty with disappointment, told himself that Peter Pan must be tired. He could hardly be bitter about the loss for his horse was flesh and blood, and had tried his best. McGrath couldn't fault the run, though he wondered strongly if a clear passage would have spelled a win. The stewards called an inquiry into Magnitas's interference, and concluded that it cost Peter Pan the race, occurring so close to the post as it did. They found Magnitas's jockey guilty of not exercising better control over his mount, and suspended him for two months for careless riding. It was vindication that Darby Munro needed, but it didn't ease the sting of the loss. As he slid off Peter Pan in the paddock, he wished he could have boasted a four-from-four record with the champion, but two gold cups and a Melbourne Stakes were good enough. Munro patted the big chestnut farewell, then headed into the jockeys' room. It was the last time he would pilot Peter Pan.

***

The end of 1934 slipped into sight with balmy summer evenings and hot nights among the mosquitoes. Swarms of white butterflies invaded Sydney, and everyone waited on the Christmas mail from Darwin. At Doonside, Peter Pan whiled away the heat, relaxed and unwound beneath the hibiscus trees and pines. His mane grew tangled and long, his coat brassy, but he was at peace, more than 11 miles of racing behind him.

29

The wildish fancy of L.K.S. Mackinnon

On the afternoon of 1 February 1935, Randwick was in the doldrums of summer. It was a hot day, bleached, stale and breathlessly still, and the tracks were quiet. The morning work was long over, and the horses gone. But the afternoon amity that had settled over the racecourse was punctured, by word from Melbourne that the VRC was about to ban geldings from weight-for-age racing. The news caught on and flashed around Randwick. It drew trainers from their lunches, even stable boys from their humble bunks.

The ban was the wildish fancy of L.K.S. Mackinnon, the ageing VRC chairman. He had decided that it was not desirable for a single horse to win all the weight-for-age races in a season, and it was much less desirable when that horse happened to be a gelding. He stated that he was trying to further the interests of breeding stock in Australia, but privately, Mackinnon was driven by a relentless dislike for geldings. It had begun a few years before when Phar Lap, useless to the breeding industry, had pillaged all and sundry. Mackinnon just didn't feel geldings were furthering the cause of the thoroughbred since they could not pass on their brilliance.

The proposal fell on Randwick like a big, black anvil. Trainers knew that the AJC was apt to follow in VRC footsteps, so they loudly decried Mackinnon's suggestion. 'The scheme is absurd,' quipped Les Haigh, because Rogilla's very future was on the line. 'It would mean that any good gelding would soon be forced off the racecourse.' Jack Cush, trainer of the Caulfield Cup-winning gelding Journal, was horrified. 'I hope I am not one-eyed when I say there's hardly one of us trainers who not does not think the suggestion preposterous and ridiculous.' In fact, there *was* one trainer: it was Frank McGrath.

McGrath saw the wisdom of Mackinnon's ways. He thought that if the chairman's intention was to improve Australian bloodstock, then he was going about it the right way. McGrath reasoned that, though in England an Epsom Derby winner was ready-set for sire duties, it was not the case in Australia. A colt over here needed to win far more than the AJC or VRC derbies to induce a full book of mares. 'In my opinion, it will give the good horses the chances they need to make a name for themselves at the studs,' he told *Truth.* 'There is no proof that our outstanding gelded performers like Phar Lap, Amounis, Gloaming and Beauford would not have been as great had they been left entire.'

McGrath had campaigned Amounis for six years, but he couldn't say that the gelding of the horse was the root of Amounis's success. Nor could it be proved that Phar Lap was as good as he was because he was a gelding. McGrath was matter-of-fact in the face of searing criticism. Wasn't racing supposed to further the interests of thoroughbred breeding?

McGrath and Mackinnon stood largely alone. The Bloodhorse Breeders' Association of Australia had presided over the issue four years ago, and had come to the conclusion that with a high percentage of colts being left entire just to compete in weight-for-age racing, the country would eventually be overrun with underachieving, undesirable stallions. Added to that, Australia, unlike England, had no export demand for stallions, so the logical outcome was that good blood, refined through years of importing stallions such as Valais and Magpie, would be diluted with second-class track retirees.

Mackinnon's proposal sought to banish the gelding from greatness. The nation's most celebrated geldings – Gloaming, Beauford, Limerick, Amounis and Phar Lap – had helped to put Australian racing on its legs and, in recent years, to keep it there. Australian racing would be much the poorer without them. The rule would turn racing on its head, altering the climate of competition remarkably for Peter Pan. There would be no Rogilla, no Lough Neagh or Journal. Winning would be easier for the great chestnut, though so much less interesting.

And so entered the first few months of 1935, with unease along the High Street barns of Randwick and unrest down Doncaster Avenue, with eyes that flicked nervously between Melbourne and Sydney, and with edgy chuckles each time Mackinnon got up from his desk. Though autumn was coming in Sydney, the sultry days of summer pressed on into March, and Peter Pan, back from Doonside since 14 January, was readying for the racing ahead.

30

'The crumbs for others'

The autumn season, after the bountiful spring, lay ahead of Peter Pan like a long golden road to conquer. He looked round but solid after his holiday, and beneath the potbelly stuffed full of western pasture, the foundations of his spring fitness lingered. Owing to the Duke of Gloucester Plate late in November, Peter had come back two weeks later than usual from Doonside, but there was only fitness to chase before his first start in the autumn. McGrath set him on a steady course to form.

He began, as was usual, with sound canters around Randwick after breakfast. Continuous drill work in long, uninterrupted sessions, and the athlete began to emerge in Peter Pan. After that, McGrath galloped him before breakfast. By the end of February, the horse was working steadily on the course proper, turning over a mile each morning in even time (15 seconds to the furlong). His work was so consistent it surprised McGrath, having pep that Peter hadn't shown at the beginning of any season. McGrath began to wonder if something amazing could happen this season. There was a seed planted in his head. The old trainer stepped up the tempo. On Tuesday 19 February, Peter Pan ran against the clock for the first time, running seven furlongs in 1.41 1/2, the last three in just over 41 seconds.

Into March, McGrath was still not bustling his champion. He varied the faster workouts with miles in even time, and sent Peter Pan over the grass and tan. The chestnut was responding well to his work, a true professional at the trackwork business. He did only what was asked and no more, rarely tugging on Clarrie Scahill for more rein, and while critics labelled it laziness, McGrath knew it was efficiency. Peter Pan wasn't a flash trackworker: he just did what he was told.

The few months of preparation had been the most seamless of Peter Pan's career. He had done everything right, and with no sign of joint problems he had bounded into racing action with hardly a hair turned. He had sparkle and zest, and a mature energy that had made his trainer's job ridiculously easy since January. All that was left for Frank McGrath was to map the season ahead, and that would begin with the Randwick Stakes on Saturday 23 March.

Peter Pan had debuted in the Randwick Stakes at the beginning of each autumn. He had won the race in 1933 and, after an 11-month layoff, was unplaced last year. The race had only been run since 1932, but had become the first big-name weight-for-age race on Sydney's autumn programme. McGrath had no qualms about tipping Peter Pan into the deep end. The trainer suspected the two-time

Cup winner would win first up, as he had in 1933, and the papers thought so too. 'CHAMPION IS LIKELY TO OUTCLASS RIVALS,' stated the *Telegraph* headline on the eve of raceday.

There would be seven other horses contesting the race, and among them were the racers that had fought Peter Pan the most. There was Rogilla, Oro and Kuvera, his three most consistent rivals, and then there was Journal, Broad Arrow, Sarcherie and Silver King. Between them, these horses had won two Melbourne Cups, two Caulfield Cups, two Sydney Cups, two King's Cups, a Cox Plate, an AJC Derby, a Metropolitan, a Toorak and a plethora of other principal races.

The conditions of the Randwick Stakes gave no disadvantage to Peter Pan in the weights. He would carry 9st 1lb along with Oro and Kuvera, while Rogilla and Broad Arrow, now aged horses, would carry 8st 12lb. Journal had 1lb less. It was a mile race, and with the speedster Silver King lining up, the pace was likely to be hot. That would suit Peter Pan, though he was the only horse that was yet to make a start this autumn. Nevertheless, McGrath was confident, and Jim Pike was back on board.

Rodney Dangar had resolved the decision about a jockey for Peter Pan. Though Darby Munro was available to ride, and had yet to be reassigned to Rogilla after the spring fiasco, Dangar was holding firm on J.E. Pike. Munro had always been clear that Pike would have first call on Peter Pan. Pike's understanding of the horse was without equal, and he was a principled jockey. He had hardly a blue stain on his record, which was important to Dangar, and when he did it was often the horse's fault. He was just the sort of rider the owner wanted. However, the reality was that Peter Pan's strike rate with the Munro brothers, and indeed Billy Duncan and Andy Knox, was just as good as Pike's, if not better. But Dangar didn't let that get in the way of his decision. Pike was confirmed for Peter Pan a week before the Randwick Stakes, and it squeezed Peter's price right down. No one could find better than even money about him, with 5/1 against Rogilla, and 8/1 the field.

***

The City Tattersall's meeting rolled around on 23 March, and was blessed with perfect weather. At half-past midday, the enclosures and grandstands were packed with excited bodies, but George Phillips and Peter Pan stopped all traffic. The pair was headed across the course to the race stalls, and Peter Pan looked like Hollywood.

The chestnut was decked out in a green silk quarter-sheet, with gold edgings and golden tassels hanging from the hems. Dangar had fashioned the rug on his green and gold racing colours, and thought it only fitting that his champion *look* like a champion now. Whether or not Peter Pan knew he was such, he certainly acted like one in his flashy new quarter-sheet. Passing the Flat patrons, he paused every few strides to look at them. Sydney's working class cheered and clapped their turf idol, and their approval followed him all the way to the stalls.

The Randwick Stakes was due off at three o'clock, and the horses were in the paddock by 2.45pm. With only half an hour between races, proceedings were quick, and Peter's beautiful quarter-sheet was whisked away to allow Jim Pike into the saddle. The thousands of racegoers that lined the paddock fences noticed a little bit of flesh on the big horse, and they thought him heavier than his rivals. Several commented that Rogilla looked dull and listless, perhaps showing his age or tired after his trip to Victoria some weeks prior. Nevertheless, money came for the Newcastle warrior in the ring. His fans backed him into 5/2, which sent Peter Pan, at 10 to 9 on, back out to even money.

At exactly 3.01pm, Peter Pan sprang from the barrier like a startled cat. He had so much spring in him that he caught Pike quite off guard, and he was the first to leave the tapes. Silver King, the speedster of the field, had to dash after the big champion to snatch the lead, but within a few strides they were level, and the pacemaker settled down on the rails to turn out the sectionals. Passing the first furlong pole, he was a length and a half ahead of Peter Pan, churning the first furlong out in 13 seconds, and dashing towards the second in 25.

On Peter Pan's back, Pike was astounded. The chestnut had energy that the jockey hadn't seen since the three-year-old days, and while Pike's instinct was to rein in the horse and settle him with the field, McGrath had reminded him before the race of Peter's sprinting talent. That, and the raw spoils beneath him, settled Pike's mind: he would allow Peter Pan to bowl along on the speed.

As Silver King rushed past the six-pole, that speed was electric. The leader was clattering down Randwick's back stretch, and had opened a two-length lead on Peter Pan. Kuvera was just inside Peter on the rails, with a further two lengths back to Oro and Journal, Rogilla and Broad Arrow trailing the field. Peter Pan was relishing the heat of the pace. With the leader some lengths out, he had space to stretch his long, straight legs, but he stayed tucked into Pike's grip, waiting to be released. As they converged on the half-mile he waited some more, and somewhere in the paddock, a *Truth* journalist waited too. When Peter Pan thundered past the half-mile pole, the journalist started his stopwatch.

It was like Peter Pan heard it, the little snap of the chronograph button. He began to dig into Silver King's lead, and Kuvera fell away, forgotten. Silver King was still running like the clappers, but into the home turn Jim Pike gave Peter Pan his head. The giant chestnut slid into the straight in full flight, and in a few kicks he had passed the leader. He belted down the home straight, the seven horses behind him falling into disarray. Two furlongs to go, he was all alone. A furlong to go, and still alone. Peter Pan flashed past the judge, and the *Truth* reporter stopped his clock.

It was an impossible time. Peter Pan had run the last four furlongs in a paralysing 46 3/4 seconds.

Randwick erupted into cheers as Australia's greatest racehorse won the Randwick Stakes first up. He had been magnificent and ruthless, and had won eased up. The official margins were a length to Silver King, and another length and three-quarters to Journal, who had fought from the back to creep past Rogilla. The time was 1:36 3/4, a second off Winooka's record. It was Peter Pan's 16th win from 27 starts. As he trotted back to scale, the ovations followed his every step. People clapped and cheered the reacquainted Pike and Peter Pan, and the veteran jockey tipped his hat to his fans. As usual, he showed no emotion, but when he slid off, he felt relieved. 'Whew, I'm glad it's over,' he said to McGrath, who laughed, then he left for the jockeys' room.

Pike was privately astounded by Peter Pan's improvement since the spring. He thought the horse as good as ever he had been, bouncing out of the machine like a two-year-old, letting loose down the straight as he had. The jockey knew the horse was older, and probably didn't want to gape about him as he had done in the past. 'It will surprise me if he is beaten in any race this autumn,' he told *Truth.*

The full measure of Peter Pan's win began to come into view. Here was a horse that was first up after a spell, winning with expert ease against horses with runs in hand. He had won the Melbourne Cup three months ago, the stiffest two-mile handicap in the country, and had now stepped back to a mile at weight-for-age, winning without pressure at a terrific clip. Where before he was deemed invincible as a stayer, now he was looking merciless as a miler. There wasn't a horse in the country within streets of his versatility. The newspapers began to label him 'Peter the Great'. Even 'Pilot', who had expected Peter to be beaten in the Randwick Stakes, admitted his error. 'In the belief that Peter Pan would suffer through lack of racing, I expected him to be beaten last Saturday,' he stated in the *Referee.* 'That idea was very wide of the mark.' On the front page of that paper, the headlines read, 'PETER PAN'S COLLECTION PLATE: THE CRUMBS FOR OTHERS'.

***

The Randwick Plate had catapulted Peter Pan back into the top spot of horse racing. The 1934 Melbourne Cup had been a career high, and many would have expected the horse to go out on it. It was the logical step for a stallion, after all. However, Dangar wasn't ready for retirement talk. Nor was Peter, it seemed. He had come back and eclipsed the Randwick Plate opposition, and he was only five, so Dangar was resolved to complete the season at the very least, which would finish with the autumn carnival. As in previous years, the owner and trainer had a specific race in mind for Peter Pan, and this time it was the AJC Jubilee Cup on 6 May at Randwick, a raceday hosted in honour of 25 years since the coronation of King George V. The race would be run like the King's Cup. It would be a set-weights affair over a mile and a half, with a gold cup valued at £100, but the first-prize purse was a rich £1350. In fact, the AJC was throwing a lot of money at its Silver Jubilee meeting. The six-race card was worth £4300, which was £500 more than the VRC was producing for its Jubilee meeting the same day.

The race would occur late in Peter Pan's preparation. Usually, by 6 May, he would be well and truly out to grass, but Easter was late in 1935, so autumn racing was late too. The AJC carnival wouldn't start until Saturday 20 April, and would conclude on 27 April. It meant that staying in training until 6 May would be no great problem for Peter Pan, as the meetings were within two weeks of each other. However, McGrath's quandary was not the Jubilee Cup. It was which races to select for Peter Pan in the meantime.

Dangar had told the trainer he didn't want Peter Pan overtaxed. He was not out to win everything with his champion; rather, he was after certain illustrious prizes which fulfilled his dreams as an owner. How McGrath got the horse to those targets was up to him. So far, Peter Pan had won all of his aimed prizes bar the 1934 King's Cup. He had scooped two Melbourne Cups, a St Leger and a Duke of Gloucester Cup. With the Jubilee Cup in sight, and under the premise that the horse was not to be over-raced, McGrath decided to run Peter Pan only once before the AJC autumn meeting – in either the Rawson Stakes at Rosehill on 6 April, or the Chipping Norton Plate at Warwick Farm on 13 April.

The Rawson Stakes was a nine-furlong contest, under weight-forage rules with allowances, and Peter Pan had tackled it twice before. In 1933, he had been caught in the tapes and finished last, and the following year he was second to Rogilla after interference settled him in the home turn. The newspapers were touting the race as his hoodoo, something that had eluded him despite his best efforts, but if McGrath elected the Rawson Stakes for Peter Pan, it wouldn't be to make good on some gremlin. It would be because Rosehill suited the loose-limbed racehorse more than the tight-turning Warwick Farm. McGrath paid up the nomination fee for Rosehill.

The entrants for the race made it a stellar competition. On top of Peter Pan there was Rogilla, Kuvera and Sydney Cup favourite Journal. Peter's stablemate Master Brierly was also in, as was Topical, a good and honest Australian Cup winner from Bill Kelso's yard. But the real sting in the Rawson Stakes was the meeting of Peter Pan and Sylvandale, because it was the proven older horse against the country's current crack three-year-old. Sylvandale had won the VRC St Leger and the Australian Cup in Victoria in recent weeks, and he was a favourite for the AJC St Leger. He was a brilliant racehorse on any day, but in the Rawson Stakes he would enjoy a three-year-old's weight advantage: he would carry 10lb less than Peter Pan.

Two days before raceday, early in trackwork, stalwart trainer Bill Kelso stood on the roof of the tote building at Randwick. He was watching his horse Topical come down the straight. After the gallop, Kelso turned to his friends and said, 'He's having a go at Peter Pan on Saturday, but I don't suppose McGrath's horse has lost any sleep on account of that.'

***

Saturday afternoon was warm and muggy over Rosehill, and Frank McGrath stood in the saddling paddock, history creeping up on him in an unexpected moment. Fifty years ago almost to the day, he had been at this very spot, a stripling at 20 years of age, waiting to ride in the first ever race meeting at the new Rosehill Racecourse. His mount had been in the last race of the day, the rich Rosehill Handicap worth 200 sovereigns. He had ridden an ageing brown racehorse called Polestar, who had also started in the first race of the day, and they had finished fifth. McGrath looked about him, and remembered Rosehill as it had been that day, neat and elegant and new. He saw the grandstand bustling with 1600 patrons, and the paddock he now stood in, then six acres of land that looked over the Parramatta River. He heard the ruffle of lace dresses, and smelled tobacco in the air, punched with the scent of horses and straw. And, like they were there again, he heard the steamers whistling on the river, ready to ferry people back to Sydneytown. Rosehill was a special spot for him today.

McGrath glanced around him, pulled back to 1935. There was the Rawson Stakes to contend with, and the horses were already in the paddock. Peter Pan looked fresh and robust as he led the field around the enclosure. He was yet to grow a winter coat, but his tail was starting to darken in the middle, though his mane was still brilliant blond. He had 9st 2lb on his back, sharing top weight with Kuvera. Topical, Rogilla and Master Brierly all had 8st 13lb, while Journal carried 8st 11lb and Sylvandale, the three-year-old, had 8st 6lb. As it stood, Peter Pan was conceding weight to almost every horse, but under the weight-for-age scale the concessions were not great. He was not at a disadvantage and Pike had the measure of things when he stood Peter Pan at the tapes. He knew he would have the goods to stay on the speed, but he suspected there wasn't a pacemaker in the field.

At 2.45pm, the seven horses lined up before Jack Gaxieu. Jim Pike, looking steely on Peter Pan, towered above his opponents, and nearby, Jim Munro, back from India (and beginning the long task of wrangling back into Sydney's jockey ranks), looked anxiously ahead on Journal. Jack Pratt was aboard Sylvandale, and towards the outside, Rogilla was giving his rider an almighty headache. The Newcastle gelding refused to stand still at the tapes, and his antics delayed the start by a minute or two. When his nose was pointed the right way, Gaxieu shouted to the field to get ready, and he threw the tapes into the air.

Peter Pan once again bounced into stride like a two-year-old. With Sylvandale, he was the first away from the barrier, and he settled into stride within the first furlong, the rest scrambling along behind him. But neither he nor Sylvandale were in a great hurry, and passing the first furlong in 12 1/2 seconds, Kuvera came around them to take the lead. Master Brierly crept up too, so as they neared the first turn into the backstretch, the seven horses were strung out like frankfurts. Kuvera showed the way to Sylvandale, with a length back to Master Brierly. Peter Pan was another length behind.

Into the backstretch they ran, and Sylvandale was finding the pace too slack. Kuvera had carved out the first two furlongs in 26 seconds, and Pratt pushed his colt into the lead. Lengths behind, Pike saw an opportunity. He swung Peter Pan away from the rails and bustled the big chestnut towards the front. Within strides, Peter Pan was bowling along behind Sylvandale, leaping over the ground in huge, effortless leagues. Sylvandale stretched himself to a two-length lead, turning out the first four furlongs in 51 seconds, and Pike simply cruised along in his slipstream.

The field swung into the far turn, and suddenly Sylvandale clattered away from the pack. Pratt was trying to steal a jump on Peter Pan. But the chestnut, who had been springing along behind him, shot away too, and the acceleration of the two front horses was so sudden and so electric that they left the others behind. They opened up a three-length lead as they pounded towards the home turn, with Peter Pan creeping into Sylvandale's lead. As the two horses swung into the straight, Peter was at the three-year-old's flanks. They straightened for home like that, the Melbourne Cup hero breathing all over the young colt.

Sylvandale was digging deep to find his finishing run. He was a gutsy competitor, but Peter Pan was about to break his heart. As they neared the two-furlong pole, Pike simply clicked to Peter Pan to get a move on, and the horse ran past the three-year-old with withering ease. He spurted to the lead, drawing away by two-and-a-half lengths, clattering through the last two furlongs in 24 seconds. He dashed past the winning post going away, with Sylvandale trailing in second and a fast-finishing Journal a head away third. Peter Pan had slashed his Rawson Stakes hoodoo. He had joined Nightmarch, Limerick, Beauford, Poitrel and Poseidon as winners of this great autumn event. As he eased up, he tugged hard on Jim Pike's reins, like he wasn't yet ready to slow down. When he returned to scale, he could hardly have blown out a candle.

'NOTHING EQUINE IN AUSTRALIA IS EQUAL OF PETER PAN,' sang *Truth* the following day. 'It is questionable if ever a better horse at all distances was seen on the course,' stated 'Musket'. The newspapers were clearing their debts to Peter Pan. They couldn't say enough about him. With the Rawson

Stakes behind him, Peter Pan's winnings climbed to £27,710 and 10 shillings. He had completed the nine furlongs in 1:52, but after the sluggish pace of the first few furlongs, he had run the last four in 49 seconds, and the last three in 37 flat. Those sectionals proved he had invented dramatic dash after the initial dawdle. It was easy to forget he had beaten terrific horses, because he had made them look so ordinary. Journal, on his third place, had crept into Sydney Cup favouritism, while Sylvandale was a certainty for the St Leger. Others in the field were heading to the Doncaster, while Master Brierly was on his way to the Cumberland Plate. Only Rogilla, whose old star seemed to be fading, didn't get the credit he deserved for finishing fourth. Everyone concluded the old warrior, now a seven-year-old, must be spent.

But a week later, as Peter Pan rested in his box on Doncaster Avenue, Rogilla snatched the Chipping Norton Plate from Hall Mark. The two horses leathered each other to the Warwick Farm winning post, Rogilla prevailing by a short head, and overnight, Peter's prospects of racing undefeated through the autumn withered a little. It looked as if his greatest rival was back.

31

The gravel in his guts

Rodney Dangar sat in his office above O'Connell Street, sensing the evening creeping in. He flicked on his desk lamp and squinted at the catalogue in his hands. It was the 1935 Inglis yearling-sale book, the buyer's guide for the forthcoming yearling sales. There were 522 youngsters, represented on crisp, ivory pages. They came from Kia Ora, Widden and Oakleigh studs, and from every corner of New South Wales, but two of them, tucked into the third and final day of selling, had come from Baroona.

Dangar looked at their pages in the dim light of his desk lamp. One of the two youngsters was a Pantheon filly out of his Irish mare Beedivine. She was a lovely type, a neat and pretty individual, but he didn't expect to break the sale ring with her. The other one, however, was a different story. Dangar had submitted for sale a half-brother to Peter Pan, the first foal Alwina had thrown since 1929.

He stared long and hard at the catalogue page. The colt was by Brazen, an imported sire that stood at Widden Stud up in the Hunter. Brazen was a 12-year-old stallion, the sire of Kuvera, but had only been at Widden for two years. Prior to 1933, he had stood at Biraganbil Stud, which was the breeding property of the Rouse family in central-west New

South Wales. Dangar's mother (who had died in 1931) had been a Rouse, and when Biraganbil was dispersed two years before, it afforded him the first opportunity to honour the family connection. Brazen was sold by the Rouse estate to Widden, and Dangar promptly sent Alwina to be covered. The resultant foal, the yearling in the catalogue page before him, had been registered as Brazilian.

The colt was one of the most well-developed yearlings Dangar had ever seen, a strapping youngster that had taken the mottled brown hide of his sire rather than the pale copper of his dam. He looked nothing like Peter Pan, and Dangar wondered why it was he had kept Peter Pan back in 1931. He could have despatched him to the Inglis yards that year as he had done these two, and he would have been none the wiser. But Peter Pan had been a stunner, a little thing that quite stole the hearts of everyone at Baroona, especially Dangar's little old mother, and as much as the owner hated to admit it, looks had been one of the factors in keeping Peter Pan. Closing the catalogue, he swung around to look out at the city below him.

***

Sydney woke with the birds on Easter Saturday, for it was one of the busiest days of the year for the city. By mid-morning, a ceaseless string of trams chugged down Anzac Parade, spilling a record attendance into the showgrounds and battling on southwards to Randwick Racecourse. After weeks of calm and clement weather, the track was in perfect order.

Peter Pan was starting in the second race of the day, the Autumn Plate over a mile and a half at weight-for-age. When he entered the parade ring a little after 1.30pm, he looked assertive and masculine, and every bit the arrogant champion. He wasn't interested in his adoring fans (though they reached over the rails for him), and he looked over them rather than at them. For the veterans that watched him, he was unlike so many of the idols they had seen before. Carbine, 40 years before, had been a little playful before races, and Amounis could have been a child's pony. Phar Lap was the most pliable champion that ever sported silk, and even Gloaming was a darling to behold. Perhaps Manfred, another irascible, strung-out stallion, had been something like Peter Pan: possessing of rare brilliance, but a horse that knew it.

Since the Rawson Stakes two weeks prior, Peter Pan had only grown more brilliant. At Victoria Park two days previously, McGrath had wound him right up for the Autumn Plate. He told Clarrie Scahill to let the horse go, and 30 feet out from the rails, Peter Pan ran like the clappers through the first five furlongs in 1:04 3/4. Bursting into the final three, he broke the mile record for Victoria Park. Trackside, the newspapers were all over it. Betting on the Autumn Plate had turned into a one-two affair, with bookies only taking money on first and second placings combined. On his own, Peter Pan stood at 5/1 on, with Rogilla closest at 5/1 against.

In the mounting yard, Rogilla looked his usual docile self. Since his winning the Chipping Norton, he had resumed work at Randwick, and had run respectable times in the mornings. But Les Haigh had had a time of it defending his Newcastle gelding from claims that he was spent to accusations that the horse was over-raced. In fact, Rogilla *was* raced heavily, but not because Haigh wanted it that way. Rogilla was a poor doer, a horse that didn't eat well and so lost condition easily. It was impossible to gallop him hard between races, as he would turn into skin and bone. As a result, Haigh trained him light and raced him often, just to keep him in trim.

Parading behind Peter Pan, Rogilla was bony about the ribcage, and looked angular and inverted. He was an ageing horse now, probably past his peak, but Haigh wasn't fooled. He didn't think his horse was a back number. The night before, he had gone through the usual schedule before raceday. Rogilla had been handfed by his groom, which was necessary just to make sure the horse had had enough to eat. The same thing had occurred this morning. Rogilla's feet were checked, because he had poor, shelly hooves, and he wore rubber pads to compensate for this. When Haigh thought about it, it was a miracle the gelding could run at all.

The Autumn Plate was the 15th time Peter Pan would meet his greatest foe. This time last year, the tallies were almost tied between the two, but this season Peter had streaked ahead. He had finished in front of Rogilla in nine of their 15 encounters now, though many were too shrewd to write off the persistent gelding. Across the ring Rogilla, who was yet to be partnered with Darby Munro since the spring, was second choice in the one-two betting, and nothing else looked dangerous. There were seven horses entered for the race. Outside Peter and Rogilla, Oro was running, and he was topweight with Peter Pan at 9st 3lb. There was Gold Trail, a former New Zealand mare and a five-year-old who had won the Auckland Cup in 1934. There was also Topical again, and King March, who had run third at Rosehill's jubilee meeting. Journal was the only other horse in the race, and it was safe to assume that Peter Pan had worried away further competition. Kuvera was scratched, and Hall Mark had been diverted to the Doncaster, due later that afternoon.

Peter Pan bounced off with what had become his usual ping. He had such power leaving the barrier that Jim Pike stood up in his stirrups to stop his ride from leaving the field behind. In protest, Peter Pan leaned all over his jockey, fighting Pike's urges to slow down, and the pair raced through the first furlong in battle. After that, Oro crept up on his inside to take the lead, and Pike managed to encourage Peter Pan into the box seat, a length and a bit behind Oro, with Gold Trail the same distance to third, and the pack chasing.

Oro bore down on the first half-mile; by the time the field swung into the backstretch, he was bounding along. Peter Pan was cruising too, not a length behind him. Pike had settled the big chestnut off the rails, and he was moving with that loose, liquid stride Pike had come to appreciate. As they left the back stretch, there was no change to the order, with Oro streaking along in front. He had blazed the first six furlongs in 1:20.

The seven horses converged on the home turn, but Pike had only to loosen his grip on Peter Pan and the favourite ran all over Oro in a few bounds. He swamped the pacemaker as they hit the straight, dashing into the lead. A roar rose up from the grandstands. Rogilla had come from nowhere after Peter Pan, and the two foes raced into the final two furlongs head-to-head. Rogilla was on the outside, with Peter hugging the rails. 'Rogilla's got him!' screamed the crowd. The gelding had poked his white face in front, with jockey Jack Pratt driving and hollering at his horse to hurry up. On the rails, Pike leaned into Peter Pan's neck. He saw the King's Cup all over again, Peter Pan's most famous loss, and he began to dig up the gravel in Peter's guts. He drove, drove with every stride. He felt Peter Pan lower, saw the chestnut's ears flatten, then saw Rogilla come back to them. Peter Pan had entered into the war.

The winning post came at the two horses in slow motion. On the stands side, Rogilla was relentlessly ridden, while on the rails, Peter Pan looked monstrous.

His head was up and his ears flat back, Pike buried in his mane. But the tiger in Peter pushed him forward. He thrust his nose into a narrow lead; two lengths from the line, he dug some more. Fighting back his old opponent, breaking him one last time, he threw his head into the lead and thundered over the line.

The cheering from the crowd rose like a hot bubble, bursting as soon as Peter Pan won. It was fever pitch, hysterical almost, and up in the Leger a gentleman swallowed his cigar butt in the excitement. Odds-on backers cheered for their tickets, men leaned over the fences waving their hats. It was a spectacle, a theatre of fans, and as Peter Pan led Rogilla back to scale, he was engulfed by applause. The two horses had produced a contest where most thought there wasn't one, and few had thought Rogilla still had it in him to frighten Peter Pan. In almost all the close finishes between these horses, Rogilla had prevailed in the dying strides. But there was new tenacity in Peter Pan this autumn. He had understood the fight, and responded like a lion.

Jim Pike and Jack Pratt had earned their laurels. They had ridden a brilliant race, and the margins proved it. The two jockeys had driven their horses to a four-length lead over Oro, who finished third, with Gold Trail another two lengths behind. The official time for the race was 2:33 3/4, which was just under four seconds off the distance record set by Oro in the Duke of Gloucester Plate the previous November. But

Peter Pan had run his last half-mile in 47 3/4 seconds, which was a titan effort, having already travelled a mile. The result threw new energy into the weight-for-age prospects for the meeting. 'Rogilla's sensational fight has paved the way for further great battles between these chestnut rivals,' wrote the *Telegraph.* Where before Peter Pan had been expected to trot through his weight-for-age programme unchallenged, now it looked as if Rogilla was renewed.

The Autumn Plate was Peter Pan's 29th start. His tally now stood at 18 wins (including a dead-heat), five seconds and six times unplaced. Curiously, he had never finished third. The purse was worth £1150, and it brought his tally to £28,860/10s in earnings. Among horses racing, he was the highest stakes-earner, and if he hadn't missed his spring engagements in 1933, there was no guessing how much he would have earned. With only a season left in him, he would probably never reach the heights of Amounis or Phar Lap in winnings, but purses had been different then.

Later that afternoon, with Peter Pan installed back at Doncaster Avenue, Hall Mark stepped out and won the Doncaster carrying 9st 8lb. It was a brilliant performance. The 1933 Cup winner, a decent stayer, had stepped back to a mile and won in a tight finish, backed for £10,000 by his trainer. Winooka, attempting a return to form, broke down in the race under Pike. With this new proficiency over the shorter courses, Hall Mark was confirmed for the All-Aged Plate on Wednesday. Though Peter Pan was nominated too, no one expected McGrath to send his champion over a mile when the longer Cumberland Plate was on the same day. McGrath, however, had different ideas.

***

On Tuesday morning, 23 April, three days after the Autumn Plate and a day before Wednesday racing, the old trainer leaned on the rails at Victoria Park and watched Peter Pan fly over a mile. He hadn't yet declared the horse for the Cumberland or the All-Aged Plate, but weight-for-age conditions stated that final declarations could be made a mere half-hour before each race. Though McGrath knew which of the two he wanted to start in, the decision rested on Peter Pan's sparkle this morning.

The chestnut was the defending Cumberland Plate champion, having won the race for the last two years. Looking at him go over the kikuyu, McGrath knew Peter Pan could win it again. But it wasn't the ease of the Cumberland that was determining the situation. McGrath had nominated Master Brierly for the race too, and he really felt this budding stayer was due for a big win. Also, starting Peter Pan in the All-Aged mile would be a statement and, if he won it, a victory without peer. It would prove what McGrath knew as simple fact: Peter Pan was lethal.

The *Telegraph* chewed over the possibilities. 'All ideas have been upset by the announcement that there is every likelihood Peter Pan will tackle Hall Mark in the sprint race. If Peter Pan is a definite starter in the sprint, why should not Jack Holt withdraw Hall Mark from that race and run him in the Cumberland Plate?' Holt, however, had no intention of bowing out. He was buoyed by Hall Mark's winning the Doncaster, and felt his horse equal to the task of racing Peter Pan over a mile. But the *Telegraph* had yet to be convinced that a Melbourne Cup winner, as both horses were, could travel a mile competitively. 'Very few horses can come from Melbourne Cup success to victory in mile company,' the newspaper stated. 'But on the other hand, Peter Pan was recently successful over a mile at Randwick. The clash of the two horses should prove one of the greatest attractions of the carnival.' The following morning, when it became public that Peter Pan would start in the All-Aged Plate, frenzy developed in the betting ring. Would it be Peter Pan, the best horse in the country, or Hall Mark, sensational winner of the Doncaster three days ago?

The All-Aged Plate had been first run in 1866, and it had decorated some of the finest thoroughbreds in turf history. Carbine had won the race in 1889 and 1890, while Wakeful had scored in 1902, Desert Gold in 1918, and Beauford in 1922. In recent years it had been won by Limerick and Amounis, while the last two runnings had seen Winooka and Chatham score. But it had become a sprinter's classic. In 69 runnings, only four Melbourne Cup winners had managed to win the All-Aged Plate, and the last one was Carbine in 1890. That meant that a true stayer hadn't clinched the race for 45 years, so the odds were stacked against Hall Mark and Peter Pan. Nevertheless, only two other horses had opted to line up against them. At two o'clock on Wednesday afternoon, 24 April, Silver King and Silver Ring stood beside Peter Pan and Hall Mark, ready to tackle Randwick's famous mile.

The four horses broke to a perfect start. Silver King, the speed specialist, dashed away fastest, leading the small field out of the chute and onto the course proper. He was flying. Hurtling down the back stretch, he carved the first two furlongs in 24 seconds, the first three in 36 1/2, and passing the four-furlong post, he clocked 47 1/2. He was running perfect sectionals – 12 seconds to the furlong.

Silver Ring was at top speed to hold second spot, and behind him came Peter Pan. Jim Pike had slotted the big chestnut in on the rails third, and he was relishing the early speed. He had found his stride and was bowling along after the frontrunners, while behind him Hall Mark was lengths away. The 1933 Cup winner was either struggling with the speed, or his jockey Keith Voitre had expected a sluggish tempo. Either way, he was hopelessly outpaced.

The field swung out of the far turn and hurtled towards the three-pole. Peter Pan was wound tight like an elastic band. The heat of the pace had him almost at top speed, and Pike knew that he could sustain it until the winning post. He allowed Peter Pan to run up to Silver Ring's heels; as they hurtled into the home turn, Silver Ring fell away exhausted. Peter Pan dashed through on the rails towards Silver King, and as they straightened for home, Pike wasted no time. He rode Peter Pan right out, and the horse devoured the pacemaker.

Down the Randwick straight he plunged with reckless abandon. Pike could see the rails whizzing past him, knew that Peter was turning out speed of a different kind. But he didn't ease his mount, and they ripped through the final two furlongs. They were two lengths clear of the pack, then three lengths clear. Peter Pan was running a merry mile. He blazed past the judge in a maelstrom of cheering, clocking 1:35 1/2 for the mile, or a new Australasian record.

Up in the stands, Frank McGrath was dazzled. His horse had chewed a quarter of a second off Winooka's 1933 mile record, and McGrath hadn't expected that. He knew that Peter Pan would easily run the distance, but break records doing it? That was a new facet he hadn't known about. In all his years of racing, the trainer couldn't remember a Melbourne Cup winner that could step back in distance so easily. Peter Pan had come from a stayer's preparation only months ago to run the fastest ever mile on this side of the world. At this very moment, as everyone at Randwick inhaled the spectacle of the All-Aged Plate, there was none to compare with Peter Pan. Dangar's horse came home fresh as summer rain. Hall Mark had finished in second spot, though only a length to the good of Silver King, but he looked beaten and tired. It was clear that as good as he was, good enough to win the Doncaster, he hadn't the constitution of Peter Pan. When Pike jumped off the champion he was breathless, and he said to McGrath jokingly, 'You'll have to tackle the Newmarket after that!'

As the flags were hoisted for correct weight, and the time pasted on the semaphore, people flicked through their racebooks to check the records. Had Peter Pan really run over Winooka by a quarter-second? Was it possible that Australia's greatest stayer was now Australia's greatest miler too? There was new lustre to this horse, new evidence of his brilliance, a brilliance that even his critics couldn't ignore. 'Peter Pan has risen to heights comparable with the mighty Phar Lap,' wrote the *Telegraph.* 'Hall Mark might have placed the seal on his versatility by winning the Doncaster last Saturday, but Peter Pan, a dual Melbourne Cup winner, has overshadowed every racehorse who has graced Australian tracks since Phar Lap.'

'Pilot' was profound in his commentary of the race: 'Peter Pan put up a performance in winning the mile All-Aged Plate which, on top of a marvellous staying record, stamps him as surely the best horse of all time. He ran a mile in 1:35 1/2, an Australasian record. His 3:23 1/4 [in the 1932 Cup] is within a fraction of the Australasian record for two miles, and he has done what no horse in the last 72 years has been capable of. He has won two Melbourne Cups.'

Peter Pan's victory had not been lost on anyone. The registering of a record in a weight-for-age race was miraculous. In handicaps, the lightly weighted horses always make the topweights carry their imposts from start to finish, so they clap on the pace from the beginning. But under weight-for-age, especially in an event with only four runners, no horse has a clear-cut advantage in the weights. As a result, the race is usually a matter of tactics, with the fast horses out to slow the field down. As it had stood, Winooka's record had been set in the Doncaster, a handicap, in 1933. Peter Pan had confounded racing form by setting a new record in the weight-for-age All-Aged Plate.

The race tipped Peter's winnings over the £30,000 mark, to £30,010 and 10 shillings. It was his nineteenth win from 30 starts, and he was unbeaten for the autumn. He had now, conclusively, proven his mettle from seven furlongs to two and a quarter miles, and had run the fastest mile ever recorded in the country. Dangar had been elevated into the highest echelons of racing, and Frank McGrath, after nearly 40 years at the top, had never trained a horse as brilliant as Peter Pan. Even the threat of Rogilla, a middle-distance champion of the day, had evaporated into the thin, cool air.

***

Two days after the All-Aged Plate, in seamless autumn sunshine, Dangar found himself seated in the Inglis auditorium at Newmarket, waiting for his two yearlings to sell. It was the final day of trading, and he was nervous, twitchy almost. His Brazen colt was due in any moment. The sale ring was full, with many who had come just to witness the sale of Peter Pan's half-brother. They chattered away quietly as Reg Inglis went through the preceding lots, and when Alwina's brown colt stepped into the ring, they fell silent. Dangar took a deep breath.

Brazilian, as the colt had been named, had never seen so many people in his young life. There were hundreds sandwiched into the auditorium, and they were a far cry from the affectionate staff of Baroona. Their faces were detached and curious, critical almost, and they watched him jitter around the sale ring under Reg Inglis. The bidding began at 200 guineas, and advanced quickly towards 700. A bid of 800 guineas was called from the far side of the ring, and Inglis asked for more. 'Come on gentlemen,' he boomed, 'a half-brother to the greatest racehorse in Australia, and a stallion when he's done.' But the faces around the ring were blank, and the bid of 800 guineas stood. Inglis raised his gavel and looked around once more. 'He'll be going home with Mr Dangar at that price,' he said. Still there was no raise. Inglis looked around at his bid-spotters one last time, and they shook their heads at him. He brought his gavel down and announced Brazilian unsold. 'Passed in at 800 guineas,' he said. 'Not nearly enough.'

The price was a decent one for an unproved yearling, and if Dangar hadn't been asking for nearly double that, Brazilian would have topped the day's sale. The reality was that buyers had no proof Alwina would throw another colt as good as Peter Pan, and though she was bred on stout staying lines, she wasn't a blueblood matriarch. In fact, if Dangar had consigned Peter Pan to sale in 1931, he probably would have attracted a very average sum. Dangar was disappointed with the result. He had thought, mistakenly, that Peter Pan's reputation would be enough to sell the colt. It was the reason he had slapped on a huge price tag. By registering a name for the colt, many thought Dangar had never wanted to sell the horse. In fact, he had wanted to sell. But in the face of an embarrassing public situation he came out with fighting words, convincing himself that he was excited to hang on to Brazilian. He was, but he had to work at it.

When the yearling sales wrapped up that Friday afternoon, 1935 showed a great improvement in bloodstock values. Averages were up, as were aggregates, and for the first time in years Heroic hadn't provided the highest priced youngster. That honour fell to Pantheon who, with a glamorous chestnut yearling, commanded a sale-topping 1700 guineas. A few days later, Chatham also went into the ring to sell as a stud prospect. His last race had been the

Melbourne Stakes of '34, which he had lost to Peter Pan. His owner, Gus Blair, had put a stiff reserve on the retired champion, but Inglis couldn't spirit the bidding above 500 guineas. It was a horror price for a horse that had proved himself the best miler in living memory. But there, plain for all to see, was that stubborn prejudice again. Chatham was Australian bred, and as good as he was, his yearlings would never command the prices that could Pantheon, or recent popular imports Silvius or Constant Son. It was a cool reality that would play on Dangar's mind in the happenings of the next few days.

32

America wants Peter Pan

The dust had scarcely settled after Peter Pan's miracle mile on Wednesday when American Al Lippe, a quick-thinking and fast-talking boxing manager, received a telegram. Lippe was in Sydney with his prized fighters Vernon Cormier and Phil Zwick, but the cable had nothing to do with boxing. 'GET THE BEST PRICE FOR PETER PAN. OFFER CONFIDENTIAL. CHEQUE TO FOLLOW.' The telegram had come from one of the leading lady-owners of the American turf, who had bestowed upon Lippe the charge of buying Peter Pan for America. She was offering him huge commissions to succeed, and Lippe thought the deal home and hosed. Later that evening, he received a banker's certified cheque for $100,000, and he made ready to approach Rodney Dangar.

Lippe wheeled in the highest social circles in America. He knew how to think big and act bigger, and as manager of some of the best American fighters this century, he had learned to negotiate. He approached the Randwick trainer Tom McGrath, who was no relation to Frank and whom Lippe had met years before on his boxing visits to Australia, and through Tom he impressed the offer upon Dangar. Lippe hoped that a fellow trainer, one not connected to Peter Pan emotionally, would sell the deal better than he.

The terms of the sale were lucrative. Peter Pan was to be retired from racing immediately and shipped straight to America to begin stud duties. Lippe was to receive 5 per cent of the monies that changed hands in Sydney, and another 10 per cent when he returned to America. He was also in line to receive 2.5 per cent of all monies exchanged on the sale of Peter Pan's progeny and, if Peter didn't produce a winner among his first crop, he would be returned to Dangar without obligation.

Lippe was positive that the offer would negotiate itself. The brash American was yet to find a man without a price. The $100,000 figure (about £30,000) eclipsed the Australian record price that had been paid for Heroic back in 1925 (16,000 guineas, or £16,800) and, if accepted, it would sit as a benchmark for decades. And Lippe's motivation was money. He well remembered the stir that Phar Lap had created in the United States in 1932, and he foresaw the same thing happening with Peter Pan. With two Melbourne Cups to his credit, and an Australasian mile record, Peter Pan's progeny would rake in the greenbacks.

Tom McGrath telephoned the offer to Rodney Dangar on Wednesday night, 24 April. The trainer, along with Lippe, was sworn to secrecy about its details, but immediately the American learned what it was to deal with Dangar. He turned him down flat, telling Tom McGrath to tell Lippe that money would not buy Peter Pan. The only official statement he made, leaked to the press the following morning, was that he had 'no intention to sell Peter Pan, and he will never leave Australia.' Lippe was confounded by Dangar's rebuttal, but not discouraged. In his experience, first offers were roundly rejected, mostly because people needed time to digest the terms. However, when Tom McGrath approached Dangar again on Thursday morning, impressing upon him that he could command whatever figure he wanted from the Americans, Dangar was even more resolute. He would not sell Peter Pan, he said, no matter the price.

Dangar didn't waver from his rejection in the next few days. Not even the failed sale of Brazilian on Friday made him wonder if he'd done the right thing. This wasn't the first time, after all, that he'd dismissed huge sums for Peter Pan. At the end of 1932, he had refused £50,000 from the Americans. But on Monday afternoon, five days after Lippe and Tom McGrath had first made representations, Dangar's resolution faltered, when Chatham fetched no more than 500 guineas at auction and was passed in. Dangar knew that Peter Pan was far more accomplished and far more valuable than Chatham, but he was forced to wonder: would his champion suffer the same indifference as a stud prospect?

Dangar was clever enough to keep his thoughts to himself. No matter his private concerns; publicly he was defiant about keeping Peter Pan, at least for the meantime. He told the *Telegraph* that he had no interest in selling his horse right now, but if Peter were to win a third Melbourne Cup in November, he might consider a sale then. No doubt the dubious response to Chatham's prospects weighed heavily on his mind. Lippe cabled to his mysterious American buyer that Peter Pan could not be bought, and he had to concede that Dangar had baffled him. 'It was a wonder offer in my opinion,' he told the newspapers when, as was inevitable, his name was associated with the affair. 'I know my client will be surprised and disappointed at not having been able to clinch the deal.' Just who the American buyer was remained a guarded secret, but by 1 May, though unconfirmed by Al Lippe, it was thought to be Isabel Dodge Sloane.

Sloane was the millionaire heiress of the Dodge motor company, and had plunged into horse racing in 1924. She was 39 now, divorced, but her wealth and tenacity had carried her to the top of American racing. The previous year she had become the first woman to lead the owners' list in earnings, due largely to her Kentucky Derby winner Cavalcade and Preakness winner High Quest. But Isabel Dodge Sloane studied pedigrees with the best of them. Her interest in racing went far beyond a social need for the winner's circle. She wanted to breed champions, and in 1929 she had purchased 850 acres of farmland in Virginia. Along with her racing string, Brookmeade Stable, she now had Brookmeade Farm.

Lippe was stunned that Sloane's name had made it to the newspapers, and he denied her involvement at every opportunity. 'I am sore about the publicity that this affair has been given,' he told *Truth.* 'It will put me in an awkward position with the lady I was negotiating for. I was practically under oath to say nothing of the transaction, or reveal the identity of the person who was making the offer until negotiations were finalised. It's got me licked how the news came out.' Though other women in American racing were also mentioned, the name of Isabel Dodge Sloane popped up again and again. If it was she who was bidding for Peter Pan, it was the top tier of American racing that had come knocking.

With the offer face down in the dirt, Al Lippe was due to leave Sydney on the *Balranald* on 4 May. Instead, he sent his two fighters ahead of him, and he booked passage a few days later so that he might see Peter Pan run in the Jubilee Cup. 'I was too busy to get out to the Easter carnival to see him,' Lippe told reporters, 'but I thought I would just like to have one look at Peter in action – the dream horse of mine whom I thought would be raking me in a small fortune.' Lippe may have lost Peter Pan, but he hadn't lost his talent for dramatics.

***

Frank McGrath had followed the American business with interest. No horse in his charge had ever commanded such an offer, and he knew that the loss of Peter Pan would be a magnificent vacuum in his stable. Nevertheless, life had to go on at Doncaster Avenue, and when it became clear that Peter Pan was going nowhere, it went on for McGrath and then some. On the last day of the autumn meeting, Master Brierly beat Hall Mark and Rogilla in the marathon AJC Plate, backing up after winning the Cumberland Plate earlier in the meeting.

Peter Pan, meanwhile, would not race again until the Jubilee Cup on 6 May. Dangar didn't want his horse overtaxed, and after the All-Aged effort, he wasn't about to risk the Jubilee Cup. Cup races were special, particularly when they possessed a royal stamp. Twice before Dangar had sent Peter Pan out after royal trophies at Randwick, in the King's Cup and Duke of Gloucester Plate, and twice he had been beaten. The circumstances of each defeat were different, but Dangar wondered if, with a fresh horse, he would have a better chance of winning.

The Jubilee Cup was a quality handicap over a mile and a half. Peter Pan had been assigned top weight of 9st 7lb. Rogilla was next closest with 9st 1lb. Oro and Journal were also nominated, and after them came a ream of excellent, and lightly weighted, challengers. The Sydney Cup winner Akuna and ex-stablemate Satmoth were in with 7st 4lb, and both were in form. There was also Rivalli who had won a mile handicap on 24 April, and Silver King had 7st 10lb. In fact, the *Referee* stated that without Peter Pan's presence, the Jubilee Cup would be a close contest. 'Take Peter Pan out and this would be a hard race to win,' the paper quipped.

Peter's 9st 7lb was 1st under his true handicap weight, but the difference in his weight as against some of his competitors was significant. He was giving Rogilla 6lb, and Silver King 25lb. Even the *Telegraph* thought that with such an advantage, Silver King could upset the apple cart. It wasn't beyond possibility for a lightweight to snatch the race, even with Peter Pan in the best form of his life. This was why Dangar was resting his horse until 6 May. He wanted nothing to go wrong this time. The *Sportsman* couldn't see anything going wrong, stating that Peter Pan was 'in such form that not a horse in the land can hope to live him over any distance from seven furlongs to two miles'. Even Darby Munro, who had been reunited with Rogilla for the race, stated he couldn't see the Newcastle gelding beating Peter Pan. In the betting, Peter was odds-on, and next was Silver King and Akuna at 12/1. It was an extraordinary business. There wasn't a punter in the land ready to bet against the champion.

The day before the Jubilee Cup, the track became a problem when the rain began to patter down. By evening it was a steady downpour. Overnight, more than nine points fell over the Eastern Suburbs and quickly Randwick's course proper became a quagmire. The following morning was no better. Thick, gluttonous clouds hung low over the course, promising plenty of rain. By the time the first race on the Jubilee card had been run, jockeys were reporting the track was a bog in certain spots.

Over on Doncaster Avenue, McGrath was readying Peter Pan for another slog through the mud. George Phillips plaited and wrapped the horse's tail into a tight stump, and they spirited Peter to the race stalls under rugs. Rain had affected racegoing attendance, but there were still thousands of people braving the conditions. They gathered in curious droves before Peter Pan's stall. McGrath knew exactly what they were looking for: they were searching for signs of lameness.

Rumours had dashed around Randwick the previous afternoon that all was not right with Peter Pan. It was a recurring annoyance in Frank McGrath's life, and this time he supposed it was due to the weather, which everyone knew didn't suit Peter Pan's shoulder. As soon as the clouds had come in, hearsay had started that Peter was sore. Immediately, his price in the ring eased, and with that came an overwhelming nervousness on the part of punters to take the odds. As much as 5/4 could be had about the champion before racing began this afternoon, but backers were reluctant. 'They know something,' came the cry, and so a brave few got very good odds about Peter Pan prior to running. By race time, he was commanding even money.

Jockey Jim Pike knew exactly what was needed to win this event. In Peter Pan he had a marvellous stayer, a horse that would stick for as long as he could keep riding. Pike knew the weight wouldn't bother him, and he knew that Peter would go on without getting tired. On proven stayers the veteran rider had one philosophy: allow the horse to stay up near the pace because there was no need, on a horse that could stay, to be left in the lurch when the speed was clapped on. Pike had ridden Peter Pan over all courses now, and he knew what the stallion was capable of. As he trotted out of the enclosure he concluded he would ride the speed from the go.

The mile-and-a-half start of the Jubilee Cup was halfway down the home straight. When the horses lined up before Jack Gaxieu there were, for the Peter Pan camp, feelings of déjà vu. The weather was ghastly, the going disgraceful, and Peter Pan was topweight with a knotted tail. Moreover, the champion had drawn the extreme outside marble again. As the 11-horse field prepared to jump, a low murmur of excitement rippled through the grandstands and across the Flat. At the jump, there was a rousing cheer.

Pike hustled Peter Pan from his outside spot and rode the chestnut hard towards the front. Peter sprinted across towards the rails, and as the field trailed past the judge for the first time he was fourth, with Silver King showing the way to Rivalli and Oro. The bustle of the first furlong had Peter Pan all wound up, and Pike had an argument with the stallion before he settled for the turn. As they swung out of the straight, though, Peter was bowling along in the slop.

Rivalli had slipped to the lead entering the backstretch, but there was little pace. The first seven furlongs took a tardy 1:34.

Peter Pan was travelling well, so well in fact that Pike allowed him to move towards the lead approaching the six-furlong pole. Oro, who hated the wet, dropped away with Peter's challenge, and Pike found himself trailing Silver King without so much as an effort. It was marvellous to feel this big horse stretch out in the mud, and they fell out of the backstretch, Peter picking off Silver King, Rivalli only a breath in front. Into the far turn they raced, Sydney Cup winner Akuna emerging from the pack. Peter Pan had drawn level on Rivalli's outside, but Akuna came with a big run; four furlongs from home, the three horses were abreast. Peter, sensing the race was on early, thrust his head in front. Rivalli was unable to keep pace and dropped out, and Peter Pan and Akuna raced into the home turn together. The pair had drawn right away from the opposition. Rogilla was almost last, Journal was not much better.

As they straightened for home, Pike had had enough of the foreplay. He sat down into Peter's neck and rode the champion home. The response was instant and brilliant. Peter dropped Akuna like a hot potato, and he shot away with insulting ease. He was out by two lengths, three lengths, and then four. At the furlong pole, Pike raised his whip and shook it in Peter's face. 'You'll get this if you ease up, sonny,' Pike yelled. Peter Pan dashed further away, and passing the judge he was alone. He won the Jubilee Cup by five lengths: daylight second.

Even in the rain, Randwick racegoers gave the chestnut a rousing ovation. He was a hero to them, one of their own, a Sydney champion that had been thrilling them since 1932. Peter Pan had raced through the autumn unbeaten, five starts for five wins, and there was nothing to compare with him. Up in the stands, Al Lippe was crushed as he watched this Australian superhorse cement his status. He was thinking of what might have been, all those dollars that had been extinguished because of an obstinate owner that clearly knew the value of his horse. Nearby, former AJC stipendiary steward Jack Higgins, now a chief advisor to the Royal Calcutta Turf Club, was visiting from India. 'Let me say that in my opinion there's not a horse in India, or any part of the world probably, that could hope to live with Peter Pan,' he told the *Sportsman.* 'I saw Phar Lap win a small race at Rosehill once, and then take the Guineas at the same track, but still I think that Peter Pan, in the condition and form he is in, is the greatest horse I've ever seen.'

Comparisons with Phar Lap came furiously after the race. 'Pilot' bleated, 'Hitherto I have been a stickler for Phar Lap as Australia's best horse, but it would now be difficult to say that Peter Pan is not equally as good.' On this argument, 'Musket' said, 'As it is impossible to bring them together to decide which is the better in a series of match races over all distances, it is useless to contend which is the better.' The matter was in little doubt in McGrath's mind. The old trainer had always held Carbine at the top of his pedestal, but Peter Pan was charging into that spot. The silver-tailed champion had been proving his mettle since the Hill Stakes of September 1932, and he had won over short courses and long courses, on dry tracks and through quagmires. He had won first up from spells, under high weights and from all barriers. He could win on the pace and off the pace, and he had beaten the best sprinters and stayers in the colony. McGrath was convinced that in his 50 years on the turf, only Carbine came close to Peter Pan's class. Dangar was elated, relieved and giddy all in the one breath.

The Jubilee Cup brought Peter's winnings to £31,360/10s. He collected £1350 for the win, plus a £100 gold cup. It was his fourth cup, bringing the value of his trophies to £600. The time for the race wasn't electric, but that was due to the deplorable state of the track. It took 2:30 3/4 to run the distance, and the five-lengths victory was his greatest winning margin yet. Immediately after the race, Dangar sent Pike a cheque for £500 to award his partnering of Peter Pan. Pike responded to Dangar in a letter dated 15 May.

Dear Mr Dangar,

Received your cheque and am very grateful for the manner in which you appreciate my services. Independent of any monetary consideration, it affords me great pleasure to win a race for you. I trust our associations will continue in the same pleasant vein and Peter Pan comes back as good as ever after his winter spell.

Yours faithfully,

J.E. Pike

The relationship between owner and jockey had become solid and honourable. After the Jubilee Cup, Pike had spoken to the *Sportsman* about Rodney Dangar. 'I would like to tell you just what I think of Peter Pan's owner,' he told the newspaper. 'He's the greatest sportsman in the world. When you are beaten on his horse, he doesn't come crying, full of complaints. On the other hand, he consoles you and says "never mind, there are other races he can win".' Pike stated it was a pleasure for a jockey to be treated like a human being, and that Dangar was even more pleasant in defeat than victory. 'It's a great way to be,' he concluded, 'and jockeys wish there were more Mr Dangars on the turf.'

Dangar was warmed by Pike's words, and reminded of how easy it was to do the right thing. He had looked after everyone connected to his horse, George Phillips included, and a few weeks before he had given McGrath a miniature, solid-gold replica of the 1934 Melbourne Cup. 'This is just a little token of appreciation for the part you have played in Peter's two Cup wins,' he had told his trainer. In days when trainers received no trophy from a Melbourne Cup victory, McGrath described the gesture as one of the proudest, most endearing moments of his life.

***

A few days after the Jubilee Cup, Dangar thought about the Americans' offer for Peter Pan. The figure involved had been wild and exaggerated, but it had been real. Another man would have taken it. A block of flats at Woollahra had sold for £12,500 the previous month, and Dangar had been offered four times that for his thoroughbred. But, as it had been in 1932, money was not the issue. Dangar couldn't imagine a life without Peter Pan now, and he was still glad he had refused the sale.

Peter Pan had been floated to Doonside that very day. Prior to his departure, Fox Movietone had sent a film crew around to take moving shots of Peter as he worked at Randwick. Clarrie Scahill had ridden the horse down the straight at a brisk half-pace, and the cameras had followed his every step, from the track to the race stalls and back to the yard. The footage would go all the way to England and America, to picture houses that showed it before feature films and theatres that ran current affairs newsreels.

Dangar had thought about sending Peter Pan to Rotherwood for the winter, to idle in the pastures around his Sutton Forest home, but in the end the champion was floated to Bungarribee, to fields that he knew and faces he recognised. Phillips was to stay with him, and McGrath had left strict orders that the stallion was not to be pampered. He didn't want Peter to turn into a house pet in his absence from racing, for the old trainer wanted to preserve some of the hardness that had developed in the horse through the last few months. He would need it in the spring: there were big plans afoot. Phillips was to ensure that the stallion was well fed and rugged at night, and that was to be the extent of any attention. For two bleak, bristly winter months, Peter Pan was at rest, the last time he would see Doonside.

33

The declaration of weights

It was 23 June 1935, and though a Sunday, the Peter Pan camp was restless. Dangar was in Brisbane, and McGrath was holidaying in Perth and Kalgoorlie, but they shared a thread of anxiety. Today they would discover how much Peter Pan would carry in the 1935 Melbourne Cup. The weights were to be released by J.H. Davis, chief handicapper for the VRC. For months, speculation had been rife over how much Peter Pan would be given for the race and, as if this year would be any different to years before, estimates came back to Phar Lap. 'When it is remembered that Phar Lap, after winning the Cup with 9st 12lb as a four-year-old, received 10st 10lb the following year, it seems probable Peter Pan will be allotted at least 10st 7lb,' stated 'Pilot' in the *Referee.* Given Peter's unbeaten run through the autumn, and the way he had won his races, it wasn't a guess without merit.

J.H. Davis had to consider Peter Pan's recent form, notwithstanding his perfect record at Flemington. Since the Melbourne Stakes of 1934, Peter Pan had lost a single race in nine starts, the Duke of Gloucester Plate at Randwick. He had given Hall Mark, a Doncaster winner, 1lb in the All-Aged Plate and a decisive beating, and had set an Australasian record while doing so. Peter had won that race by three lengths, and with something to press him he would have reduced the record even further. Days later he had come out in a quality handicap under top weight and sauntered home by five lengths. The question for Davis, however, was how did Peter Pan stack up to those that came before him?

When Phar Lap had carried 10st 10lb in 1931, it was most that a horse had been allotted in recent history. The task had been beyond him. Carbine set the weight record for a Melbourne Cup in 1890, lumping 10st 5lb to victory. But few horses had ever been allotted 10st or more. Eurythmic had been given 10st 5lb in 1921 and was unplaced. Poitrel had won the year before with 10st. Poseidon, with 10st 3lb in 1907, had failed, as had the great mare Wakeful and Malua with 10st. But even these were pale weights against The Barb's allotment in 1869, when he was given 11st 7lb, or Archer's 11st 3lb in 1863. Neither horse started. Even J.H. Davis knew that no horse would ever be given that sort of weight again, because no horse would ever win a Melbourne Cup under a steeplechaser's weight. But it was Davis's job, unenviable that it was, to level the field. What to give Peter Pan...

The VRC handicapper came out that evening with 10st 6lb for Peter Pan. Hall Mark was rated next in the weights with 9st 6lb, so Peter was to carry 14lb above any other horse in the race. Though Dangar and McGrath suspected the penalty, and had told themselves they were ready for it, the reality of the task set their horse crashed down upon them thereafter. No horse had carried this much weight to victory in a Melbourne Cup. 'Everything will have to go right with him,' said Dangar. 'He cannot afford to put a foot wrong, either in his preparation or in the race.' Even Jim Pike, faced with piloting the horse, confessed his fears. 'The danger will come from a really good staying three-year-old with a three-stone advantage in weight,' he said. Still, Dangar was reasonable about the allocation, refusing to blame the handicapper for the impost, as many owners often did. 'Peter could hardly have got less,' he said. 'He won last year with 9st 10lb, and his Australasian mile record had to be considered.'

Trainer Isaac Foulsham thought that Peter was not badly treated by J.H. Davis. 'If he trains on, he will take all the beating in the world,' Foulsham said. 'He is such a strong fellow and so big-boned that his weight is not likely to trouble him.' The conclusion among racing folk was that Peter Pan would overcome the burden, with some even thinking the horse had not been given enough weight. Sydney trainer Dan Lewis thought Peter Pan was in too light, and declared that on a horse of Peter's size, weight made little difference. But amid the sceptics, there was overwhelming support for Peter Pan to make history. Jack Holt, trainer of Hall Mark, declared, 'If he wins, it will be a well-deserved victory, and I will say good luck to him.'

When the list of weights was released, it was clear that several horses, and not just Peter Pan, had advanced in their handicaps. Sarcherie, who had run second to Peter the previous year, had also received a 10lb increase, though she still had 38lb less than Peter Pan with 7st 12lb. La Trobe, who had run third the previous year, had gone up 15lb to 8st 3lb, though it had to be remembered he had been the lightest horse in the 1934 field. Of the excellent horses, however, only Peter had risen to new heights. Hall Mark received just 4lb more than his Cup weight the previous year, although he had won the Doncaster, and Journal had risen only 3lb. After these analyses, pre-post betting was opened on the Melbourne Cup, and Peter Pan fell into favouritism right away. He was 7/1 when books opened, with Hall Mark and Silver King behind him. But these were fool's figures, and even Dangar thought so. With the Cup so far off, he declared 7/1 a prohibitive price on his champion. There were months of racing yet to go.

Peter Pan had been raised 10lb from his Cup win the previous year, while Phar Lap had been raised 12lb in 1931. The obvious conclusion was that Peter Pan was 4lb inferior to Phar Lap (based on the actual weights they carried). However, applying the weight-for-age scale, Peter Pan was being penalised 2lb more than his rival had ever been. When Phar Lap was allotted 10st 10lb in 1931, he was a five-year-old. Under weight-for-age figures, a five-year-old was allowed a 5lb improvement. A six-year-old, however, was allowed only a 1lb improvement, and Peter Pan would be a six-year-old in November. By this rigid reckoning, and adjustment of the two horses' weights, the son of Pantheon was 2lb worse off in his attempt this year than Phar Lap had been in 1931. It was a crucial detail that almost everyone would forget.

34

'Is he so much class?'

The Great Western express train was about to pull out of Kalgoorlie with Frank McGrath seated in its dark steel belly, waiting for the long journey back to Sydney. He was a preoccupied man, and he barely noticed as the train slipped into the desert. He was consumed. How was he going to fit a horse to run two miles at the end of the spring with a record-setting weight? For the few days it took him to cross Australia, he thought hard, until his mind was sore and contorted. When he arrived back in Sydney it was 24 July, and one of the coldest days in the history of the state.

The temperature at first light had been little above freezing, and by midday the city's teeth were chattering. The cold was shaking the shutters of Doncaster Avenue, and horses shivered in their boxes. When McGrath arrived home, he checked that Peter Pan wasn't one of them. But he needn't have worried, for the dutiful George Phillips had doubly rugged the champion, and Peter was knee-deep in straw. The corners of his box were packed against the draughts, and the electric light above his stall was on.

A light frost clung to the trainer as he made his way to the yard the next morning. The stable boys were clustered in a group, cowering into the collars of their coats, and George Phillips was in the middle of them with a scalding cup of tea. It was 6.15am, a late rising for Peter Pan. Phillips gulped his tea, then unlatched the door of the box. McGrath followed him in to inspect the horse. Moments later, Peter Pan walked out into the bitter morning. Within the hour, Clarrie Scahill had trotted the horse around the tan before breaking into a steady canter. Rodney Dangar had joined McGrath to watch the morning's work, and the two men squinted into the still, freezing fog, searching for anything irregular in their champion.

Peter Pan pulled up clean that morning without a hot mark on him. He didn't sweat in winter, and so was never hosed in the cooler months. When he returned to the yard, he was put in the sandbox, where McGrath, Dangar and Phillips watched him roll with an energy unbecoming of the conditions. He didn't favour any shoulder, turning right over, and when he got to his feet he shook himself like a fit horse. McGrath and Dangar had to be pleased. They left Phillips to rub and dress the horse, and by 7.45am they were seated in the trainer's kitchen. McGrath was worried still.

He didn't need to remind Dangar of the woes that came for Peter in cold weather. The snap that had settled on Sydney was one of the worst in living memory, and as the champion had left his box this morning, McGrath had stood on the nearside. The trainer had noticed – though it was almost, just almost, invisible – an awkwardness when Peter Pan had stepped out. By the time the horse had left the yard it was gone, melded into the medley of movement. But the signs were there, and McGrath told Dangar that he feared the worst. That morning, the two men concluded that if Peter Pan went wrong, his Cup chances were shot.

July rolled into August without a break in the weather, and the new racing season was met with rainsqualls, hail and northwest gales. The skies, from the Blue Mountains to the coast, were a thick blanket of grey matter every day, and Doncaster Avenue was swept by horizontal showers. As one storm passed out to sea, another seemed to follow it in. McGrath ordered that Peter Pan be kept in when it was damp, so for what seemed like days the champion was holidayed in his box. Phillips led him out whenever the rain broke, and at intervals the horse picked at grass and rolled in the sand. But the flipside of the rest bore itself out in no time. By Saturday 3 August, Peter Pan was tied up in his near shoulder.

The horse had started to leave his box first thing in the morning cramped. His action had become scratchy, and to any eye but McGrath's, Peter Pan was lame. When the near foreleg reached out, Peter ducked from it. For him, stretching that shoulder joint was like trying to mould solid rock. The team set to work with the usual repairs: hot fomentation, steamed blankets and liniments. However, McGrath continued to exercise the horse, and each morning Peter Pan reached the track in suspect order. When trotting began, the trainer watched as the shoulder trouble slowly fell away. By the time Peter broke into a canter, he was moving with that familiar, fluid stride of his. Such was the fickle nature of the trouble, with its comings and goings for years now, that McGrath refused to believe it would affect Peter Pan's preparation.

It didn't take long for the newspapers to spot the problem. Peter Pan was working under rugs again, often with his shoulder packed, and reporters started knocking on McGrath's door. If they couldn't reach the trainer they tried Rodney Dangar, who politely showed them the door. McGrath, however, remained resolute, at least in public. 'The soreness which affects Peter Pan has not prevented him from winning races,' he told a posse of pressmen one morning. 'It is not likely to do so this season.' The trainer was half right. Peter Pan had been troubled in that shoulder at Flemington the previous year, but it hadn't prevented his sweeping the board down there. Nonetheless, the same soreness had sidelined the horse from all his spring engagements in 1933, and there was no reason it wouldn't happen again.

Peter Pan's ailment grew worse. By Wednesday 7 August he was in terrible straits, and McGrath was convinced the horse was in pain. Peter hobbled out of his stable each morning, and it was taking longer and longer for him to drop the cramp in his action. Scahill reported that Peter was shaky on the track, that even though he improved into the exercise there was no sign of the clean lines the rider was used to.

McGrath declared to reporters that he was very concerned now. He announced that if Peter Pan showed no improvement in the next few days he would be scratched from the Melbourne Cup, and likely from all spring events. The bountiful dreams of a third Melbourne Cup tilt were withering for Rodney Dangar.

The furrows in McGrath's face were deep and tight these days. He was an anxious man, and speaking to *Sportsman* he stated he was not at all happy about Peter Pan's future. 'Unless there is definite improvement within the next few weeks I am afraid he will be withdrawn from training,' the trainer said. 'Needless to say, everything will be done to get Mr Dangar's champion fit, but no risks will be taken. His career as a sire will not be jeopardised.' At this stage of Peter Pan's life, the men around him had to think about his extended career. He was an entire, a valuable one, so anything that would risk his next life at stud had to be taken seriously. But despite the gravity of Peter's current condition, McGrath also remembered that he had worked through this ailment before. 'Peter's recuperative powers are such that he might pull through,' the trainer added. 'His constitution is that of an ox.'

Dangar was at the yard every morning, and it didn't take a horseman's eye to see Peter Pan was struggling. In the afternoons, Dangar would return to Doncaster Avenue, and for what seemed like days he stood by the shed row, his arms crossed, inspecting his champion and assessing the options. The facts were that Peter Pan had not been right almost from the moment he had returned from Doonside, but still he wasn't about to rush to judgement. Instead, Dangar issued a warning to punters not to place pre-post bets on Peter for the Melbourne Cup, and he rested a little easier knowing he wasn't going to rip off the public.

By the weekend, the wild and squally weather that had battered Sydney for weeks had moved out to sea, and temperatures floated upwards. The draughts and frosts were gone from the mornings, and finally the last few weeks of winter grew pleasant and balmy. Immediately, Peter Pan's constitution responded. By Saturday 10 August, not less than two days after McGrath was considering scratching, the horse was moving like a racehorse. Sending him off on a light canter, McGrath could hardly see the shoulder ailment. 'I don't think any stranger to the horse could have detected any lameness at all,' he told the press boys after the workout that morning. All they needed now was for the weather to keep up to put Peter (and their aspirations) back on track for spring racing.

By the last few days of August, it was clear that the horse would stay in work. He was in good heart, lively and pliant each morning, but McGrath knew that the shoulder issue had set them back about three weeks. Most of the spring horses would be starting their campaigns now, or at the latest during the first week of September, but Peter Pan wouldn't be fit enough to contend these early races. The trainer guessed that the champion would make his spring debut either at Victoria Park, in the Sir Herbert Maitland Stakes on Wednesday 18 September, or he would wait until the Hill Stakes at Rosehill the following Saturday. Either way, McGrath had a little over two weeks to fit his horse.

***

With the first week of September came the debut of racing's biggest names. There was a meeting at Warwick Farm and at Canterbury, and on Saturday 14 September, Randwick held its first spring meeting. Peter Pan was absent from its Chelmsford Stakes, which was his usual step into the season. In his non-appearance, Rogilla, Sylvandale and Journal were given their chances. 'It might be wise for the next-best weight-for-age horses to make hay before Peter Pan arrives to cast a shadow,' wrote the *Referee* on 5 September. They did. Rogilla, whose perpetual appearances suggested he might go on racing forever, dead-heated with Silver King for first in the Warwick Stakes on 31 August, and Sylvandale poached the Chelmsford.

Into the month, McGrath remained undecided about the Herbert Maitland or the Hill Stakes. One was a seven-furlong dash, the other a mile, and both were weight-for-age contests. In both races, Peter would meet Young Idea, who was touted as the best three-year-old in the land. Young Idea had won every two-year-old classic there was the previous year, including the Sires' Produce Stakes. The younger horse, in all their meetings, would have a huge advantage in the weights. In the Hill Stakes, Young Idea was nominated with 7st 12lb against Peter Pan's 9st 3lb, but as his horse was a six-year-old now, McGrath couldn't hope for it to be any better. Two days before the Maitland, the trainer made his decision, scratching Peter Pan from the Victoria Park race. He felt that the horse needed the extra furlong to build his fitness. On 18 September, Young Idea was a dazzling one-length winner of the Sir Herbert Maitland Stakes, and the Hill Stakes became not only the debut of Australia's idol thoroughbred. It became a match race between Peter Pan and Young Idea.

The newspapers had been watching Peter's programme carefully; in the last few weeks the champion had run very fast times in the mornings. 'Peter Pan's early spring preparation was interrupted,' reported the *Telegraph* on the eve of the Hill Stakes, 'but by his recent gallops he showed that condition excuses cannot be made for him if he should be beaten tomorrow.' The paper believed that Peter's work proved his brilliance of last season was unimpaired, and it told its readers that his victory seemed certain. The *Sportsman* told a similar tale, albeit theatrically. 'HILL STAKES LOOKS A GIFT FOR DANGAR'S FREAK,' the headline read. Inside, the paper said, 'Can Pete, without a race tucked inside him, break through the guard of those other champions? Is he so much class that he can commence his 1935 season at such a disadvantage and get away with it? We think he can.' The other champions the paper was referring to were Young Idea, Journal and Lough Neagh. The latter had won first up a few weeks before in the Tramway Handicap. There was also a horse called Berestoi entered, and Synagogue who, on a firm track, was expected to be a big noise. In total, there were nine horses entered in the Hill Stakes, but in the betting there were only two. Peter Pan was 11/8 on, with Young Idea next at 9/2.

The opposition didn't worry Frank McGrath. He had doubts about Young Idea's ability to stay and anyway, every year there was a three-year-old that the papers lauded as a David to top Goliath. Last year it had been Sylvandale, and this year the trainer was sure that Peter Pan, on form, would run a merry mile with Young Idea. The champion chestnut had been scintillating in his trackwork of late, the shoulder trouble of a few weeks before almost a memory. Peter Pan had given McGrath no cause to worry that he wouldn't return to the winner's circle as easily as he had done last autumn.

***

The morning of the Hill Stakes was wet and windy, and many racegoers looked out their windows and changed their minds about making the trip to Rosehill.

When the gates opened to the western Sydney track, the crowds were thin, but by late morning the weather front was moving on and people began to arrive in droves. When the hurdle race kicked off at 1.15pm, the stands were packed.

The jockeys guided their horses to the mile start of the Hill Stakes, and Jim Pike eyed his opposition. He had ridden Silver Ring to second spot behind Young Idea in the Maitland Stakes, and he knew the colt's style. He suspected that Andy Knox, Young Idea's regular pilot and Peter's former hoop before his sensational replacing after the Caulfield Cup, would try to steal a jump on the unseasoned Peter Pan, making him carry every pound of his 9st 3lb. Pike would have to keep Peter close enough to the lead, but not expend his energy if the pace was fast. Young Idea, Lough Neagh and most of the others had racing up their sleeves. Young Idea had started three times already this season for two wins. If he was going to beat Peter Pan, this race was his opportunity.

The nine horses stood up before the tapes. When they jumped, Silver Jubilee took Lough Neagh into an early tussle for the lead. Fred Shean, on Lough Neagh, wasn't in a hurry to show the way, but inside the first two furlongs the pace was lazy. The field was only lumbering, and it was obvious that Silver Jubilee was applying the brakes to the race. Lough Neagh came around the leader and plunged to the front, ticking through the first half of the race in 51 seconds.

Peter Pan sat midfield of the nine horses, keeping Young Idea in his sights in front of him. The going was sticky after the rainfall, but he was travelling with ease, and Pike was happy to sit off the leaders and wait. Lough Neagh led from Silver Jubilee, with Young Idea a few lengths back in third, but the order changed as they raced into the home turn. Young Idea made a sudden charge on the lead, and with brilliant speed he gathered up the leaders as they hit the straight.

Pike had seen every move that Knox had made, had predicted them all. He swung Peter Pan away from the field, and around the turn Peter was racing four wide. The chestnut began to stretch his long, straight legs, carrying Pike towards Young Idea in a moment. A furlong and a half from home, the two horses were one, charging down the Rosehill straight like old foes. But Peter Pan was playing. Pike shook his whip in the air, and the champion cruised ahead. He was travelling with reckless abandon, breaking 47 seconds for the last half-mile. As he galloped past the post, he was a length to the good of Young Idea, with nearly two lengths back to Lough Neagh. The Hill Stakes had been little more than an exercise gallop.

The crowd lifted the roof of Rosehill with its cheering. Peter Pan had continued on his winning wheel: the turf idol of Australia was back. As he trotted to scale, there were ovations and screeches for the dazzling son of Pantheon. Women leaned over the fences to touch him as he passed, and everyone clapped heartily, even if they hadn't backed him. Peter had not lost a race now since 22 November 1934, and most people at Rosehill that afternoon couldn't see him being beaten again.

The Hill Stakes brought Peter Pan's winnings to £31,810. It was win number 21 (including his dead-heat) for 32 starts, and he had run the mile in 1:39, three and a half seconds outside of his own record. Young Idea had not been disgraced, for he had beaten all but the best horse home. However, because of the ease of the win, the race was reported as being somewhat dull. 'Banjo' Paterson wrote simply that 'Synagogue and Lough Neagh took on Peter Pan in the weight-for-age race, so it is not so much a matter of how they ran as how they looked'. This was generous praise from Paterson, for he had been queerly quiet about Peter Pan since the 1934 Melbourne Cup. 'Musket', who adored the champion, was much more liberal in his coverage. 'PETER THE GREAT,' he titled his article in the *Mail.* 'As it was Peter Pan's first race of the season, Young Idea was expected to prove a tough proposition for the great son of Pantheon. He ran a great race too, but he was no match for Peter Pan.'

McGrath saw it that way too. Peter Pan hadn't been extended, and while Knox had ridden Young Idea furiously to stave off defeat, Pike had sat still and let Peter Pan run his own race. Later in the afternoon, the trainer heard it said that Peter's ways of winning were different from those of Phar Lap. Phar Lap would run to the lead and let the pack chase him. He had won races by breathtaking margins. Peter Pan, on the other hand, made things easy for himself. He let others do the pacemaking, then ran over them in the straight. When he reached the lead, he tended to forget his task, staring about with obvious boredom. Compared to Phar Lap he was probably a lazy fellow, an opinionated, economical winner of races, albeit a beautiful one. But it was clear to McGrath, as it was to most that day, that Peter Pan and Phar Lap were two sides of the same coin.

For Peter Pan, the next event would be the Spring Stakes on the first day of the AJC spring meeting, Saturday 5 October, followed by the Craven Plate four days later. After that, it was to Melbourne. Ideally, McGrath would have preferred a longer lead-in to the AJC races, because Peter Pan would benefit when it came to the southern campaign. However, the shoulder problems had put paid to that, and the old trainer couldn't change the way things had gone. He could only hope that luck would step in to fill the gaps that might be left come November.

35

'That's the sort of horse to back ... He never lets you down'

There were certain races throughout the year that could boast magnificent histories. They weren't always the most valuable, and they usually weren't the oldest. They didn't have gold cups dangling from them, or purses that would dazzle the average man, but for whatever reason, be it time of year or distance, they attracted legends. The Spring Stakes was one such race. Since its inception in the spring of 1870, it had been won by the most decorated thoroughbreds in Australian history. Chester, Malua, Carbine, Newhaven and Positano had all won it before the turn of the century, and after them had come Wakeful, Poseidon, Trafalgar, Comedy King and Poitrel. In recent memory there had been Beauford, Gloaming, Windbag, Spearfelt, Limerick and Phar Lap. The Spring Stakes was a glittering, red-letter roll of honour, and it was missing only Peter Pan's name.

It wasn't that the chestnut hadn't tried. He had contested the race the previous year and had lost by a nose to archrival Rogilla. But it had also been one of Peter's most disgraceful races, costing Jim Pike his spring in Melbourne. This year, Peter Pan was a cleaner, more professional galloper, and Pike was certain they could win without a hitch. Cliff Graves thought so too. Writing in the *Referee,* he guessed, 'With the Hill Stakes in his belt, Peter Pan should be as fit as a fiddle for the Spring Stakes.'

If Frank McGrath had doubts about Peter's winning the race, it was on the score of the horse being unseasoned enough for the mile and a half. Nominated for the Spring Stakes was Rogilla, who had had four outings already and so was fighting fit. Also, there was the consistent Sylvandale, who had raced twice already. Sylvandale was out to prove his worth as a weight-for-age horse, and Rogilla had been handy in all his starts this season. McGrath, however, didn't think either horse would throw Peter Pan in the final half-furlong. The champion was so good that even with a disadvantage in starts, he was lengths better at this stage of his life than any horse in the country.

With two weeks between the Hill Stakes and the Spring Stakes, the trainer got busy with making up lost ground. Peter Pan's trials each morning were encouraging, proving he was no worse off for his lack of racing. As the Spring Stakes approached, the newspapers predicted him the winner, and it was only a matter of who would run second. But the race would also be a form guide for the Melbourne Cup, for Peter Pan was so disadvantaged in the weights for the big two-miler that if any horse ran him to a close second in the Spring Stakes, their Cup chances had to be good. 'If Sylvandale can finish within a length or two of the champion,' wrote the *Telegraph* on 4 October, 'he might depose Peter [as Melbourne Cup favourite].'

Opinions of Sylvandale grew greater as 5 October approached. The morning of the race, the *Telegraph* suggested that Peter's brilliance would be threatened. 'Sylvandale has risen to staying heights, and his potential greatness cannot be overlooked.' The four-year-old had won the Chelmsford a few weeks back, but in his only meeting with Peter Pan, in the Rawson Stakes in the autumn, he had been clueless. The *Telegraph* was therefore counting on the horse's maturing, and that Peter Pan might be no better than in the autumn. But the paper was forgetting that Peter had been ruthless that autumn. It was impossible to improve on it, and he had shown in the Hill Stakes that he was as good as he had been. He was undefeated in six starts now. To McGrath's mind, that wasn't about to change this day.

When the first day of the AJC meeting kicked off at Randwick, Synagogue won the Epsom by a neck. Peter Pan had beaten Synagogue decisively at Rosehill, and his Epsom win was a line through Peter's brilliance. It proved he wasn't beating average horses – he was beating first-class gallopers. As the time came for the Spring Stakes field to enter the mounting yard, the cup of confidence in the Peter Pan camp was spilling over.

The chestnut looked strapping as he led the field around the enclosure. It was a beautiful day, and in the sunshine his pale chestnut coat was glittering, buffed and brushed by George Phillips. It never took Peter long to drop his winter wool, so that at this time of year he never looked better. In saddlecloth number one, he was to carry 9st 6lb in the Spring Stakes, and because Jim Pike had wasted to 8st 10lb to meet his Derby weight, Peter carried 10lb of lead under his saddle. The connections of Sylvandale mingled in the paddock, and they weren't confident of beating Peter Pan, despite the newspapers. They did hope their horse would make a fight of it down the straight, so had taken the 5/1 offered about the four-year-old. Some of the crowd had followed their lead, as stranger things had happened. The Derby result had been a dead-heat, which hadn't happened since 1919 and was only the second such occurrence in Derby history, while Synagogue had had to survive a protest before his number had been hoisted for the Epsom. Peter Pan then, at odds-on, was a prime candidate to come unstuck.

There were eight horses contesting the Spring Stakes. Oro shared top weight with Peter at 9st 6lb, while High Cross and Rogilla each had 9st 3lb. Berestoi had 9st 2lb, and the four-year-olds Sylvandale, Theo and Contact each had 9st. Contact was choice for Monday's Metropolitan, while Theo, last season's dual-Derby winner, had yet to run into form. In the betting, Peter Pan was 3/1 on, Sylvandale 5s against, Rogilla was at 8/1, Berestoi was next at 20/1, and Oro was wide at 33/1. Punters were also taking the one-two odds for Peter Pan and Oro, some getting as much as 15/1.

As the jockeys and horses filed on to the track, Peter Pan was given a rousing cheer. There were 68,000 people in the stands, on the lawns and across the Flat, 12,000 more than 1934, and they couldn't be hushed while the field circled at the mile-and-a-half start. Jack Gaxieu could hardly be heard as he sorted the horses at the barrier. Peter Pan had drawn widest in alley eight, with Berestoi on his inside. Oro was fifth off the rails, with Rogilla, looking lean and race-fit, in postposition three. The Newcastle gelding gave Gaxieu his usual trouble, but a few moments after three o'clock the field was ready. Gaxieu sent the tapes up, and the Spring Stakes was off and going.

A huge cheer sent the eight horses down the straight for the first time, with Oro dashing to an early lead inside the first three furlongs. Pike was in no hurry with Peter Pan, and he settled the champion midfield. As they swung into the first turn, Peter was fourth, with Sylvandale, Berestoi and Contact behind Oro. Rogilla was on the rails towards the back, with High Cross on his outside and Theo bringing up the rear.

The eight horses ran into the back stretch, Oro bowling along in front. Sylvandale and Berestoi had let the leader slip ahead by two lengths, and behind them Contact was running on the rails. Peter Pan was behind him, but Pike had swung the big chestnut out.

Peter's long legs were carrying him on to Contact, and as he moved out he found more room. He eased up alongside the Metropolitan fancy, and they swung out of the back in that order. Oro was kicking along two lengths to the good of Sylvandale and Berestoi, with Contact and Peter Pan together a length behind, while Rogilla brought up the chasers.

Pike eased his grip on Peter Pan as they swung towards the four-furlong pole. Peter began to eat into the leaders, running up to Sylvandale and Berestoi. He raced around them three-wide, and with only Oro in front he surged into the home turn on the hunt. Pike began to drive Peter Pan with hands and heels, and the champion kicked into gear. He accelerated away from the pack, running past Oro with such speed that the white-faced leader was behind him in a matter of strides. An almighty cheer rose from the grandstands. In the saddling paddock, the bandsmen picked up their instruments and began to play Handel's *See, The Conquering Hero Comes.* Peter Pan was winning the Spring Stakes as he liked. He went out by a length, then two lengths – there was no catching him. He shot past the judge in the time of 2:32, nearly three lengths back to Oro, Berestoi and Rogilla.

The crowd burst into a cacophony of shouts and whistles, cheering the result with all the volume it could muster. The bandsmen had whipped the paddock patrons into a frenzy, for racegoers couldn't remember the last time a horse at Randwick had been ridden home to such a soundtrack. In the betting ring, bookmakers felt like they'd been robbed. Peter Pan had started at 3/1 on, and they had begun to pay out, even as the horses trotted back to scale. One punter, who had laid £300 to £100, skipped towards the ring to collect his ticket. 'That's the sort of horse to back,' he was heard to say. 'He never lets you down.'

As Peter Pan returned, he looked fresh and toey. The gallop had taken little from him, but McGrath noticed right away that there was an ugly cut on the heel of his near foreleg, and abrasions on his off-hind pastern. Peter had overreached on his heel, and at some point possibly been galloped on. Pike couldn't pinpoint when the injuries might have occurred to cause the cuts on his hind leg, but after inspection, McGrath wasn't worried. The abrasions were superficial, and once the foreleg cut was cleaned it wouldn't look so nasty. Peter Pan was stripped and sent back to the race stalls in one piece.

Pike took his saddle and leads into the weighing room, and within moments the red flag was hoisted for the winner's correct weight. However, when Oro's jockey stepped onto the scales, he was found to be 4lb short. A hullabaloo ensued in the jockeys' room. The stewards called an enquiry, trying to ascertain how Oro had managed to carry nearly 4lb less than his allotted weight. Neither owner-trainer Jack King or jockey Robert Maxwell had any explanation. They swore to good faith and appeared as mystified as the stewards. Through lack of evidence, little could be done by the officials. They disqualified Oro from second place, and Berestoi and Rogilla were promoted to second and third. The bookmakers who had paid out on tickets before weights were declared lost hundreds, and at 15/1, punters weren't hurrying to return their winnings. It was an expensive blunder for the bag swingers, for they then had to pay out on the Peter Pan–Berestoi tickets.

With Peter Pan's name now on the honour roll for the Spring Stakes, his earnings climbed to £32,935 and 10 shillings. He had bypassed Carbine, Nightmarch, Desert Gold, Manfred and Heroic on the winnings list, and there were only seven ahead of him – Windbag, David, Eurythmic, Limerick, Gloaming, Amounis and Phar Lap. If his stakes had been to the value of Phar Lap's day, Peter would have shot into the top five already. The Spring Stakes was his 22nd win in 33 starts, and his seventh successive victory. In his last 10 starts, he had lost a single race. It was a ridiculous record, one that boasted stamina, speed, consistency and versatility, and a record that had sprung from an era of champions. McGrath could assert that afternoon, without second guessing his judgement, that Peter Pan was proving himself as great as Carbine.

On Monday, that assertion meant much more when Oro and High Cross battled for the finish of the Metropolitan Handicap. Peter Pan had outclassed both horses in the Spring Stakes, but High Cross won

Monday's race by a neck, only to lose it to Oro on protest. Lough Neagh was on song for his second Randwick Plate the following Saturday, and Synagogue had already won the Epsom. Time and again, Peter's beaten brigade were proving their worth in other races, but at this point in 1935, they were no match for the champion.

***

Wednesday's Craven Plate crept up quickly after the Spring Stakes, and with it a nervousness that Sydney might be seeing Peter Pan for the last time. Dangar had stated that after the Craven Plate, his horse would not run again until the Melbourne Stakes on 2 November. But after Peter Pan's third attempt at the Melbourne Cup, no plans had been announced for him, and Sydney racegoers had little clue if their idol would be retired, or return to finish the season in the autumn.

Dangar himself wasn't sure about it. Even thinking about the end of the road produced a stomach-turning emotion. Peter Pan's career, his very life, had been uplifting, life-changing. It was like having another child. But there were practicalities to consider. Dangar was certain that Peter Pan would meet his stud duties in 1936, for by then the horse would be a seven-year-old. It was only tractability that was keeping the stallion in training. But Dangar also found it challenging to think about retirement when Peter Pan was still winning. He was seven for seven at the moment, with a history-making third Melbourne Cup just over the rise. How could he think about retirement?

The Craven Plate was a mile-and-a-quarter weight-for-age contest, and Peter was competing in it for the second time. The previous year he had lost by less than a length to Chatham, and this year he had to contend with Rogilla, Oro, Lough Neagh, the Derby dead-heater Homer, and two other moderate gallopers in The Raider and Sporting Blood. All had won races, and all were fit for the distance, but the public saw only two horses in it – Peter Pan and the three-year-old Homer. Peter Pan was paying 7/1 odds on, with Homer at 8/1 against. Metropolitan winner Oro was next at 15s, Lough Neagh was paying 20/1, and no one wanted a price about Rogilla. The writing was on the wall for Les Haigh, but he was yet to read it. Peter Pan was carrying 9st 4lb with Oro. Lough Neagh and Rogilla each had 9st 1lb, while Homer had a distinct advantage with 7st 11lb. Though no one thought Peter Pan would come unstuck, nothing was a certainty in horse racing. 'Sometimes, the unexpected happens to champions,' suggested the *Telegraph.*

McGrath felt that the unexpected had already happened that week. Peter Pan had overreached on his near-heel quite badly in Saturday's race, and upon closer inspection back at the yards the trainer had found an inch of flesh cut away. He had called in Dr Stuart Pottie right away, who cleaned and dressed the wound on Saturday afternoon. Peter wasn't lame, he wasn't even favouring the foot, but it was an awkward spot for a cut. The heels of the forefeet took a lot of pressure in galloping, and the wound would be opened every time Peter Pan stretched his legs. But by the morning of the Craven Plate, McGrath was satisfied that the skin had closed. He wouldn't even need to wrap the foot for racing.

Yet again, the AJC had been blessed with perfect spring weather on Wednesday, and Randwick came alive to the rattle of tramcars and the excited hum of racegoers. Over 25,000 people arrived to watch the racing, 3000 more than 1934. At one o'clock, things kicked off with the hurdle race. An hour later, the horses were leaving the paddock for the Craven Plate, and thousands of spectators dashed from the tote windows and bookie stands to watch the race. The length of the straight, a sea of people jostled for positions just before two o'clock.

Peter Pan stood quietly in the centre of the field as he waited for Jack Gaxieu to send them away. The Raider, a difficult horse at the tapes, was on his own on the extreme outside, but when the barrier flew up he shot across the track to take the lead. As they left the first furlong, he led from Oro and Lough Neagh, with Peter Pan settling down in fourth. Pike found the pace wanting. They clocked the first furlong in a tardy 13 seconds, and as they headed away from the grandstands, the jockey had to ease Peter Pan out. The Raider was deliberately slowing the field;

when they passed the mile-post, he had run the first two furlongs in 26 1/4 seconds.

Pike had yet to find a situation that Peter Pan couldn't adapt to, and today was no different. Entering the backstretch, the champion had slowed down under his jockey's grip and was ambling along with the rest of the field. But as they straightened down the back, The Raider picked up his game. Maurice McCarten whipped the leader up, and they set off with new speed. Oro was second, bringing Lough Neagh and Peter Pan along with him, while the Derby colt Homer was just behind Peter. Rogilla, some lengths back, brought up the tail with Sporting Blood.

The Raider's new tempo brought the field through the first six furlongs in 1:15. As they swung into the far turn, Homer had moved up on Peter Pan's outside and looked to be sprinting towards the lead. Pike let Peter run on a little, and the big chestnut stayed with the colt, but as they left the five-furlong pole, Pike heard a sickening snap. For a millisecond of terror, he thought the sound had come from Peter Pan's legs, but it was the Derby winner who suddenly faltered. Homer began to bob furiously beside him, and his rider Keith Voitre swung the horse away from Peter Pan's flanks. Pike saw no more of him, but he didn't need to be told what had happened. The young horse had snapped a foreleg.

Oblivious to the commotion, Oro had run up to The Raider, and as they entered the straight he had gone clear by two lengths. The Raider was left in second, with Lough Neagh closing in on him in third. Peter Pan was travelling so well by the turn that Pike simply eased his big horse around Lough Neagh, and as he ran into the straight, he picked off the leaders at his leisure. His gait was so easy, so tireless to the eye, that he looked quite lazy. Under hands and heels from Pike, he drew alongside a desperate Oro at the furlong, and drew away from him with insulting ease. At the judge, Peter Pan won the Craven Plate by a length and a half to Oro, with Lough Neagh another length and a quarter back in third, and Rogilla had plugged on for fourth. Poor Homer, who snapped a fetlock in running, would later be destroyed.

For the second time of the meeting, Randwick erupted into cheers for its all-conquering blond champion. Peter Pan had returned racegoing faith yet again, and thousands deserted the rails to collect on their tickets. They had sent certain bookies broke. The tote had taken so much money on Peter Pan that its odds barometers fell down on the job. At one point, they had wrongly displayed 6/4 against Peter Pan for the race, and when hapless punters came to draw their winnings, thinking they had gotten the best ever odds about Peter Pan, they realised they were getting only 11 shillings for 10 shillings on the win and their money back for a place. Worse still, the final dividends were not displayed on the tote boards until nine minutes after the race was over, which was a long time for queuing customers. Disgruntled, tote punters flocked to the bookies for the next race.

The time for the Craven Plate was 2:04 1/4 seconds, which was two seconds outside of Phar Lap's record and a second slower than Chatham's win the prevoius year. But The Raider had held up the field for the first three furlongs, and the track was a little giving after the AJC had watered it. With a purse of £1125, the race brought Peter Pan's earnings to £34,140 and ten shillings. It was his eighth win in a row – 23 from 34 race starts – with five seconds, and he was only six times unplaced.

After the race, Pike addressed a posse of journalists about Peter Pan's performance. One of the reporters asserted that Peter had had to be pushed along to win by a length-and-a-bit, but Pike rebuffed the suggestion. 'I often have to keep Peter Pan moving towards the end of his races,' he responded. 'I cannot remember having ridden a horse who can go to a leader with such brilliance, but once he hits the front he starts to play about, loaf and veer towards the inside. Today, I kept Peter's mind on his job to prevent his going across on Oro, not because I had any thought that he would be beaten.' Pike added that he couldn't see how Peter Pan could lose the Melbourne Cup, even with his monstrous weight. 'Peter is probably better now than ever before, and he has already won two Cups,' Pike said. 'He can now gather pace like a Newmarket winner, a thing he couldn't do earlier in his racing career. I can't see what's to beat him unless some good three-year-old comes to light.'

The three-year-olds' Cup chances had fallen to Young Idea following Homer's death after the Craven Plate. The accident had left a terrible blemish on the race, and also robbed Melbourne's spring events of a Derby winner. Les Haigh, also, was battling demons. Rogilla had become very sour. His run through the spring had been disastrous, and his unruliness at the barriers had grown worse. The Newcastle trainer saw no point in shipping his gelding to Melbourne on such poor form. After the Craven Plate, Haigh scratched Rogilla from the Caulfield Cup, and then from all engagements at Flemington, and he sent the old warrior for a rest.

***

On Friday evening, 11 October, two days after the Craven Plate, Peter Pan was loaded into a boxcar that would take him to Melbourne. McGrath was wasting little time in shipping the champion, along with Master Brierly, to his Melbourne engagements. The livestock platform at Central Station was buzzing with Sydney horses vying for fortune and glory in the southern state and the chatter of men that were there to safeguard their chances. There were strappers, stable lads and watchmen dashing everywhere. In Peter Pan's camp, there was George Phillips, Clarrie Scahill, Maurice McGrath and bodyguard Tom Breen.

Frank McGrath had booked passage for Peter Pan in the forward car of the Melbourne Express, just behind the engine. The rear cars could sway dangerously on a journey as long as this one, and the trainer was taking no chances with injury. The chestnut was rugged and his legs wrapped in bandages. After Phillips had made the horses comfortable, he fixed a bed for himself in the corner of the boxcar. A little after six o'clock, the train eased out of its dock and began the long and straight track to Melbourne.

36

The fate of all champions

It was the afternoon of Wednesday 23 October, a drizzly, miserable Melbourne day. Peter Pan had been installed at the Mackinnon & Cox yards for just over a week, and on this day a crowd had gathered along the shed row. George Phillips was there, along with Maurie McGrath, Clarrie Scahill and a number of McGrath's stable boys, as was the VRC veterinarian S.O. Woods. Tom Breen stood close to Peter Pan's box, and Frank McGrath was scurrying in and out of Australia Fair's stable.

The little horse was on his last legs. Australia Fair had been in Melbourne for several weeks, running third in the Toorak Handicap the day Peter Pan had arrived. On the morning of 17 October, however, he had collapsed after trackwork and was diagnosed with diabetes. McGrath had nursed the horse through his infirmity that morning, and by the following day it seemed all would be well. But on 19 October he lapsed again. He couldn't stand on his own, and his jaw had swollen to gross proportions, so he wasn't eating or drinking. With each day that passed, he trotted closer to death. By Wednesday 23 October, the little Heroic horse had been fighting for his life for seven days.

Australia Fair died that afternoon, leaving McGrath stricken with grief. People saw him and looked away.

His eyes were glassy and his complexion pale, and he looked all of his 69 years. It was the third time he had lost a foal out of Fair Rosaleen. The first had broken a leg and the second had died shortly after birth. He wondered if his fine mare was cursed or simply unlucky. When the van came to remove Australia Fair's body, McGrath ordered that Peter Pan and Master Brierly be closed up in their stables so as not to see the sight. The old trainer left the yard for the evening. It was a disastrous start to the Melbourne campaign.

Rumours flew around Flemington that Australia Fair had been poisoned, and McGrath had to admit that the horse's deterioration was symptomatic of such a thing. Was it possible his racehorse had been given something intended for Peter Pan? At first reluctant to allow a post-mortem of Australia Fair, McGrath eventually consented, and the following day the results disproved the conspiracy. The son of Fair Rosaleen had died from an abscess on his kidney, complicated by his diabetes.

The morning following the death, a stiff chill settled over Flemington, and McGrath watched as Master Brierly set off with Allunga and High Cross for a mile gallop on the course proper. They had travelled but three furlongs when the big gelding faltered and appeared to break down. Scahill pulled up right away and found the horse in a distressed state. Master Brierly was floated back to the yard, where McGrath discovered that a suspensory injury had wiped out his chances of competition for the spring. Two days later, just before eleven o'clock on the morning of Saturday 28 October, McGrath entered the VRC offices to scratch Australia Fair from engagements, and Master Brierly from the 1935 Melbourne Cup.

The trainer left the VRC building that morning with the weight of the world on his shoulders. He had lost two horses in 24 hours, one of which was his own, and there was a part of McGrath that wanted to curl up in a quiet room and forget the spring carnival. He lit up a cigarette and began the short walk back to the yard. By the time he reached it, he was sweating and frustrated. The Melbourne Cup was 10 days away, and though Peter Pan was still standing, something was not right with the champion.

***

Peter had travelled from Sydney in good repair, settling at the Mackinnon & Cox yards with his usual aplomb. He had begun work right away, because it was at the forefront of McGrath's mind that the horse hadn't had the same quantity of racing as in the previous year when he had begun his Cup campaign. For the first few days, Peter Pan had looked imposing. He had stepped on to the track each morning in boisterous form, and McGrath had set him some searching gallops around Flemington. The course proper was fast going, and Peter had galloped over nine and 10 furlongs, pulling up sound and looking as unstoppable as 1935 had so far found him to be.

On 20 October, the weather changed, and the storm clouds moved in over Melbourne. Temperatures dropped, and rain began to dribble into the stables around Flemington. Overnight, Peter Pan responded. He began to battle with his shoulder. He walked out of his box stiff and awkward in the mornings, and it took him a few minutes into his gallops to right himself. Though the problem was not a new one, McGrath was much more alarmed this time. Peter Pan seemed a little flat, almost stale; he went through the motions each morning not because he wanted to, but because he was asked to.

The bipolar nature of Melbourne's weather persisted. The mornings were very cold for October, and George Phillips had to apply hot blankets and liniments to keep Peter Pan sound. But to the untrained eye, the horse wasn't sound at all. He left the yard with an obvious limp, and though it was hard for a horse of his size to look flat, he was certainly that. Phillips saw it and McGrath saw it, and the morning Master Brierly broke down, the track watchers saw it. Peter Pan was beaten in a gallop by Sylvandale.

McGrath had instructed Scahill that morning not to knock the champion about, and the two horses had set off for a mile in steady time. Within a furlong or so, the free-moving Sylvandale had a good advantage on the rails over Peter Pan. As they turned for home, Scahill niggled at Peter to catch up. The champion had to make hard work of it to get within a neck of his younger rival, and the two horses eclipsed the final two furlongs in 24 1/4 seconds. They had taken 1:44 1/2 for the distance. Sylvandale won the trial, though not by much, and Peter Pan had conceded the four-year-old 12lb. Peter had started wide on the course, and was also heavily shod. His plates weighed 34 oz (over 2lb), and McGrath found himself counting on all these things to excuse the defeat. The reality was that in his right form, not even these disadvantages would have slowed Peter Pan.

McGrath discounted the gallop to the newspapers, stating that track trials were not a reflection on Peter Pan's chances in the Melbourne Cup. The Sydney papers continued to give Peter Pan a winner's chance, with Cliff Graves even saying that Peter would show on 5 November that horses like Carbine could still be produced. The Melbourne press, however, was dubious. The *Sporting Globe* declared that the Sylvandale trial was evidence that Peter Pan was not up to 10st 6lb over two miles, and in the Melbourne betting markets, the champion eased a point or two from favouritism. In his place, the four-year-old Marabou, who had run third in the Caulfield Cup, rushed into contention. Even McGrath had to admit that a nicely weighted youngster had a great advantage against Peter Pan. 'A good four-year-old with such a big pull in the weights is always a danger in any race,' he told the *Globe,* 'and if Marabou goes on improving, his chances of beating Peter Pan next week will become more apparent. And I will also say this, if there's a three-year-old in the big race as good as Prince Foote, Artilleryman or Trivalve, Peter would not have an earthly chance of winning. He could not possibly concede the weight.'

Peter Pan would give Marabou 37lb in the Melbourne Cup, or a fraction under 2 1/2st. Sylvandale would receive 16lb, and the closest to Peter Pan's 10st 6lb was Hall Mark with 1st less. Even with optimism, the task set the champion was monumental. When a horse's weight tipped over the 10st mark, the extra burden became cumulative. Though Peter's admirers knew he was only up 10lb on his 1934 weight, that extra 10lb (which was nearly 1st) would be so much more tiring. At a cumulative rate, the poundage was a hell of a lot more serious on 10st than 9st. If the pace were fast in next week's Cup, Peter would carry his weight for every furlong of those two miles. How could he expect to have fuel enough to motor over horses with more than 35lb less than him at the finish? If the time for the Cup were anything near the 3:22 3/4 that stood as the record, the champion would have shouldered his weight at high speed for 16 furlongs. It was only his greatness that made anyone think he could do it.

Veteran trainer James Scobie had trained four Melbourne Cup winners, the most recent being Trivalve in 1927. The old trainer (he was 75 now) knew what it took to win Australia's famous race, and he didn't discount Peter lightly. 'No one ranks Peter Pan higher than I do,' Scobie declared. 'He is a beautiful mover, a brainy horse with a lot of character and a fine stayer. However, even superhorses may be set impossible tasks.' The veteran added that horses could not carry burdens of 10st 6lb against rivals of the present day travelling at the speed they did. He quoted Phar Lap's weight in 1931 as an example. He said that Peter Pan was such a horse that would accommodate himself to the conditions of the race, be it a big field, at high speed or through the mud, but that any check in running would cost him lengths and lengths. 'Peter Pan is as kind as a child, and an ideal horse to train. He is beautifully tempered, and these are the essentials of a champion, but there is a serious doubt in my mind as to whether Peter Pan can give 37lb to Marabou, who is a very solid thoroughbred and possesses an undeniable chance of success.'

'Pilot' also selected Marabou over Peter Pan, believing that the severity of Peter's task would prove too much. 'Great as was Phar Lap, 10st 10lb proved too much for him,' the journalist said. 'Peter Pan has recently done all that was asked of him, but in those races he was carrying over 1st less than he has to put up in Australia's greatest long-distance handicap. If the race is solidly run, his weight is bound to tell against him.'

Within days of the Cup carnival, bookmakers reported that no huge fortunes were at stake on the 1935 Melbourne Cup. An outsider had come home in the Caulfield Cup, so doubles backers had been isolated, and prior to this week, the price about Peter Pan had been too prohibitive to induce big wagers. And, despite the rumours about Peter's condition, the champion remained at cramped odds because bookies knew that no matter the quotations, the public would still come for their idol.

No one knew this fact better than Rodney Dangar, for he had been drowning in letters from the public for weeks now. Hundreds of notes and cards had arrived at Arlington wishing Peter Pan luck in his third attempt at Cup victory, and they had come from every corner of Australia. Dangar's personal favourite came from an 18-year-old boy in Adelaide who flew pigeons, and who had named his aviary 'The Peter Pan Loft'. Dangar sent him a mounted picture of Peter Pan and a £1 donation for his pigeon club. It took the champion's owner hours to answer the mail that he received from fans, and it became a comedy for the Sydney papers. The *Sun* ran an illustration by cartoonist Tom Glover of Dangar sitting at a typewriter outside Peter Pan's stable, the champion clutching his two Melbourne Cups and a 10st 6lb anvil on the ground in front of him. Dangar cut out the cartoon and kept it.

He had not invested a penny on Peter Pan winning, but rather than lack of faith, he felt it a gesture of reason. No one knew what was going to happen in the race, and because of that he felt he could not regard Peter Pan as unbeatable. He recalled all too easily the despair he had felt in 1934 when he had inspected the track before the Cup, and this year maybe the insurmountable would be weight. Dangar also wondered if Peter Pan's previous glories had led them all on a goose chase this year. How, after all, could they dare to hope for such wondrous victory again? But sometimes it felt like there was nothing this horse couldn't do and that was why, in the face of overwhelming odds like weight, distance and history, Dangar was still confident. Peter Pan was yet to let him down.

The hopes of Sydney followed Rodney Dangar south. Outside the hundreds who had written to the horse's famous owner, Canon Robert Hammond, minister of St Barnabas Church in Broadway, said a special prayer for him. Canon Hammond was the founder of Hammondville, a settlement for Sydney's poor and unemployed in the western districts, and he was well acquainted with Dangar. 'I don't know anything about the racing game,' he said, 'but Mr Dangar deserves any luck that may come his way. I have never known a more big-hearted or generous man. Altogether this year, he has given us more than £4000.'

Dangar had a special spot for the work of Hammondville, and at the end of 1934 he had visited the settlement to inspect the 50th home opened to an unemployed family. While there, he had noticed that the home had expended the last tract of land the charity had, so he bought the 150 acres across the road and handed it over to Canon Hammond the following day. The purchase cost him £3750, a terrific amount of money for the charity, but Dangar wanted no recognition. Instead, he was delighted when the Hammondville settlement named Peter Pan Park in his horse's honour.

***

With only three days to go before the start of Flemington racing, Peter Pan was still proving a mixed bag. It was obvious his shoulder was giving him trouble, so obvious in fact that everyone outside his camp was now convinced he was lame. McGrath noticed that the cramps were more pronounced when he walked, and as he climbed into his paces, the champion moved more loosely. The trainer clung to the opinion that the problem would not inhibit Peter Pan's chances in racing, as they hadn't at the beginning of the spring or this time last year. The horse verified this in the final week of gallops when he ran an easy mile, 30 feet out from the rails, in 1:45 1/2. But McGrath couldn't account for Peter Pan's attitude. The horse was not giving trouble, but he wasn't tackling his trials with his usual bulldog tenacity. He wasn't off his game, but he wasn't bright either. None of his symptoms was serious enough to scratch him from racing, and there would be a public outcry if he was scratched, but still McGrath was perplexed.

On Thursday afternoon, 31 October, the trainer made his way to the VRC offices to declare Peter Pan's acceptance for the Melbourne Stakes on the Saturday. Immediately following it, McGrath waited anxiously with nearly a dozen trainers outside the stewards' room to learn of the Melbourne Cup barrier draw. When he discovered that Peter Pan had drawn postposition 14, the sandwich spot of 28 runners, the old trainer was not disappointed. 'I'm glad he's out from the rails,' he told 'Cardigan', who was standing with the trainers. 'I don't want him to get boxed in and unbalanced early.'

The number-14 start was the best of a bad lot really, and if pushed, McGrath would have admitted that an outside draw would have been better. He wanted Pike to ride the champion fairly wide this year, in that way giving him every chance to find his feet under that terrible weight, but much would depend on the tempo of the race. Even with a jockey riding to instruction, anything could happen over two miles.

In the final days of the preparation, McGrath tried to put his concerns aside. If there was anything wrong with Peter Pan, it would render itself apparent in the Melbourne Stakes. On the morning of that race, the champion went through his usual raceday routine. He loped an easy mile around Flemington and ate well, and the cramps in his shoulder were no worse than they had been since he arrived. But when he appeared out of the Birdcage on his way to the saddling paddock in the afternoon, the trouble began.

Phillips and McGrath were used to Peter Pan's limp when he started moving, but the public wasn't.

Racegoers didn't understand the problem, nor did they realise that Peter Pan would shake it off when he settled down into his race. All they saw was a sore, lame horse. Peter Pan stepped short each time he reached out with that near foreleg, and people were outraged. A few threw comments of cruelty at Frank McGrath, and many more were surprised that Dangar, with his fine reputation among men, would start his horse in such a condition. For the owner and trainer, nothing could be done about the way people felt. Dangar couldn't change what they thought, and their ignorance of the facts was leading them to conclusions. But it injured the owner to think of their criticisms. Peter Pan was like his son; he would never put him in danger.

Peter Pan stepped around the parade ring until Jim Pike was legged into the saddle. The jockey knew of Peter's preparation since the Craven Plate, but he didn't think their chances were affected in the Melbourne Stakes. Peter Pan had been sore from his ailments before, but like McGrath, Pike believed that Peter's constitution was iron. He trotted the chestnut down the lane to Flemington's course proper, and it was as obvious to him as it was to racegoers that Peter Pan was limping. He also didn't think the horse was as strong under him as he had felt in the autumn, or indeed as he had been a few weeks prior. Nevertheless, as the champion cantered to the start along the back stretch, he limbered up as Pike thought he would.

The weather was settled and pleasant for the first day of the VRC carnival. With only a splattering of rain in the morning, the going was good on the course proper. Peter Pan had top weight of 9st 3lb with Hall Mark, and the only other competitors were Contact, Berestoi, Sylvandale and Marabou, each with 9st. Peter Pan had beaten all of these horses in the preceding 12 months, though his one and only meeting with Marabou had been in the 1934 Melbourne Cup. On paper, therefore, and on form alone, he looked the certain winner.

The six horses stepped forward for the walk-up start of the Melbourne Stakes, and up in the stands Frank McGrath was nauseous with nerves. The confidence that had always sprouted before Peter Pan's races had deserted him, and instead he was left with a churning stomach and a busy mind. And yet, he thought his champion would win. Peter Pan had not lost a race in almost a year, after all. He watched through his field glasses as Peter Pan strode forward, and then he could hear his own thoughts no more. They were carried away by a chorus of cheers across Flemington.

The six horses set off from an even break, Berestoi the fastest into stride. He breezed away from the field, but was quickly joined by Sylvandale, and as they ran out of the first furlong, these two led with Peter Pan on their heels. The horse had also broken smartly, so smartly in fact that Jim Pike had had to restrain him.

The jockey found nothing wanting in Peter Pan's action. They were striding out in third place along the rails as they ran out of the back stretch. Sylvandale had stolen a huge lead up front, bursting clear by five lengths to Berestoi. Peter was a length behind him, with Hall Mark and Contact another two lengths behind. At the back, Keith Voitre had taken a huge hold of Marabou. The four-year-old had been right on the speed in the Caulfield Cup a few weeks before, and had been left behind in the straight. Voitre was determined to bring him from the back this day.

The horses made the long sweeping arc into the home turn, and Pike let the reins slip out. Peter Pan began to pick up with his usual charge, and a swell of voices rose from the crowd as the champion was seen to overhaul Berestoi. They saw him coming, and they cheered for him, beckoned for him to steal the race as he had done each time he had appeared at Flemington.

But then Peter Pan's charge died on its legs. Pike felt the champion stop running beneath him, like someone had suddenly, violently, pulled the plug that fuelled the big chestnut. Pike began to ride vigorously. Drawing the whip, he hit Peter Pan once, then again. Nothing. It was like the horse didn't even feel the cuts. Up in the stands, the crowd fell quiet. It watched, stunned, as Berestoi ran past Peter Pan again, then Hall Mark and Marabou. Only Contact stayed behind the champion. As the leaders dashed past the judge in a bunch, Pike didn't even know who had won the race. He was in shock. He and everyone at Flemington that day.

When Peter Pan pulled up to a walk, Pike found the horse was lame, and it wasn't the brittle action of cold muscles. It was soreness. Peter had never been lame after a race in his life, and the jockey knew that he could account for today's loss. Pike would not forgive Peter Pan for sourness or dishonesty, as he wouldn't forgive it in any racehorse, but these were not factors on this day. The chestnut was not right, and Pike hurried the horse back to scale.

Sylvandale had run to a narrow victory in the Melbourne Stakes, but he was afforded only moderate applause when he trotted back. Flemington was in a state of astonishment that the odds-on favourite, the victor of his last eight races and an undefeated horse on this course, had been beaten so soundly. A hum of disapproval spread through the crowd, and it had nothing to do with the thousands that had been lost on the horse. It had everything to do with the fact that Peter Pan had hobbled back to scale.

George Phillips looked upset as he snapped the shank on Peter Pan's bridle, and when Pike removed the saddle McGrath threw a rug over the horse. The trainer looked less confounded by the circumstances than anyone, for as he had suspected, if something was amiss with the champion, it was going to present itself in the Melbourne Stakes. McGrath spoke with Jim Pike for a few short moments, and then he followed Phillips back to the Birdcage. He inspected

Peter Pan thoroughly at the stall, and though the shoulder joint seemed troubled, Peter Pan was all right. He wasn't distressed or dehydrated, and he wasn't in pain. McGrath left to talk with Rodney Dangar.

In these moments of disappointment, Dangar was seen at his best. He had a stiff upper lip, a radar for rising above the obvious. When McGrath found him, he was talking to a dozen reporters. 'Racing does not worry me a bit,' Dangar said. 'You must be ready for surprises on the turf. Of course, the signal defeat of Peter Pan was amazing, but we do not know how a horse feels inside. In my youth I was an athlete, and there were some days when I couldn't do anything. A human being is able to explain in these circumstances, but a horse cannot.' Dangar had practiced athletics in his teenage years; he knew the foibles of a fading body. The reporters wanted to know what he thought of Peter Pan's chances now, and they fired their questions at him in a muddle of voices. Dangar waited for them to be silent, and then continued, 'On his running today, I cannot give my horse a chance in the Melbourne Cup.' He sounded glib, but inside he was churning. 'Peter Pan will run in the race, unless anything unforeseen happens in the meantime, but Marabou or Feldspar now seem more likely to win.'

Peter Pan's condition inspired a lot of questions, and it was obvious that reporters had heard the disparaging comments that had floated around the racecourse. 'Perhaps the nip in the air caught Peter

Pan in the shoulder today,' Dangar suggested, 'but he seemed to pull up alright. When he was going out to race, I didn't like the look of him, and made a remark to this effect to Frank McGrath. But the manner in which Peter Pan limped before the last Melbourne Cup was awful, and he hasn't been as bad as that this spring.'

When the posse of writers noticed McGrath, they turned their attention to him, pressing him for comment on Peter Pan's appearance. 'He doesn't look as burly as he did in the autumn,' McGrath admitted, and for the first time he cast public doubts on the champion's preparation. He questioned himself. 'Although I have not overtrained him...' and his voice trailed off. 'I think he may have begun to feel the strain of racing. He'll be given a spell at Bacchus Marsh after the present carnival is over.' Stunned at the admission, the reporters pressed for more. But McGrath left it at that, hardly as keen to feed the newspapers as Dangar. Owner and trainer left the little group, and they weren't seen again until after the Derby result.

The newspapers were agog in their coverage of the race. 'How to account for the downfall of Peter Pan,' wrote the *Sporting Globe.* 'Possibly the greatest sensation of all time in a weight-for-age race at Flemington occurred when the great Peter Pan, who was regarded as a certainty for the race, beat only one horse home in a field of six.' Up in Sydney, the *Referee* was also shocked. 'Peter Pan's defeat must be taken seriously,' the paper stated. 'There must be something wrong with Peter, for no champion can fall from grace overnight. Has he become burned out?'

That question played on Frank McGrath's mind for the rest of the day. With each race that passed that afternoon, he craved for the day to be over. He was weary of the questions that followed him around, exhausted from the way he felt. When he retired to the yard in the evening, he wondered if he had underestimated the spring preparation. Peter Pan had started in the Melbourne Stakes a race short on the previous year's campaign. He had missed the Chelmsford, and started fast work a full three weeks later than what he had in 1934. In compensating for that, had McGrath brought Peter Pan to a peak too early? In addition, the shoulder complaint had complicated things again, only this time Peter Pan seemed unable to get past it. The trainer had said it himself back in September: if anything went wrong with Peter Pan, his Cup chances were shot. Well, things *had* gone wrong, and even with a sound horse, 10st 6lb was a monstrous task. With a troubled one, it was nigh impossible.

That night, Peter Pan was unfairly credited with providing the greatest shock in horse racing. Few stopped to remember that in the history of the Melbourne Stakes, there had been many odds-on horrors. In 1925, Windbag had been 6/4 on in the ring when he was beaten. Most champions had shocked the world at some stage. Poseidon, who was arguably the best three-year-old Australia had ever seen, was beaten in the 1908 Autumn Plate when he was 10/1 on. Even Carbine was not beyond disgrace, for he was not undefeated through his career. Phar Lap, also, had displeased everyone in his Melbourne Stakes of 1931, winning by a mere half-length under pressure.

McGrath knew that night that Peter Pan had met the fate of all champions – that of downfall – and though his heart was crushed by it he battled on towards Tuesday's Melbourne Cup. On Sunday, Peter Pan galloped as usual, and late on Monday morning, after all work was complete, he was bedded down until the afternoon. McGrath left the yard, Dangar departing too, and all fell silent, save the solitary figures of Maurice McGrath and George Phillips. In no time, however, the sanctum of the yard was shattered by two strangers in department-store suits.

***

Maurie McGrath first noticed the men when he found them standing some feet away from Peter Pan's box. Tom Breen had been relieved of guard duties since the Melbourne Stakes, and it was only the presence of Carlo, McGrath's Alsatian dog, that had prevented the two strangers from walking right into the stable and leading the champion out themselves. Maurie asked the two men what they were doing, bellowing at them that they had no business being so close to the horses. One of the men stepped forward and introduced himself as Allan Latham, secretary of the Victorian Society for the Prevention of Cruelty to Animals.

Latham explained, in a dry and matter-of-fact manner, that he and his sidekick, Society inspector Benjamin Wilmott, had arrived to investigate allegations that Peter Pan was being raced lame. Complaints had arrived at the Society after the running of the Melbourne Stakes, and Latham stated that it was his and Mr Wilmott's job to determine if the reports were true. He demanded that Peter Pan be removed from his box so that a thorough inspection could be made of the champion, and that if his wishes were complied with, the process would be over and done with in no time.

Maurie's first inclination was to call his brother Frank, and when George Phillips came around the shed row to see what the commotion was about, he agreed that McGrath should be telephoned. Though Maurie had been left in charge of the yard in McGrath's absence, orders were that Peter Pan was not to be removed from his stall until three o'clock exercise. The horse had lived by that routine since 1932, and no circumstances were supposed to change it. Maurie told Latham and Wilmott that he wasn't going to disturb the horse, and he would not allow him to be inspected without the presence of the trainer. Latham, now irritated, insisted that he wasn't going to wait until Frank McGrath arrived later in the afternoon, and added that there was a duty to allow

Peter Pan's inspection. On top of numerous public complaints after Saturday, several published statements had declared the horse was lame, and Latham asked Maurie what it was he was trying to hide. The secretary had his hands on his hips, convinced now the pair was guarding a suffering horse.

The confrontation went on for a long time, and Maurie didn't know what to do. He knew that his brother would be less than pleased if he disturbed the horse, but he also recognised that Latham and Wilmott were officials of a respected organisation. Their interests were not in disturbing the peace, but in the welfare of Peter Pan. Reluctantly, he told George Phillips to bring Peter out of his box.

The inspection was thorough but ultimately unnecessary. Wilmott had the horse trotted up and down the shed row, and he watched from all angles as Peter Pan moved. He ran his hands over the troubled shoulder, then checked for heat in Peter's legs. He inspected each shoe, took temperature and pulse readings, and even made weight calculations. The whole process took nearly an hour. By the end of it, neither Wilmott nor Latham could find anything wrong. The horse looked as well as any horse in the yard, so they pronounced him sound and fit to fulfil his Melbourne Cup engagement the following day.

As the two officials left the yard, the insult of the incident began to settle on Maurie. Who were these people to announce themselves at a racing yard and demand an inspection of a racehorse, without the owner or trainer present? They had no comprehension of this level of horse racing if they thought McGrath would race an unfit horse, and they obviously had no idea of Mr Dangar's track record. When McGrath arrived at the stable a little before three o'clock and learned of the incident, he was furious. He telephoned Rodney Dangar right away, and the two men shared sentiments. They were filthy over what had happened, and went straight to the newspapers.

'I consider it gross impertinence,' Dangar told the press that afternoon. 'The Society's action is an affront to Peter Pan's trainer, and to me. If there were anything seriously amiss with Peter Pan, I would be the last man in the world to overtax him. The horse is all right, and he will take his place in the Melbourne Cup field tomorrow.'

Frank McGrath found it hard to be polite over the incident, as nothing so insulting had ever occurred to him in all his years of training. He was also very incensed with Maurie. 'My brother paraded Peter Pan for inspection, but the horse should not have been taken out of his stable until his customary time of three o'clock, when he is exercised,' McGrath stated. 'They could have examined him thoroughly then, and I strongly resent their action.' The training community at Flemington was resounding in its support for McGrath. The Society's action had been just as Dangar described it, an affront to the trainer, and everyone knew that Frank McGrath had a flawless record in handling champions at the highest levels of racing.

Latham and Wilmott were condemned among trainers for their actions that afternoon, and they were forced to defend themselves.

'The examination was carried out merely as a matter of routine,' Allan Latham stated. 'It was our duty to satisfy ourselves that no cruelty would be involved in allowing Peter Pan to race in the Cup. My society investigates all cases of reported cruelty simply on their merits, and without consideration of the type of horse concerned or the person who owns it. We are glad to have been able to confirm the owner's declaration about the fitness of the horse, and our visit conveyed no insinuation. Allegations have been disproved, so everybody should be satisfied.'

Latham would not reveal the identity of the people who had made complaints about Peter Pan's condition, but it was obvious that most of them were the racegoing public who had been alarmed that the champion had been limping on Saturday. When they witnessed his inability to fight his way home in the Melbourne Stakes, their suspicions had been compounded, and they had acted on them, probably with the best of intentions, but still ignorant of the facts. Latham said that if he had found Peter Pan to be lame on Monday morning, he would have secured the authority to prevent the horse's starting in the Melbourne Cup. But as he and Wilmott had found the horse in good order, no such action was necessary. Latham also had to admit, 'No one owning a valuable racehorse would be likely to run the risk of injuring it by running it when it was not fit.' For Dangar, Latham's realisation had come a little too late to be excused.

It took hours for the dust to settle on the whole incident. The injury to the Peter Pan camp was palpable, and it was the last thing that should have been clouding McGrath's mind the day before the Melbourne Cup. He had fostered hope that Peter Pan's great stamina would come to his assistance in the next day's race, but now he just felt deflated. Pike would be instructed to win if he could, but if victory were impossible, Peter Pan was not to be knocked about. Dangar held the same opinion, and the owner, even more than the trainer, was realistic that glory was unlikely.

37

The 1935 Melbourne Cup

Cup Day broke with a stiff southerly breeze and scattered clouds, and it was cold. The temperatures were barely in double figures as crowds began to pour through Flemington's turnstiles. Still, it wasn't raining, and a carnival spirit prevailed across the racecourse. VRC secretary Arthur Kewney suspected that for the first time since 1928, more than 100,000 people had come to witness the Melbourne Cup. They packed the Hill stand, the lawns and the grandstand, and the Birdcage was abuzz with horses and curious onlookers. Six entrants had been scratched from the race, including Young Idea, Satmoth, High Cross, and the Caulfield Cup winner Palfresco. It meant 22 horses would go to post for the 1935 Melbourne Cup.

Peter Pan was in stall 77 in the Birdcage, and at 2.45pm he was being saddled for the big race. At first light, Jim Pike had ridden the horse in work around Flemington, and Peter Pan had been no worse and no better than he had been on Saturday. As McGrath placed the saddle on Peter's back, he straightened the number-one cloth and brushed the hairs flat with his hand. There was more than 1st of lead under the saddle, and McGrath didn't want it on Peter Pan any longer than it had to be. As George Phillips led the chestnut to the mounting yard, he was clapped and cheered by racegoers. Lesser men wouldn't have started the champion when he had little chance, but Dangar had always done the right thing by racing. Peter Pan's backers would get a run for their money, and though it was ambitious, he knew, Dangar prayed to his good God for a little miracle.

The racetrack officials were 10 minutes behind schedule as they marshalled the Cup horses into the paddock. The VRC had allowed old Shadow King to lead the field for this year's Melbourne Cup. The bay gelding was making his sixth start in the handicap, and because his record boasted four placings in five runnings, he had become a local legend. Though he bore saddlecloth number 7, Shadow King strode out in front of Peter Pan as they entered the paddock, and no one knew if the cheers were greater for Australia's champion racehorse or for the 10-year-old bay gelding.

Standing in the middle of the enclosure with their jockey, McGrath and Dangar said little. Once the scene of so many triumphs, the paddock now felt like someone else's patch. It was a sobering feeling for the pair. They gave Pike few instructions. The old hoop knew Peter Pan better than any rider, and he was a kind man with a horse. If he saw no chance of success, he would not push, and he left the two men with only one instruction. He was to keep Peter Pan as wide as possible to avoid any scrimmages. As he trotted behind Shadow King down the lane to the course proper, Pike remembered how it felt to ride a champion to certain defeat in Australia's biggest race. The 1931 Cup aboard Phar Lap was still a gaping wound for the jockey. Over a mile, he thought, a horse might win with Peter Pan's weight this day. But over two miles in a field of 22 with a horse that wasn't quite right, Pike was certain it would be 1931 all over again.

As the horses lined up at the barrier, down the chute of the straight six, the voices in the crowd began to rise over Flemington, and from their various spots around the racecourse, Peter Pan's people held their collected breath. Rodney Dangar clutched Elsie's nervous, twitching hand, and McGrath was nearby, his field glasses raised and his heart thumping. Down in the saddling paddock, George Phillips looped Peter Pan's lead rope around his fingers, then unlooped it and did it again. He was so worried about his horse getting through the run soundly he thought he might throw up. VRC starter Rupert Greene arranged the 22 horses in their positions, and ordered them to walk forward. Clear Art had replaced Satmoth on the rails, and inside him came Hot Shot. Old rival Yarramba was next, and Marabou was in postposition 10. Sylvandale was on Peter Pan's inside, with Allunga on his outside. Hall Mark and Sarcherie were wide out, and Feldspar was widest of all.

The clerk of the course raised his flag to signal that all was well behind the field, and a cheer broke out across Flemington. It was 3.10pm, a full 10 minutes behind the advertised time for the race, and

Rupert Greene got ready to send the field away. They stepped nearer to the tapes, all 22 horses striding in an awesome procession, and when the tapes flew up there was a tremendous charge of horseflesh. Peter Pan's third Melbourne Cup was underway.

The non-racing man had little idea how much effort it took for a horse to raise a gallop with 10st 6lb on its back. Though Pike tried as hard as he could to help Peter Pan into stride, the big chestnut was anchored by his colossal weight. All around him, horses shot away. Sarcherie, Sylvandale, Hot Shot and Marabou bounced off to early positions, and as the field ran down the straight for the first time, Peter Pan was ahead of only five horses. Pike had swung him to the outside, though he was only a horse off the rails, and the jockey was hoping that Peter would find his stride quickly as they left the straight.

The pace in the first quarter was muddled, with Sarcherie hoping for a pacemaker to steal her lead. They lumbered through the first four furlongs in 54 seconds, but as they swung into the backstretch, Sarcherie began to bowl along. Her jockey had no choice but to run the race that would suit her, and she began to clatter down the river side. The second half-mile was covered in 50 1/2 seconds, the third half-mile in 49 1/2 seconds, and by the abattoirs, Peter Pan was carrying every pound of his immense weight. Pike knew the load was getting heavier and heavier with each furlong that passed, and he rode the champion as lightly as he could.

When they turned into the straight, the leaders were more than 10 lengths to the good of Peter Pan. Though Pike asked the horse for an effort, Peter's response was poor. Pike felt the chestnut reach out further, try to dip his neck and go faster, but it was no good. Peter Pan was anchored under 146lb, and he didn't pass a single horse. After Marabou burst over the line the winner, within a second of the Melbourne Cup time record, Peter Pan carried on into 14th place, a breath away from Hall Mark who finished 13th.

Dangar and Elsie stood up straight away. Their chests were heavy, and they hurried out of the stands towards the Birdcage. Frank McGrath didn't even remember seeing Marabou win. His glasses had been fixed on Peter Pan for the entire race, and when the champion had passed the judge, the trainer left the stand to meet George Phillips in the paddock. There was a rousing reception for Marabou, who had returned the 9/2 favourite, but when Peter Pan trotted in, he too was clapped for his effort. He was a tired horse, and his coat was brassy with sweat. Phillips spirited him to the stalls as soon as the saddle was off. After the race, Jim Pike could say only that something was wrong with Peter Pan. 'He simply plodded along at the rear of the field from the start, and never gave me the impression that he could win.

That's not like him,' Pike said. 'There's obviously something the matter.'

McGrath found that, though spent, Peter Pan looked all right. He was no more cramped than he had been on Saturday, but the horse's spirit was flat. Maybe it was tiredness, McGrath thought, or maybe Peter was tiring of racing. The old trainer wondered, for the umpteenth time that week, had he asked too much of the horse this spring?

Phillips spent most of the evening massaging Peter Pan's weary frame, applying hot blankets to his shoulder and helping the horse recover from his gruelling effort. The old strapper was hurting too, knowing well that his horse needed a rest now, and if anyone knew that Peter Pan had lost his sparkle, it was Phillips. He feared most that a broken spirit would be hard to mend. McGrath didn't think the race had taken too much out of Peter Pan, and he told the *Referee* that the champion had pulled up better than he had expected. 'I'm pleased with him in the circumstances,' McGrath said, but still he hurried to arrange the horse's summer spell. Peter Pan would stay in Victoria, and go to Underbank Stud at Bacchus Marsh. Arrangements were made for the end of the week.

***

On Friday morning, 8 November, in a light spring drizzle, the horse float pulled up to take Peter Pan to Underbank. The stud was a few hours' drive from

Melbourne, and belonged to racing identity Sol Green, one of the biggest and most well-known players in the racing game. As Peter was loaded for the journey, McGrath watched on, and realised that Melbourne may well have seen the last of Peter Pan. He looked away before his face betrayed his sadness.

The float ambled out of Flemington a little after ten o'clock, chugging through the northwest suburbs of Melbourne until the factories and houses disappeared and the rolling vales of countryside lined the road. The smell of grass filled Peter Pan's nostrils, and he sucked in the fresh air that came through the vents. Not an hour later, he was let loose in the stud's giant paddocks, with wild flowers and grass to his knees. They were the same paddocks that Phar Lap had enjoyed during the tenure of his life, and it took Peter Pan mere moments to abandon the traumas of the racetrack and learn to be a horse again.

38

Something had happened

The end of 1935 rolled on, to Rodney Dangar, like a slow tide, November merging lazily into December. The fresh, wispy days of spring became the hot, oily nights of summer, and two weeks before Christmas, Dangar set off from Sydney for Baroona. He was to welcome there, on 15 December, Cinesound Productions and a film crew of 55 for the shooting of scenes on the feature film *Thoroughbred.*

The picture was the latest big-budget production by Cinesound's director Ken Hall, and its star was Hollywood actress Helen Twelvetrees. It was the story of a rundown racehorse that becomes a racetrack star, and would feature race footage of Peter Pan's collision in the 1932 Melbourne Cup. Hall and Twelvetrees were travelling with the Cinesound entourage, and they arrived at Baroona in total darkness, on a stale and still night in Whittingham. The following morning, they woke to startling views of the Upper Hunter Valley at dawn. 'I would not have missed that Australian sunrise for any money,' Twelvetrees said.

For the next few days, Baroona charmed its movie visitors and stunned the American actress. 'The panoramas are wonderful,' she exclaimed. 'One can see for miles and miles.' Each morning, Baroona's magpies landed on Twelvetrees's windowsill, clattering their noisy morning welcome, and she felt as though they had turned it on just for her. 'Your birds, I just love them,' she gushed to Dangar, and for days, with a giggling, excited Roslyn on the sidelines and Elsie fussing over her guests, the grand homestead buzzed like a Hollywood film set. Footage was shot on the piazza in front of the house, in the paddocks and at the stables. The film's star racehorse, Antique, mingled with Alwina and her weanling filly Tinker Bell. Dangar watched it all and was proud.

When the Cinesound team departed Baroona, the Dangars retreated to Rotherwood for the Christmas holidays. Walking among his orchard trees, Dangar recounted the events of the past year. Peter Pan had run in 10 races in 1935, and had won eight of them. He had landed every prize he had competed for in Sydney, in both the autumn and spring meetings, and his only failures had been at Flemington. What a shame it was, Dangar thought, that he had not been able to finish with a win.

The champion's form reversal was still a mystery to his owner. Was it possible that McGrath had underestimated the preparation this time? For, seasoned as McGrath was, trainers did make mistakes. Peter Pan had been in scintillating form at Randwick in the weeks prior to Melbourne, and the horse had not been winning by a hair's breadth. He had been winning as he liked, in some cases eased up by Jim Pike. Had Peter Pan found himself too suddenly dumped into a fast-run two-miler with a tonne on his back?

Dangar had a good racing mind, and he knew the difference between a moderate performer and a superhorse like Peter Pan. He knew that a track star was a tightly wound machine, much more keyed up than the average racehorse, and he wondered if too much strain had been placed on Peter Pan after the Craven Plate. In McGrath's anxiety to produce the horse for the Melbourne Cup after the Randwick meeting, had he placed too much pressure on an already taut Peter Pan, only for the horse to come apart? It was the only conclusion Dangar could arrive upon.

Since 1929, he and McGrath had enjoyed a professional friendship. There would be nothing that McGrath could do to make Dangar question his trainer's abilities, and he would never think more highly of another trainer. But no man was perfect. Earlier in the year, in the winter months prior to the Melbourne Cup, he and McGrath had had a disagreement over a horse, and Dangar had removed his second-stringer, Merrie Miller, to another yard. It had been a simple situation in the owner's eyes – Merrie Miller had not been winning. Dangar suspected that he wasn't getting enough attention. So one afternoon when McGrath was out, the horse was moved to another trainer where he would get the extra coaxing he would need as a slightly average horse. Enraged, McGrath had marched into Dangar's office that very afternoon, demanding an explanation. He exclaimed that if Dangar had such little faith in him, he should remove Peter Pan too. Calmly, and with his usual aplomb, Dangar replied that if McGrath were not to train Peter Pan, no one would.

The incident brought a smile to Dangar's face these days, for business was still business when it came to racehorses. Merrie Miller won his first start under new trainer E.D. Lawson, but the incident had not blemished Dangar's faith in Frank McGrath. He had still sent Brazilian to the trainer, and McGrath would continue to receive Dangar's best racehorses. Nor was Dangar in the mind of blaming McGrath for Peter Pan's failures at Flemington. Whether the trainer had erred or not, that was racing. Peter Pan had been competing since 1932, and in that time had won the greatest prizes Australia had to offer, some of them twice. McGrath would be forgiven for making mistakes, for he had made none up until now.

After the Cup, Marabou had been touted as the new star of Australia. 'He might soon be ranking among our best staying weight-for-age horses,' the *Referee* had stated, 'now that Peter Pan apparently has gone off the boards as the champion.' It stunned Dangar how the merit of Marabou's single win had wiped the verity of Peter Pan's 23 victories. But very few men had bothered to measure Peter Pan's Cup defeat as it should have been measured. In the last 15 years, four horses had been asked to carry more than 10st in the Cup, and each had run in the

Melbourne Stakes on the Saturday and all had failed on the Tuesday. Eurythmic, in 1921, broke down in his Cup with 10st 5lb. In 1926, Manfred also broke down, though after running in the Stakes. Phar Lap had won his Melbourne Stakes by a whisker, and could manage no better than eighth in the Cup with 10st 10lb. Peter Pan had suffered the same fate. Like Phar Lap, Peter had been unbeatable at Randwick in the weeks prior to Flemington, only to travel south and meet with disgrace.

Jim Pike had stated in 1931 that he was so confident of Phar Lap winning the Cup that year that the race could be run however it was run and it would make no difference. He had uttered the same confidence this year in reflection of Peter Pan's chances, and Pike was not a man to toss confidence about. On both accounts, his horses were defeated. Manfred, Phar Lap and Peter Pan had all arrived at Flemington with glittering form, only to have it drip away from them for the biggest race of their lives.

Up in Brisbane, the turf writer for the *Courier-Mail* newspaper was thinking similar things. Writing as 'The Harvester', he believed that the pace at which some Melbourne Cups were run these days made it impossible for any horse carrying more than 10st to win. Only Carbine had managed it way back in 1890. 'I think any fair-minded man will agree that ten stone should be the maximum weight in a Melbourne Cup,' he stated. If a horse was entered for the Cup, 'The Harvester' argued, that horse had to be capable of running two miles in the time of 3:22. To run that time with more than 10st required either a Pegasus, he argued, or a horse prepared on a very careful programme.

Dangar knew that Peter Pan was no Pegasus, as Phar Lap had not been, but champions didn't expire overnight. Something had happened at the end of this spring, and it had happened between the Craven Plate on 9 October and the Melbourne Stakes on 2 November. Dangar would never know what it was, and it would remain one of the mysteries of his life. His historic third Melbourne Cup had expired in a heated rush. But on that afternoon at Rotherwood, among the orchard trees, he decided he had thought about it for the last time.

In those final, summer weeks of 1935, Marabou was sold at auction in Melbourne. Upon his entrance to the sale ring, the auctioneer called for an opening bid on the new hero of Australia, and the crowd erupted into laughter when a woman cried, '50 guineas!' Actual bidding began at 2000 guineas, and trainer Jack Holt, acting on behalf of Hall Mark's owner, Charles B. Kellow, secured the horse for 5500 guineas. It was an expensive affair for Kellow. Marabou would never win another race.

39

'A great heart cannot carry a doubtful leg'

It was only hours before the turn into 1936, and a horse float rattled down Doncaster Avenue. It eased to a stop outside Frank McGrath's yard, and a little party of men gathered on the street. They were dusty and grubby from the afternoon's stable chores, but they had stepped out to welcome Peter Pan home. The chestnut came off the float with George Phillips, and even clad in rugs he was massive. He had reached 1100lb in weight, a titan stallion now, and he looked robust and lusty as he strode across the yard into stable number six.

McGrath's first observation was how heavy the horse had become. In Peter Pan weight was deceptive, for though he was a tall horse, he was still narrow. That narrowness made him appear much lighter than he actually was. When looked at sideways, he was a different specimen. He had an enormous, powerful shoulder and a huge girth now; it must have been nearly 77 inches around. His neck was short and set and, as from the day he had been born, his legs were as straight as organ flutes. That afternoon on New Year's Eve, McGrath pulled out the measuring stick.

Peter Pan, from the point of his shoulder to his hindquarters, was shorter than the height of his withers to the ground. That meant that he was taller than he was long, which had been the case since he was a colt. He stood a shade above 17.1 hands now, not much higher than he had been as a five-year-old, and he was beautiful in conformation. His quarters rose higher than his withers, and he had a perfect back outline. He was also very clean in the skin. He had no saddle sores or girth galls, and he had never been fired. His feet were tough, having never suffered from quarter cracks or greasy heel. In fact, outside his shoulder ailment (and the nail accident that had occurred as a two-year-old) Peter Pan had been very healthy. But McGrath knew the risks of having a horse with these dimensions. Peter Pan was so big now that the strain placed upon his heart and forelegs would be amplified in his racing this autumn. At high speeds, the risk of injury would be so much greater.

Dangar had decided to resume the training of Peter Pan because he couldn't see the wisdom of retiring the horse after two losses at Flemington. He had reasoned that losing was not a cause in itself for retirement, and he wanted to allow Peter Pan an opportunity to renounce his Melbourne form. Because the horse was declared all right after the Cup, Dangar had seen to it that after the break at Bacchus Marsh an itinerary was mapped for the autumn. Though no one knew if Peter Pan would manage the preparation, McGrath suggested he might be aimed at the Futurity

Stakes at Caulfield. That race was due off on 22 February.

The Futurity was a full three weeks ahead of Peter Pan's usual autumn debut. Since 1933, Dangar's horse had not appeared in silks until the middle of March, usually in the Randwick Stakes. The Randwick Stakes was a weight-for-age event, and a nice entrance back into racing, but the Futurity was an altogether different target. Not only would it occur in February, it was also a weight-for-age race with penalties. Amounis and Phar Lap had carried huge weights in their Futurity races, 10st 4lb and 10st 3lb respectively, and it was safe to assume that Peter Pan would be given a high impost too, regardless of his form. It was a strange race to suggest for the ailing champion, and implied that McGrath really didn't think Peter Pan was faltering.

The trainer had nominated the horse for other interstate races this autumn, among them the King's Plate at Flemington on 4 March, and the C.M. Lloyd Stakes two days later. He had also nominated Peter for the King's Cup in Adelaide on 16 May, but he didn't know if these were realistic targets. It would be ideal to have Peter Pan chase big prizes in his last season on the turf, but everything would hinge on the champion's form. If he could return to his former steel, Peter Pan could chase any race he wanted. But not long into February, the threads of McGrath's plans unravelled.

***

Peter Pan began the road to autumn fitness with his usual light work after breakfast. He first appeared on Randwick's tracks on New Year's Day, and he surprised many watchers that morning with his immense size. He was now carrying a lot of scope, and even Clarrie Scahill could feel it. The rider was piloting a six-year-old stallion now, a horse that was far bigger and more powerful than the average thoroughbred scampering around Randwick. Peter spent his mornings trotting on the tan, working off the weight he had gained at Underbank. Summer temperatures were keeping the shoulder problem at bay, and he was in jaunty spirits, even frisky in the mornings. When January fell into February, and Peter began light gallops before breakfast, there was every possibility that he would breeze into condition.

Peter stepped out for a distance of just over a mile on 11 February, covering seven furlongs in 1:40, whipping the last two in 25 seconds. It was his most extensive piece of work since returning from Bacchus Marsh, leaving McGrath very pleased. The horse was running out of his skin, and had set off on the gallop very freely. But when the trainer inspected him after the work, McGrath found heat in Peter Pan's off foreleg. The area was also tender, and Dr Stuart Pottie was called in right away.

Inspections of Peter Pan revealed soreness in the suspensory ligament. Pottie suspected trouble there but, because the champion was not lame, just sore, he didn't think the ligament had been properly damaged yet. He advised McGrath to take Peter Pan out of fast work, and to wrap the front legs any time the horse stepped out. Pottie suggested that McGrath knew as well as he did how serious the problem was, and McGrath did.

The suspensory ligament is one part of the suspensory apparatus of the foreleg. It is a band of strong tissue that stretches behind the horse's shins, from the top of the cannon bone to the fetlock region. It acts like a spring during movement, and its purpose is to prevent the horse's fetlock from over-extending during motion, or dropping to the ground under pressure. Injury to the suspensory ligament usually occurs when the load placed on it is greater than can be handled (for instance, during fast galloping), causing the fibrous bundles that comprise the ligament to fray and tear.

Peter Pan displayed early symptoms of suspensory ligament damage. On the outside of his off foreleg, there was heat followed by swelling, and when McGrath touched the area, Peter would flinch. But neither Pottie nor McGrath could find symptoms anywhere else. The problem was restricted to the outer region of the foreleg, and that meant that the damage had occurred quite specifically.

In a horse's foreleg, the suspensory ligament, as it travels down the shin, splits into two branches that run either side of the fetlock: one on the outside, the other on the inside. These branches are more susceptible to injury because they are comprised of fewer fibres than the rest of the ligament, and branch injury is identifiable by its occurrence low on the foreleg, just above the fetlock. Early diagnosis is essential, and in most cases in thoroughbred horses, it spells the end of racing.

Peter Pan's injury became a typical suspensory case overnight. His body, in response to the damage, began to send blood to the area, which resulted in ugly swelling by morning. But because the fibres of the suspensory ligament are so tightly bunched, and so contain few blood vessels, it was impossible even for internal bloodflow to clean away the debris of damage, which was what it was supposed to do. McGrath could only hope to isolate the harm, and prevent further destruction of the branch. He telephoned Dangar right away to tell him what had been discovered, and explained the seriousness of the situation. The trainer had no idea if the ligament would withstand any level of pressure, and if they tested it by sending Peter Pan over a quick trip, it might tear completely. If that happened, Peter Pan's racing career would be over. Worse, the destruction could be so grand as to render the horse incapacitated. It would be the end of his stud career, but it could also spell the end of his life.

Dangar told McGrath that he would take Peter Pan out of training before he would see the horse break down. He said that he was happy to retire the champion immediately if that was what McGrath advised, but the trainer was in two minds. In one respect, the potential for carnage was great. But on the other hand, Peter Pan was only sore. He had also been to the edge of breakdown several times before, and had thrust his way back with his iron spirit. So the trainer suggested that they persevere for two weeks, and reassess the situation then.

For the next few days, Peter Pan emerged on Randwick's tan track for light, easy exercise. For the first time in his life, his two forelegs were wrapped in bandages, and if reporters didn't notice that, they noticed McGrath's dejection. On Monday 17 February, 'Pilot' met the old trainer at the track. 'What's the news?' he asked McGrath as Peter Pan trotted past them.

'Bad news,' McGrath said. 'I doubt Peter Pan will stand another preparation.'

'As serious as that then?' the journalist queried, turning to face the trainer, stunned.

McGrath nodded. 'I'll keep him at easy exercise and unless there is a marked improvement it is probably the end of his racing career.' After a moment of silence, he added, 'This is very serious, but I've not abandoned all hope yet. Let's just wait and see.'

As McGrath watched Peter Pan trot around the tan that morning, he marvelled at the way the horse moved that splendid, big frame of his. But this was half the trouble. Peter Pan had furnished into such a tremendous beast that a weak foreleg was now a serious flaw. At two stages of a gallop, Peter Pan's whole weight would be on one foreleg, then the other, so that for a quarter of the stride, the troubled off fore would bear his whole weight.

'Pilot' reflected on Peter Pan's future in that week's edition of the *Referee.* 'Peter Pan continues among regular workers and shows no signs of lameness,' he reported. 'However, his trainer is not optimistic. He is afraid of what will happen when the chestnut is asked for a little extra, and that will soon be necessary in order to fit him for autumn racing at Randwick.' 'Pilot' also identified the deceptive nature of suspensory problems. 'In the past I have seen various horses with ligament trouble go along nicely until they had to be subjected to the winding up process, and then that was the end of them. While it may not be so in Peter Pan's case, it will be a pleasant surprise if he proves an exception.'

By 19 February, Peter had been stepped up to a tentative three-quarter gallop. He was still exercising on Randwick's tan, where the cushioning was good, and McGrath was more pleased with him than he had been since 11 February. 'You never know when a heavy-topped horse shows signs of soreness in the joints of a foreleg whether the trouble can be overcome,' he told the press boys that morning. 'But, I am more pleased with him today than I was yesterday.' Despite this, McGrath scratched Peter Pan from his Melbourne engagements a few days later. Dangar was not happy to risk the horse when he was not fully sound. It was ambitious to think he would be forward enough to travel to and race in Victoria, let alone win. When questioned about the withdrawals, McGrath replied that Peter Pan was in no state to race yet. 'He is no better and no worse,' he said. 'He has not been out of a canter, so it is impossible to say definitely what the future holds.'

February became March, and with the Randwick Stakes only two weeks away, the situation became critical for Peter Pan. He was yet to move any faster than a three-quarter gallop, and in condition he was still much above himself. There was no way he would be ready for the Randwick meeting on 14 March. McGrath decided that while the horse was no better, he was no worse either. The foreleg was still hot, and it was still puffy, but Peter was not lame. During his morning work he moved with his usual elasticity, and he pulled up sound after each outing. He was also in great spirits, so McGrath began to test the horse. On 7 March he sent Peter Pan on a strong canter around Randwick's tan, and with a week to go before racing, he took the champion to Victoria Park. On 12 March, Peter Pan was breezed over six furlongs, and running on the centre of the track he covered the distance in 1:18 1/2, a phenomenal time for a horse that was, admittedly, half fit.

After the gallop, McGrath's optimism was soaring, and he and Dangar agreed that while Peter Pan was an unlikely winner of Saturday's Randwick Stakes, he would need the race to fit him for the AJC autumn meeting. Dangar, who still held reservations about the health of his horse, was relenting to the trainer's advice.

***

14 March was a warm and pleasant Saturday in Sydney, and Randwick had attracted a big crowd. Peter Pan had had a mortgage on the meeting since 1933. He had won the Randwick Stakes twice in its last three runnings, proving with each victory that winning first up from a spell was not beyond him. This year, however, the situation was very different. Peter Pan had galloped but once in his preparation, and with the condition he still carried, he was not fancied. 'That Peter Pan could be fit to run in the Randwick Stakes seems unlikely,' reported Cliff Graves in the *Referee.* 'Even if he runs in order to provide a test of his capacity to stand further training and racing, it is incredible that he should be ready to win it.'

The race was more open than it had been for years. Peter's old nemesis, Rogilla, was back to complete his season, and Les Haigh had hurried the old gelding's preparation so that he looked like one of the most forward horses in the parade ring. He hadn't raced since his poor fourth in the Craven Plate the previous October, but Haigh still thought his horse had wins left in him. It was a dubious decision, for the Randwick Stakes was Rogilla's 70th start, and better judgement was that he was due for a permanent rest. He had soured considerably, dumping his rider in the mornings and refusing to stand at the barriers, but he was also just shy of turning nine. It was clear to everyone, though Haigh was taking his time with admitting it, that Rogilla had had enough.

The Randwick Stakes had attracted Oro and Lough Neagh, and Master Brierly had recovered from his spring injury to return that autumn. The competition, however, would come from Sarcherie and Contact, two horses that had crept into form since the spring. Sarcherie had run second behind Marabou in the Melbourne Cup, after the same placing behind Peter Pan in 1934, and the five-year-old mare was due for a win under weight-for-age conditions. Nevertheless, she could be found at as much as 10/1 in the ring, because the public had come foolishly for Peter Pan. He was getting odds of 6/4, with 6/1 about the four-year-old Gay Blond. The Sydney bettors were still behind their idol.

Before Jim Pike set off with Peter Pan for the start, McGrath instructed the jockey that Peter Pan was not to be knocked about. If he noticed anything amiss in Peter's stride, Pike was to pull up straight away. It was explained very carefully to him that this was the first time the damaged off foreleg would carry the strain of racing, and Peter Pan had been wrapped and bandaged for the effort. When he cantered away to the barriers, McGrath and Dangar were restless with worry. Horses had broken down during races with lesser injuries.

Peter Pan had drawn the widest alley of 10 horses, and as he took his place at the tapes, he stood with the poise of a professional. When Jack Gaxieu sent the field away, Peter bounced out with his usual tenacity, crossing over to take third position in the early running. Master Brierly had missed the start altogether, while Limarch was also away badly. King's Head had adopted an early lead, with Sarcherie bowling along in second.

For the first furlong, the pace in the Randwick Stakes was a dawdling one, and Pike felt Peter Pan shuffling along comfortably. It would have been ideal for the chestnut if it had stayed that way, but Sarcherie grew impatient and snatched the lead from King's Head. As she had done in the Melbourne Cup, she clattered down the backstretch, so that the first half-mile of the Randwick Stakes was run in 49 1/2 seconds. Immediately, Peter Pan felt the sting of the pace. Gay Blond and Contact came around him nearing the home turn, and Pike was almost afraid to ask for an effort. Peter was labouring to stay in touch, too unfit to stay with the pace. As they ran into the straight, Sarcherie stole a lead of three lengths.

Pike didn't panic on Peter Pan. He allowed the big horse time to find his stride in the run for home, and

Peter did find it. Two furlongs from the judge, though the race was lost, he mustered an effort that carried him to his rivals in an instant. His speed was so electrifying that the crowds in the Leger hollered for him to win. But Gay Blond and Contact veered wide across Peter's track, and Pike had to check the horse to prevent him being carried across too. The big chestnut became unbalanced again; his stride was lost. As Sarcherie crossed the line a half-length to Gay Blond, Peter Pan was a length-and-a-quarter from Contact back in fourth.

There was little disgrace in Peter Pan's defeat. The horse had battled on through the Randwick Stakes, and despite his impositions of fitness, injury and weight, Peter Pan had finished better than Oro and Lough Neagh, seasoned gallopers who had no excuses for defeat, while Rogilla had run well back. Master Brierly had finished last, and Limarch had broken down in running and was pulled up. Peter had spotted Sarcherie 8lb in weight, and the placegetters 9lb and 6lb respectively. And, while Peter's former brilliance may have deserted him, his courage hadn't. He had pushed through his limits to finish where he did. No one could have asked for much more.

When he returned to scale, his condition was showing. He was breathing heavily, thick mats of sweat bunching on his neck and under the saddlecloth. McGrath, however, attributed that to fitness. The Randwick Stakes was run in the good time of 1:36 1/2, only a second outside of Peter Pan's own record, and he would have had to have been a fit horse to win it. Jim Pike agreed. He was encouraged by the dash that Peter displayed in the straight, and he told the press, 'I think he will come back to his best form now, provided he stands all right. As there were no signs of soreness and he never faltered in the race, I feel sure he is sound again, and there are good prospects of his getting fit.'

Back at the race stalls, George Phillips slowly unravelled the bandages on Peter Pan's forelegs. The suspensory injury on the offside looked shocking. The area was very swollen and unsightly, the surface rough and ugly, but McGrath recognised that it had become calloused, covered in thick, hardened skin. The trainer did not believe that the way the joint *looked* was the way that it *felt,* and he said so to Rodney Dangar. Like anyone that looked at the leg, Dangar was horrified when he saw it that afternoon, exclaiming that no horse should be run looking like that. He was mollified only when McGrath assured him that Peter was not lame. The trainer could touch the area, could stretch the leg and flex the fetlock, and Peter Pan remained relaxed through the inspection.

Dangar was getting nervous now. To him, it felt like his champion was falling to pieces. Peter had open sores on his foreleg, shoulder ailments that had ruined his spring, and a lagging spirit. The old fire was gone. Even if McGrath was missing that, Dangar could see it clearly. But the trainer hadn't lost his mind. He hadn't suddenly forgotten how to do his job. Peter Pan was clocking decent times in the morning. He was eating and drinking, and doing all the correct mechanical things a racehorse should do. Perhaps Dangar was too sentimental, whereas McGrath had learned to distance himself from such things long ago. The owner put it down to that and pressed on, albeit reluctantly.

McGrath, in another spectrum altogether, felt more confident about the champion's future. He wondered if Peter would be as good as he had been the previous season, for he had been lethal then, but the Randwick Stakes had at least proved the horse could stand up to racing, that the damaged branch of the suspensory ligament was not about to fray and tear in half. McGrath suggested to the press that when fit, it was quite acceptable to hope that Peter Pan would beat the rest of his opposition that autumn.

Les Haigh had no such thoughts. At the other end of Doncaster Avenue, at the stables on 11 Bowral Street, the Newcastle trainer was tending to Rogilla. The old gelding had come out of the Randwick Stakes very distressed, soreness having affected him in running. He was also suffering from round bone issues, caused by concussion on the front feet, poor conformation and nutritional disparities. The years had finally taken their toll on the gangly eight-year-old. Heartbroken, Haigh announced the retirement of Rogilla that afternoon, and Peter Pan's greatest rival, the horse that had run him to more close finishes than any other, departed the track with 26 wins from 70 starts, and more than £22,000 in prizemoney. His destiny had been spun around Peter Pan's since 1932, and it was a sign to Dangar's champion that the end might be near too.

***

The week following the Randwick Stakes, McGrath took Peter Pan to Victoria Park each morning. The champion's next race was the Rawson Stakes at Rosehill on 28 March, and the trainer had two weeks to bring Peter Pan to racing condition. The constitution of the champion was incredible. He was clocking times consistent with a horse that had been fit for weeks, and certainly a horse without ligament trouble. The following week, he ran a stiff six furlongs with Master Brierly at Victoria Park, and towed the younger horse home by four lengths. McGrath couldn't time the work because fog had settled over the track, but he could see that it was Peter's fastest effort since the spring. The off fore was holding up, and the champion was sound when he came to a stop. He seemed a stronger horse by the morning of the Rawson Stakes, a horse much more like himself.

The Rawson Stakes was the nine-furlong contest that Peter Pan had won for the first time the previous year. This year, it had attracted as good a line-up as any. Peter shared topweight honours with Oro at 9st 2lb, Sylvandale was entered with 9st, while Lough

Neagh and High Cross had 8st 13lb. There were six other horses in the race, among them an excellent three-year-old colt called Garrio, and they completed a field of nine. McGrath told Pike to win the race this time if he could, and he legged the jockey into the saddle a few minutes before the three o'clock start.

It was a hot, still afternoon when Peter Pan left the mounting yard for the Rawson Stakes. As he trotted on to the course proper, a huge cheer swept up from the grandstand for the champion, and he cantered to the start with all of Rosehill behind him. Pike knew that if Peter Pan was going to win again in his career, it would be today, and the jockey couldn't predict the hysteria if he pulled it off.

Up in the stand, Rodney Dangar was trying to muster the same faith. Lingering in him, he had feelings that winning was beyond Peter Pan. Notwithstanding Peter's loss of form in Melbourne, a great heart, a heart even as titanic as Peter's, could not carry a doubtful leg, and Dangar had only to look at that limb to see that something was wrong. He tried to cast away his feelings that Peter Pan was not right, for McGrath had assured him that there was no risk to his horse still running. The track times were evidence of that, he had said. But still there was something. Dangar wondered if he was doing the right thing by Peter Pan. He watched through his field glasses as the chestnut lined up in postposition five. Peter stood quietly under Pike, ready for the task at hand. When the tapes rose, he lurched into stride with the rest of the horses, but the pace was so slow in all of them that Lough Neagh, who was never forward in a race, hit the front running.

The Queensland horse led the field through the first furlong in 14 seconds, just outside of even time. It was a disgraceful crawl, and back in the pack, the slower horses had plenty of time to find their feet. Spear Prince came right around the field to run with Lough Neagh, and with two furlongs travelled he took the lead narrowly. Peter Pan had settled himself in sixth.

From the stands, it looked like the son of Pantheon was labouring. He hadn't been this far behind in a weight-for-age race since 1934, but Pike was using the extended distance to balance the champion. He was content to sit him off the speed, then race him from behind in the closing stages. It had been a winning formula during his battles with Rogilla, and Pike was determined it would be so today. The jockey kept a close eye on the proceedings up front, particularly on Garrio, as he waited for the business to be done in the turn for home.

Four furlongs from home, Spear Prince ran past the four-furlong pole with Lough Neagh still at his flanks. Behind them, the field had bunched into a tight group, with Peter Pan sitting at the back. As they turned into the straight, Pike swung the chestnut out on to the course and Peter began to motor around horses. The effort wasn't momentous, as Pike had him wound up, but the champion was travelling so quickly inside the final two furlongs that he looked like the old Peter Pan. He swooped on the leading horses, and was within two lengths of Lough Neagh when Garrio, on the rails, went to make his run. But Pike drove Peter Pan alongside the colt, and the hole closed. Garrio had nowhere to go. Riding and driving, Pike urged Peter Pan up to Lough Neagh; Peter inched up. He was trying with all his heart, heaving and digging to pass the leader, and he ranged alongside. But the winning post came too soon. Peter Pan lost the 1936 Rawson Stakes by a neck.

The crowd gave Lough Neagh fitting applause, but when Peter Pan returned to scale he received an ovation. It mattered nothing to Rosehill's patrons that day that he hadn't won. They had seen the champion try, and they knew of the struggles he was racing through. Their outburst was vociferous; they didn't stop cheering until Jim Pike slid off the horse. The occasion made the tears swim in Rodney Dangar's eyes. Even in defeat, his beloved Peter Pan was still a Sydney idol. He left the stands to greet the horse in the mounting yard, and he too clapped as Peter strode away from them, heading for the stalls.

The Rawson Stakes was Peter Pan's 38th race, and the sixth time he had run to second place. He earned £80 from the effort, which brought his winnings to £34,140/10s. After meeting Lough Neagh on many occasions since the Hill Stakes of 1932, it was the first time the Queensland gelding had gotten the better of him. Even now, the margin of finish was so close, and the advantages so favourable to Lough Neagh, that there was no disgrace. Peter had given the gelding 4lb in weight, a huge head start, and he was not a right horse. McGrath could declare him fit until the cows came home, but something had gone from Peter Pan.

***

Deep inside the chestnut's system, a lesion had occurred in the last five months, a physical change in Peter Pan's body as a result of some injury or overexertion. The lesion was making it impossible for him to win, impossible for him to garner the same devastating speed that had helped him set the Australasian mile record the previous year. It had brought him back to the playing field, had made horses like Lough Neagh and Sarcherie, good horses but not champions, defeat him on the racetrack. It was discrediting Peter Pan as a legend, chipping away at his brilliant record.

Dangar had stated after the Melbourne Stakes the previous October that Peter Pan was stale from racing, and it was generally felt in training circles that a rested horse would recover from fatigue. But Peter had been holidayed for six weeks after the Cup and was yet to find his form, and it was clear to all who handled him that he had not soured from competing. He was energetic during trackwork and he did not shirk his duties when he hit the racecourse. In the

Randwick Stakes and the Rawson Stakes, he had wanted desperately to win, but had been unable to muster the ability to do it.

The injuries that could have caused Peter Pan's lesion started with the nail that been driven through his foot in 1932. That incident had resulted in infection and blood poisoning so pronounced they almost claimed Peter's life. In veterinary circles, such infections were considered lethal in racehorses. They resulted in inflammation of the heart's muscles, and often a horse was never right again. In Peter Pan's case, he had seen himself through the infection, and there was no evidence to suggest he had carried any ill effects from it. However, the exertion it had taken his young constitution to recover, and the fact that five months later he was sent out to win the Melbourne Cup, which he did in extraordinary circumstances, could have left some damage that was only now telling on him. It was a wide suggestion, but not an impossible one.

The near-shoulder trouble was a more realistic cause. Though Peter Pan had been spelled when the problem first arose in 1933, he had been raced through it ever since. McGrath had relied on Peter's ability to limber up during fast work, and it was a correct move from the trainer. Peter Pan had won almost every major prize in Sydney throughout that time, but had that period now taken its toll? Veterinary surgeons believed that a change took place in a racehorse's heart when he was overworked, or when overexertion took place. Evidence suggested that a horse could do all ordinary work, and even show some brilliance doing it, but when presented a task that required a great effort, as at the finish of a race, the horse would never again rise to the occasion.

Peter Pan had not been over-raced, and there was no horse at Randwick that had been more carefully prepared. McGrath had shown vigilance all the way through Peter's life, but it was possible the horse had been overtrained when he was weak prior to the Melbourne Stakes. On its own, this might not have been so affecting, but Peter Pan had then run two miles with a grandstand on his back. It was only speculation, but the effort might have been so enormous as to strain his heart, the symptoms of which were that now he was unable to perform the way he used to.

Sooner or later, every racehorse shows symptoms of deterioration. It becomes obvious when a previously excellent galloper begins to lose races that had been easy for him the previous season. In geldings, it was often age that caused it, as had been the case with Amounis. Geldings, unlike stallions, had a longer lifespan on the track, and were often more stout in their ability to keep winning. Stallions, like mares, with their physiology turning their minds to stud duties, were usually off the track by five or six years of age. But whether it be because of age or sex, it is inevitable that all racehorses begin to expire. The problem with Peter was that the deterioration had been sudden, and during a time when he was largely unbeatable.

After the Rawson Stakes, it became obvious that the champion had mustered a splitting effort to get within a neck of Lough Neagh. The suspensory injury became more pronounced after the race, hotter and uglier than it had been before, and Peter showed all the physical signs that his heart had barely managed the race. He was heaving in the paddock, and Dangar grew more alarmed for his horse. It was no longer enough for him that Peter Pan had run to within a whisker of winning. All he could see was distress. He wanted it over now, and hung dangerously close to announcing Peter's retirement.

In the *Sydney Mail,* 'Musket' was concerned about Peter's condition. 'The question now arises whether the hard race will affect the injured foreleg, or whether the great showing Peter Pan made will prove that he is not so lame as was feared,' the journalist wrote. 'But the fact that he could not concede 4lb and a beating to Lough Neagh proved conclusively that he was not the horse he was 12 months ago.' On Thursday 2 April, five days after the Rawson Stakes, the reality of Peter Pan's situation was broadcast in the *Referee.* Though Cliff Graves had always been a fan of the big chestnut, and it saddened him to write the words, he said, 'The old Peter Pan brilliance is missing, and if he wins at all this autumn it might be against the slow plugs in the longer weight-for-age races. Absence of the fast sprinters in those will give him a chance to issue an effective challenge over the final stages.' It was not the eulogy Peter Pan deserved, nor the way that Rodney Dangar wanted to see his horse go out.

40

The last start

Jim Pike sat in the jockeys' room at Randwick, fastening the buttons of his green and orange silks. His brittle, bony fingers pushed each button through its hole, then he tucked the jacket inside his ivory breeches. When he heard an eruption from the grandstands outside, the muffled cheer of thousands of racegoers, he knew the winner of the First Hurdle had come in. It was almost time, then, for the Autumn Plate. He glanced around the jockeys' room, and saw Billy Cook and Maurice McCarten in conversation. Andy Knox was there too, and Edwin Tanwan. In a corner, Keith Cook was climbing into Master Brierly's silks. It was a scene Pike had looked upon for nearly 30 years, a Randwick play he had been cast in since 1906.

The 44-year-old veteran was on the brink of retirement. He had announced he was to retreat from racing when Peter Pan did, but as he adjusted his spurs and brushed the scuffs off his boots that afternoon, he had little idea if it would be today. Peter was running in the Autumn Plate in a half hour or so, and his effort would decide if he would race in the All-Aged Plate on Wednesday. Pike had another riding engagement that afternoon for his old mentor, trainer William Kelso, but beyond that his books were clear. If Peter Pan raced on, so would Pike. But this might just be the last time he left the jockeys' room with the famous Dangar silks.

He snatched his green cap and riding whip, and strode out of the sanctum towards the mounting yard. He emerged into a sea of activity at Randwick. It was the first day of the AJC autumn meeting. The horses were in the yard for the Autumn Plate, and there were neat huddles of owners and trainers everywhere. He could hear the chants of the bookies in the ring, and the excited babble of 50,000 racegoers. They were jammed around the fences, in the grandstands, and packed into the Flat enclosure like so many sardines. Some of them hollered his name and wished him luck as he picked his way towards Peter Pan's connections.

A little way away, Peter Pan seemed robust as he walked around the ring, and when Pike joined McGrath and Dangar, he exclaimed as much. Dangar nodded, though he was austere, but McGrath was confident and verbose. The trainer said that Peter Pan had made terrific progress since the Rawson Stakes two weeks ago, and the only thing likely to beat him at this meeting was his dubious foreleg. McGrath had only the facts to read, and over the previous fortnight the facts had been promising.

After his close finish to Lough Neagh, Peter Pan had been sent to Victoria Park the following week for trackwork, where his efforts were excellent. For this reason, McGrath had predicted nothing less than a win this afternoon. Pike had only McGrath's wisdom to work from, and on raceday, if a trainer says a horse is a good thing, the jockey believes him. Before Pike was legged into Peter Pan's saddle, he gave old George Phillips a pat on the shoulder. Peter's dearest friend didn't look confident, but Phillips never said much. Pike tucked his feet into the irons, and picked up the reins from his horse's neck. These were gestures he had made a thousand times before, robotic manoeuvres almost, but he delivered them today with deliberateness. It might be the last time he rode a champion like this.

Pike and Peter Pan left the mounting yard, swinging away from the grandstands to perform their preliminary gallop before the race. A moment later, they were cantering past the judge and back down the home straight towards the mile-and-a-half start of the Autumn Plate. The crowds gave them a sporting cheer as they passed, and the champion had been backed into odds-on. Peter Pan was commanding 10/9 on because of his close finish in the Rawson Stakes, and the newspapers, hearing of Peter's good work during the week, had declared their faith in the horse. 'Grand and glorious Peter Pan will come into his own again at Randwick on Saturday,' said the *Referee.*

Jack Gaxieu began to shuffle the horses into their postpositions. There were nine runners for the weight-for-age event, including Oro, Sarcherie, Silver Ring, Contact and Master Brierly. Pike didn't pay much attention to them. He brought Peter Pan forward; the chestnut stood before the tapes, peering down the straight ahead of him. Pike got ready for the jump, and it happened at 1.55pm.

Peter Pan sprang off his hindquarters with the agility of a three-year-old, the rousing cheers of Randwick Racecourse pouring into his ears. He was the first to leave the line of a perfect start, and as he shot away down the straight, Pike stood in his irons and eased the big horse, coaxing him back to the field. Spear Prince came around to take the lead out of the straight, and going into the first turn, Peter was ahead of only three horses. He had settled at the rear, but the field was running only 14 seconds to the furlong. They ran into the backstretch, tightly bunched but slow.

Down the long run of Randwick's back straight, Pike began to ease Peter Pan around horses. The chestnut dropped into his loose, long stride, and Pike hunched quietly over the horse's neck. Peter's blond mane flew in the jockey's face, its wiry texture tickling his skin, but the horse and rider moved as one. They picked off the leading division, until Peter Pan was off the rails in third position, with only Spear Prince and Contact ahead of him. Peter Pan was running with his old tenacity. Dangar watched from the stands as his racehorse poised to run into the straight. The owner's heart was pounding, a cocktail of excitement and nerves, of a desire for victory sedated by the worry of breakdown. As Peter Pan galloped into the home turn, Dangar could hardly breathe. He followed his horse as he swooped on

Contact, then on Spear Prince. Peter Pan stuck his nose in front. The crowds around him raised the roof. 'Here he comes!' 'Here comes Peter Pan!' Two furlongs from home, Peter Pan had kicked into the lead.

Pike began to ride with hands and heels, urging the champion down the home straight. The time had come for Peter's final effort in the race, for the withering finish that would leave the field far behind. The champion was looking for it, and Pike could feel him trying, but then Peter Pan's heart failed. The mechanics of his system could not sustain the effort. On the rails, Sarcherie ran past him into the lead.

Pike kept urging Peter Pan. The oxygen in his muscles was low now, and he adjusted his stride to cope with the effort. He was labouring, his pace shortening by six inches each time. His forelegs were hitting the ground more heavily, and the suspensory injury began to throb. Pike sensed the struggle in the champion, and he stopped riding right away. Alarmed, he eased the big horse down. Silver Ring dashed past them in the dying strides, and just before two o'clock on that afternoon of 11 April 1936, Peter Pan struggled third past the post in the Autumn Plate, a sore, distressed horse.

Jim Pike heard the confused chatter of the race crowds as he pulled up after the judge. His heart was swollen with emotion, with disappointment and concern for Peter Pan. The horse was in pain, and as Pike turned him around to return to scale, he knew the off-foreleg was gone. He could feel it in Peter's gait each time the limb touched the turf, which meant the horse had come home lame. Pike hoped the champion had carried silks for the last time. When he turned the chestnut over to George Phillips, who was about to topple into nervous hysteria, he heard a few calls. Though his expression never revealed it that day, he hoped so too. It had been a moderate, slowly run weight-for-age race, yet the big horse had not been up to the effort. Pike knew there was no hope of Peter Pan returning to his illustrious form of former seasons.

Pike lifted the buckles of the girth and slid his saddle from Peter. When he spun around to weigh in, Dangar and McGrath were waiting for him under the eaves of the grandstand. They looked grieved, and the jockey told them that Peter Pan was sore and sorry. It was a wonder, he explained, that they had clung on for third place. Dangar patted his shoulder and told him he had ridden a fine race, and Pike strode sullenly away from the two men. He suspected they would announce Peter Pan's future that afternoon, and when they did, Dangar would send for him. In the meantime, Pike weighed in, and returned to the jockeys' room from whence he had come not half an hour earlier.

***

It was idle time for Jim Pike when he was summoned out of his quarters later that afternoon. Outside the jockeys' room, Rodney Dangar awaited him, and before Pike even reached Peter Pan's owner, he knew what was afoot. The sadness was written all over Mr Dangar's face. His wonderful horse had been retired. Dangar and McGrath had conferred on the state of the champion after the Autumn Plate, and McGrath had finally admitted that Peter Pan was in no fit state to race again. Dangar announced the horse was done, and then sought out his jockey immediately. He wanted to thank Pike for his role in Peter Pan's life, and the moment was honest and intimate. Pike, almost always steely and poker-faced, was overcome that afternoon. For 30 years he had ridden on the backs of winners, but today it had ended. His last champion, 'the grand and glorious Peter Pan', was finished with racing, and so Pike was finished too.

The old jockey looked morose as he perched on his seat in the jockeys' room, reflecting on Peter Pan's career. For the rest of his days, he would be amazed how the son of Pantheon had returned from two Melbourne Cup wins to become one of the fastest milers in Australia. Pike had suspected after the 1934 Cup that the distressing effort of winning that race would slow the horse down in speed, because it was normal in the case of true stayers that staying campaigns made them slower. But Peter Pan was the only horse in Pike's long and lavish memory that had furnished into some sort of sprinter after three years of being a champion stayer. The revolution, which Pike described as 'something of a miracle in the history of thoroughbred racing', had fairly bamboozled him.

Pike had enjoyed Peter Pan's life for three-and-a-half years, and he tried to grasp the conclusion of his relationship with Mr Dangar. He told anyone who asked him that Peter's owner was cut from the cloth of the best, and Pike could not recall any owner in all his years who had paid him so quickly, who had rewarded him so generously, and who had thanked him so sincerely. Pike had received huge money for armchair rides on Peter Pan, and still to this very afternoon, he admired Dangar's humility. The man had won without boasting and lost with good grace. 'Win or lose,' Pike would say in an interview many years later, 'he was the daddy of them all.' He was a league in front of Phar Lap's connections who, Pike remembered, had won twice the prizemoney yet had half the generosity.

The wiry old jockey left his quarters later on for the Vaucluse Handicap, announcing his retirement to William Kelso, who subsequently broadcast it to the Randwick public. Pike rode the welter galloper Golden Gate to fifth place. But as he eased up on Kelso's horse that day, a small irony eluded James Edward Pike. He had ridden his last winner a few days before in the Mascot Welter Mile at Ascot, on an ordinary entrant called Babili, the very horse that had shared the honours with Peter Pan in his first race win at Warwick Farm in August 1932.

41

'Au revoir, Peter Pan'

Night settled on Randwick Racecourse, and the grandstands were hushed and still. The voices were gone, the enclosures silent, and fruit bats whistled in the air, whooshing across the tracks and disappearing into the darkness. In the vacuum of raceday, the day that Peter Pan retired, the place was different. It was emptier, a lonely tract of land without its champion. The battle cries for the son of Pantheon were dead and gone forever.

Peter Pan had retired from racing with 23 wins. After 39 starts, he had six seconds, a solitary third, and was only nine times unplaced. His winnings had reached £34,210 and 10 shillings, placing him eighth on the list of stakes winners in Australia, and he had trophies to the value of £600. The gold alone was worth the price of a worker's cottage in Darlinghurst. He had won two Melbourne Cups, an AJC Derby, a St Leger, a Craven Plate, a Duke of Gloucester Cup and Jubilee Cup, the Autumn Plate twice, the Cumberland Plate twice, and the Melbourne Stakes twice. He held a myriad of other stakes wins across Sydney. He had beaten the crowned sprinter of the nation one afternoon at Victoria Park, humiliating Chatham in a seven-furlong dash in course-record time, and he had run the fastest mile ever recorded on an Australasian racetrack. He was the second horse, and the only horse in 72 years, to win the Melbourne Cup twice, and he had beaten every top horse that had raced in Australia since 1932.

The whirlwind was over now, but the legacy was planted in Randwick's fair turf. Peter Pan had established himself as one of the greatest stayers in Australian history. He had started over two or more miles on five occasions, losing only once. His weights had varied from 7st 6lb to 9st 10lb, and fast going or quagmire, it had all been the same to him. McGrath was convinced that the horse could have run three miles, perhaps further, if he was pushed. He believed Peter Pan was built on the same stout lines as Carbine, iron horses that possessed second and third winds deep in the bellies of their being. Peter Pan was built like a stayer, a lean, ferocious machine with lines that threw back to the finest sticking blood in history. He had St Simon three times through his pedigree, and he had Musket, Goldsbrough and Yattendon through him. Breeding authority William Allison, who had posthumously published the family numbers work of his friend Bruce Lowe, had said, 'Let them [Australian breeders] hold on to their old Musket, Fisherman, Yattendon, Tim Whiffler and Goldsbrough strains, and then they will find the imported racing horses not a serious menace.'

Peter Pan's reputation as a stayer was set in stone, for it was in his pedigree and his racing record. But as a miler, he ranked with the best that had been seen in years. From 1932 to 1936, he had started over the mile course eight times, winning six and setting an Australasian record in the process. Neither Chatham nor Winooka, the two fastest milers of years past, had registered a quicker time than he, and the day he did it he won going away from Hall Mark, last-start winner of the one-mile Doncaster Handicap. Peter Pan had run it in 1:35 1/2, breezing off by three lengths and pulling up as fresh as cut grass.

The horse was a miracle in racing, an animal that had demonstrated tenacity enough to begin his career under a stayer's preparation, and complete it with withering wins over seven and eight furlongs. He didn't know what it was to be one or the other. Peter Pan had wanted to be everything, a stayer and a sprinter alike, and he had been brilliant in either guise. McGrath had never trained a more tractable thoroughbred, a horse more versatile over any distance, under any weight, and through any conditions. Peter Pan was intelligent, the ideal horse to train according to James Scobie, and though McGrath described him as haughty and aloof, he placed only Carbine above him in ability.

Australia had not been ready for another legend so soon. At the time of Peter Pan's three-year-old season, the nation was wounded from Phar Lap's death. The Red Terror had met a terrible end, so his deeds, magnificent as they were, became national treasures. It was incomprehensible to the nation that one just as brilliant could come along so soon, not even six months later. It was like an insult to Phar Lap's legend. As a result, Peter's early deeds were soiled by heavy criticism. The defamations had not ceased until his second Melbourne Cup victory, after which the chestnut's form became so devastating as to make racing history. Peter Pan, as a five-year-old, raced 13 times for nine wins and three seconds. He was unplaced just once, and by such time his greatest critics, namely 'Banjo' Paterson and W.J. Stewart McKay, had gone to ground. These were men who had spat in the face of overwhelming evidence and written Peter Pan off for the Cup of '34.

The power of legend is such that the son of Pantheon stood no chance when it came to being crowned the greatest horse of the 19th century. Peter's deeds were, at certain points in his career, better than any Phar Lap had achieved. But Phar Lap's end had catapulted him into a stratosphere that no horse could reach, because he had not lived to grow old and expire. He had died at the top of his game, and his last start had resulted in a famous victory overseas.

But many believe that there is no better analysis of a champion than that which discusses who he defeated. While there have been seasons on the Australian turf that have been vintage down to their bones, Phar Lap's were not considered among them by many in racing. Amounis was the best that famous horse encountered between his years of 1929 to 1932, and Amounis beat him twice. His other good opponents, Nightmarch and Limerick, had been well past their prime. 'That Phar Lap was a great horse there is no denying,' stated 'Musket' in the *Sydney Mail* on 15 May 1935, 'but his greatness was emphasised by the poor class of opposition he encountered in most of his races.' Of Phar Lap's great effort in the 1931 Futurity Stakes, a race that Jim Pike said was the red horse's greatest, the *Referee* said, 'Phar Lap beat only moderate welter horses.'

'Musket' was emphatic that Rogilla was a better horse than Phar Lap had ever had to oppose. Rogilla remained the only horse to win the Caulfield Cup, the Sydney Cup and the Cox Plate, and yet Peter Pan trounced him on so many occasions. Phar Lap had also never had to race against opposition like Hall Mark and Chatham. Chatham's deeds were spectacular, but little Hall Mark had been a superstar. He had won the Champagne as a two-year-old, then both Derbies, the Melbourne Cup, and the VRC St Leger as a three-year-old. At four, he won the Doncaster with 10st 4lb, and sprinkled around his record were wins in the Underwood Stakes (twice), the King's Plate (twice), the Memsie Stakes, and the C.B. Fisher Plate. He had never, however, won a race against Peter Pan.

Phar Lap remained the highest stakes earner in Australian racing history. He had died amid earnings that made poor men weep in the streets. But though he had raced through the Depression, it was not until 1932 that stakes had been slashed significantly. They were still at paltry levels by 1935. Peter Pan, therefore, had had no chance to compete with Phar

Lap on that account. But if fate had not borne the son of Pantheon in 1929, and instead had dropped him into the roaring twenties, his earnings would have simmered at about £40,000, which would have placed him among the top-four earners on the Australian turf. It also had to be remembered that Peter Pan had missed the spring prizes of 1933.

Because of the proximity of Peter Pan's life to Phar Lap's, it was easy to compare their records. The first thing that stood out was how many more times Phar Lap had raced than Peter. As a two-year-old, Peter Pan had started only once because of Dangar's concerns that he was under-mature. Phar Lap had been just as gangly and underdeveloped, yet he had been raced five times in the autumn of his two-year-old season. As a three-year-old, Peter Pan started 11 times, while Phar Lap started 20 times. When Phar Lap died in the autumn of his five-year-old year, he had gone to the post on 52 occasions. At the same point in his career, Peter Pan had raced 31 times. This, in a large way, accounted for the wide gap in earnings between the two champions.

On Melbourne Cup records alone, Peter Pan stood head and shoulders above his great rival. The facts were that both horses had started in three Cups, and Peter Pan had won twice, Phar Lap once. But the times recorded were more interesting. In 1929, when Phar Lap placed third as a three-year-old, the race was won in 3:26 1/2, and Phar Lap finished four lengths behind the winner. Peter Pan, in his three-year-old attempt, not only won the race after tripping, but ran it in 3:23 1/4. It was a mere half-second off the race record, but it was also the fastest time ever clocked by a three-year-old in the history of the Melbourne Cup.

The two horses' second Cup efforts were very different, because even though they carried similar weights, the 1934 track was the worst that many had ever seen. The honours were Peter Pan's, for he lumped 9st 10lb through the mud, running wide on the course from the widest alley. Darby Munro declared it the best effort he had ever experienced from a racehorse. Peter Pan was the only horse that day with more than 7st 2lb to act in the going, and he won by three lengths, the same distance by which Phar Lap won his Cup, through good going, in 1930.

Both horses were defeated in their third Melbourne Cups, and both were handed imposts far too heavy for a two-mile handicap. There was no disgrace in either of their defeats, but in Peter Pan's case it was impossible to tell if the weight had really beaten him. He had already been beaten by his weakened constitution in the weeks or days before the race. But as far as records in the Melbourne Cup went, Peter Pan's was superior to Phar Lap's, and he should have been appreciated for that. Instead, because of his hapless timing in 1932, he would never be given what was due him.

***

The champion stirred in his box that night of 11 April, not knowing that he had taken his final bow before Randwick. George Phillips had been slow with taking him back to Doncaster Avenue. The faithful attendant had been quiet and low spoken, hiding his emotions from the stable lads. Four wonderful years were over for Phillips, and he was about to release Peter Pan to his stud duties. Somehow, the days would be less colourful for him, and the yard emptier. Peter had been such a personality horse. He had been demanding and arrogant, but never nasty. He had known his worth, and no one around him was made to forget it, save Phillips, his friend.

Peter would remain at the McGrath racing yard until 29 April, when he would be ferried to Baroona by train. Until then, he would let down at Randwick, enjoying mild exercise in the late mornings, and rolling in the sandbox in the afternoons. His suspensory injury had necessitated veterinary attention that afternoon, but rest would repair the ravages done. His mind would settle without racing, and his body would thicken, and he would meet the duties of a stallion by August. In time, he might forget his deeds on the track.

Having followed Peter Pan's life since 1932, the Sydney newspapers were glad to see him retired. 'Everybody loves a champion,' the *Sportsman* said, 'and even though we all know that even a Peter Pan must, at some time, come to the end of his tether, the spectacle of seeing him struggling valiantly against horses whom he could have conceded stones to a little time back is indeed sad.' The paper commended Dangar for retiring the horse, and stated that though the Australian turf could not afford to lose a champion with such sterling worth as Peter Pan, 'the humane side of the picture comes up in bold relief. There's not a man among real lovers of the thoroughbred who did not welcome the news of Peter's retirement.' *Sportsman* declared that the son of Pantheon, striking and talented as he was, would remain an everlasting memory for all who watched him race, 'and as great as Phar Lap was, he never rose to the heights Peter did by winning two Melbourne Cups'.

The *Referee* gave the horse a fitting tribute: 'Peter was a beloved champion. His great consistency won him a place in racegoers' hearts ... and now he slips off the turf into the legion of past champions, but not to be forgotten.' The newspaper highlighted one of Peter Pan's most popular qualities. 'He is the only champion of his curious blending of dark chestnut coat and flaxen, or platinum, mane and tail. Trafalgar was a chestnut and silver, but Peter Pan had a colour scheme all his own.'

Frank McGrath, like George Phillips, was an emotional man after the Autumn Plate, as the whirlwind had come to an end for him too. He would be 70 years old in a few months, and how many more years could he expect to flip around after racehorses? The ageing trainer sat in his living room that night, recounting to himself the impact of Peter Pan. He believed that he would never train another horse like him, and he couldn't be shifted from his view that the Pantheon horse was the greatest galloper since Carbine. He had seen Carbine with his own eyes, and he believed that horse was immortal. But Peter Pan, who had propelled the trainer into even greater fortune and glory, had been a machine. He was, McGrath thought, a better horse than Phar Lap.

McGrath knew that racing men had short memories. The Cup winner of today, so 'Cardigan' had said once, was forgotten tomorrow, and it was the fashion to idolise the latest champion. But McGrath had never been like that. When people had asked him, he had said that Phar Lap was not Carbine. He believed that over two miles the Red Terror would have been no match for Peter Pan. He would stick to that conviction for the rest of his life. A good horse asks no favour of pace or track, and Peter Pan had lived up to that axiom in the Melbourne Cup of 1934. Distance, going, weight, rider, opposition ... they had all been the same to Peter.

For Dangar, the decision to retire the champion had been easier, for Peter Pan was not deserting his life. The chestnut would return to Whittingham and enjoy a beautiful existence, a serene second career among the jacaranda trees and oleanders of Baroona. But like Phillips and McGrath, Dangar had felt a deep regret in his gut that afternoon, a sadness, he presumed, that Peter Pan would not race again. It had been the greatest few years of Rodney Dangar's life, and now it was over. He knew that he would never own another horse of this class. 'It is too much to expect the mare to produce another as good as Peter Pan,' he said of Alwina. 'I am not going to make the error of regarding my geese as swans.'

Peter Pan had given Dangar the credit he had craved in breeding circles. Albert Augustus's son could now say that he had bred a two-time Melbourne Cup winner in the paddocks of Baroona. He was proud that Peter Pan had been born and raised in the very pastures where he had first seen the light of life, and Dangar had joined his uncles and cousins at Neotsfield in the breeding of turf immortals. Peter Pan had joined Poseidon as a Dangar-bred champion, and he would soon join Positano as a Dangar stallion. It was the circle of life, Rodney Dangar thought, and now Peter was coming home.

Across Randwick and Kensington, in the early hours of that night, Peter Pan disappeared forever. He would never win again, and he would never be cheered again, and he became a memory, that huge, beautiful beast stamped in the minds of the racing public. There were children who had seen him that would grow up with the champion first in their minds, and there were women who swore there would never be a lovelier horse. There was a punter who was convinced, as he had been after the previous year's Spring Stakes, that no other horse would prove as reliable a punt. Peter Pan, on the afternoon of 11 April

1935, had left the course proper, and stepped into the halls of Randwick history.

Epilogue

George Phillips woke early on the morning of 29 April. Slowly, he climbed into his best suit, a dark brown cotton weave, single-breasted with waistcoat and pocket watch, and he made his way to the yard. It was still dark, though in the east there were tiny swathes of navy and blue. The yard was silent. The horses were still dozing in the back of their stalls, the boys yet to jump from their bunks. Phillips walked across the yard to stable six, and peered in at Peter Pan. The stallion nickered a greeting, a throaty, rumbly hum that floated through his nostrils. Phillips thought how he would miss that sound in the mornings, how it had started his day for years. He felt his chest grow tight with sadness, and his eyes water. He hurried away to the feed room to stop himself from sobbing.

The yard came alive in no time, and before Phillips had fixed Peter Pan's breakfast, the stable lads were scurrying here and there, with rugs and saddles, body brushes and currying combs. Each of them stopped at Peter Pan's box that morning, bidding him cheerio with heavy hearts. No one wanted to lose him, for he was a light that they all had basked in, but that was racing. A horse didn't last forever. By the time they filed out of the yard for the morning's trackwork, the sky had turned a magnificent pink, and the key players in Peter Pan's life were the only ones standing in the yard.

The stallion was rugged and booted for his long trip home to Baroona. McGrath circled the horse, checking his straps and boots. The moment had come to say goodbye. He slid his hand under the horse's white mane, felt the curve of Peter's neck and the warmth of his skin. He patted the horse, and saying nothing, McGrath left the stable.

George Phillips led Peter Pan out of stable six for the last time. A horse float was thrumming out on Doncaster Avenue, and a little before 6.30am that pale Wednesday morning, Frank McGrath watched as Peter Pan stepped out of the yard and up the ramp away from him. The float doors swung closed, and the champion was suddenly gone.

Peter Pan's train eased out of Sydney a little after 8am and George Phillips, who planned to stay at Baroona for a week, sat with the chestnut for the long journey to Whittingham. He thought about the change that would occur in his life now, and the horses that he would tend when he returned to Sydney in a week's time. He thought of his financial fortunes, and how they had changed because of this horse. There were the bonuses he had received from Mr Dangar, and the gifts from Jim Pike. 'Good ol' Jimmy,' Phillips thought. 'He never forgot me.'

The train wound north throughout the morning, and Peter Pan began to sense the change in the air. Deep in his memory he knew these smells, the rich scent of Hunter Valley grass, of unspoilt river flats and gentle hills. When the train pulled up at the

Whittingham station siding, the big horse was rippling with excitement. He came out of his boxcar with a clatter, and was ferried the short trip to Baroona. Up the long, magnificent driveway, Peter Pan breathed in the old smells of home. He sensed the broodmare band and the dairy herds, and the lure of broad pastures.

Rodney Dangar was there to see his horse home. Later in the afternoon, over 100 people arrived at Baroona to welcome the champion back to the district. Dangar had organised a garden party for Peter Pan, but philanthropist that he was, it was all in aid of charity. Locals mixed with Singleton aristocrats and Sydney visitors on the lawns in front of the mansion. Later on, Peter was presented to the crowd, where he was warmly, politely cheered. The president of the Dangar Cottage Hospital stepped forward to give the champion a few loose lumps of sugar, followed by a carrot, and George Phillips was not forgotten. The women of Singleton had arranged a basket of flowers and fruit for Peter Pan's friend, and it trailed with yellow marigolds and foliage, and green and orange streamers.

That first day home at Baroona rolled into the next day, and the next after that. The big chestnut grew into his old surroundings. He had a large paddock to himself during the day, and he began to leave the racetrack far behind him, lost in the rural paradise that he found himself in. For Phillips, with each night that passed so approached the moment when he would say goodbye. He felt the regret in his stomach. He sat in the tall grass of Peter Pan's paddock, watching him graze and gambol like a two-year-old. He slipped him carrots from the pockets of his trousers when he passed, and laughed out loud when the horse shoved him for more. Dangar watched them, and was saddened that they would be separated.

But the time came for the strapper to return to Sydney. McGrath was expecting him, and Phillips stood with the horse a long time before he could say goodbye. It was extraordinary how a thoroughbred could reduce a solid man to tears, and as George Phillips walked away for the last time, Peter Pan gazed after his old, ageing friend.

***

Autumn sidled into winter at Baroona, and Peter Pan's coat grew thick and dark. Each day he felt the sun on his skin, and freedom was becoming of him. He snorted with pleasure in the fresh mornings, and in the afternoons he dozed on the hillside pointed towards the western sun. By the time August rolled around and the breeding season began, he had let down into a magnificent stallion. He had a definite crest, and the taut muscles in his hindquarters had relaxed and rounded. 'As an individual he is the ideal type of sire,' so the Inglis catalogue described him in 1939, 'of commanding appearance and full masculine character.' The suspensory injury was hardly visible anymore.

Alec Young began to prepare the horse for stud duties. Dangar had arranged for a light season for Peter Pan, about 30 mares, and he and Young were selective about the outside bloodstock that was sent to Baroona. Peter Pan stood his first two seasons for 200 guineas (about £210), which was as high a fee as any stallion in Australia. The tall chestnut sired some very useful horses in his first few years, and immediately they were stamped with his likeness. In 1937, 11 foals by Peter Pan were dropped at Baroona, and seven of them carried their father's impressive and unusual colouring.

The years were not long passing in idyll surrounds. In the Easter of 1939, Peter Pan's first yearlings were sent to the Inglis yards at Newmarket. There were only four, for the others had been retained by either Dangar or the broodmare owners. The interest in Peter's offspring was high. No greater racehorse had entered stud since Carbine. But in Dangar's zealousness to breed the best to Peter Pan, he closed the book to many outside mares, believing strict selection would produce only the best foals. In so doing, Peter Pan's foal numbers were well down. It resulted in inflated prices for his yearlings, but it did little to help the stallion produce winners on a large scale.

The young Peter Pans matriculated into the racing game in 1939. Some were a sparkling success. Pretty Blue started at Newcastle in a two-year-old maiden and ran four-and-a-half furlongs in Australian record time. The broodmare Sequoia, who had gone to Baroona for two seasons, produced Panover who, in 1940, won her first start. Sequoia's second foal to Peter Pan was infinitely better. Named Peter, he won the Eclipse Stakes at Caulfield in 1944, and ran Sirius to a neck in the Melbourne Cup. In 1943, Precept, a colt from Peter Pan's third crop, won the VRC Derby. Precept would go on to sire Fire Dust, winner of the 1955 Doncaster. By 1940, Peter Pan had sired serious winners. The *Herald* stated he 'was an immediate success. No sire could have done better in his initial stud season'. With limited opportunity, he was producing very classy horses, and though the foal numbers were low, it made his offspring much more exclusive.

Dangar, who felt his stallion had hit the ground running, set about making Baroona one of the premier breeding farms in the Hunter Valley. Though he continued to race the odd horse here and there, he now threw his energies behind the farm. His broodmare band swelled from 19 in 1936 to 30 by 1940. By the 1941 Easter yearling sales, Baroona had a draft of 13 yearlings, and double that the following year. The seasons, one after another, fell away with slow, blissful rhythm.

***

The characters in Peter Pan's life slowly scattered. Pantheon continued on his march through the record books, becoming the most successful sire of runners in Perth. He produced four winners of the West Australian Derby before 1939, and along with Peter Pan, these youngsters made him a sensation. By the time he was pensioned at the age of 19, he had sired 420 winners worth £131,327 in earnings, a staggering sum for the times. He had remained at Kia Ora Stud since 1928, but in May 1940 he was sent to Willaroo, the pastoral home of Patrick Osborne, AJC committeeman and friend of Kia Ora studmaster Percy Miller. Pantheon had been a splendid servant, and in return Miller granted him peace and pasture, an old horse's treasures. He survived but two months. On Monday 29 July 1940, Pantheon suffered a twisted bowel and died.

In the grand shadows of the Baroona homestead, Alwina grew old with the broodmare herd. Of the mares belonging to Dangar, she was the most special, the single one that had produced a racehorse more sensational than any before. She produced five foals, and all were winners, but none proved as exceptional as Peter Pan. Dangar ensured her a wonderful life. She was covered sparingly, usually every second year, and Dangar would run his finger over her pedigree chart, tracing her stout staying lines through St Alwyne, through Boniform and Musket, and Yattendon and Chester.

He wondered how it was, of all the horses at the yearling sales of 1925, he had been so lucky to poach her. What was it, he asked, that had brought her to create a freak like Peter Pan? Late into the night of Sunday 3 September 1939, Alwina began foaling to The Buzzard. At 16 years of age she was getting along, so trouble was to be expected, but lying on the floor of her stall that night, wrenching with effort, Alwina haemorrhaged and passed away.

George Phillips returned to Frank McGrath, but craved the dizzy heights that came with champions. He thought about his involvement with Amounis and Peter Pan, and wondered if he was a common denominator. At the end of 1936, he uptook stables at Victoria Park and took out a trainer's permit with the AJC. He registered a combination of yellow, green and purple silks, a medley of the colours that Amounis and Peter Pan had raced under, and early in the mornings he was seen riding his own small team over the kikuyu. In February 1942, however, Victoria Park closed to race meetings, and the weather-beaten, gracious Phillips was lost in the void that rushed in.

Frank McGrath's good fortunes rolled on as they always had. New horses flowed in to replace the old ones, and in 1939 his yard was transformed once again with the arrival of a New Zealand colt called Beau Vite. For the next few years, Beau Vite carried the old trainer back to his stamping ground at the top of the racing game, with multiple wins in the Cox Plate, Craven Plate and Mackinnon Stakes (formerly the Melbourne Stakes), and victories in nearly every principal race in Sydney. When Beau Vite retired in 1942, McGrath was 76 years old.

The trainer carried his age gracefully. He pottered around Randwick with his familiar smile and round spectacles, a slight stoop in his shoulders and a short step here and there. Thoughts of retirement slipped into his mind at the close of World War II. He relinquished his stable to his son, Frank Jr, in the winter of 1946, and for little more than a year he passed his retirement on Doncaster Avenue. But he suffered heart trouble, and illness eventually confined him. On 28 October 1947, before first light over the grandstands of Randwick, Frank McGrath slipped away at home.

***

In the fair paddocks of Baroona, Peter Pan hardly noticed the years passing. His life was a simple one, a satisfying mix of females and freedom, and he knew nothing of age, of wars or the passing of time. He whiled away his days picking grass between his feet, resting in the afternoon sun or sniffing the wind that blew past him. On the morning of 17 March 1941, he left his box with careless abandon, playing and dancing at the end of his lead rope. He was in high spirits, and as soon as he was released, he set off for the other end of his paddock.

Stud groom Will Shade and his son Noel watched the big stallion dive and buck his way around the enclosure, cavorting like a foal on brand new legs. Then the unthinkable happened. Peter Pan buckled, and was snatched by gravity, his big frame crashing to the ground. He got up right away and stood startled at the end of his paddock, but he had heard a tiny snap and felt searing pain. He held his near foreleg in the air.

Dangar was summoned from Sydney, and he brought with him the Randwick veterinarian Roy Stewart. They confined Peter Pan to his stall, and discovered that the stallion had broken a small bone at the back of his knee. It was a fracture that would heal, but it had punctured the skin, so Stewart set the joint in plaster and bandaged it, feeling no need for a splint. The break would set, he said, in a few weeks, and provided it knitted perfectly, Peter Pan would be able to bend his knee in a matter of weeks.

It was an impossible task, persuading an 11-year-old stallion to stay confined. Peter was walked around the lanes of Baroona, and put on a long line to graze in the afternoons, but the constant attention, handling and restraint frustrated him. He wasn't used to it now, and he became listless and difficult. Worse, the break did not heal. As the weeks passed, the horse became dull in his coat, and fractious. By the first week of May he wasn't eating, and Dangar, Young and Roy Stewart were at a loss. The injury turned septic, and before their eyes, maddeningly, Peter Pan began to die from blood poisoning.

Dangar sat with his great horse, stroking the blond mane and wiping the sweat from his flanks. He couldn't imagine how this could be Peter Pan's final battle. The life of his grand stallion was dripping away, an agony he could hardly watch. But Dangar stayed right to the bitter end. On the morning of Monday 5 May 1941, as the dawn drove warm, willowy shadows over Baroona, the last light vanished from Peter Pan, and he was dead.

A man cannot be measured by a racehorse, and yet Rodney Dangar could be measured by Peter Pan. His champion had lived a magnificent life, had fought titanic battles and was rewarded for them. He had never seen an auction block, nor felt the sting of human rejection, and he had lived without need and died among friends. When he was removed from his stable for the last time that morning, he was taken to his favourite paddock overlooking Baroona. The grave pointed east, towards the rising sun, and Peter was placed in the ground by men with heavy hearts and long, long memories. The gravestone placed over the champion recited the Duke of Gloucester's words: 'A very gallant horse.'

Dangar tried to repair the void that gushed in Peter Pan's wake. He purchased two-time Sydney Cup winner Mosaic to stand at Baroona, but the new stallion failed as a successor. He didn't produce a single stakes winner, and within a year of Peter Pan's death, Dangar was selling up his mares. By the following year, Elsie had fallen ill with respiratory failure and could no longer leave the city. The inevitable occurred. Dangar sold Baroona, his childhood home, and on 1 October 1943, the last of the horses were sold: six fillies, two colts and a gelding, all by Peter Pan. Dangar left Baroona, but his heart remained up on the hillside, facing east.

Elsie died in Sydney on 26 March 1944, and Dangar settled at Arlington for the last few years of his life. He purchased the country property St Clements at Kurrajong Heights, but by 1948 he was too ill to enjoy it. He was suffering from chronic carditis, an inflammation of the heart. It confined him, in the same way Peter Pan had been confined in his final weeks of life. With daughter Roslyn looking over him, and the lure of release in his tired heart, Rodney Rouse Dangar died at Arlington on 24 October 1950.

Three days later, a young man walked into the Commercial Banking Co. of Sydney, at the offices of 343 George Street. He was a valuer with the auction firm James R. Lawson Ltd., and he was in search of a bank vault that had appeared in Dangar's will. When he found it, he popped the lock and peered in at the contents. Dusty, dull from years of lonely capture, were the 1934 Melbourne Cup, the 1934 Duke of Gloucester Cup and the 1935 Jubilee Cup. They were the last surviving pieces of Peter Pan, fragments of the grand and glorious racehorse who had made mere men his slaves.

Peter Pan's Racing Record

Racing statistics have been compiled from the *Australasian Turf Register* (issues 1932 to 1936), which outlines official race times, finishing margins, prizemoney, etc. The *Turf Register,* popularly known as 'the blue book', was the authoritative record on all races held in Australia, and was produced annually by the *Australasian.*

Note on records: The Australian racing season begins on August 1 and finishes on July 31. In the detailed record below, sw denotes 'set weights', H'CAP denotes 'handicap', QTY H'CAP denotes 'quality handicap', and WFA denotes 'weight-for-age'.

Includes dead-heat

	Starts	1st	2nd	3rd	Unpl.	Earnings
1931–32 (Age Two)	1	0	0	0	1	£0
1932–33 (Age Three)	11*	9	0	0	2	£14,218
1933–34 (Age Four)	6	2	2	0	2	£1767/10s
1934–35 (Age Five)	13	9	3	0	1	£15,375
1935–36 (Age Six)	8	3	1	1	3	£2880
Total	39	23	5	1	9	£34,240/10s

* Includes dead-heat

***

Two-Year-Old	
UNPL.	SYDNEY TATTERSALL'S TWO-YEAR-OLD HANDICAP, Saturday May 14, 1932. Randwick. 6f. Diamond de Rouge (R. Reed) 8.0, Vista (F. Hickey) 7.8, Delmond (J. Paul) 8.0. Peter Pan (E. 'Jock' Reynolds) 7.7 unpl. (8th). Time 1min.11 3/4. Margins 1/2 length, 4 lengths. Betting 6/1 Tingalba, King Pin, Diamond de Rouge (Peter Pan beyond 20/1). 17 ran.

Three-Year-Old	
WON (dead-heat)	NOVICE HANDICAP, Saturday August 27, 1932. Warwick Farm. 1 mile. Peter Pan (A. Knox) 7.10, Babili (E. Britt) 7.6, Samian King (N. McLachlan) 7.9. Time 1min.40. Margins dead-heat, 3/4 length. Betting 5/2 Peter Pan, 9/2 Archmel, 5/1 Babili. 20 ran. Winnings: £99 (stake halved in dead-heat).
WON	HILL STAKES (WFA), Saturday September 17, 1932. Rosehill. 1 mile. Peter Pan (A. Knox) 7.7, Nightmarch (R. Reed) 9.3, Johnnie Jason (S. Davidson) 9.4. Time 1min.42. Margins 1/2 length, 3/4 length. Betting 6/4 Veilmond, 9/2 Johnnie Jason, 5/1 Peter Pan. 8 ran. Winnings: £405.

Three-Year-Old	
WON	AJC DERBY (SW: 3YO CLASSIC), Saturday October 1, 1932. Randwick. 1 1/2 miles. Peter Pan (A. Knox) 8.10, Oro (J. Munro) 8.10, Kuvera (M. McCarten) 8.10. Time 2min.34. Margins 1 1/2 lengths, 3 lengths. Betting 9/4 Gaine Carrington, 3/1 Peter Pan. 11 ran. Winnings: £4420 and £250 breeder.
UNPL.	CAULFIELD CUP (H'CAP), Saturday October 15, 1932. Caulfield. 1 1/2 miles. Rogilla (G. Robinson) 7.12, Segati (J. Stocker) 6.12, Top Hole (W. Duncan) 7.2. Peter Pan (A. Knox) 7.7 unpl. (4th by short head). Time 2min.34 1/4. Margins 3 1/2 lengths, 3 lengths. Betting 3/1 Induna, 7/2 Peter Pan, 10/1 Rogilla. 20 ran.
WON	VRC MELBOURNE STAKES (WFA), Saturday October 29, 1932. Flemington. 1 1/4 miles. Peter Pan (W. Duncan) 7.11, Rogilla (D. Munro) 9.1, Middle Watch (J. Munro) 9.0. Time 2min.08 1/4. Margins length, 1 3/4 lengths. Betting 6/4 Peter Pan, 4/1 Middle Watch, 7/1 Rogilla. 9 ran. Winnings: £525.
WON	VRC MELBOURNE CUP (H'CAP), Tuesday November 1, 1932. Flemington. 2 miles. Peter Pan (W. Duncan) 7.6, Yarramba (A. Knox) 7.3, Shadow King (E. Baxter) 8.12. Time 3min.23 1/4. Margins neck, 2 lengths. Betting 4/1 Peter Pan, 7/1 Rogilla, 20/1 Yarramba. 27 ran. Winnings: £5000 and £200 gold cup.

Three-Year-Old	
WON	CITY TATTERSALL'S RANDWICK STAKES (WFA), Saturday March 18, 1933. Randwick. 1 mile. Peter Pan (E. Bartle) 8.6, Rogilla (D. Munro) 8.12, Lough Neagh (J. Munro) 8.11. Time 1min.36 1/4. Margins length, same. Betting 7/4 Peter Pan, 3/1 Rogilla. 8 ran. Winnings: £389.
UNPL.	RAWSON STAKES (WFA), Saturday April 1, 1933. Rosehill. 9 furlongs. Lough Neagh (E. Tanwan) 8.11, Kuvera (M. McCarten) 8.6, Dermid (W.J. Smith) 8.11. Peter Pan (E. Bartle) 8.6 unpl. (last, caught in starting tape). Rogilla unpl. Time 1min.53. Margins neck, 3 lengths. Betting 3/1 odds-on Peter Pan, 6/1 Rogilla, 12/1 Lough Neagh. 8 ran.
WON	AJC ST. LEGER (SW: 3YO CLASSIC), Saturday April 15, 1933. Randwick. 1 1/2 miles. Peter Pan (J. Pike) 8.10, Oro (W. Cook) 8.10, Kuvera (M. McCarten) 8.10. Time 3min.02. (Unofficially, Peter Pan shaves a second off the circuit record.) Margins 1 1/2 lengths, 3/4 lengths. Betting 2/1 odds-on Peter Pan, 4/1 Braeburn. 7 ran. Winnings: £1580.
WON	AJC CUMBERLAND PLATE (WFA), Wednesday April 19, 1933. Randwick. 1 3/4 miles. Peter Pan (W. Duncan) 8.4, Johnnie Jason (G. Robinson) 8.11, Oro (M. McCarten) 8.4. Time 3min.05 1/4. Margins 2 lengths, 1 1/4 lengths. Betting 7/2 odds-on Peter Pan, 5/1 Oro, 16/1 Johnnie Jason. 4 ran. Winnings: £775.

Three-Year-Old	
WON	AJC PLATE (WFA), Saturday April 22, 1933. Randwick. 2 1/4 miles. Peter Pan (W. Duncan) 8.2, Lough Neagh (E. Tanwan) 8.11, Johnnie Jason (J. Simpson) 8.11. Rogilla unpl. Time 3min.55. Margins neck, length. Betting 7/4 odds-on Peter Pan, 2/1 Rogilla, 14/1 Lough Neagh. 6 ran. Winnings: £775.

Four-Year-Old Peter Pan missed 1933 spring racing due to shoulder ailments. He was spelled from September to December, and returned to racing in the autumn, March 1934.	
UNPL.	CITY TATTERSALL'S RANDWICK STAKES (WFA), Saturday March 3, 1934. Randwick. 1 mile. Chatham (S. Davidson) 9.1, Lough Neagh (E. Tanwan) 8.12, Blixten (A. Stead) 8.1. Peter Pan (D. Webb) 9.0 unpl. (first up after 11-month absence). Time 1min.36. Margins 4 lengths, 1 length. Betting 5/4 odds-on Chatham, 3/1 Peter Pan. 5 ran.
2ND	RAWSON STAKES (WFA), Saturday March 17, 1934. Rosehill. 9 furlongs. Rogilla (D. Munro) 8.13, Peter Pan (D. Webb) 9.0, Lough Neagh (E. Tanwan) 8.13. Chatham unpl. Time 1min.50 1/2. Margins 3/4 length, 1/2 neck. Betting 3/1 odds-on Chatham, 3/1 Rogilla, 20/1 Peter Pan. 5 ran. Winnings: £80.

Four-Year-Old Peter Pan missed 1933 spring racing due to shoulder ailments. He was spelled from September to December, and returned to racing in the autumn, March 1934.	
UNPL.	CHIPPING NORTON PLATE (WFA), Saturday March 24, 1934. Warwick Farm. 1 1/4 miles. Silver Scorn (S. Cracknell) 8.11, Closing Time (A. Knox) 9.3, Blixten (M. McCarten) 8.4. Peter Pan (J. Pike) unpl. (6th). Time 2min.04 1/4. Margins length, 1/2 head. Betting evens Peter Pan, 4/1 Lough Neagh, 7/1 Silver Scorn. 8 ran.
WON	AJC AUTUMN PLATE (WFA), Saturday March 31, 1934. Randwick. 1 1/2 miles. Peter Pan (J. Pike) 9.0, Silver Scorn (S. Cracknell) 8.11, Peter Jackson (A. Ellis) 9.0. Time 2min.38. Margins 2 1/2 lengths, 3/4 lengths. Betting 10/9 Silver Scorn, 6/4 Peter Pan. 7 ran. Winnings: £1000.
WON	AJC CUMBERLAND PLATE (WFA), Wednesday April 4, 1934. Randwick. 2 miles. Peter Pan (J. Pike) 9.0, Oro (J. Pratt) 9.0, Heroic Prince (M. McCarten) 9.1. Time 3min.39 1/4. Margins 1 length, 1 1/4 lengths. Betting 9/4 odds-on Peter Pan, 11/2 Silver Scorn, 20/1 Oro. 5 ran. Winnings: £387/10s (total stake of £1000 was reduced in half because the race was not run in the stipulated time of 3min.35 or better).

Four-Year-Old Peter Pan missed 1933 spring racing due to shoulder ailments. He was spelled from September to December, and returned to racing in the autumn, March 1934.	
2ND	AJC KING'S CUP (QTY H'CAP), Saturday April 7, 1934. Randwick. 1 1/2 miles. Rogilla (D. Munro) 9.3, Peter Pan (J. Pike) 9.5, Kuvera (M. McCarten) 8.9. Hall Mark unpl. Time 2min.32. Margins short head, neck. Betting 3/1 Peter Pan, 4/1 Rogilla, 10/1 Kuvera, Hall Mark. 11 ran. Winnings: £300 (Rogilla's squeeze through the hedge at the finish instigated the removal of the hedge at Randwick).

Five-Year-Old	
2ND	SYDNEY TATTERSALL'S CHELMSFORD STAKES (WFA), Saturday September 8, 1934. Randwick. 9 furlongs. Rogilla (D. Munro) 9.8, Peter Pan (J. Munro) 9.11, Gladswood (E. Britt) 7.2 (car. 7.3). Time 1min.52 3/4. Margins 1/2 length, 2 1/2 lengths. Betting 11/8 odds-on Rogilla, 9/2 Nightly, 7/1 Peter Pan. 9 ran. Winnings: £150.
WON	SIR HERBERT MAITLAND STAKES (WFA), Saturday September 19, 1934. Victoria Park. 7 furlongs. Peter Pan (J. Munro) 9.3, Chatham (J. Pike) 9.3, Duke Caledon (A. Knox) 7.2 (car. 7.4). Time 1min.24 1/2 (course record). Margins neck, 3 lengths. Betting 4/1 odds-on Chatham, 7/1 Peter Pan, 33/1 Duke Caledon. 9 ran. Winnings: £400.

Five-Year-Old	
2ND	AJC SPRING STAKES (WFA), Saturday September 29, 1934. Randwick. 1 1/2 miles. Rogilla (D. Munro) 9.3, Peter Pan (J. Pike) 9.5, Oro (A. Knox) 9.5. Time 2min.32. Margins head, 2 lengths. Betting 7/4 odds-on Peter Pan, 2/1 Rogilla. 9 ran. Winnings: £200.
2ND	AJC CRAVEN PLATE (WFA), Wednesday October 3, 1934. Randwick. 1 1/4 miles. Chatham (S. Davidson) 9.4, Peter Pan (J. Munro) 9.4, Rogilla (D. Munro) 9.1. Time 2min.03 1/2. Margins 3/4 length, 1 1/2 lengths. Betting 10/9 Peter Pan, 6/4 Rogilla, 8/1 Chatham. 5 ran. Winnings: £250.
WON	VRC MELBOURNE STAKES (WFA), Saturday November 3, 1934. Flemington. 1 1/4 miles. Peter Pan (D. Munro) 9.3, Hall Mark (F. Dempsey) 9.0, Nightly (M. McCarten) 9.0. Chatham and Rogilla unpl. Time 2min.05 3/4. Margins length, head. Betting 5/2 Peter Pan, 3/1 Chatham, 9/2 Hall Mark, 5/1 Rogilla. 8 ran. Winnings: £700.
WON	VRC MELBOURNE CUP (H'CAP), Tuesday November 6, 1934. Flemington. 2 miles. Peter Pan (D. Munro) 9.11, Sarcherie (D. Lightfoot) 7.2, La Trobe (W. Cox) 6.10 (car. 7.2). Rogilla unpl. Time 3min.40 1/2. Margins 3 lengths, neck. Betting 9/2 Sir Simper, Nightly (both last), 14/1 Peter Pan. 22 ran. Winnings: £8000 and £200 gold cup. (Heaviest track in living memory, Peter Pan drawn widest.)

Five-Year-Old	
WON	VRC DUKE OF GLOUCESTER CUP (QTY H'CAP), Saturday November 10, 1934. Flemington. 1 1/2 miles. Peter Pan (D. Munro) 9.7, Broad Arrow (H. Skidmore) 8.9, Hyperion (A. Knox) 7.5. Time 3min.04 3/4. Margins 1/2 length, 2 lengths. Betting 9/4 odds-on Peter Pan, 9/2 Nightly, 20/1 Broad Arrow. 7 ran. Winnings: £1400 and £100 gold cup.
UNPL.	AJC DUKE OF GLOUCESTER PLATE (QTY H'CAP), Thursday November 22, 1934. Randwick. 1 1/2 miles. Oro (J. Pratt) 7.13, Mr. Kerry (J. Simpson) 7.0 (car. 7.1), Magnitas (R. Carter) 7.0 (car. 7.3). Peter Pan (D. Munro) 9.5 unpl. (6th). Time 2min.29 1/2 (course record). Margins 1/2 length, same. Betting evens Peter Pan, 20/1 Oro. 15 ran.
WON	CITY TATTERSALL'S RANDWICK STAKES (WFA), Saturday March 23, 1935. Randwick. 1 mile. Peter Pan (J. Pike) 9.1, Silver King (S. Weiss) 8.1, Journal (A. Knox) 8.11. Rogilla unpl. Time 1min.36 3/4. Margins length, 1 3/4 lengths. Betting evens Peter Pan, 5/2 Rogilla. 8 ran. Winnings: £245.
WON	RAWSON STAKES (WFA), Saturday April 6, 1935. Rosehill. 9 furlongs. Peter Pan (J. Pike) 9.2, Sylvandale (J. Pratt) 8.6, Journal (J. Munro) 8.11. Rogilla unpl. Time 1min.52. Margins 2 1/2 lengths, long head. Betting 5/2 odds-on Peter Pan, 7/1 Sylvandale, 1 4/1 Journal. 7 ran. Winnings: £380.

Five-Year-Old	
WON	AJC AUTUMN PLATE (WFA), Saturday April 20, 1935. Randwick. 1 1/2 miles. Peter Pan (J. Pike) 9.3, Rogilla (J. Pratt) 9.0, Oro (M. McCarten) 9.3. Time 2min.33 3/4. Margins long head, 4 lengths. Betting 5/1 odds-on Peter Pan, 5/1 Rogilla. 7 ran. Winnings: £1150.
WON	AJC ALL-AGED PLATE (WFA), Saturday April 24, 1935. Randwick. 1 mile. Peter Pan (J. Pike) 9.1, Hall Mark (K. Voitre) 9.0, Silver King (D. Munro) 8.8. Time 1min.35 1/2 (Australasian record). Margins 3 lengths, 1 1/4 lengths. Betting 6/4 odds-on Peter Pan, 2/1 Hall Mark. 4 ran. Winnings: £1150.
WON	AJC JUBILEE CUP (QTY H'CAP), Monday May 6, 1935. Randwick. 1 1/2 miles. Peter Pan (J. Pike) 9.7, Akuna (H. Hanley) 7.4, Satmoth (D. Lightfoot) 7.4. Rogilla unpl. Time 2min.39 3/4. Margins 5 lengths, 1 3/4 lengths. Betting evens Peter Pan, 12/1 Silver King, Akuna. 11 ran. Winnings: £1350 and £100 gold cup.

Six-Year-Old	
WON	HILL STAKES (WFA), Saturday September 21, 1935. Rosehill. 1 mile. Peter Pan (J. Pike) 9.3, Young Idea (A. Knox) 7.12, Lough Neagh (F. Shean) 9.0. Time 1min.39. Margins 1 length, 1 3/4 lengths. Betting 11/8 odds-on Peter Pan, 9/2 Young Idea. 9 ran. Winnings: £450.

Six-Year-Old	
WON	AJC SPRING STAKES (WFA), Saturday October 5, 1935. Randwick. 1 1/2 miles. Peter Pan (J. Pike) 9.6, Berestoi (H. Skidmore) 9.2, Rogilla (E. Bartle) 9.3. (Oro placed 2nd, but disqualified after weighing in 4lbs light). Time 2min.32. Margins 2 lengths, neck. Betting 3/1 odds-on Peter Pan, 5/1 Sylvandale, 8/1 Rogilla. 8 ran. Winnings: £1125.
WON	AJC CRAVEN PLATE (WFA), Wednesday October 9, 1935. Randwick. 1 1/4 miles. Peter Pan (J. Pike) 9.4, Oro (J. Pratt) 9.4, Lough Neagh (F. Shean) 9.0. Time 2min.04 1/2. Margins 1 1/2 lengths, 1 1/4 lengths. Betting 7/1 odds-on Peter Pan, 15/1 Oro, 20/1 Lough Neagh. 9 ran. Winnings: £1125.
UNPL.	VRC MELBOURNE STAKES (WFA), Saturday November 2, 1935. Flemington. 1 1/4 miles. Sylvandale (J. Pratt) 9.0, Marabou (K. Voitre) 9.0, Hall Mark (H. Skidmore) 9.3. Peter Pan (J. Pike) 9.3 unpl. (5th). Time 2min.08 1/4. Margins 1/2 length, neck. Betting 4/1 odds-on Peter Pan, 7/1 Hall Mark, 12/1 Sylvandale, 20/1 Marabou. 6 ran.
UNPL.	VRC MELBOURNE CUP (H'CAP), Tuesday November 5, 1935. Flemington. 2 miles. Marabou (K. Voitre) 7.11, Sarcherie (F. Shean) 7.12 (car. 7.13), Sylvandale (J. Pratt) 9.4. Peter Pan (J. Pike) 10.6 unpl. (14th). Time 3min.23 3/4. Margins 2 1/2 lengths, 1/2 length. Betting 9/2 Marabou, 6/1 Sarcherie, 8/1 Peter Pan. 21 ran.

Six-Year-Old	
UNPL.	CITY TATTERSALL'S RANDWICK STAKES (WFA), Saturday March 14, 1936. Randwick. 1 mile. Sarcherie (R. Maxwell) 8.7, Gay Blond (J. Pratt) 8.6, Contact (C. Maher) 8.9. Peter Pan (J. Pike) 9.1 unpl. (4th). Rogilla unpl. (last start). Time 1min.36 1/2. Margins 1/2 length, long head. Betting 6/4 Peter Pan, 6/1 Gay Blond, 10/1 Sarcherie. 10 ran.
2ND	ROSEHILL RAWSON STAKES (WFA), Saturday March 28, 1936. Rosehill. 9 furlongs. Lough Neagh(F. Shean) 8.13, Peter Pan (J. Pike) 9.2, Garrio (K. Voitre) 8.4. Time 1min.51 1/4. Margins neck, 1/2 length. Betting 2/1 Garrio, 9/4 Peter Pan, 5/1 Lough Neagh. 9 ran. Winnings: £80.
3RD	AJC AUTUMN PLATE (WFA), Saturday April 11, 1936. Randwick. 1 1/2 miles. Sarcherie (W. Cook) 9.1, Silver Ring (A.E. Ellis) 9.0, Peter Pan (J. Pike) 9.3. Time 2min.34 1/4. Margins 3 lengths, 1 length. Betting 10/9 odds-on Peter Pan, 7/2 Silver Ring, 12/1 Sarcherie. 9 ran. Winnings: £100.

Bibliography

This book is indebted to the State Library of New South Wales, including the Mitchell Library, for access to rare and out-of-print reference books, *Sands Directory* microfiche, and original and microfilm newspapers including the *Sydney Morning Herald,* the *Sydney Mail,* the *Referee, Truth* (Sydney), the *Arrow,* the *Telegraph,* the *Sun,* the *Sunday Sun & Guardian,* and *Smith's Weekly,* and the regional newspapers the *Singleton Argus,* the *Maitland Mercury,* the *Barrier Miner,* the *Mercury,* the *Town & Country Journal* and the *Pastoral Review.*

From the State Library of Victoria, newspaper sources included the *Age,* the *Australasian,* the *Argus,* the *Sporting Globe,* and *Truth* (Melbourne). Magazines included *Sporting Life, Sporting Novels, Racetrack, Turf Monthly* and the US-based the *Blood Horse.* Information was also sourced from Trove, the online resource of the National Library of Australia, and the libraries of the Australian Jockey Club and Australian Racing Museum, as well as the New South Wales State Archives. Also, Registry of Births, Deaths and Marriages (New South Wales), and the *Australian Dictionary of Biography.* Climate data was acquired from the Bureau of Meteorology, from records for Sydney (Observatory Hill, station 66062) and Melbourne (Regional Office, station 86071).

Secondary Resources

Ahern, Bill (1982) *A Century of Winners: The Saga of 121 Melbourne Cups.* Boolarong Publications: Brisbane.
Anderson, Joseph (1985) *Tattersall's Club Sydney 1858–1983.* Koorana Ltd.: Sydney.
Australasian Turf Register (1932–36) The Australasian: Melbourne.
Barrie, Douglas M. (1956) *The Australian Bloodhorse.* Halstead Press: Sydney.
Barrie, Douglas M. (1960) *Turf Cavalcade.* Australian Jockey Club: Sydney.
Barrie, Douglas M. & Pring, Peter (1973) *Australia's Thoroughbred Idols.* The Discovery Press: Penrith.
Beltran, David Jimenez (2004) *The Agua Caliente Story: Remembering Mexico's Legendary Racetrack.* Eclipse Press: Lexington, Kentucky.
Binney, Keith R. (2003) *Horsemen of the First Frontier (1788–1900) and The Serpent's Legacy.* Volcanic Productions: Sydney.
Bland, E. (ed.) (1950) *Flat-Racing Since 1900.* Andrew Dakers Ltd.: London.
Britt, Edgar (1967, reprinted 2000) *Post Haste.* Pan Macmillan: Sydney.
Cairns, Steve (1994) *'London to a Brick On': A Salute to Australian Race Calling.* The Australian Bloodhorse Review: Richmond.
Carter, Isobel (1964) *Phar Lap.* Landsdowne Press: Melbourne.

Cavanough, Maurice & Davies, Meurig (1960) *Cup Day: The Story of the Melbourne Cup 1861–1960.* The Specialty Press: Melbourne.

Chittick, A.J. (2001) *Jim Pike, The Master: His Life and Times 1892–1969.* Moss Vale.

City Tattersall's Club (1970). Sydney.

Church, Michael (2006) *The Derby Stakes: The Complete History 1780–2006.* Raceform: Berkshire.

Collis, Ian (2007) *Sydney: From Settlement to the Bridge.* New Holland: Sydney.

Collis, Ian (2008) *Old Sydney: A Pictorial History.* New Holland: Sydney.

Cuffley, Peter (1989) *Australian Houses of the Twenties and Thirties.* The Five Mile Press: Rowville, Victoria.

Curby, Pauline (2009) *Randwick.* Randwick City Council: Randwick.

Day, William (1891) *Reminiscences of the Turf.* Richard Bentley & Sons: London.

Dexter, A.W. (1947) 'My double Cup winner was better than Phar Lap', *Sporting Life,* November, p.5.

Dexter, A.W. (1947) 'The greatest Melbourne Cup ever', *Sporting Life,* November, p.3.

Ellis, Tom (1936) *The Science of Turf Investment.* The Federal Capital Press of Australia: Canberra.

Fairfax-Blakeborough, J. (1932) *The Turf Who's Who 1932.* The Mayfair Press: London.

Fiddian, Marc (2005) *The Williamstown Cup.* Galaxy Print and Design: Melbourne.
Fitzwygram, F.W. (1901) *Horses and Stables.* Longmans, Green & Co.: London.
Gould, Nat (1909) *The Magic of Sport: Mainly Autobiographical.* John Long: London.
Griffiths, Samuel (1933) *A Rolling Stone on the Turf.* Angus & Robertson: Sydney.
Hall, Dixon Henry 'The Druid' (1862) *Scott and Seabright.* Rogerson & Tuxford: London.
Hall, Sandra (2008) *Tabloid Man: The Life and Times of Ezra Norton.* Harper Collins: Sydney.
Hayes, Capt. M. Horace (1877, 18th reprint 2002) *Veterinary Notes for Horse Owners.* Simon & Schuster: New York.
Hewitt, Abram S. (1977, reprinted 2006) *Sirelines.* Eclipse Press: Lexington, Kentucky.
Hickie, David (1986) *Gentlemen of the Australian Turf.* Angus & Robertson: Sydney.
Hitchins, Max (1995) *Fact, Fiction and Fables of the Melbourne Cup.* Sydney.
Hobson, Warwick (1992) 'Peter Pan – even Banjo was puzzled', *Turf Monthly,* January, p.32.
Hobson, Warwick (1973) 'Peter Pan – he beat the best', *Turf Monthly,* November, p.8.
Hobson, Warwick (1986) *Racing's All-Time Greats.* The Thoroughbred Press: Sydney.
Hobson, Warwick (1972) 'Stable of Champions', *Turf Monthly,* March, p.8.

Howe, Graham & Esau, Erika (2007) *E.O. Hoppe's Australia.* W. Norton & Co.: New York.

Huntington, Peter, Myers, Jane & Owens, Elizabeth (2004) *Horse Sense.* Landlinks Press: Collingwood.

Hynes, Matt (1950) *The Melbourne Cup Down the Years: Champions from 1861 to 1950.* Adelaide.

Inglis, Clive (1950) *Horsesense.* Halstead Press: Sydney.

Inglis, Clive (1959) *More Horsesense.* Halstead Press: Sydney.

Justice, Charles (2008) *The Greatest Horse of All: A Controversy Examined.* Author House: Bloomington, Indiana.

Lawrence, Joan (2001) *Pictorial History: Randwick.* Kingsclear Books: Sydney.

Lemon, Andrew (2008) *The History of Australian Thoroughbred Racing: Vol. I.* Hardie Grant Books: Melbourne.

Lemon, Andrew (1990) *The History of Australian Thoroughbred Racing: Vol. II.* Southbank Communications Group: Port Melbourne.

Lemon, Andrew (2008) *The History of Australian Thoroughbred Racing: Vol. III.* Hardie Grant Books: Melbourne.

Lillye, Bert (1985) *Backstage of Racing.* John Fairfax Marketing: Sydney.

Mackaness, Caroline & Butler-Bowdon, Caroline (2007) *Sydney Then and Now.* Cameron House: Wingfield, South Australia.

McKay, W.J. Stewart (1933) *Staying Power of the Racehorse.* Hutchinson & Co.: London.

Names Registered for Racehorses: Vols. I to VIII of Printed List. Registrar of Racehorses (Australian Jockey Club), July 31, 1918.

Names Registered for Racehorses: Vols. XVII to XXII of Printed List. Registrar of Racehorses (Australian Jockey Club), August 1932.

O'Hara, John (1988) *A Mug's Game: A History of Gaming and Betting in Australia.* University of New South Wales Press: Sydney.

Pacini, John (1988) *A Century Galloped By: The First One Hundred Years of the Victorian Racing Club.* Victoria Racing Club: Melbourne.

Painter, Martin & Waterhouse, Richard (1992) *The Principal Club: A History of the Australian Jockey Club.* Allen & Unwin: Syndney.

Paterson, A.B. (1986) *Off Down The Track: Racing and Other Yarns.* Angus & Robertson: Sydney.

Peake, Wayne (2006) *Sydney's Pony Racecourses: An Alternative History.* Walla Walla Press: Sydney.

Pierce, Peter (1994) *From Go to Whoa: A Compendium of the Australian Turf.* Crossbow Publishing: Melbourne. Poliness, Grania (1985) *Carbine.* Waterloo Press: Sydney.

Pollard, Jack (1971) *The Pictorial History of Australian Horse Racing.* Paul Hamlyn: Sydney.

Potts, David (2006) *The Myth of the Great Depression.* Scribe: Melbourne.

Pring, Peter (1977) *Analysis of Champion Racehorses.* The Thoroughbred Press: Sydney.

Reason, Michael (2005) *Phar Lap: A True Legend.* The Museum of Victoria: Melbourne.

Rolfe, Costa (2008) *Winners of the Melbourne Cup: Stories that Stopped a Nation.* Red Dog: Melbourne.

Sharpe, Alan (2000) *Pictorial History: City of Sydney.* Kingsclear Books: Sydney.

Sharpe, Harry (1913) *The Practical Stud Groom.* The British Bloodstock Agency Ltd.: London.

Spearitt, Peter (2000) *Sydney's Century: A History.* University of New South Wales Press: Sydney.

Stallion Register Volume I. (1939) *The Sydney Morning Herald:* Sydney.

Stone, Gerald (2003) *1932.* Pan Macmillan: Sydney.

Sydney Thoroughbred Yearling Catalogue 1939. William Inglis & Son: Sydney.

They're Racing: The Complete Story of Australian Racing (1999). Penguin Books: Melbourne.

Thoroughbred Yearlings Catalogue 1928. H. Chisholm & Co.: Sydney.

Thoroughbred Yearlings Catalogue 1934. William Inglis & Son: Sydney.

Walker, R.B. (1980) *Yesterday's News: A History of the Newspaper Press in New South Wales from 1920 to 1945.* Sydney University Press: Sydney.

Warne, Catherine (2005) *Pictorial History: Lower North Shore.* Kingsclear Books: Sydney.

Acknowledgements

Samuel Johnson, the English author, once said that what is written without effort is, in general, read without pleasure, and having come to the end of telling Peter Pan's tale, I can see what he meant. There are so many challenges in writing history, but along the way I have had some extraordinary help, and I would like to acknowledge that.

First and foremost, my thanks to Ellen Montgomery, née McGrath, granddaughter of trainer Frank McGrath who lives a skip from Peter Pan's original stables on Doncaster Avenue. For years, Ellen took my telephone calls, visits and questions, and dug deep into her family vault for answers. Her kindness and sincerity is rare indeed. Secondly, my appreciation to Timothy Ritchie, grandson of Rodney Rouse Dangar, and his wife Yvonne, who granted me access to the Dangar family archive. Their extraordinary material has been the root of my research and I can't thank them enough.

I feel privileged to have visited all the places that were central to Peter Pan's story, so my thanks to Colin and Judy Peterson for initial access to Baroona and Peter Pan's final place of rest. My thanks also to Ken and Liz Cooper of Rotherwood, who allowed me to spend a glorious morning in the once country home of Rodney Dangar, and to Neville and Andrea for showing me around Neotsfield. Thank you also to Steve Rawling of St Clements, though I never made it there, and John Moore, the extraordinary Bungarribee historian. I must offer extra special thanks to Rob Waterhouse for his unique knowledge and historical context, and the sandwich in North Sydney that afternoon. Also, to his wife Gai, for access to Frank McGrath's old yard. We live in hope that Peter Pan's racing home might be saved.

I would like to thank Sid and Rosemary Reynolds, living descendants of J.H. Keys, and Michael Fitzgerald for their information on Bengalla, and R.L. 'Tig' Moses for his photographs and memories of the 1924 dispersal of Arrowfield Stud. Also, my appreciation to Biddy Oquist of Arrowfield who, during a busy time, copied and forwarded to me the history of that grand stud.

In bringing Peter Pan's life to the page, I have dealt with some extraordinary people, among them Glen Shade of the Singleton district, son of Noel and grandson of William Shade who attended to Peter Pan at Baroona. At any time, Glen was at the end of the highway or the telephone, ready to answer my questions. Also, my thanks to his nieces Michelle Hills and Christine Burne in Hobart, who allowed me access to their special inheritances. Very special mention must go to Les Haigh and his father John, grandson and son of Rogilla's trainer, who brought to life Peter Pan's greatest rival once more, and who gave tirelessly of their time and resources for my benefit. Their help has been critical, and their generosity breathtaking. Thank you also to veterinarians Dr Leanne Begg and Dr Percy Sykes of Randwick Equine Centre, and Dr

John Auty, who answered my questions about Peter Pan's ailments. Also, special thanks to Rod Ritchie whose interest and assistance was greatly appreciated, and to Tom Brassel, former turf journalist of the *Daily Mirror,* for his insight into times long since passed.

To bring the puzzle of Peter Pan's story together, I have dealt with all sorts of organisations in Australia and around the world, and I am indebted for their respective help. Thank you to Kevin Gates and Liz Brown of the Australian Racing Museum, and VRC historian Andrew Lemon. A very special mention must go to Sue Hutchinson of the AJC (now ATC), without whom I would have been in terrible trouble, and to Sue Ormsby of the Australian Stud Book who never failed my requests for ancient and obscure pedigrees. Also, to Michael Ford, Keeper of the Stud Book. My gratitude to the excellent staff of the State Library of New South Wales, who are exemplary in every way. Also, thanks to the Bureau of Meteorology, to the pictures departments of News Ltd and Fairfax, to the National Film and Sound Archives, and to the staff of the City of Sydney archives. I would also like to mention Hugh Stowell, of the Australian Club in Sydney, who helped to dig up Dangar's membership. In Singleton, special thanks to Alton Heuston and the wonderful Singleton Historical Society, and to Diane Sneddon, editor of the *Singleton Argus.* In England, my thanks to the staff of Weatherbys, in particular Lyn Price and Rob Marriott, who worked very hard when I needed them, and to Alan Grundy of the

National Horseracing Museum at Newmarket. Also, thank you to Paul Brown of the Mary Evans Picture Library for access to *Tatler* magazine.

In obscure places, I found some very worthy friends. Unending thanks to the romance girls – they know who they are – who for years now have been my private cheerleading squad, and who gave me critical advice and friendship in the writing world when I needed it most. Special thanks to John Dyer of Horseman's Bookshop in Melbourne. Through online auctions, I met many likeminded folk, so my thanks to Dave Maher of Wellington, and Trish des Bouvrie of Quanah Park in Western Australia. I must thank the lovely John and Pauline Hoffman, and also the former editor of *Turf Monthly* Warren Wruck, along with John O'Hara, author of *A Mug's Game.* Special mention must go to the racing boys of Slattery Media – Geoff Slattery and Stephen Howell, and in particular Danny Power, to whom I owe a great deal. But there are two people who deserve special accolades for the assistance and wisdom they have provided this book, and they are Graham Caves, racing historian and writer with *Racetrack* magazine, and Wayne Peake, author of the inimitable *Sydney's Pony Racecourses: An Alternative Racing History.* Neither man will ever know how grateful I am to them. Finally, how can I ever thank Peter McGauran, CEO of AusHorse? He took this bulging, unedited manuscript in its earliest days and read it from cover to cover. There is no greater gentleman in racing.

There are so many people who gave me their time throughout this project, and I couldn't possibly mention them all. To anyone I have left out here, know that your input hasn't been forgotten. I must acknowledge the writers who made this journey before me, especially Michael Wilkinson, whose 1980 book *The Phar Lap Story* is where it all began for me. I need to thank my literary agent Margaret Gee, who was charming and enthusiastic from the moment she got the manuscript, and my exquisite publisher Alison Urquhart, who fell in love with Peter Pan as quickly as I did. May I also mention my editor at Random House, Maisie Dubosarsky, who has spirited this book from its submission to polished piece. She has been an angel, and I can't wait to do it all again.

Thank you to my perfect parents James and Kate Owers, who have delighted in my writing since I was seven years old, and to my courageous sister Sonya. Thank you also to my wonderful brother-in-law Philip O'Carroll, and to Stefano Lucia, my friend. But I am indebted, above all others, to Maurice Lombardo, who endured this book with me every step of the way, who loved it and believed in it as much as I did, and who carried me through it for many years. I'm not sure what it would be without him.

Last of all, Rodney Rouse Dangar and Frank McGrath cannot be forgotten, and I thank them for the lives they lived and the trail they left for me to blaze. Also, the magnificent city of Sydney, which was spun through this story like a silent character, and the stunning, seductive racehorse Peter Pan, the reason for it all.

Jessica Owers
Sydney, November 2011

Back Cover Material

In 1932, they said there would never be another Phar Lap. Yet that same year there came a racehorse so wildly brilliant that he was instantly compared to the dead champion. He was Peter Pan.

Within months of Phar Lap's death, Peter Pan had won the Melbourne Cup, and two years later he won it again – the first horse in 72 years to clinch a second. He then broke the mile record in Australia. The nation's greatest stayer became the nation's greatest miler. The newspapers of the day called him a 'superhorse' and declared 'another Phar Lap takes the stage'. But over the long years, Australia forgot its new champion.

Peter Pan: The Forgotten Story of Phar Lap's Successor is the tale of the horse that came next – the brilliant, speedy Peter Pan. Casting off the shadow of Phar Lap, it is a story of triumph during the Great Depression and the coming of a champion when Australia least expected one.

It is time to restore the standing of our other great racing hero.

A

B

D

E

F

G

H

K

L

M

N

O

P

Q

R

W

Y

Books For ALL Kinds of Readers

At ReadHowYouWant we understand that one size does not fit all types of readers. Our innovative, patent pending technology allows us to design new formats to make reading easier and more enjoyable for you. This helps improve your speed of reading and your comprehension. Our EasyRead printed books have been optimized to improve word recognition, ease eye tracking by adjusting word and line spacing as well as minimizing hyphenation. Our EasyRead SuperLarge editions have been developed to make reading easier and more accessible for vision-impaired readers. We offer Braille and DAISY formats of our books and all popular E-Book formats.

Printed in Great Britain
by Amazon

44090900R00384